Christopher Marlowe

and

English Renaissance Culture

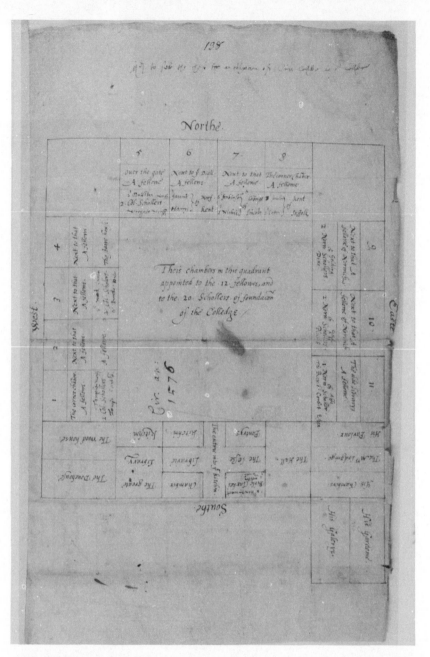

A plan of Corpus Christi College, Cambridge, *circa* 1576. The chamber (the 'stoare house') which he shared with other Parker scholars from Canterbury shortly after his arrival in 1580 is shown in the top left hand corner. [Reference: CCCC Archive misc. no. 138]

Christopher Marlowe

and

English Renaissance Culture

Edited by
Darryll Grantley
and
Peter Roberts

Ashgate

Aldershot • Brookfield USA • Singapore • Sidney

First published in hardback (ISBN 1 85928 260 1) under the Scolar Press imprint, Ashgate Publishing Ltd.

Published by
Ashgate Publishing Ltd
Gower House, Croft Road
Aldershot
Hants GU11 3HR
England

Ashgate Publishing Co
Old Post Road
Brookfield
Vermont 05036–9704
USA

British Library Cataloguing-in-Publication Data
A catalogue record for this book is available from the British Library.

US Library of Congress Catalog Card Number: 96–68684

ISBN 0 7546 0025 4 (paperback)

Printed and bound in Great Britain by MPG Books Ltd, Bodmin, Cornwall

CONTENTS

Contents

The drawing in the frontispiece and the putative image of Marlowe are reproduced by kind permission of the Master and Fellows of Corpus Christi College, Cambridge. The editors would like to thank Christine Wilson of the Computer Centre at the University of Kent for considerable and expert help in the preparation of camera-ready copy, and to acknowledge the kind assistance of Paul Pollak, Archivist of the King's School Canterbury.

PREFACE

To the question, 'Who and what was Christopher Marlowe?' there are plain answers and polemical ones. The dramatist, poet, intellectual and roisterer was also possibly both a subversive and a spy, was reputed to be an atheist, and was almost certainly homosexual. If he is to be characterized as a man of his time, it must principally be in relation to its turbulence and contradictions. Ever since Leslie Hotson made his archival discoveries with their pointers to undercover work for the Elizabethan regime, it has been possible to sketch a documentary profile of Marlowe's life and the manner of his death, and this has in turn stimulated critical interest in his work. While the more scholarly of the recent biographical and literary studies of Marlowe have resisted the temptation to reduce him to the status of an avatar of 'the Renaissance spirit', they have explored in his life and writings the signs of discordances and dissidences that were inherent in the ideologies and cultural dynamic of the period.

The essays in this volume are a selection of contributions to a conference held in 1993 at the University of Kent at Canterbury to mark the four hundredth anniversary of Marlowe's death. In a range of papers on dramaturgy, textual criticism and biography which focus on Marlowe and the English Renaissance, an interdisciplinary element is inescapable, and several of the contributions exemplify the variety of approaches which may be taken to the writing of cultural and intellectual history.

The circumstances of Marlowe's family background have been explored in William Urry's pioneering study on *Christopher Marlowe and Canterbury*. This was a posthumous publication which Andrew Butcher prepared for the press and on which he builds his present study of Marlowe's childhood that takes account of new archival evidence on questions of identity and community.

Contemporary commentators were aware that those best placed to take advantage of the greater social mobility in Elizabethan England belonged, like Marlowe, to a middling rank in the commonwealth. One such observer was the educationalist Richard Mulcaster, who argued:

> The midle sort of parentes which neither welter in to much wealth, nor wrastle with to much want, seemeth fittest of all, if the childrens capacitie be awnswerable to their parentes state and qualities: which must be the leuell for the fattest to fall downe to, and the leanest to leape up to, to bring forth that student, which must serue his countrey best.'[1]

If in the final analysis the trajectory of Marlowe's brief life was extraordinary, the path he had followed – from grammar school to university to living on his wits in the capital – was commonplace enough among the young men of his generation who took advantage of the new educational opportunities available to the laity after the Reformation. As a scholarship boy he curtailed a course of study which should normally have led to ordination in the church, and he arrived in London at a time when new conditions were being worked out by the playing companies and by the authorities for the practice of the craft which he chose to pursue instead of an established profession.

A number of the essays in the collection examine Marlowe's place in the network of connection radiating from Canterbury and Kent to Cambridge and London. Peter Roberts explores the question of his social identity and aspirations in the successive milieux which he inhabited, and considers the different kinds of dramatic activity which he may have encountered in his home town and in Cambridge. What Marlowe's business in Deptford may have been leads Richard Wilson to investigate the ramifications of the Muscovy Company, whose agent was Anthony Marlowe and which was 'in reality a cartel of Kent families', and to uncover a hitherto unsuspected dimension to *Tamburlaine*. Charles Nicholl argues for a Dutch first edition for Marlowe's *Ovid* and, in the charge of counterfeiting levelled against Marlowe the 'scholar' apprehended in the Netherlands in 1592 he intimates a 'dangerous collusion' between his work as a poet and as an intelligencer.

Several essays uncover tropes of resistance and dissidence in Marlowe's work. In his study of erotic passion in *Edward II*, Lawrence Normand relates the plays to broader cultural discourses of homoeroticism in the period, and makes an argument for a contemporary parallel in James VI of Scotland. In a discussion of Marlowe's sources for *The Massacre at Paris,* David Potter also looks at the French King Henri III's reputation for sexual ambivalence. Michael Hattaway considers homosexuality as part of an agenda of dissidence in Marlowe's plays, with particular reference to *Edward II*, *Tamburlaine* and *Dido, Queen of Carthage*. The allegations of atheism made against Marlowe are examined by Nicholas Davidson in an extensive analysis of evidence for the existence of religious scepticism in Renaissance England. Gareth Roberts considers the possible influence of Agrippa of Nettesheim on Marlowe's Faustus within the complex interplay of history and fiction in texts representing magic in the Renaissance.

If heterodoxy of belief and ambivalent sexuality inform Marlowe's plays, also present in his work is a familiarity with other forms of knowledge produced by the expansion of trade and global exploration. The world was becoming not only better known in his lifetime, but more fully chartered and documented. Nicholas de Somogyi discusses the emergence of geographical study and cartography with reference to geopolitics and warfare in *Tamburlaine*, while Thomas Cartelli uses the same plays to illustrate the perspectives on the conquest and possession of territories in the New World to be found in Marlowe. Five of the essays thus explore Marlowe's engagement, in person or imaginatively, with other lands and cultures: Scotland, the Low Countries, France, Russia and North America.

Roger Sales contemplates the theatricality of the exercise of power through public executions, with specific reference to *The Jew of Malta* and to the staging of actual executions in late sixteenth–century England. Alexander Shurbanov studies the same play alongside *Tamburlaine* in a dissection of the ironies inscribed in Marlowe's construction of dramatic character. In an anatomy of the trope of theatricalism and its possibilities for the subversive representation of political and theocratic power, Darryll Grantley considers the uniqueness of Marlowe's aesthetic in English Renaissance culture.

In the course of the collection, the focus ranges over all of Marlowe's dramatic *oeuvre* and some of his poetry. In all cases fresh perspectives are offered by adducing new historical materials, or by rereading his work in the context of Renaissance culture in general or the writing culture that was his chosen métier. The very diversity of the approaches, methodological and philosophical, recognizes and, it is hoped, will contribute to continuing debate.

DRG
PRR

Note

1.   Richard Mulcaster, *Positions Wherin those Primitive Circumstances be examined which are necessarie for the training vp of children*, Thomas Vautrollier, London, 1581, 140

CONTRIBUTORS

Andrew Butcher teaches History at the University of Kent. His published work has been concerned with urban and rural society form the eleventh to the seventeenth centuries and with relations between literature and society in the fourteenth, fifteenth, and sixteenth centuries. In 1991 he published (with Peter Brown) *The Age of Saturn*, as study of society and literature in Chaucer's *Canterbury Tales*, and he is the editor of William Urry's *Christopher Marlowe and Canterbury*.

Tom Cartelli is Professor of English and Chair of the Department of English and Humanities at Muhlenberg College, USA. He is the author of *Marlowe, Shakespeare and the Economy of Theatrical Experience*, as well as a number of articles on English Renaissance drama and post–colonial appropriations of Shakespeare. The best know of these is 'Prospero in Africa: *The Tempest* as Colonialist Text and Context'.

Nick Davidson is a lecturer in History at the University of Leicester. He is currently completing a study of the Inquisition in sixteenth–century Venice and has been commissioned to write a new history of Italy 1500–1800 by Oxford University Press.

Darryll Grantley is a lecturer in Drama at the University of Kent. He has published several essays on medieval and Renaissance drama, including a contribution to *The Cambridge Companion to Medieval English Theatre*, edited by Richard Beadle.

Michael Hattaway is Professor of English Literature at the University of Sheffield. He has taught at the Universities of Kent, British Columbia, and Massachusetts. Among his publications are *Elizabethan Popular Theatre* (1982), and editions of Shakespeare's *1–3 Henry VI* for the New Cambridge Shakespeare and Jonson's *The New Inn* for the Revels Series.

David Potter is a Senior Lecturer at the University of Kent. He has published studies on politics, aristocracy, army and diplomacy of sixteenth century France. His recent work includes *War and Government in the French Provinces: Picardy 1470–1560* and *A History of France 1460–1560*.

Charles Nicholl, an author and journalist, has written various books about the Elizabethans. These include a biography of Thomas Nashe, *A Cup of News*, and a reconstruction of Sir Walter Raleigh's first expedition to South America, *The Creature in the Map*. His investigation of the death of Christopher Marlowe, *The Reckoning*, won the James Tait Black prize and the Crime Writers' Association Gold Dagger award.

Lawrence Normand teaches English at Middlesex University. He has published on Renaissance drama and gender theory, and with Gareth Roberts is writing *Witch–hunting* in Early Modern Scotland. He is also currently working on a book on W. H. Davies.

Gareth Roberts lectures on Renaissance Literature at the University of Exeter. He is the author of *The Open Guide to Spenser's Faerie Queene*, and *The Mirror of Alchemy*. With Lawrence Normand he is writing *Witch–hunting* in Early Modern Scotland, editing *The Comedy of Errors* for the Arden Shakespeare, and with Peter Wiseman translating Ovid's *Fasti*.

Peter Roberts lectures in History at the University of Kent at Canterbury, and writes on Tudor Wales and on the Elizabethan court and stage and the restrictions on playing legislated between 1572 and 1648. He is joint editor of *Religion, Culture and Society in Early Modern Britain: Essays in Honour of Patrick Collinson*.

Roger Sales is a Senior Lecturer in English Studies in the School of English and American Studies at the University of East Anglia. He has been Visiting Professor of Cultural Studies at the University of Munich. His *Christopher Marlowe* was published in 1991. In addition to other books on and editions of Renaissance drama, he has also published widely on the literature and history of the Romantic period. His *Jane Austen and Representations of Regency England* was published in 1994.

Alexander Shurbanov is Professor of English Literature at the University of Sofia. He was the founding President of the Bulgarian Society for British Studies. He has published critical books on Shakespeare's sonnets and Marlowe's drama, and is also a poet and translator of poetry, including English medieval and Renaissance verse. He is currently writing a book on Shakespeare's drama and genre theory. Professor Shurbanov is the recipient of honorary doctorates from the universities of Kent and Surrey.

Nick de Somogyi has recently completed a Cambridge doctorate on Shakespeare and military history.

Richard Wilson is Professor of Renaissance Studies at the University of Lancaster, and author of *Will Power: essays on Shakespearean Authority*, a study of *Julius Caesar*, and many essays on Elizabethan Drama. He has edited *New Historicism and Renaissance Drama* and *Christopher Marlowe* for the Longman Critical Reader series, and is currently completing *Gothic Shakespeare*, a study of drama and the evil eye.

1. 'onelye a boye called Christopher Mowle'[1]

ANDREW BUTCHER

On 20th May 1573, Elizabeth Dyer, a domestic servant of John Bynge, of the parish of St Dunstan, the extra–mural parish lying to the north of Canterbury, beyond the Westgate, gave evidence in a case of sexual assault which she had brought against John Roydon (CCA, MS DCc X.10.4, fos.165v–66)[2]. Elizabeth gave her age to be nineteen years. She claimed to have lived for four years in the parish of St Dunstan and, before that, for three years in the parish of Hernehill. It would seem likely that her family had moved to Hernehill when she was about twelve years old and that she had then been sent into service in Canterbury when she was fifteen. She said that she had known John Roydon, whom she described as of Westgate parish (probably the parish of Holy Cross, Westgate), for four years, knowing him to be a married man, 'And a young woman to his wif', keeping a victualling house and selling beer.

One day she had been sent by her master, at about nine o'clock in the morning, to Roydon's victualling house to buy beer. When she arrived, there seemed to be no one about except a young boy that lived with Roydon, although she could hear that there were guests in the parlour. When Roydon eventually appeared, she asked for a halfpenny pot of beer. Roydon asked her to come down into the cellar to fetch the drink and the boy went with them to draw a pot of beer for the guests in the parlour. Once in the cellar, Roydon ordered the boy 'to fill his pot quickly and to get him out of the seller' and, when the boy had gone upstairs to the guests, Roydon's alleged assault upon Elizabeth Dyer then took place.

The single surviving deposition in this case gives tantalizingly little more to prevent the exercise of the imagination but it does reveal the age and name of the silent and innocent boy witness. Elizabeth gave his age to be twelve years and his name to be 'Mowle', 'onelye a boye called Christopher Mowle'. Though the age is wrong and the name is wrong, the possibility exists that the boy may have been Christopher Marlowe. Various forms of the name 'Marlowe' coexisted in sixteenth century Canterbury and its hinterland including 'Marley' or 'Marle' and Elizabeth Dyer may not have known the boy's name well or accurately have remembered the sound which the clerk attempted to render in the deposition.[3] In May 1573, moreover, Christopher Marlowe would have been only nine years and three months old but Elizabeth Dyer's twelve is unlikely to have been an informed and precise description, more likely a means of indicating a threshold, in this case, perhaps, the customary threshold of service; and though Christopher may have been a big boy for his age he was still young enough to be called a 'boye' by a maid of nineteen years.

If it was the boy Christopher Marlowe in Roydon's victualling house, Elizabeth Dyer's deposition provides us with the only known evidence of his existence between the time of his baptism on 26 February 1564 and his becoming a scholar at the Cathedral School at Christmas in 1578. If it is such evidence, what is its value? Implicit in the biographical enquiry is the notion of the connection between the child and the man, and, in the instance of literary biography, the connection between the child, the man, and the work – the search for a certain psychological explanation which satisfies the desire to see the subject as working out some kind of special destiny or articulating the critical influences upon him in the formative years of his life. Childhood, in this scheme of interpretation, constitutes those formative years, the years in which self and person are so constructed that the course of individual development is critically determined. The value of this deposition evidence, then, might be to contribute to a reconsideration of those formative years and the assumptions made about them. This is not to suggest that the incident in Roydon's victualling house warrants consideration as some kind of decisive childhood trauma (how much did Christopher Marlowe *really* witness of the assault upon Elizabeth Dyer in the dark cellar?), nor would I want, for more than a moment, to play with the irony of the childhood witness of an assault in a victualling house, carrying his pot of ale from cellar to parlour, ending his life murdered in the parlour among the guests of a similar establishment. The significance of the described episode is rather that it lends access to structures and processes without knowledge of which it is difficult to understand the social constraints upon life in a sixteenth–century English town; and that it emphasizes the neglected role of the contingent and the particular in the construction of historical identity. Such an investigation, moreover, is all the more worthwhile in the attempt since Christopher Marlowe's childhood and youth in Canterbury constituted more than half his life. Indeed, by the then current, conventional description of youth in the topos of the seven ages of man, Christopher Marlowe was scarcely more than an adolescent when he died (Brigden, 1984, 77).

Contemporary perceptions of gender, family, neighbourhood, community, and identity are all implicit in the court's record of Elizabeth Dyer's testimony. At the heart of her allegation was a public defence of reputation, a defence all the more important because it touched directly the reputation of not only herself but her master, John Bynge; the landlord of the victualling house, John Roydon; and even the 'boye called Christopher Mowle'. By implication, it also affected the reputations of the families, households, and dealings of all those involved, even those unseen guests drinking in the parlour. Within the parishes of Holy Cross and St Dunstan, and no doubt further afield, the common fame of the incident disturbed the manifest and tacit mutual understandings which acted to sustain social order, and demanded their renegotiation. Not only Roydon's establishment but all victualling houses were damaged by these allegations. The necessary reevaluation of the perceived identities within neighbourhood and wider communities of the principal actors was a complex process of the redefinition of moral worth inextricably enmeshed with local and regional religio–political struggles as well as matters of national and international moment. At all social levels Roydon's assault upon Elizabeth Dyer became symbolically dynamic in a reciprocal process of cognitive exchange in which social knowledge was subtly transformed in the course of the re–establishment of the social equilibrium.

For Elizabeth Dyer, the defence of her social standing had a particular significance. As a domestic servant her very livelihood in the parishes of St Dunstan, Holy Cross, and beyond, might depend upon the honesty of her reputation. As a young woman of nineteen years, her prospects of marriage might seriously be affected by the damage caused to her, prospects with significant consequences for her family and kin. The vulnerability of the servant, and especially a recent immigrant to the town, with little more than a master's household to provide immediate protection, was never greater than when that servant was female. In explaining that she had known Roydon since she had been fifteen years old and that he had a young wife, she was describing the complexity of the sexual politics of their relationship. Having known him for four years and, presumably, having dealt with him on behalf of her master, she had developed a relationship of trust from when she was no more than a child to her present condition as a young woman. It may be that in describing the youth of his wife she was indicating Roydon's own maturity but she was also making clear that there was no excuse for his behaviour. He was not a young unmarried man nor a mature unmarried or widowed man for whom some public excuse might be made for exploitative behaviour. The relationship was of long standing, he was mature and responsible, and by any expectations his sexual appetites should have been capable of fulfilment. His behaviour was entirely reprehensible, she was guiltless, and her reputation ought to remain unsullied or, since that was impossible in such circumstances, the damage done to her reputation should be limited, the extent of its social consequences confined and the balance of advantage maintained in the process of renegotiation. All that Roydon stood for should receive the moral opprobrium of the community. The ecclesiastical court, moreover, exercised a special function in permitting the public examination of certain issues of this kind in the context of its role as an instrument of religious and moral reform in the sixteenth–century town.

Parallels can be drawn between the position of Elizabeth Dyer and that of the Marlowe family, as what was true for Elizabeth Dyer was in its own way true also for the Marlowes. In the community, the situations of servant and immigrant were especially vulnerable. Both were involved in the development of personal and public relationships which would determine the success or failure of their careers within their chosen communities. Reputations established in their early years might stay with them for the rest of their lives. Social memories in such societies were long and the past was continuously renegotiable.[4] As recent immigrants to the city, Christopher Marlowe's mother and father faced extreme difficulties of social adaptation.[5] Yet the notion of the boy genius arising from the bosom of the indigent shoemaker's family is probably more the stuff of popular mythology (past and present) than the product of a careful reading of the surviving evidence. From the beginning, indeed, John Marlowe's career is characterized by success. For most migrants entering provincial towns in this period, intent on setting up in business and entering the privileged freemen body, failure was the common experience, especially within the first two or three years, with a probable consequent social descent into the ranks of the labouring poor or, in debt, enforced flight from town authorities and landlords. In Canterbury, it was possible for some to retain trading privileges for a while by annual payment of a fine but without gaining the full social, economic and political rights of the freemen elite, though very few succeeded for any length of time in this marginal existence (Butcher, 1979, 1–10). For some, apprenticeship was the course of entry to the freedom; for some, the marriage of the freeborn daughter of a Canterbury freeman; and for some, freedom was inherited as the freeborn son of a citizen. Such entrances were, however, relatively unusual and by far the majority of those gaining the freedom did so by payment of a special fine. This freemen elite, therefore, was selectively composed of families of sufficient wealth, influence, and reputation, and included those thought suitable as marriage partners as well as those few who might be deemed fit to perform service and receive training in the households of freemen with the recognized possibility of their becoming members of the governing body of the town. That John Marlowe should have been admitted as an apprentice in 1559–60, let alone as a freeman in April 1564, was no small achievement in this small provincial town.

It has been suggested that John Marlowe's apprenticeship has the appearance of 'a fiction designed...to circumvent the stringent demands of full apprenticeship and to make a back–door entry into the city's freedom' (Urry, 1988, 13). If so then such an admission should be seen as specially favoured and in keeping with the shoemaker's notable economic progress which enabled him to undertake marriage in May 1561 and, two months after the birth of his second child, Christopher, to enter the freedom in April 1564 as a member of the Shoemakers' Company and establish a business in his own workshop.[6] His further commercial success and confidence would seem also to be confirmed by the size of his family and the regular recruitment of apprentices to his household. Under normal circumstances, the nature of the life–cycle of the family economy would suggest that the accumulative capacity of the family unit, based on the difference between labour production and consumption per year of the marriage, would show a steady decline and prolonged deficit after the first few years, exacerbated by an increasing number of children (Smith, 1984, 68–72, esp. Table 1.9 [after Chayanov]). This negative characteristic helps account for the persistent failure of the family economies of peasants and artisans, their inability to accumulate, and their tendency to remain small and underdeveloped. Between 1561 and 1580, when Christopher Marlowe left for Cambridge, John and Katherine Marlowe, however, managed to produce seven surviving children, and establish a business and family respectability, John Marlowe's standing acknowledged in his holding of office in his trade company and his parish church as well as in securing a small loan from the Wilde Charity (Urry, 1988, Ch.2 *passim*).

The success of these opening years of their long career in the city was crucial to their later progress and there may recently have been too great an insistence on John Marlowe's modesty of means, lack of business competence and social marginality: 'rowdy, quarrelsome, awkward, improvident, busy, self–assertive and too clever by half' (Urry, 1988, 28). The evidence of the courts may often more appropriately be read as a testimony of social, economic, and administrative record and control than of criminal activity, and the remarkable volume of surviving detail for the life of John Marlowe may well indicate the extent of the involvement of a respected freeman craftsman, recognized as office–holder in trade company, parish church, and ward administration, as well as security in financial dealing. The temptation to reconstruct John Marlowe retrospectively from the supposed temperamental extravagance of his son in order to provide the son's psychological inheritance must be resisted.

What is known of the family's pattern of residence, moreover, may indicate not an impecunious restlessness but stages in the process of social and economic integration and a certain upward social mobility.[7] The Marlowes made at least four moves for which we have evidence: to St George's parish (c.1560), to St Andrew's (c.1584), to St Mary Breadman (c.1594), and to All Saints' (c.1603). The significance of the establishment of household and workshop in St George's parish has already been noted and it seems likely that the subsequent moves to the parishes of St Andrew and St Mary Breadman marked a recognizable shift to more prosperous neighbourhoods associated with those at the centre of the town's economic, governmental, and administrative life. The final move, and the licence taken out 'to kepe comon victualing in his nowe dwelling howse' in 1604, may well have been associated with retirement at the end of the working life–cycle and, indeed, the inventory taken of his house in 1605 shows no sign of his craft activities as a shoemaker (Urry, 1988, 38–40). For many migrants who managed to establish a household and maintain themselves in business, the working life–cycle might begin and end in a small, poor, one or two room tenement and, if they were fortunate, in between times, a degree of prosperity might make possible a more substantial house and workshop in a more distinguished quarter. The Marlowes' house in 1605 perhaps suggests a modesty of means and a 'precious word–picture of a household which must have been similar to that in which Christopher Marlowe grew up'(Urry, 1988, 39). Yet the house described, with its belongings, is probably distinctly more comfortable than that in which the Marlowes' seven children were raised in the 1560s and 1570s. The low value of the inventory (£21 14s 2d) and the bareness of the provisions of John Marlowe's will should not be allowed to detract from the quality of the house itself (Urry, 1988, 133–34, 137–39). With a small parlour next to the street as well as a hall, separate kitchen and cellar, and with a great and small chamber, this was a house with some pretension to style for the retiring household of a former craftsman and one readily adaptable in rooms and furnishings to the needs of a victualling house, not so different, perhaps, from the 'Vernicle' in which the Marlowes had sat drinking in St George's parish in 1565 or from the house of John Roydon.[8] The house in All Saints' parish occupied by John and Katherine Marlowe, though probably inferior to those occupied in the two previous parishes, may nonetheless serve as some kind of indicator of social progress.

The marriages of the Marlowe daughters in the 1580s and 1590s might also provide valuable evidence for the family's social status in the city. Whatever the success in business and the growth of reputation and influence, none of the daughters' marriages created affinal connections with families of established status in the city, their partners were drawn not from the children of those already members of the freemen elite but rather from those seeking to enter that elite as respectable immigrants. Such prospective partners within Canterbury society were clearly not to be spurned but their standing would seem to suggest the social limitations of the Marlowes' advancement. These were marriages by newcomers to those who had not sufficiently managed to escape their own recent origins as migrants. They were marriages, moreover, that carried with them the prize of admission to the freedom as the husband of a freeborn daughter of a freeman. Without the appeal of such a prize, perhaps, the Marlowes' attractions of wealth, honour, and connection, were not enough to enhance their ambitions. Jane Marlowe's marriage to John Moore, a migrant from Ulcombe and Faversham, in 1582 did, it is true, reinforce pre–existing connections between the respectable family of the Moores and the Marlowes (Urry, 1988, 15–19), but her pregnancy at 12 years old, followed by the death of her child and herself in childbed, probably did little for her sisters' marriage prospects. Margaret, Anne, and Dorothy all married in the church of St Mary Breadman between 1590 and 1594 in their early twenties. Margaret's husband, John Jordan, a shoemaker, brought the respectability of a former servant in the household of the Bishop of Dover and Dean of Canterbury. Anne's husband, however, John Cranford, a tailor, had arrived in Canterbury in the year before his marriage as a migrant born in Henley–on–Thames who had made his way via Cambridge, Rye, and Ashford in Kent. Thomas Graddell, Dorothy's husband, a glover, had made his way from Preston in Lancashire before arriving in Canterbury in 1585 (Urry, 1988, 31–35). These were men, whatever their personal qualities, in search of fortune, reputation, and connection, not bringing them. The principal dowry they were to receive from their brides was freedom and the status and associations already won by the Marlowes among kin and fictive kin, among friends and neighbours, in craft and trade. Their life stories demonstrate the workings of the urban marriage market in recruitment and social promotion at the outer margins of the freemen elite in a small, provincial city.

Whatever limited success the Marlowes had won and strove to secure in the 1580s and 1590s had been founded upon their achievements in the 1560s and 1570s. Not that such achievements are likely to have been easily made. The nature of the marriage of John Marlowe to Katherine Arthur in 1561 itself suggests a precariousness of social position which might be converted to advantage only with difficulty. Though John might have some support from family and kin in Ospringe and in Canterbury and its hinterland, his own position, in the late 1550s, aged in his early twenties, perhaps as servant to Gerard Richardson, an impoverished, alien shoemaker, provided an inauspicious beginning. It may be, indeed, that the good fortune which seems to have followed his marriage in St George's parish owed more to his wife and her family than to his own enterprise.

Katherine's own family origins in Dover are, however, obscure and her status uncertain but it is notable that, through her kinsman, William Arthur of Dover, and his business interests in Canterbury, she appears to have had connections with St George's parish from at least the late 1550s; and her brother Thomas, who before his death in the epidemic of 1593 had served as office–holder in various positions of responsibility in Canterbury and its environs, had interests in the city from at least as early as 1564 (Urry, 1988, 14, 16–18). Relations between the Marlowes and the Moores, moreover, were replicated in those between the Moores and the Arthurs. Katherine's brother, Thomas Arthur, married Ursula Moore following her family's move to Canterbury from Ulcombe and her father, Richard's, purchase of freeman status as a blacksmith in 1573. Richard may well have been a citizen of recognizably greater substance in Canterbury than the Marlowes and the Arthurs. Richard's son Thomas, indeed, had married Mary, sister of the prosperous Canterbury grocer and later innkeeper, George Aunsell, whose marriage to Ann Potman at Ulcombe brought even 'some tone of gentility to a circle of small craftsmen and tradesmen' (Urry, 1988, 16–20). This was a connection which, however indirectly, might significantly enhance the status of the immigrant blacksmith and his family, a status to which Katherine's brother Thomas might have gained access as representative of local authorities but to which John Marlowe and his family might only aspire, whatever the quality of Katherine's name and fame. It was a connection which made possible the movement from the periphery of the freemen body to its élite core, a delicate weight in the scale of influences which determined dignity and worth in the distribution of power among those few families who, over generations, came to determine the identity of this small provincial city, even if George Aunsell's moral reputation as 'drunken knave and whoremaster knave' might somewhat compromise that possibility (CCA, MS DCc X.1.10, fo. 67; CKS, MS PRC 39/11 and 39/26, fo. 4).

Obligations of kinship and the need, at the very least, to maintain a mutual dependence in the interests of preserving social standing, ensured the continuing involvement of the Moores, the Arthurs, and the Marlowes in each other's affairs. The occasion of the reading of Katherine Benchkin's will in November 1585, now well known for Christopher Marlowe's involvement, reading 'plainely and distinktly', is perhaps more significant for the presence as witnesses of John Marlowe, Thomas Arthur, John Moore, and Christopher Marlowe, kinsmen acting together at the request of Katherine's son John Benchkin (Urry, 1988, 123–29). The death of Thomas Arthur and his wife in 1593 inevitably involved the same families again in the complex administration of his estate, the Marlowes taking into their household as maid Dorothy, the daughter of Katherine Marlowe's brother and of Richard Moore's daughter (Urry, 1988, 17–18). The construction and maintenance of such alliances were reinforced by those only slightly less important among neighbours and friends, like the Plessingtons and the Applegates, involved with the Marlowes in the administration of Thomas Arthur's will and on various other occasions, neighbours and friends whose intimate engagement with the family's development included their role in the frequent gatherings of women at the childbed of Katherine in the 1560s and 1570s and the bringing of the children to baptism.[9] And, in this same period, it was necessary to find a place in those vertical structures of production and consumption without which a business life might not be sustained.

To gain acceptance among their fellow tradesmen and craftsmen in these early years of their life in Canterbury meant acknowledgement of John Marlowe's skill and honest dealing among the members of the trade company of leatherworkers which he joined in 1564. This implied not only the recognition of other shoemakers, competitors in a market of small margins, but the trust of craftsmen in the chain of production which reached from farmers, butchers and graziers to tanners, tawyers, curriers, and to saddlers, glovers, cappers, and others, representatives of the families of Ashenden, Augar, Bennet, Doggerell, Free, Grave, Grenleff, Holland, Stockden, and Umberstone, all of whom served as craft officers with John Marlowe, to say nothing of Graddell and Jordan. The goodwill of such men was essential to business prosperity and in the moral economy of the sixteenth–century town that goodwill might be determined as much by perceived political and religious allegiance as by wealth, status, or family connection. To enter the necessary network of credit relations, to find honest customers, to identify reliable suppliers of raw materials and finishers, involved a complex process of social negotiation, meant learning a language of participation in this field of common experience and developing a sensitivity to the balances of power distributed among its members. Public and personal identities were pervaded by occupational considerations. John Marlowe's relations with his leather supplier, the currier, Leonard Doggerell, who served as Master of the Leatherworkers' Company, provide one example of the influence of these vertical structures of connection. The ties of kinship between Katherine Benchkin and the Grenleff family in the person of Thomas, one time Master of the Leatherworkers' Company, appointed overseer of Katherine's will, provide another and suggest further reasons for the presence of Christopher Marlowe in the widow's house in November 1585 (Urry, 1988, 21–3, 124–25).

The world of Christopher Mowle in the parlour of Roydon's alehouse was the world of such social negotiations, just as, in the year of Christopher Marlowe's birth, the conversations in 1564 in John Marlowe's workshop between Marlowe and Laurence Applegate, the tailor, or in 1565 in the 'Vernicle' between Lora Atkinson, wife of Thomas, the barber, Goodman Harmon Verson, the glazier, Goodman Michael Barton, basketmaker, and John and Katherine Marlowe, were conversations which, concerned with the reputation of Godelif Hurte and Laurence Applegate, the tailor, contributed to the process of social integration and adaptation and a mutual comprehension of person and self in a society undergoing significant conflicts and discontinuities in the local distribution of power. Even as the sign of the 'Vernicle' itself, with its origins in the popular beliefs of saints' cults, relics, and pilgrimage of the later middle ages, was changing its meanings. The formative years of Christopher Marlowe were inevitably influenced by the translation, in domestic terms, of the tensions of these processes of transition. Mediating the national and local political and religious struggles of the 1560s and 1570s these translations gave added significance to the strict Calvinist education he was to receive among the socially diverse sons of local landowners, local clergy, professional men, royal servants, farmers, tradesmen and artisans.

9

If these social processes of mediation are to be understood, however, and if the influence of the inheritances of successive generations in the course of the Reformations of the sixteenth century are to be fully appreciated in a town like Canterbury, then it is important to recognise the role of individual responses within these processes.[10] For the Marlowes, the 1560s and 1570s involved the dangerous cross–currents of radical and conservative religious groupings struggling for ascendancy, Protestants enlisting the Privy Council in their support against conservative leaders seeking to manipulate tradition and popular culture to humiliate their enemies; and if from the early 1570s Protestant control was increasingly assured there were still those for whom that control was repugnant even during the Sabbatarian regime of the 1580s. There were, furthermore, those like John Marlowe and Katherine Arthur who, arriving as immigrants in the 1550s, might interpret the developments of the ensuing decades through the prism of Marian reaction. Recalling his youth in the city of Gloucester in the 1560s or early 1570s, Willis described being taken by his father, standing 'betweene his leggs, as he sate upon one of the benches', to see a morality play called 'The Cradle of Security' in which a Prince was seduced from good counsel by the blandishments of three female courtiers, rescued to judgment by two old men, and finally carried off by wicked spirits.

> This Prince did personate in the morall, the wicked of the world; the three Ladies, Pride, Covetousnesse, and Luxury, the two old men, the end of the world, and the last judgement. This sight tooke such impression in me, that when I came towards mans estate, it was as fresh in my memory, as if I had seen it newly acted.[11]

How much more traumatic were the dramas played out in the sandy hollows of Wincheap, outside the walls of the city of Canterbury, where forty–three men and women were burnt as Protestant martyrs before the crowds in 1556 (Butcher, 1989, 23–5). If we are to understand the construction of Christopher Marlowe's identity, then the assimilation of such a morality by his future parents is of central psychological importance.

The whole notion of inter–generational 'transference' in the formation of identity is of special interest in a society such as Reformation Canterbury which achieved continuity in the face of forces making for radical dysfunction and the repeated erasure of legitimating categories of action.[12] If it is true that 'To a large extent.....the identity of a person or a community is made up of these identifications ['by which the other enters into the composition of the same'] with values, norms, ideals, models, and heroes, *in* which the person or a community recognizes itself' (Ricoeur, 1992, 121), then the processes of acculturation and the construction of identity in the 1550s, 1560s, and 1570s, in this provincial city, must be recognized to have been peculiarly unstable. Seeking stability, continuity, and acceptance must have involved both John and Katherine Marlowe in frequent silences and suppressions, creative of anxieties in their children about past, present, and future, which were likely to become obsessive in their desire for resolution.

No doubt there were many cultural forms which acted therapeutically to express such personal and social tensions. When William Doggerell, of Canterbury, died, in the year of Elizabeth's accession, his bequest to his sons Leonard and Isaacke, in the context of this discussion, seems symbolically to be peculiarly appropriate. The bequest included:

> ii chestes wheryn my players garmentes do lye and my said garmentes with all and everye suche thynge and thynges as to the same garmentes dothe belonge and appertayne to be had and holden to them.....together wythe all suche gaynes and advantages as shall from tyme to tyme ryse growe and come at anye tyme or tymes by hyrynge or lettynge forthe the saide garmentes and all other the thynge and thynges to them belongynge.
> (CKS, MS PRC 17/32, fo. 241)[13]

In passing on such costumes for his sons' own use or for purposes of economic benefit through hire, it would seem that he was passing on not costumes associated with a specific role or play but costumes which identified a player and, therefore, gave special significance to that player's performance, whatever it might be. The understanding of the player's performative skills was dependent upon the interpretive context of the performance. The costumes allowed a range of performances and interpretations within generic limits, providing continuity (even from generation to generation) while permitting change. Alternatively, they might be seen as a bequest from one generation to another which, however enabling, was essentially restrictive, predetermining the form of expressive response. And the nature of this inheritance is all the more intriguing since Leonard Doggerell was to become the currier who acted as John Marlowe's supplier of leather and, eventually, held the office of Master of the Leatherworkers' company.

It has been argued that 'Costume in fact was a language, a system of signs, whose meanings derived from its own codes and not from congruence with reality' (Hattaway, 1982, 86).[14] Doggerell's bequest might then be understood as the transmission of a recognized means of expression and understanding, implying a shared system of values between father and sons. Between the father who spent his last years in Marian Canterbury and the sons who came to maturity in the Elizabethan city, however, such interpretive continuities should not be too readily presumed. Dress, dressing, and costume constituted, undoubtedly, a distinctive system of signs operating at all cultural levels but changes in its operative contexts necessitated changes in signification. It has been suggested, indeed, that dramatic use of costume and disguising, dependent on this system of signs, permitted the exploration of contradiction:

> This device...was already commonplace in medieval moral drama, but it was ubiquitous in the Reformation interludes from Bale's time onwards, and *was* so because of the dilemma experienced by English audiences of discerning between true and false representations of truth in times of tumultuous religious change. (White, 1993, 76)

And since the direction of that change was locally perceived as far from certain, subject to discontinuity and reversal, often assimilated in resistance, the system of signs was highly unstable, multi–valent, ambiguous. Characteristic was the use by players of clerical garments rented by English churches and the dramatic advantage taken of the controversies over church vestments and ceremonies which were of such widespread public concern during the 1560s and 1570s (White, 1993, 89–92, 142; Collinson, [1967] 1982, 92–7). When the polemicist, Anthony Munday, asked: 'As for those stagers, are they not commonlie such kind of men in their conversation as they are in profession? Are they not variable in hart, as they are in their parts?', he was not simply voicing traditional views against the theatre as part of that Puritan onslaught which sought to redefine and redirect Protestant culture, but was also representing those contemporary anxieties, widely experienced, which the players expressed in the destabilizing effects they had on the audience's sense of self, in producing an uncontrollable variability; such also underlay the motives of those who, significantly, rejected as an abomination the practice of boys playing female roles (White, 1993, 170–71; Barish, 1981, 104[15]; Collinson, 1988, 112). The chests of Doggerell's bequest were more like Pandora's boxes.

If the meanings of costume were subject to such particular variations, they were also more generally expressive of a dramatic tradition which, as has recently been identified, though having its origins in medieval drama, was a Protestant cultural form, vigorous, innovative, and popular, in creating 'a new religious and moral drama of its own for its own propagandist and didactic purposes' (Collinson, 1988, 102, 98–106 *passim*; White, 1993, 2–4, 163–74). Co–existing with civic, parish, and other popular productions, it became part of an expressive medium in the period c.1530–1580 which, perhaps especially in urban society, helped to articulate personal and social tensions in time of conflict, only slowly developing from a time in which 'Protestantism was still a religion of protest, at ease with the culture of the streets and of other public places, including inns and alehouses and..."vintners' and barbers' shops"'(Collinson, 1988, 107). Though in the discussion of sixteenth–century drama there is a danger in attributing to the provinces what were essentially the experiences of London, it seems likely that Canterbury was caught up in these cultural processes, not least because of its special role in the course of the Reformation. The presence of John Bale, early in Elizabeth's reign, still writing satirical sketches in the cathedral precincts 'with which to hammer home the recent and still fragile Protestant *revanche*, and which were performed by the boys of the king's grammar school', is a potent reminder of circumstances in this city in the 1560s, as is the preference of Alderman Okeden's son for the Whitsuntide mystery plays of New Romney rather than the works of Bale, circumstances intimately contributory to Christopher Marlowe's inheritance (*pace* Collinson, 1988, 103–04).

But just as the 1560s and 1570s in Canterbury were characterized by political and religious struggle, so the dramatic medium which gave expression and direction to that struggle was undergoing a significant transformation. To speak of a cultural phase of the English Reformation, epitomized in its Protestant drama, coming to a close in 1580 is seriously misleading. The first two decades of Elizabeth's reign were characterized, in the provinces, by the changing relationship between the Protestant drama and other forms, by the decline of traditional civic and parish practice and by the growing importance of visiting professional troupes; the Protestant drama itself became increasingly controversial in these years, losing some of its support as a central instrument of reform; but that drama, nonetheless, continued to be performed, albeit in reduced volume, down to the Blasphemy Act of 1605/6 (White, 1993, 163–74; Collinson, 1988, 100, 112–13). If the role of the drama in the political, religious and moral changes of these years is fully to be appreciated then it is the local processes of its transformation as it involved men and women in provincial urban society which are critical. To argue that changes in certain elite Protestant cultural values in some way 'emancipated the English theatre' and made it possible for writers such as Christopher Marlowe 'to explore the moral and social complexities of the human condition on their own terms and in their own language' (Collinson, 1988, 114)[16], begs so many questions as to be essentially ahistorical, ignoring as it does issues of continuity and the intimate reciprocal relationships between drama, society, and audience. For those who lived through the turmoil of the 1550s, 1560s, and 1570s in Canterbury it was the capacity of a complex and changing dramatic medium in a variety of ways to express social and personal tension and anxiety which was the measure of its therapeutic value, its contribution to acculturation, and its role in the construction of identity. Even before he attended the King's grammar school,

Christopher Marlowe was aware of the integral role of dramatic performance in the lives of his parents, their kin, friends and neighbours, fellow craftsmen, and, indeed, in the lives of all those who inhabited their world. His developing intelligence of the moral and social complexities of the human condition was inescapably fashioned before the 1580s, even in the domestic sphere, by the interaction of the susceptible sensibilities of John and Katherine Marlowe as vulnerable and ambitious immigrants and the often ambiguous and contradictory systems of signs, discourses, and ideological concerns of competing traditional and modern dramatic productions.

When I return to the case of *Dyer versus Roydon*, as I have done on many occasions since first reading Elizabeth Dyer's deposition, I realize that it exercises a powerful hold on my imagination. Above all, it is the presence of the silent witness, Christopher Mowle, which I find myself trying to recover. The narrative is tantalizingly unresolved. I picture the boy descending to the gloomy cellar, following his master and the young servantwoman as they exchange pleasantries, thinking as he slowly fills his pot with ale, of returning with the others, only to be brusquely excluded by Roydon, ordered out, upstairs to the guests waiting in the parlour. I see him climbing the stairs and try to imagine his bewilderment, even pain, his disturbed awareness of some violation, some sin, translated perhaps into a sense of guilt, associated with exclusion, the closed door, the faint and muffled sounds of a struggle. As he approaches the parlour, carrying the pot of ale, fearing to spill a drop, he hears new sounds of voices gossiping, joking, exchanging adult knowledge, discussing reputations, and he experiences a different sense of exclusion and anticipates the act of courage it will require to enter the adult intimacies of the parlour and deliver the ale. Between the cellar and the parlour in this alehouse there is a liminal journey which he undertakes and which, henceforth, he may undertake with a special trepidation. And whether Christopher Mowle is Christopher Marlowe or not, the liminality is that of the childhood and youth which, in various ways, has been the subject of this paper, a liminality too which extends to the peculiar experiences of Christopher Marlowe's parents as immigrants, and to the extraordinary transitions of Reformation Canterbury in the 1550s, 1560s, and 1570s. If Christopher Marlowe's contribution as a dramatist is to be fully understood it is to these years that we must return.[17]

Notes

1. This essay is a detailed reconsideration and, to some extent, a reinterpretation of evidence previously considered in Urry, 1988, ix–xl. I would like to record my thanks to Bill Watson for raising with me many issues central to the following arguments in the course of many discussions in Eliot College, in those times before administrative fiat made such conversations impossible to sustain. I have still to tackle the most substantial of his questions in attempting to demonstrate the ways in which social processes are translated into textual expression in Marlowe's work.

2. I am grateful to Dr Diana O'Hara for drawing my attention to this case.

3. For further discussion of the name see Urry, 1988, 150, n.2.

4. See, for example, the case of *Lobly v Yetman* in 1574, discussed in Urry, 1988, xxxvii–xxxix.

5. The following biographical details are based on Urry, 1988, xv–xl,1–41.

6. For more usual progress from apprenticeship see Ben–Amos, 1994, 229–30.

7. For valuable suggestions about the link between dwelling place and life–cycle stage see Boulton, 1987, 138.

8. For the characteristics of Canterbury's ale– and victualling–houses see Clark, 1983, 64–5. For the evidence of the drinking party in the 'Vernicle' see CCA, MS DCc. Y.4.12, fo.10.

9. For important exploration of the nature and significance of women's groups in sixteenth and seventeenth century Canterbury see Elizabeth Hallam, 1994, esp. ch. 3. I am grateful to Dr Hallam for discussion of these matters.

10. This argument is strongly sympathetic to approaches taken by Cohen, 1994. Felicity Riddy's powerful criticisms of another version of this paper have also influenced my perceptions of the need to distinguish self *and* person in historical analysis.

11. R. Willis, *Mount Tabor, or Private Exercises of a Penitent Sinner*, 1639, London, 110–14, quoted in Bevington, 1962, 13–14, Hattaway, 1982, 65–6.

12. For a stimulating discussion of these issues see Fischer, 1986, 204–08. I am also grateful to Judith Waller for suggestions made in discussion of these matters.

13. I have benefited, in the assessment of this and related evidence, from discussions with Catherine Richardson.

14. Similarly, writing of Bale's audiences, White argues: 'Bale could also count on their previous play experience to recognize visual significations of meaning transmitted through costumes, gesture, movement, and properties, as well as the conventions of disguise, parody, and inversion, that were staple features of English drama for centuries.'
    (1993, 31)

15. Citing Munday, *A Second and Third Blast of Retrait from Plaies and Theaters*, (1581).

16. See also White, 1993, 174: 'the new conditions and freedoms inspired Marlowe, Shakespeare and the other major playwrights of the time to offer a more complex and problematic view of the human condition than their clerical predecessors had done.'

17. With thanks, as ever, to Peter Brown.

2. The 'Studious Artizan':
Christopher Marlowe, Canterbury and Cambridge

PETER ROBERTS

To the Elizabethan Protestant antiquary, William Lambarde, the former centres of pilgrimage like Canterbury and Walsingham were no better than the Cities of the Plain. In his *Perambulation of Kent* (1576) Lambarde wrote that 'these harborowes of the Devill and the Pope... in horrible crimes contended with Sodome, in unbeliefs matched Ierusalem, and in folly of superstition exceeded all Gentilitie.' Divine vengeance is visited in all ages 'not onely upon the persons, but upon the places also, where his name was dishonoured, striking the same with solitude and exterminion.'[1] He attributed Canterbury's decline in prosperity and population since the Reformation to God's wrath, rather than to the dissolution of the abbeys and the destruction of Becket's shrine. A pall of retribution thus hung over the place where Christopher Marlowe was born.

Lambarde's view of the decadence of Canterbury was shared by John Bale, who in 1561, shortly after his appointment as a prebendary of the Cathedral, deplored the popular ceremonies and superstitious observances which persisted in the City after the Elizabethan church settlement. The fervent Protestant who in an earlier phase of the Reformation had developed English drama as a potent instrument of religious propaganda lamented the prevalence of May games, bonfires in the streets and bell ringing on saints' days. The 'preachers of Gods sacred wurde' who had condemned the pagan superstitions from their pulpits had been mocked for their pains. The greatest delinquent was a jester–minstrel, Richard Borowes, *alias* 'Raylynge Dycke' who, armed with a drum, had led a hundred boys to a bonfire at the Bull–Stake in Burgate. He was '... an unshamefast ribalde and commen smelfeast, a generall jester or mynstrell also for baudy songes at all bankettes of the papistes, and an ydle vagabonde, upholden amonge them only to that ende, for other wurke he doth none, as the commen fame goeth.' Bale denounced the civic authorities who countenanced the 'settyng fourth those unruly pageauntes,' and prayed that 'God sende that cytie better, and more godly governours'(Baskerville, 1993, 240–48). The ending of the wealth that came with the pilgrims and the abbeys had led to urban decline, but the Canterbury described by Bale was evidently still a populous and vigorous, if in his eyes an unruly, community.

There had been gains as well as losses at the Reformation for the City which became the primatial see of the Church of England. The 'King's School' established in 1541 as part of the new foundation of the Cathedral was re–endowed by Cardinal Reginald Pole in his will and flourished under its first headmaster, the antiquary John Twyne (Edwards, 1957, 62–7). Twyne had been mayor of Canterbury and a burgess of parliament for the City in 1553 and, as a recalcitrant Catholic, was one of Bale's adversaries in the stirs of 1561. Most of the free school's brightest pupils seem to have been sent to Oxford (Twyne had been at Corpus Christi College) until Archbishop Matthew Parker endowed a series of tied scholarships at Cambridge colleges. As Primate, Parker was as much concerned to reform the institutions and religious life of the see as he was to provide for the education of the clergy. In 1569 part of the revenues of Eastbridge Hospital in Canterbury, which had previously been misappropriated by the Masters, were assigned for the maintenance of two scholars from the Canterbury School at Parker's old college of Corpus Christi. In 1571 he provided for 'the foundation of one Scholar or Student in physic' from the School at Gonville and Caius (a place that was to be taken up in 1593 by William Harvey). At Parker's death in 1575 three further scholarships were endowed at Corpus, under the terms of his will, for boys from Canterbury and Norfolk, and the 'stoare house' at the college was to be fitted out as their chamber. The Archbishop had already made provision for the bulk of his library to be bequeathed to Corpus, whither they were conveyed in 1576.[2]

The main objective of Parker's endowments and bequests was to staff the established church with suitable ordinands. In Latin letters dimissory issued in 1568 he defined the qualities to be looked for in an ordinand: 'good character, knowledge of Scripture and of Latin, and that he should not have been educated in "illiberal" arts' (cited in Brook, 1962, 222). This was the vocation to which Marlowe seemed destined when he went to Cambridge as one of the first Parker scholars, for which he was prepared with a grammarian's grounding in the liberal arts. His name first appears on the Ladyday list of fifty 'grammar boys' for the Christmas quarter 1578–9, when he was almost fifteen years of age, receiving an allowance of £4 a year, paid in arrear. He may have been a commoner at the School before that date. The headmaster since 1566 was John Gresshop, the inventory of whose library drawn up at his death in 1580 attests to the breadth of his learning and his committed Protestantism. Gresshop possessed a copy of *The Fal of the late Arrian* (1549) by John Proctor. Manuscript extracts from this book, describing the Arian heresy which the author proceeded to confute, were to be discovered in 1593 in the 'chamber' in London which Thomas Kyd shared with Marlowe: it formed part of the incriminating, if circumstantial, evidence for Marlowe's alleged atheism. Gresshop's executors enumerated over 350 volumes in his library. William Urry has drawn attention to the fact that Marlowe's headmaster 'had a larger private library than almost anyone outside of the circles of bishops and noblemen, far greater than the private collections of university dons.'[3] This does not make it as important as Matthew Parker's collection, but it is remarkable that the libraries of two of the most assiduous collectors or bibliophiles of the age were attached to Marlowe's school and college. Gresshop's books were kept in 'the upper study by the schoole doare' and in 'the lower study'. These may have been more accessible to his pupils than Parker's books were to the students, as distinct from the Fellows, of Corpus, for under the terms of the bequest the latter books were protected by strict regulations against loss.

The acting of plays was well established at the Canterbury School before Marlowe's time and not always, it seems, as part of the curriculum. Some of John Bale's satirical interludes attacking the friars were acted by the pupils early in Elizabeth's reign. In May 1560 one of these was given a public performance before a fee–paying audience in one of the more commodious dwelling houses in the City.[4] The earliest extant record of plays performed at the school is an entry dated late 1562 in the Chapter Act Books, Miscellaneous Accounts, of a payment made towards the charges of the grammar school for the 'settyng forthe of Interludes...' This is closely followed by a sum of £3 6s. 8d. to the headmaster, Anthony Rushe, towards the expenses 'in setting furthe of [tra]gedies, Comedyes and interludes this next [Christ]mas, and the same to be done by th'advise [and] consent of Mr vicedeane.'[5] Nothing has survived in the accounts about any dramatic activity under John Gresshop, but there is evidence dating from the playwright's lifetime that playing had become such an accomplished diversion among the schoolboys that it posed a problem of discipline.

II

In January 1592, when Marlowe was in the Netherlands, two players, one Edwards and William Symcox, were arraigned before the Court of High Commission for the diocese of Canterbury for having 'inveigled' some of the scholars of the King's School 'to go abrode in the countrey to play playes contrary to lawe and good order.' The case was heard before Richard Rogers, suffragan bishop of Dover, in the precincts of the Cathedral, of which Rogers was also dean. The players had persuaded the pupils to disobey their masters, not once but twice, for the boys had ignored one warning and been apprehended and put in the precincts prison, where the two players 'came to them and there dyd anymate' them to perform again. And so the boys had 'hanged owte a sho or a pott to beg wythall'.[6] This of course brought them within the danger of the act of 1572 in restraint of vagabonds and beggars, which imposed severe penalties on common players of interludes who did not have a licence to play.[7] Symcox and Edwards 'dyd anymate the said boyes so ffarr that they should have as good recompense as they should have by the scole yf they did gyve over or lose theyr place.' In other words, the prospect of a livelihood of at least £4 a year as members of a company of players was dangled before them: a rare clue perhaps to the average earnings of

19

Elizabethan boy actors in the adult companies. The matter was determined in May 1592, when the two players confessed their misdeed, promised to reform and were dismissed with a caution; the boys presumably went back to their studies.[8] It looks as if the bishop was using the court to fulfil his responsibilities as dean for the government and welfare of the school under the terms of Archbishop Parker's injunctions of 1574 to the dean and chapter.[9] It was not the first time that the Cathedral authorities had had to intervene to correct laxity in the running of the school. In 1588 the headmaster, Anthony Shorte, was reprimanded by the chapter for neglecting his duties, which led to a marked decline in learning, good manners and civility among the boys in his charge. By 1591 Rufus Rogers, the dean's nephew, had been installed as lower master, though he manifestly failed to prevent the lapse in scholarly discipline in 1592.[10] However, for all the attentions of the Court of High Commission, a full–blown scandal seems to have been averted, and it may be significant that no moral objections were registered on this occasion to the performance of plays.

Who were these players? Edwards has not been identified (unless he was a superannuated Richard Edwardes, Master of the Children of the Chapel Royal from 1561 to 1566 and author of *Damon and Pythias* and *Palamon and Arcite*),[11] but Symcox later turns up in the records as a member of the Duke of Lennox's company of players, who acted in Canterbury in the first year of James I's reign.[12] In 1592 they may both have belonged to the Queen's Men: there is an entry in the City accounts of 20s. paid to this company on 9 January 1591 and the same sum again on 30 March 1592 (Dawson, 1965, 17–18). If Symcox and Edwards wore the royal livery, this might explain their lenient treatment by the Court of High Commission. It was an established tradition for Cathedral choristers, if not the pupils of schools of royal foundation, to be recruited into royal service under licence by choirmasters from St George's, Windsor, or the Chapel Royal, although such impressments were, not surprisingly, resented by the depleted choirs.[13] For the Queen's Men (if that was the culprits' affiliation) to adopt such recruiting tactics was obviously an abuse of their privileges. The Canterbury case must be considered alongside the other known instances of the abduction of schoolboys for the purposes of acting. In 1575 it was brought to the attention of the Privy Council that one of Sebastian Westcote's boys, 'beinge one of his principall plaiers, is lately stolen and conveyed from him,' presumably by a rival (Hillebrand, 1964, 123–24). In the notorious Star Chamber case of 1601 the Master of the Children of the Chapel Royal was accused by an indignant parent of having abused his royal warrant to search for singers for the choir by kidnapping the plaintiff's son and other boys so as to recruit them for the playhouse at Blackfriars.[14] There is no suggestion that the Canterbury boys were choristers, but the episode of 1592 does show that there was a lively interest in acting among the pupils of the school during Marlowe's lifetime – and indeed a talent for it which Symcox and Edwards may have first spotted during the performance of a school play.

III

Besides the academic drama, both English and classical, which was studied and acted at Marlowe's school, there were the public spectacles and shows of these years which attested to the citizens' new–found loyalties and belated acquiescence in the Elizabethan regime. When the Queen visited Canterbury in 1573, Christopher Marlowe was nine years old, and the pageantry which (it is not too fanciful to suggest) he may have witnessed on that occasion would have been his first experience of the mystique and theatricality of power. Elizabeth was accompanied on her progress as far as Canterbury by envoys from France, with whom she dined in state in the former abbey of St Augustine's, now a standing house or royal palace. She attended evensong at the Cathedral where, after 'the grammarian' from the school in the Precincts had made his oration to her 'upon her horseback,' she alighted, to be greeted by the Archbishop, with the Dean and Chapter in their chimers and rochets. They then knelt down and said the collects of the day and the psalm *Deus misereatur* in English, before the Queen processed into the Cathedral under a canopy 'borne by four of her temporal knights,' while the choir 'brought her Majesty up with a square song'.[15]

The shows put on by the privileged companies of players who visited Canterbury regularly from early on in the reign, receiving payments from the authorities of both City and Cathedral, could hardly vie with such magnificence. But even they brought something of the Court with them, for their rewards can be construed in part as tributes paid to the actors' patrons, the Queen and her courtiers. The City Chamberlain's accounts reveal that the Earl of Leicester's Men visited Canterbury almost annually from 1559 (before 1564 as Lord Robert Dudley's players), and the Queen's Men from their foundation in 1583 until 1595. The Lord Strange's players were paid 10s. on their visit in the accounting year Michaelmas 1580–1 (Dawson, 1965, 16). (Marlowe was at school for only the first six weeks or so of that period, and so he may have missed them). There is a gap in the series of payments to players in the Chamberlain's accounts for 1577–9 during Marlowe's schooldays; the accounts are full, but no payments were made to players. However, the Chapter Treasurer's accounts show that Leicester's Men made at least one visit during this period, and were paid 30s. Again in 1588–90 (20–21 Elizabeth) the Lord Admiral's players, who were then on the point of amalgamation with Lord Strange's Men, were paid by the Dean and Chapter, rather than the City, for their performances. The Queen's Men, on the other hand, seemed to have been paid by both City and Cathedral for their visits in these years.[16] Marlowe's *1 Tamburlaine* was printed in 1590 as 'shewed upon stages in the City of London' by the Admiral's Men (Chambers, 1923, vol. 2, 136). If it remained in the repertoire for their last provincial tour as an independent company, there is the intriguing possibility that this was the play performed in Marlowe's home town at the expense of the Dean and Chapter. The Lord Strange's players returned to Canterbury on 13 July 1592, 'when they playd in the courte hall before Mr Leedes, maior & other his brethren'.[17] Philip Henslowe's diary records that *The Jew* and *2 Tamburlaine* were in the repertoire of Strange's Men during their London season between March and June of that year, and they may well have performed one of these plays on this occasion in Canterbury, to receive a reward of 30s., whereas the Queen's Men had been paid only 20s. earlier in the year.[18]

The evidence of these institutional records suggests that in his formative years as a Canterbury schoolboy in the later 1570s Christopher Marlowe would have had ample opportunities to experience drama in the form of academic exercise and public theatre. At the same time he may also have learnt something of the hostility to the stage which had intensified since the setting up of permanent, purpose–built playhouses in London in 1576. While the Cathedral authorities, as overseers of the school, may have been ambivalent in their attitude to public performances and professional players, three Canterbury men were foremost among the critics of the stage in these early years of the emergence of 'the quality' of playing as a profession or business. In a sermon preached at Paul's Cross on 24 August, 1578, John Walsall, who had been a Six Preacher at Canterbury Cathedral in the previous year, inveighed against dancing, players and minstrels as well as usurers and the oppressors of the poor.[19] In 1579 Thomas Twyne, son of the former master of the Canterbury School, embellished his translation of Petrarch's dialogue, *Physicke against Fortune*, with a digression on the playhouses in contemporary London, the Theatre and the Curtain, which 'are well knowen to be enemies to good manners: for looke who goeth thither evyl, returneth worse...'[20] Of the two Canterbury playwrights, John Lyly and Stephen Gosson, who may have been early exemplars or role models for Marlowe, the latter had already turned his coat and denounced actors and plays. Gosson's *The Schoole of Abuse* was entered on the Stationers' Register on 22 July, 1579.[21] All these three publications, with their dire warnings about the iniquities of plays, players and playhouses, appeared during Marlowe's time as a scholar at the Canterbury School.

IV

Marlowe left Canterbury for the University of Cambridge in December 1580 and on 7 May 1581, according to the *Registrum Parvum* of Corpus Christi College, he was elected and admitted in place of Christopher Pashley, also from Canterbury School. Marlowe had probably been nominated before he went to Cambridge by John Parker, the Archbishop's son, as one of the three scholars provided for under the terms of Matthew Parker's will. For some reason Pashley did not release his stipend until this late date. 'Marlin', as he appears in the books, formally matriculated in March 1581.[22] We do not know who provided for him in these early months in Cambridge. The suggestion that he was the protégé of a Kentish patron, Sir Roger Manwood, Chief Baron of the Exchequer, rests on the claim that the poet composed a Latin epitaph for the judge on his death on 14 December 1592, but the only extant copies of these verses date from the seventeenth century (Maclure, 1968, 259 & apx.; Prideaux, 1885, 15; Wraight, 1965, 34–6; Urry, 1988, 81). We can safely assume that Marlowe moved into the chamber in the converted 'stoare house', reserved for the Parker scholars, once the dilatory Pashley had packed his bags. The 'stoare house' is shown on a plan of the college drawn up *circa* 1576 to indicate the rooms allocated to the 12 fellows and the 20 foundation scholars.[23]

On his arrival in Cambridge Marlowe would have found that the University was less indulgent to visits from the sponsored companies of players than the City and Cathedral authorities were in Canterbury. When in June 1580 Burghley recommended that the Earl of Oxford's players be given leave to spend four or five days in Cambridge to perform the plays which they had shown publicly in London and before the Queen, the Chancellor's request was politely but firmly turned down by the Vice–Chancellor, Dr John Hatcher, on the grounds that Leicester's Men had recently been refused a similar permission. He reminded Burghley that assemblies in open places were forbidden within five miles' compass of the town by a Privy Council order of 1575, the pestilence had still not abated on the eve of the midsummer fair and the time of commencement was at hand, which, he primly added, 'requireth rather dilligence in stodie then dissoluteness in playes.'[24] An entry in the University Audit Book for 1583–4 records a sum of 50s. given to the Queen's Men 'forbidding theim to playe in the towne & so ridd theim cleane away'. The Vice–Chancellor looked more favourably on academic drama, or at least was concerned on one occasion to discipline a scholar who had taken his objection to violent extremes. In December 1579 Dr Hatcher described for Burghley the antics of one Punter, a former scholar of St John's who had gone round the colleges maliciously disturbing the performances during a season of plays held the previous year. We are not told what his motives were, but Punter seems to have been a serial gatecrasher and heckler rather than a serious critic of the drama. After having plucked off the visor of one of the stagekeepers of Caius, he had disrupted 'the first playes ye same yeare at Trinitie colledge', and then in retaliation for his expulsion thence had 'privily crept into Benet colledge' (Corpus) and, donning the clothes of a stage–keeper, had assaulted a Trinity man in front of the audience.[25]

Most of these college performances were probably of Latin rather than English plays, but at Corpus both seem to have been encouraged and not merely tolerated by the Master and Fellows. In the accounting year 1577–8 the Master, Robert Norgate, was paid by the college to travel 'into Norffolk about the comedyes.' Regular payments 'to the musitians' occur in the Corpus accounts for these years, including 10s. in 1586–7 to William Byrd, who as a university wait had received a piece of commercial sponsorship in 1583 when he was appointed 'the lord of tappes' at Stourbridge Fair. He was engaged 'for the saffetie of the boothes & profitt of the merchauntes ... by sound of some Instrument [to] gyve notize to shutt & open their shoppes' at sunset and sunrise. Only two items in the college accounts relate to dramatic activity during Marlowe's years at Corpus. In the accounts for 1581–2 a payment of 20p was made to Lamb and Porter, who were possibly college servants, 'for making houses at the Comaedie' and, perhaps on the same occasion, another 20p 'In Largeis to the Actors for a Beaver'.[26] In his 'A Treatise on Playe' of *circa* 1587, Sir John Harington recalled his days as a student at King's from 1576 to 1581 and defended interludes against their censurers:'I thinke in stage–playes may bee much good, in well–penned comedies, and specially tragedies; and I remember, in Cambridge, howsoever the presyser sort have banisht them, the wyser sort did, and still doe mayntayn them.'[27] The society at Corpus seemed to have been of 'the wiser sort' in this respect.

V

The surviving evidence for Marlowe's student years at Corpus, his attendance and absences, has been well rehearsed in modern studies since the publication of the researches of Moore Smith and F.S.Boas in the college archives (Moore Smith, 1909, 167–77; Boas, 1940, 13–14). The college accounts and buttery books indicate prolonged periods of absence from Corpus, and presumably from Cambridge, in the third or fourth terms of 1584–5, and the third term of 1585–6, his expenditure in the buttery in the latter year being conspicuously higher than normal. The pattern of irregular residence and of indulgence rather than subsistence suggested by the records has prompted speculation about Marlowe's movements during the intervals of absence.

On 29 June 1587 the Privy Council sent a letter to the University authorities to scotch the rumour that 'Christopher Morley' had entertained plans to quit the realm and to settle in Rheims, presumably at the English college for missionary priests. On the contrary, it was declared, he had behaved honourably in the service of his Queen and country; 'in all his accions he had behaved him selfe orderlie and discreetelie, ... and deserved to be rewarded for his faithfull dealinge.' He was therefore to be admitted to the degree he was due to take at the next commencement – that is, his MA. The Privy Councillors who authorized the letter were Burghley, Archbishop Whitgift, Lord Hunsdon, Sir James Croft and the new Lord Chancellor, Sir Christopher Hatton.[28] It was Leslie Hotson who verified the identification of the subject of the conciliar letter as the Corpus Marlowe and not the 'Christopher Marley' then in residence at Trinity College, and the possible reasons for the Council's intervention have exercised the minds of Marlovians ever since (1925, 59).

The 'constitutional' significance of the episode may be illuminated by reference to the changes that had recently been made to the residential requirements for students and fellows. Between March 1584 and July 1587 Marlowe, though formally resident, appears to have been absent from the University a number of times. A judgement of 1608 by the Vice–Chancellor and heads of houses was to stipulate that it had been 'continual practice' since the University Statutes of 1570 were framed to allow 'discontinuance' between the BA and the MA. For those nine terms candidates for the higher degree were not 'strictly tied' to residence in Cambridge but could be 'discontinuers', studying privately and (it may be) supporting themselves by parish work or as schoolteachers. In this way (it was declared in 1608) they could be of 'great use' in church and commonwealth. To qualify for the degree they must supply the Vice–Chancellor with testimonials from their landlords and three clergymen to certify that during their absence they have 'lived soberly and studiously the course of a scholar's life'. They were obliged to perform the necessary public disputations, exercises and declamations in the Old Schools, before proceeding to the degree.[29] Thus absences from Cambridge, for whatever reason, were not abnormal by the 1580s if they were vouched for under these rules; they were in order at a University requirement level. The Privy Council testimonial was presumably a substitute for the landlord/parson certificate.

It may also have been called for to overcome another impediment relating to the recently revised College Statutes. Robert Norgate, Master of Corpus between 1573 and 1587, had at one stage called in the Vice–Chancellor, Dr Andrew Perne, with two senior doctors of divinity, Edward Hawforde and John Whitgift (then Master of Trinity) to interpret a clause of Statute XVI obligating the Fellows of the college to assume holy orders within three years of their admission. The three divines also adjudicated on other points at issue, such as 'that no Fellow or Scholar can absent himself from College without leave of the Master or his Deputy' (Masters, 1753, 114). These formalities had evidently not been observed in Marlowe's case and Burghley, as Chancellor of the University, and Whitgift, who as Vice–Chancellor had been instrumental in devising the University Statutes of 1570, would have been particularly concerned that the rules of discipline of both the College and the University should be scrupulously observed.[30] However, an inadvertent infringement of them, such as seems to have happened in this case, was to be overlooked on the grounds of reasons of state, and the Privy Councillors set about to put the record straight as far as the University regulations and Marlowe's reputation were concerned.

VI

Most attempts to explain Marlowe's involvement with the Elizabethan secret service have concentrated on his relationship with Thomas Walsingham. More recently it has been suggested that (on the analogy of the modern practices of MI6 and the KGB) there may have been a recruiter of spies into the intelligence network who had Cambridge connections. In *The Reckoning*, Charles Nicholl speculates that Nicholas Faunt, one of Sir Francis Walsingham's secretaries, may have fulfilled this role in Marlowe's case. 'He is the only one of Walsingham's regular officers to have attended Cambridge, and his college was the same as Marlowe's: Corpus Christi' (1992, 119). When on leave from Cambridge in the summer of 1572 Faunt had witnessed the events of St Bartholomew's Day in Paris, and he was one of the first to bring a detailed account of the massacre of the Huguenots back to England. After entering Walsingham's service around 1578, Faunt became his 'confidential clerk'; he was in correspondence with English agents on the continent, and in 1587 he was sent by his master to Paris to check on the dealings between the English ambassador, Sir Edward Stafford, and the English Catholic exiles. His mission coincided with one of the intervals when Marlowe was absent from Cambridge.

Faunt was to become a close associate of Anthony Bacon, a fellow 'intelligencer' and the son of the old Lord Keeper, Nicholas Bacon (another *alumnus* of Corpus, though his sons Frances and Anthony were sent to Trinity). It was in a letter of 1 August 1582 to Anthony Bacon that Faunt described the nature of his duties at Court: 'here I see into the inward course of things and very cabinet of secrecies, indeed not common to many'. He was obliged to be a 'continual courtier' but disapproved of the moral laxity of the Court, 'where is so little godliness and exercise of religion, so dissolute manners and corrupt conversation generally, which I find to be worse than when I knew the place first...' Almost exactly a year later he again confided to Bacon his disillusionment with life at Court, 'where sin reigneth in the highest degree' (a hint perhaps that the rumours of a scandalous intimacy in the relationship between the Queen and the Earl of Leicester may have been true) (Wright, 1754, vol.1, 26, 39). If the puritan Faunt's fastidiousness does not mark him out as a natural companion for Marlowe, it did not prevent his friendship with Anthony Bacon, who like his brother Francis was sexually ambivalent; nor did it affect his loyalty to him after Anthony's unfortunate escapade in France in September 1586. Bacon had been on a diplomatic mission when he was imprisoned by the magistrates of Montauban on a charge of committing an act of pederasty with his page. He was released after a successful appeal addressed to Henry of Navarre and the matter was kept quiet, though Faunt must have been privy to the cover–up.[31]

In drawing attention to a possible network of agents recruited from the University of Cambridge, Charles Nicholl may have written truer than he knew, in the sense that the connection between Faunt and Marlowe is closer than hitherto suspected. For Faunt also came from Canterbury and not, as the *Dictionary of National Biography* has it, from Norwich. He was one of the first scholars from Canterbury School to go to Cambridge under the Parker foundation of 1569. In fact he went first as a pensioner to Caius and then transferred to Corpus as a scholar in the same year, 1572, proceeding to his BA in 1575–76. His name appears on the college plan drawn up in his last year there; his room was in the north–west corner of the court 'next to the Diall' and to the gateway leading out to St Benet's Church.[32] This is adjacent to the 'stoare house' on the north side of the same corner of the quadrangle where the Parker Scholars were to keep, and where Marlowe was presumably to move shortly after his arrival in Cambridge within five years of Faunt's departure. Whether their paths crossed in Canterbury, Cambridge or London, sober history does not relate, but it is legitimate to speculate whether a 'Cambridge connection' worked at this level as a route to a covert career in the intelligence service open to the talents of the university wits. The setting up of a 'Cambridge connection' certainly worked for the Catholic opposition as a means of recruiting seminary priests, if we are to believe the boast of Father Robert Parsons, SJ, that in 1581 he had insinuated a priest as a 'mole' into the University 'in the guise of a scholar or a gentleman commoner', who within a few months 'has sent over to Rheims seven very fit youths.'[33]

VII

For the last thirty years or so the image of Marlowe has been fixed for us by the putative portrait of him which now hangs in the Hall of his old college. It has become an icon for Marlovians, and no account of Marlowe's Cambridge years would be complete without some consideration of its significance. The attribution is plausible at best, based as it is on the circumstances of its discovery in rubble removed in 1953 from the modern Master's Lodge in the New Court, the matching of the date of the painting, and the age of the sitter ('ætatis suae 21 1585') with those for Marlowe, the intriguing motto and the ambivalent posture. Since its restoration the portrait has been read emblematically, and as in the case of *imprese* the motif seems deliberately mysterious. The college has been careful not to associate itself with the attribution, while Sir Roy Strong interprets what he describes as 'the portrait sometimes called "Christopher Marlowe"' as an example of the contemporary fashion for depicting the melancholy of the disappointed or rejected lover (compare Dickens, 1966, 24–5; Purdon, 1967, 261–62; Strong, 1969, 353). The motto '*Quod me nutrit me destruit*' (that which nourishes me destroys me) reinforces the impression and, although the studied ambiguity has been assumed to chime with Marlowe's reputation for heterodoxy, no–one has suggested that the disdainful creature who was the object of the infatuation was other than a woman.

One of the objections which has been made against the claim that the portrait is of Marlowe and that it once hung in the old Master's Lodge, is that the college would hardly have accepted the likeness of a shoemaker's son or displayed it in a gallery reserved for academic worthies, the great and the good.[34] For a student from such a humble background to dress himself in such finery would be an infringement of the sumptuary laws against excessive apparel. These Acts of Parliament, designed to keep such people in their place and to discourage extravagance in the commonwealth, were continually renewed by royal proclamation and had been enforced in Cambridge in 1585.[35] However, it has been argued, these laws continued to be flouted until they were repealed early in the next reign. Marlowe at the age of twenty–one may well have been capable of a defiant gesture against convention, but would he have been in a position to do so in 1585, before he had made his mark in the world of the theatre? The evidence for a sudden access of prosperity during his absences from Cambridge may be taken quite plausibly to suggest that he was already earning a living in the underworld of espionage. There are few pointers to his acknowledged social status or his own sense of selfhood in these hidden years. In his brushes with the law at the Middlesex sessions in 1589 he was designated by the clerk of the court first as 'yeoman' and then as 'gentleman'.[36] Not long settled in London, his rank in society still uncertain, Marlowe was patently no longer destined for the church, but as one of the university wits even a craftsman's son, a 'studious artizan', was entitled to the suffix 'gent.', according to Sir Thomas Smith's sardonic definition of a gentleman.[37] If the correction in the court records was in recognition of his status as a university man, rather than a playmaker, it was a description to which he had been formally entitled since he had become 'Dominus' at Cambridge in 1583–4.

Poets, playwrights and players did have their portraits painted in this period, like successful merchants and theologians, to signify their 'arrival' in their chosen vocation. In the gallery of new men in new professions, we have the likenesses of actors like James Burbage, Nathan Field, Edward Alleyn, Ben Jonson, and the purported likeness of Shakespeare. In some of these cases it was perhaps a mark of achievement, and of acceptance in contemporary society, to have a portrait painted, especially for those of more humble origins. For the creative artists, it may also have been a matter not merely of the projection of their self–image but of its invention. The lutenist Thomas Whythorne tells us in his 'Autobiography' how and why he had three portraits made at different times of his life. The first was of himself playing the lute, painted as a decoration on his virginals, to match a picture of Terpsichore, the muse of dancing, holding a lyre (c. 1549); the second was a year later, on his recovery from the ague, to see how far the disease had altered his appearance. The third was much later, and shows the mature man, bearded, wrinkled and hollow–eyed. None of these portraits has survived, but a fourth one has, and this was the basis of the woodcut of 1571 which embellishes Whythorne's songbooks. His aim this time, he tells us, was to display the 'outward marks as in the inward man', and he is duly portrayed in the dress and armorial bearings of a gentleman. The professional musician, who was so concerned in his memoirs to stress the distinction between his kind and the humble minstrel of English tradition, had at last arrived (Osborne, 1962, 305–6).

As it was with the more conventional *arrivistes*, so too with the adventurers, the impulse to project a contrived image of themselves for posterity could be compelling. It was not unknown for those engaged in 'underground' activities at this time to have portraits painted as mementos of their endeavour. In 1586 Anthony Babington and his fellow conspirators commissioned portraits which were intended to serve as a record of their sacrificial service to Mary Queen of Scots and the Catholic cause. After the plot was exposed by Walsingham's 'intelligencers' (among them Marlowe's associate, Robert Poley), prints of these portraits were reproduced to accompany a proclamation to apprehend them on their flight – perhaps the first 'Wanted' posters in English history.[38]

Do we then have in the Corpus portrait an instance of 'Renaissance self–fashioning' in paint? It displays an obscure conceit of the kind normally associated with depictions of courtiers and gallants. Those who would identify the sitter as the poet son of a Canterbury shoemaker see in the portrait an 'aspiring mind' that was not content with the attainment of mere professional recognition or the status of a gentleman. There is no more than suppositional proof that the sitter is Marlowe and the temptation to accept it uncritically as the authentic likeness should be resisted. To adduce it as evidence to confirm an alleged correlation between the works of the poet's imagination and his reported lifestyle and beliefs, would be to fall into 'the fallacy of hypostatized proof.'[39] The only artist associated with late sixteenth–century Cambridge for whom any evidence survives is Edward Norgate, son of Robert Norgate, Master of Corpus in Marlowe's time. Edward Norgate went on to be a herald painter in King James's reign; like Nicholas Hillyard he was mainly a miniaturist and, like Hillyard, he too wrote a discourse on 'the art of limning'. He was to be described by Thomas Fuller as the 'the best illuminer and limner of his age'.[40] But Norgate was only a boy when his father died in 1587, and he is too young to be considered a candidate for the artist of the portrait of 1585. A portrait could have been commissioned elsewhere, in England or abroad; most paintings which have survived from this period are anonymous in the sense that it has not been possible to attribute them to their artists. In the present state of the evidence neither is there a plausible alternative candidate for the subject of a work of art which may have been created to convey the sitter's identity only to an inner circle. Marlowe was still a student in 1585 (even if a non-resident or 'discontinuer' for part of the year), and however precocious or outrageous his 'high aspiring mind', there is no independent evidence to connect him with this painting. Whether the portrait depicts a brooding aristocrat or a posing upstart poet, the young man remains in quiet possession of his secret, and the only scholarly verdict possible at present on the claim that he is Marlowe must be 'not proven.'

Notes

1. William Lambarde, *A Perambulation of Kent: Conteyning the description, Hystorie and Customes of that Shyre* (compiled in 1570; London, 1576), 236.

2. See C[anterbury] C[athedral] A[rchives] U24 (unsorted MSS), fos. 418–19, for the indenture of 22 May, 11 Eliz., between the Master of Eastbridge Hospital and the Master, Fellows and Scholars of Corpus; J.Strype, *The Life and Acts of Matthew Parker*, 4 vols., Oxford, 1821, vol. 3, 333–40 (for Parker's will), 350–55 (for his gift to Cambridge colleges); also Woodruff and Cape, 1908, chs. 3 & 4; Urry, 1988, 53.

3. 1988, apx.11, 108–22. The inventory still awaits a modern bibliographical study.

4. See Collinson, 1988, 104 and n.28; also Andrew Butcher's essay in the present volume.

5. CCA, Acta Capituli, 1561–8, fos. 21, 28v. (the original MS is mutilated): a transcript of these entries made by B.K.Jeffery in 1957 and preserved in the King's School Archives, corrects the extracts given in Woodruff and Cape, 1908, 80. This payment was also entered in Dean & Chapter Misc. Accounts, no. 40 (1540–76), fo. 219r. The chapter accounts for 1563–4 also show that a sum of 3s 4d was paid to John Johnson, presumably a servant or craftsman, 'yn tyme of the playe' (fo.289v). I am grateful to Mr Paul Pollak, Archivist of the King's School, for invaluable help in tracing these records.

6. The only forensic details given in the record are that Symcox alone was delated before the court on 14 Jan., on 16 March evidence was given in English, and on 11 May both Symcox and Edwards were dismissed (Kent Archives Centre, Maidstone, High Commission Act Book, Diocese of Canterbury, 1584–1603: PRC 44/3, fols. 103–8). The court sat in the bishop's residence in the Cathedral precincts. Richard Rogers was suffragan bishop of Dover 1568–96 and dean of Canterbury from 1584. He owed his preferment as dean to the patronage of Lord Burghley, to whom he sent a new year's gift in acknowledgement on 1 Jan. 1585 (*Calendar of State Papers, Domestic, 1581–90*, 222).

7. For a discussion of the significance of the act 14 Eliz., c.5, see Roberts, 1994, 29–55.

8. The scholars for the years 1588–90 are listed in the Cathedral Treasurer's Accounts, but there are no known lists for 1591–1598. I have not been able to match any of the names in the extant lists with those of known professional players of this or the next generation. Compare *A Dictionary of Actors*, ed. E. Nungezer, *passim*, & 346 for Symcockes.

9. 'You are to take care that each scholar when admitted to the foundation be assigned to the care of the Dean, or one of the Prebendaries or Preachers, who shall act as the boy's tutor or guardian, and provide him with all necessary things.' Translated from the Latin in Woodruff and Cape, 1908, 88.

10. Cowper, 1900, 46–51. Roger Raven's appointment as headmaster to succeed Shorte in 1591 had been at the recommendation of Archbishop Whitgift (Woodruff & Cape, 1908, 91–3).

11. *Damon and Pythias* was produced in 1565 and published in 1571 (Chambers, 1923, vol. 2, 33–4).

12. As 'Symcockes' (Chambers, 1923, vol. 2, 241; vol.4, 193; *Henslowe's Diary* ed. R. Foakes and R. Rickard, Cambridge, 1961, 194).

13. Successive masters of the Chapel Royal, including Richard Edwards in 1561, had been granted the right to enlist children into their choirs, and comparable privileges ('to take upp suche apte and mete childrene as are most fitt to be instructed and framed in the arte and science of musicke and singinge') were extended to Thomas Gyles for St Paul's on 26 Aug.1585 (BL Sloane MS 2035b, fo.73; Chambers, 1923. vol.2, 33–4). For instances of Canterbury choristers being thus removed, and of the efforts made to recover them, see Woodruff and Danks, 1912, 458; Collinson *et al.*, 1995, 432.

14. PRO, Star Chamber Procs., Eliz.C46/39: Clifton *vs* Robinson *et al.*, printed in Fleay, 1890, 127–32; see also Hillebrand, 1964, 123–24, 160–63.

15. Archbishop Parker described the scene in a letter of 17 March 1575 to Grindal of York: *Parker Correspondence 1535–75*, ed. J. Bruce and T. Perowne, Parker Society, 1853, 475–76. Compare A. L. Rowse's comment on the possible significance of the procession, '...the Virgin Queen where not so long before the Virgin Mary would have been borne

in state under her canopy: a measure of secularization, not without its hieratic overtones' (1971, 94). However, kings of England are known to have processed under such canopies even before the Reformation.

16. Canterbury Cathedral Archives: New Foundation, Treasurer's Accounts: TA 9, fo. 122 (20–21 Eliz.); TA 10 (31–32 Eliz.) fo. 132.

17. Dawson, 1965, 17; the entry is mistranscribed in Murray, 1910, vol.2, 229.

18. *Henslowe's Diary*, 16–18; Dawson, 1965, 17. By 1595 the court of Burgmote had become less tolerant of plays, and ordered that none be performed on Sundays, or after 9 pm on week–days, or for more than two days at a time, or at intervals of less than 28 days. The order made no distinction between common players and privileged ones, while its preamble deplored the profaning of the Sabbath, which was highly displeasing to God, while the 'contynuance of them so longe tyme' was inconvenient and hurtful to the state, quiet and prosperity of the City. Extract from Burgmote Books, 15 April 1595 (Murray, 1910, vol.2, 233).

19. '...And as in the countrie minstrels thus seduce & bewitch the people, so it hath bene sayd (I trust it be reformed) that vaine plaiers have had about this citie of London farre greater audience then true preachers.' John Walsall, *A Sermon Preached at Paul's Cross* (5 Oct. 1578) sig. Eiij. in Hill, 1982, 32–3.

20. *Physicke against Fortune, as well prosperous, as adverse...*, Thomas Twyne, London, 1579, book 1, 42.

21. *The School of Abuse: conteining a pleasaunt invective against poets, pipers, iesters, and such like caterpillars of a comonwelth*, Stephen Gosson, London, 1579, sigs.B1r, B3v, C7v. In this first tract Gosson was obviously trailing his coat; his subsequent attacks on the stage became more virulent. Gosson was admitted a scholar of the King's School in 1567; John Lyly's school is not known but his younger brother William was at King's in 1578 (Urry, 1988, 10, 102).

22. Urry, 1988, 54; Boas, 1940, 13–14. The accounts for the year ending Mich. 1581 show that 'Marlin' had paid an admission fee of 3s. 4d.; not yet a scholar, he is listed in the middle category of students (poor scholars, paid 12d.). Pashley vacated his place in the spring; Marlowe's

name appears at the end of the list of Parker scholars for the first term, 1580–81, but is crossed out and Pashley's name written above (receiving 9s.), suggesting that the clerk had made a mistake. 'Marlin' is entered in the second term (receiving 12s.) in a group of 8 scholars. CCC, Cambridge, Archive: Audits, 1578–80.

23.   The plan exists in rough draft and a final version: CCC, Cambridge, Archive Misc. Doc. 138 dated '*circa* 1576'. A modern drawing of the plan is reproduced in *John Josselin, Historia Collegii Corporis Christi*, ed. J. Clark, Cambridge, 1880. 'The olde Librarye', 'The Lesse Library' and 'The greate Library' are clearly marked in the finished plan on either side of the Master's Lodge and the Hall situated in the south east corner of the court; it was probably in the 'greate Library' that Parker's collection was installed in this very year.

24.   Leicester's Men had come armed with letters from the Lord Chancellor and the Earl of Sussex. The Vice Chancellor informed Burghley that he had dismissed Oxford's players with a payment of 20s., having failed to persuade the University to be more generous. (Nelson, 1989, vol.1, 289–91). This reluctance on the part of the University to oblige the Privy Council and the Court in matters concerning plays and the privileged companies persisted at least during Marlowe's lifetime. In Dec. 1592, when the Queen's Men were prevented by the plague from performing at Court, Burghley was informed by the V.C. and six heads of houses that the University was unable to accede to the V.C.'s request to prepare a comedy in English to be acted before Elizabeth over the Christmas season. Though willing to please her majesty, they pleaded that the University actors had 'no practize in this Englishe vaine, and beinge (as we thinke) nothinge beseeminge ouer studentes, specially oute of the University... and do finde ouer principal actors... very unwillinge to playe in Englishe'. They asked that they be allowed to play in Latin, and for adequate time to prepare (Heywood & Wright, 1854, vol.2, 40–2). In 1593 the Privy Council banned 'common players' from acting at both Oxford and Cambridge and instructed justices not to grant them licences. The reasons given were the hazard of the plague to the health, and of the plays (being 'full of lewde example and moste of vanity') to the morals of the students. The preamble to the order recognised the changing function of the universities in post–Reformation England. They were the nurseries of youth in good learning, civil education and honest manners, 'whereby after they maie serve their Prince and contrye in divers callinges...[and] the State and Commonwealthe maie receive hereafter greate good' (Dasent, 1901, 427–9). Compare Curtis, 1959, 76.

25. Nelson, 1989, vol. 1, 311, 289. Harington later recalled how, when he was a 'truantly scholar' at King's, 1576–81, 'our stage–keepers in Cambridge, that for fear lest they should want company to see their comedies, go up and down with vizors and lights, puffing and thrusting, and keeping out all men so precisely, till all the town is drawn by this revel to the place; and at last, tag and rag, fresh men and sub–sizers, and all be packed in together so thick, as now is scant left room for the prologue to come upon the stage'. J. Harington, 'An Apology' [1814 edn, 21] cited in *The Letters and Epigrams of Sir John Harington* ed. N. McClure, 1977 reprint, New York, 9).

26. Moore Smith, 1923, vol.2, pt.2, 210; Nelson, 1989, vol.1, 280, 305–6, 309–12. The conditions for staging academic drama seem to have been stricter in some of the other colleges, e.g. St John's, where chapter 10 of the Statutes prescribed that students were permitted to perform in comedies or tragedies to be held at the discretion of the Reader in Humane Letters and the 'other examiners.' The interpretation of this clause by the Master became a bone of contention in the college in 1587–8 (ibid. vol.2, 115).

27. Cited from *Nugae Antiquae* in Chambers, 1923, vol.4, 245. The tract deals mainly with games of chance.

28. PRO, Privy Council Registers, Elizabeth, vi. fo.381; Dasent, 1890–1907, vol.32, 130. The entry is reproduced photographically in Wraight & Stern, 1965, 88. Their lordships' letter can be read as a denial, not necessarily of the allegation that Marlowe 'was determined to have gone beyond the sea to Reames,' but of the report that he had contemplated settling there, and thereby defecting to the enemy camp.

29. Dyer, 1824, vol.1, 289–92. I am grateful to Dr Harry Porter for bringing this source for the 1608 judgment of the Vice–Chancellor and Heads of Houses to my attention.

30. Whitgift as Archbishop did not relax the close scrutiny of University affairs that he had exercised as Master of Trinity and Vice–Chancellor. He had 'attempted to press a court–oriented curriculum upon the university' in the new Statutes of 1570 (Heywood & Wright, 1854, vol.1, 5). The Archbishop was particularly anxious to ensure that Dr Copcoats was elected Master of Corpus in succession to Norgate on the latter's death in 1587, and to forestall any attempt to present another candidate to the college (Whitgift to Burghley, 3 Nov.1587: PRO:

SP12/205/7).

31. Du Maurier, 1977, 66–8. If the evidence can be construed to suggest the existence of a 'Cambridge connection' of deviant sexuality in the intelligence network, Faunt was obviously not a procurer!

32. CCCC Archive, Misc doc. 138. At Caius he was assigned to a *cubiculum* or chamber under the supervision of his tutor and surety, Dominus Stephen Purse (Brooke, 1987, 57–67; Venn, 1897, vol.1, 69).

33. Parsons to Aquaviva, General of the Society of Jesus, 24 Aug. ?1581 (Taunton, 1901, 88). If news of such a popish plot had leaked out and was still in circulation in Cambridge, the conciliar letter of 1587 might have been intended to exculpate Marlowe from suspicion of being one such 'fit youth' recruited to the English College at Rheims.

34. 'A Canterbury Scholar could scarcely have afforded a portrait by a good artist, or even to have dressed as well as the young man of the picture' (Dickens, 1966, 24–5). Urry is equally sceptical (1988, 61). For a contrary view, see Wraight and Stern, 1965, 63–71; Nicholl, 1993, 5–7.

35. Every scholar was to 'absteyne to weare in his apparell anye stuff, colour, or fasshion that shall not be playne and schollerlike' on pain of being deprived of his weekly commons and allowance (Heywood & Wright, 1854, vol.1, 397–405).

36. Jeaffreson, 1972, 189; Urry, 1988, 62–4. Sir Roger Manwood, Chief Baron of the Exchequer, was on the bench at Newgate sessions on 3 Nov. 1589 when Marlowe was tried as an accomplice of Thomas Watson on a charge of the manslaughter of William Radley, and set at liberty.

37. '... as for gentlemen, they be made good cheape in England, For whosoever studieth the lawes of the realme, who studieth in the universities, who professeth liberall sciences, and to be shorte, who can live idly and without manuall labour, and will beare the port, charge and countenaunce of a gentleman, he shall be called master...' Thomas Smith, *De Republica Anglorum*, London, 1583, 27. Compare *Edward II*, 3.2.242–3: 'My name is Baldock, and my gentry / I fetch from Oxford, not from heraldry.'

38. *State Trials*, I (1809), 28 Eliz., 1138. When Ballard was arrested, Babington went to a barber's 'without Billingsgate, where were his own, Titchbourne's and Savage's pictures; and on Babington's picture was written, "*Hic mihi sunt Comites, quos ipsa pericula jungunt*". But then misliking that, was written: "*Quorsum haec alio properantibus*"' (MacCaffrey, 1970, 230–31). The would–be assassins were 'pictured to the life, and Babington in the midst of them, with this Verse...'(Hughes and Larkin, 1964–69, vol.2, 525–6, draft proclamation, 2 Aug. 1586).

39. In which a hypothesis, with repetition, is taken to be a fact: see Fischer, 1971, 55–6.

40. *A Treatise Concerning the Arte of Limning by Nicholas Hilliard, together with A More Compendious Discourse Concerning ye Art of Liming by Edward Norgate*, ed. R. Thornton and T. Cain, Ashington, 1981, 36–41.

3. 'At Middleborough': Some Reflections on Marlowe's Visit to the Low Countries in 1592

CHARLES NICHOLL

Our knowledge of Christopher Marlowe's activities in the early 1590s is based on a handful of historical documents. Probably the most important to have emerged in recent years, and certainly the most tantalizing, is the letter found by Professor Bruce Wernham in 1976, during his cataloguing of the Foreign State Papers at the Public Record Office in London (PRO, SP84/44, fo.60; Wernham, 1976, 344–5).

It is a letter from Sir Robert Sidney, the younger brother of the late Sir Philip. He was the governor of the port of Vlissingen, or Flushing, in the Netherlands, which was at this time an English possession: a 'cautionary town' handed over by the Dutch in return for English military assistance against the Spanish. On 26 January 1592, Sidney wrote from Flushing to Lord Burghley, who was broadly speaking his employer back in England. His letter concerned a young man whom he describes as a 'scholar' named Christofer Marly, and who was without any shadow of doubt the poet and playwright Christopher Marlowe.

In January 1592, we learn, and perhaps for some while before, Marlowe was lodging in a 'chamber' in Flushing. There he was arrested on a charge of coining, or counterfeiting money. According to the charge he had 'induced' a goldsmith named Gilbert to the forgery. A Dutch shilling had already been 'uttered', or circulated, and other counterfeit coins were found at their lodgings. Marlowe and Gilbert were hauled before Governor Sidney and examined. Marlowe admitted the crime, but claimed he had only done it out of curiosity: 'to see the goldsmith's cunning', as Sidney puts it. On 26 January they were deported back to England to be interrogated by Lord Burghley. The document discovered by Professor Wernham was Sidney's covering letter, reporting what he knew of the case. It was delivered to Burghley, together with the two prisoners, by Sidney's 'ancient', David Lloyd, who received payment of 40 nobles (£13 6s 8d) for the job (PRO, E351/542, fo.169 v; Nicholl, 1992, 239).

One interesting revelation in the letter is that Marlowe's 'chamber fellow' in Flushing, and the man who actually informed on him, was the spy Richard Baines, who a year later provided the authorities with a detailed list of Marlowe's alleged heresies and blasphemies – the notorious 'Baines Note'. Knowledge of this earlier encounter between Baines and Marlowe has added new perspectives to that crucial and sinister 'Note'.

Among the accusations which Baines laid against Marlowe in Flushing was that he 'had intent to go to the enemy', in other words that he intended to defect to the Spanish side in the Netherlands. A defector might sign up with one of the renegade English regiments fighting under the Spanish flag; or he might join one of the cliques of English Catholic exiles, mainly based in Brussels, who were busily plotting the overthrow and assassination of Queen Elizabeth. The latter is more probably the logic of Baines's accusation.

So the charges against Marlowe are serious. The coining (which he admitted) was itself a capital offence, under the heading of 'petty treason'. The intention to 'go to the enemy' (which he did not admit) made it doubly so. It seems significant, therefore, that Marlowe escaped any serious punishment for his crime. He was certainly free by May, for in that month we happen to know he was tangling with the constables of Shoreditch, and was bound over to keep the peace towards them.[1] If he suffered any punishment at all, it can have been no more than a couple of months' detention.

Far more likely – as I have argued at length elsewhere (Nicholl, 1992, 234–56) – is that he suffered no punishment at all because he was working once again as an agent of the English government. We know he had done so previously, in the mid 1580s, when he was praised by the Privy Council for his 'faithful dealing' in 'matters touching the benefit of his country'.[2] It is quite probable he was now working for Lord Burghley himself, or for Burghley's son, Sir Robert Cecil, who had charge of undercover operations: working for them, at least, in that floating, semi–official way so characteristic of the Elizabethan intelligence service.

I see this as the true subtext of the Flushing episode: that Marlowe's efforts as a coiner were not done with criminal intent, but as a means of infiltrating those exile groupings in Brussels. His purseful of forged money might itself be a way into those groups, whose grand revolutionary plans were chronically starved of cash. This is a twist to the Sidney document, but by no means an exceptional one. There were hundreds of Englishmen flitting around the front lines of the Low Countries, playing the meddlesome game of the 'intelligencer' or 'projector'. Marlowe was one of them, not a very successful one perhaps, but able to claim that his 'intent to go to the enemy' was a matter of espionage rather than of treason.

I relate this, in turn, to Marlowe's connection with Ferdinando Stanley, Lord Strange. In the Sidney letter Marlowe is quoted as saying he is 'very well–known to my Lord Strange', and we know from other sources[3] that Strange was a patron of Marlowe's in the early 1590s, and that his troupe of players – Lord Strange's Men – gave the first known performance of *The Jew of Malta*, and perhaps of other Marlowe plays. Lord Strange was the son and heir of the Earl of Derby. He was not himself a Catholic, but he came from an ancient and deeply Catholic family, and he was blood related to the Queen through both his father and his mother. This made him an ideal figurehead for Catholic plotters – a Catholic pretender to the throne, albeit a reluctant one – and there is plenty of evidence of the Catholic hopes heaped upon his shoulders, and of the government's vigilant surveillance of him, and his retinue of followers, as a result. Chief among these pro–Strange plotters was his cousin, Sir William Stanley, who had defected to the Spanish in 1587, and whose headquarters was now in Brussels. It was this Stanley clique in Brussels, I believe, that Marlowe was intending to 'go to' when he was arrested in Flushing in 1592.

This is an interesting crossover between Marlowe's career as a writer and his career as an intelligencer or spy. It is as a writer that he finds a place in the Strange circle, but once he has that *entrée* he is of use to the government, as an intriguer, as a pretend–plotter, as an infiltrator into this penumbra of conspiracy that surrounds Lord Strange. There is another crossover, of course, in the sheer theatricality of espionage. In this glimpsed scenario, in this little comedy of the Dutch Shilling, we seem to find Marlowe living out the kind of tawdry, convoluted fictions which he put on stage in plays like *The Jew of Malta*, first performed by Strange's Men in February 1592, just a few weeks after his ignominious return from Flushing.

II

It is against this backdrop of Low Countries intrigue that I wish to pose the central question of this essay. There is, I believe, another literary connection to this episode which has not yet been explored. It concerns the printing of one of Marlowe's books: the undated and rather mysterious first edition of the *Elegies*, his translations of the love poems of Ovid. These translations, from the Latin collection known as the *Amores*, are often said to have been written while Marlowe was still a student at Cambridge. There is no direct evidence for this assumption, but it is certainly likely that they were early works. They are sometimes rough, but they have that marvellous Marlovian speed and spareness of style; one of them, the famous 'In Summer's Heat', is recognized as a classic of Elizabethan erotic poetry.

The first edition of the *Elegies*, the one that interests me here, contained only ten of the poems. The full complement (fifty eight) did not appear until the third edition, which was published sometime in or after 1602.[4] In all the early editions, six in total, Marlowe's elegies appear together with a selection of epigrams by the poet John (later Sir John) Davies. Whether Marlowe and Davies actually collaborated on the book is unknown. It is generally assumed they did not: there is no internal evidence of collaboration, and it is rather more likely that the poems were printed from separate authorial manuscripts, or from a single intervening manuscript in which the poems were already collected together. Neither the printer nor the publisher of the book is named.

The title page of the first edition reads as follows:

E P I G R A M M E S

and
E L E G I E S
by I.D. and
C.M.

And then, beneath two horizontal blocks of type ornaments, the imprint: 'At Middleborough'. And so we come to the two words which I have taken for the title of my paper, and to the question which they have raised in my mind since the discovery of the Sidney letter.

This 'Middleborough', of course, has nothing to do with the English town of Middlesborough, which was then an obscure Teesside fishing village, and which contained no printing presses of any sort. It refers, rather, to the Dutch town of Middelburg, the capital of the province of Zeeland, where there had been for some while a small but thriving printing industry. Despite the actual existence of Middelburg printers, however, the consensus view about the provenance of the *Epigrams and Elegies* is that the Middleborough imprint is a decoy, a false imprint, designed to conceal the circumstances of an unlicensed printing, in England, of poems considered too salacious, too objectionable, to be issued in more regular fashion. The use of a false foreign imprint was a common enough ruse in such circumstances.

With the basic premise of this view – the 'objectionable' nature of the poems – there can be no quarrel. They were, by Elizabethan standards, pretty hot stuff. This is demonstrable, for in the summer of 1599 a list of books to be banned, and indeed burned, was drawn up by the Archbishop of Canterbury's censors, and at the head of this index of 'unseemly' works was the *Epigrams and Elegies*.[5] This decree came some time after the initial publication, and was probably aimed at the second edition, but it shows that the publisher of the first edition (or the authors themselves) had good enough reason for avoiding the legitimate, closely censored, channels of publication. The selection of elegies in the first edition, it has been noted, concentrates on the fruitier, more erotic material, which further suggests that the book had a deliberately risqué intention as – dare one say it? – a kind of upmarket pornography.

So this is undoubtedly a clandestine printing, but the deduction from this – that the Middleborough imprint is therefore false – seems to me much shakier. Certainly the use of a decoy imprint was conventional when putting out 'subversive' material (usually extremist political tracts), but so too, of course, was the actual use of foreign printing presses to produce work that could not be printed in England. So what I am now asking is this. As we now know – which earlier experts like Bowers and Gill did not – that Marlowe was present in the Low Countries in the early 1590s, is it not possible that the Middleborough or Middelburg imprint is, after all, a genuine one? The town of Middelburg is, in fact, only a few miles away from Flushing, where Marlowe had his lodgings in early 1592. The towns are virtually contiguous now, about half an hour's bus ride from centre to centre, and even in Elizabethan times it cannot have taken very long to ride or boat between them. We can now virtually locate Marlowe himself 'at Middleborough', so it seems reasonable to suggest that his 'unseemly' elegies were indeed printed there, as the title–page proclaims.

III

The true test of this suggestion must be bibliographic: a systematic forensic study of the output of Middelburg printers in the 1590s, in comparison with the first edition of the *Epigrams and Elegies*, which survives in a unique copy at the Huntington Library in California. One of the Middelburg printers, Richard Schilders, is already quite well known (Dover Wilson, 1912, 3–20; Aarssen, 1969, 104–8). He had English connections: he had served apprentice in London to the printer Thomas East in the 1570s, and among his productions at Middelburg were books in English. As these were markedly Puritan works (he was particularly associated with the separatist Robert Browne) it is perhaps unlikely that he would have anything to do with a selection of erotic lyrics by the anti–Puritan Marlowe, so we should perhaps look elsewhere. But at least Schilders serves to show the general plausibility of an English text emanating from Middelburg. (Of course, the decoy hypothesis in itself supposes the plausibility of the book being printed there: a false imprint was a disguise, and had to be plausible to be effective.) The bibliographic investigation of the case awaits someone with the skill and patience to undertake it. In the meantime, as a prelude and (I hope) an encouragement, I offer a few pointers that seem to reinforce, circumstantially, my suggestion that the Middelburg imprint may be genuine.

The first concerns the movements of Marlowe's co–author, John Davies, for I note with interest that in the summer of 1592, just a few months after Marlowe's departure from Flushing, Davies was himself in the Netherlands (Eccles, 1982, 36–7). Davies was at this time a student at the Middle Temple. Early in 1592, he and two fellow students, Richard Martin and William Fleetwood junior, were in trouble for rowdy behaviour at the 'Lord of Misrule' revels, held at the Inns of Court on Candlemas Night. They had all been fined the previous year, on the same charge, and this time they were suspended, or 'put out of commons'. That summer, all three crossed over to the Netherlands, and enrolled as students of law at the University of Leyden. If they travelled together, they must have arrived some time before 23 July 1592, on which date Richard Martin enrolled at Leyden. Davies himself did not enrol until 3 September. He did not stay long, it seems, for on 20 October an acquaintance of his there, Paul Merula, wrote a letter to England saying that Davies and his friends were preparing to return home. He was certainly back at the Middle Temple before the end of the year.

The idea that Davies had personal dealings with a Middelburg printer remains a conjecture, but as with Marlowe his physical presence in the Netherlands in 1592 makes it an attractive conjecture. As noted, Marlowe's elegies are thought to be early works: certainly earlier than 1592. What do we know about the date of composition of Davies's epigrams? Not a lot, admittedly, but what we do know tends to support the possibility that they were composed by the time he arrived in the Netherlands. External evidence shows that they were definitely written by 1594: a transcript of them bears that date.[6] Internal evidence is sparse, but at least three of them can be fairly confidently dated, and in each case the evidence points to 1591 or 1592 as the date of composition.

The first is the epigram 'Ad Musam', in which Davies speaks of 'Lepidus's printed dog'. This 'Lepidus' is Sir John Harington (as Harington himself tells us in one of his own epigrams[7]) and the dog is his illustrious pet pooch, Bungey. The description of the dog as 'printed' alludes to the woodcut portrait of Bungey which adorns the title page of Harington's translation of *Orlando Furioso*. This was published in mid 1591, which is therefore the earliest possible date for Davies's epigram. Given the topical nature of the epigrams, the probable date of 'Ad Musam' is 1591.

Another epigram, 'In Paulum', tilts at Sir Walter Raleigh. (It is once again Harington who unlocks the cypher: he frequently used this name for Ralegh in his own epigrams.) Paulus, Davies writes,

> Derives out of the Ocean so much wealth
> As he may well maintain a Lord's estate;
> But on the land a little gulf there is
> Wherein he drowneth all that wealth of his.
> (Epigram 41, ll.3–6)

This clearly glances at Raleigh's fall from royal favour in 1592. The 'ocean' suggests his relationship with the Queen (as in his poem to her, 'The Ocean's Love to Cynthia'), and the 'little gulf' – a periphrasis for the vagina – refers to his love affair with Elizabeth Throckmorton, which was the cause of his disgrace. Rumours of the liaison were circulating in early 1592; their illegitimate child was born in March; they were under house arrest in June. The probable date of the epigram is mid 1592.[8]

A third datable reference occurs in the epigram 'In Dacum', which quotes from Samuel Daniel's sonnet sequence, *The Complaint of Rosalind*, published in early 1592. In these three cases, at least, the evidence suggests a date of composition prior to Davies's arrival in the Netherlands in the summer of 1592.

As to why Davies might have chosen a Dutch printer to publish his epigrams, the reason is much the same as with Marlowe's elegies: the probability that an English edition would not get past the censor. They are tart, cynical poems; their satire is aggressive in a way that had not yet become familiar. They are also fairly racy. One describes a sado–masochist: 'His lust sleeps and will not rise before / By whipping of the wench it be awaked'. Others are humorous in a ribald way: whores, pox, farts, etc. It was for this sort of reason, no doubt, that they fell foul of the censor in 1599. Some of the language Davies uses was still unacceptable three centuries later, as witness the many omission–marks in Grosart's Victorian edition of 1869.

So what we can now say is this. We have documentary evidence that both the authors of the *Epigrams and Elegies* visited the Low Countries in the year 1592; we have at least some evidence that the poems in the book had been written prior to their visits; and we have a coherent motive, retrospectively justified by the suppression of the book in 1599, for it to be printed abroad rather than in England. All this seems to strengthen the possibility that the book was genuinely produced in Middelburg, from manuscripts acquired by a printer during, or as a result of, the authors' physical presence in the area. If so, we might be looking at a publication date of around late 1592 or early 1593 for the first edition of the *Epigrams and Elegies*.

IV

This is, I repeat, conjecture: an interesting possibility. But let us see how it works when viewed from other angles and when placed in other contexts – particularly those which so often shade dangerously together in Marlowe's career: the literary and the political.

The literary context takes us straight back to that elusive figure, Lord Strange, whom we know to have been one of Marlowe's patrons in 1591–2. It strikes me straightaway that Lord Strange is exactly the kind of patron who would have enjoyed Marlowe's Ovidian elegies, and who might even have encouraged him to publish them. As noted, the choice of elegies in the first edition goes for the more explicitly sexual material, and we happen to know that Lord Strange was something of an enthusiast of erotic verse. This can be inferred from the fact that Thomas Nashe, another member of Strange's literary circle at this time, dedicated to him a bawdy epic called *The Choice of Valentines*, popularly known as 'Nashe's Dildo'.[9] There is no doubt that Strange is the 'Lord S' referred to in Nashe's dedication, and even Nashe is unlikely to have offered him such a salacious poem without some prior knowledge of his fondness for that sort of thing. Nashe seems confident that Strange will 'smile at what I write': it is not unlikely that the piece was commissioned.

Interestingly, Nashe's poem is filled with references to Ovid. In his dedication to Strange, he describes it as a 'wanton elegy'. In the course of it he likens the drooping lover to 'one with Ovid's cursed hemlock charmed', referring to a description of detumescence in the *Elegies*. And in the concluding sonnet, again addressed to Strange, he adds:

> Yet Ovid's wanton muse did not offend;
> He is the fountain whence my streams do flow.
> (*Works*, vol.3, 415)

In these allusions Nashe may simply be thinking of Ovid *per se*, the past master of erotic poetry, but I suspect there is actually a more specific allusion to Marlowe's translation of the *Elegies*, and to Lord Strange's favourable opinion of them (they 'did not offend'). There is a world of difference between the sleek sexuality of Marlowe's Ovid and the raunchy doggerel of Nashe's Dildo, but although he can hardly be claiming Marlowe's poems as his model, Nashe may well be claiming them as a kind of precedent.

This would fit in with the kind of dating I am proposing for the printing of the *Epigrams and Elegies*. Nashe's dirty Valentine was probably written in 1592, which is when he was connected with the Strange circle. It was certainly known to Gabriel Harvey by early 1593, when he refers to Nashe's 'unprinted packet of filthy and bawdy rhymes'.[10] The poem, with its clear references to the *Elegies*, belongs precisely to the time of Marlowe's known involvement with Lord Strange; to the time of his visit to the Low Countries; to the time when, as I believe, the *Elegies* first saw the light of day in print, in an unlicensed edition smuggled into England from Middelburg.

Nashe and Marlowe, of course, were personal friends. They may also have been collaborators: their names appear together on the title page of *Dido Queen of Carthage*, and it has been suggested Nashe contributed to the comic scenes in *Doctor Faustus*. It is worth noting that Nashe was also acquainted at this time with John Davies. He is thus a personal link – the only one of which I am so far aware – between the two authors of the *Epigrams and Elegies*. Nashe probably knew Davies as part of the circle around the historian Robert Cotton, who was Davies's room–mate at the Middle Temple,[11] and he mentions him rather amicably in his pamphlet *Strange News*, published in late 1592. In the dedicatory epistle, addressed to a certain William 'Apis Lapis' (i.e. Beestone or Beeston), Nashe writes:

> By whatsoever thy visage holdeth most precious I beseech thee, by
> John Davies's soul and the Blue Boar in the Spittle I conjure thee,
> to draw out thy purse.

(*Works*, vol.1, 255)

This is an interesting remark, since 'John Davies's soul' almost certainly refers to Davies's best known work, *Nosce Teipsum*, a long metaphysical poem whose sub–title and subject matter was 'Of the Immortality of the Soul'. The poem was not published until 1599, so Nashe must have known it in manuscript.

Nashe's dedicatee, Master Beeston, is a shadowy figure, but one judges from the tone of it all that he too is a friend of Davies – he holds Davies's poem to be at least as 'precious' as his favourite tavern, the Blue Boar in Spitalfields – and from another remark we gather that he is himself a legal man who moves among 'men of judgement in both laws [i.e. canon and civil law] every day'. We get that offhand, intimate note so valuable in Nashe: this is a casual reference among Inns of Court friends. But it carries also a topical frisson. The dedicatory epistle before *Strange News* can be dated quite precisely: it was written in early November 1592, which is just about the time that Davies returned from the Netherlands, to take up his old quarters at the Middle Temple. The full title of Nashe's pamphlet is: *Strange News of the Intercepting Certain Letters and a Convoy of Verses, as they were going privily to victual the Low Countries*. Nashe is always a tease, and of course the title actually refers to the letters and poems of his enemy Gabriel Harvey, and – via the hackneyed puns on 'privily' and 'low countries'– to their suitability for use as toilet paper. I find it more than a coincidence, however, that in his writings from this year of 1592, Nashe gives us a dirty Ovidian elegy, a puff for the poems of John Davies, and a joke about a 'convoy of verses' on their way to the Netherlands. Strange news indeed.[12]

V

I began this essay with a discussion of the Flushing episode, and briefly advanced the idea (fully explored in my book, *The Reckoning*) that Marlowe the coiner was actually Marlowe the government spy or projector; that his supposed 'intent to go to the enemy' was actually an attempt to infiltrate Catholic exile circles in Brussels; and that this was the reason he escaped any punishment after his arrest and deportation by Sir Robert Sidney. I now conclude by returning to this political context, and thinking of how this notion of a genuine Middelburg edition of the *Elegies* might fit in with it. It would fit in rather well, I think. It would provide another aspect to Marlowe's undercover work in the Low Countries: an involvement in clandestine printing.

From the English government's point of view, the chief danger posed by those Catholic exiles in the Netherlands was not their endless, pipe–dreaming conspiracies in favour of Lord Strange and others, but their skill in propaganda. They pumped out anti–government tracts, both in Latin and English, both serious and scurrilous. These were printed in the Netherlands, smuggled across to England, and dispersed through the country by secret 'carriers' or 'colporteurs'. Among the most influential was the work of the great Jesuit propagandist, Robert Persons. His Latin polemic, *Responsio ad Edictum*, published in Antwerp in 1592, was an eloquent rallying cry, and was widely read by disaffected Catholics in England. Even more popular was the English digest of it, generally known as the *Advertisement*. This was written in a racy, humorous, scandal sheet style, *à la* Martin Marprelate, and it enjoyed much the same clandestine vogue as the earlier 'Leicester's Commonwealth' – that is to say it was enjoyed by a wide range of readers, not just by dyed–in–the–wool Catholics. It contains the famous smear about Ralegh running a secret 'school of atheism', though the principal target of its mockery is Lord Burghley.

There is no doubt that the government feared the damaging influence of books like this emanating from the presses of the Netherlands. Among the tasks of English intelligencers was to learn about the mechanics of this operation, in particular – really the only part of it that the government could hope to disable – the methods and routes whereby the books were smuggled, via a network of couriers and contacts, into England. The government's interest in this area is clear, both from the interrogations of captured Catholics, and from the records of certain intelligence operations.[13]

Among those involved in trying to crack the Catholic book–smuggling routes were two English spies working under the Burghley umbrella – Robert Poley and Michael Moody.[14] Their despatches at this time frequently mention 'seditious books', indeed Poley's cypher key for Low Countries intelligence, dated *circa* 1591, has a specific symbol for 'books'. Moody was himself in Flushing in late 1591, pestering Sir Robert Sidney with complex and dubious plans for the ensnaring of Catholics. In January 1592, he sent a certain book to Sidney, promising he would soon learn the author of it. In March he wrote to Burghley that the 'new answer to the proclamation is coming forth', clearly a reference to Father Person's *Responsio ad Edictum*. A couple of months later, 'divers books of sedition' were seized among the luggage of a Flemish merchant landing at Sandwich; bundled up with them were despatches from Moody, addressed in code to Lord Burghley and Sir Thomas Heneage. Poley was urgently summoned to Sir Robert Cecil's office to discuss their contents.

These are brief details of just one operation; there were many others, in the opportunistic, tail–chasing way of Elizabethan espionage. These are English spies at work in the Low Countries, and among their purposes is to wheedle their way into the covert network of book–smuggling that fuelled the Catholic cause back home. And amidst them one glimpses Christopher

Marlowe, in his 'chamber' in Flushing: a young man who is conveniently an author as well as an intelligencer, and who is arranging for a certain manuscript to be published by a Dutch printer, and thence smuggled back into England. One notes in this scenario a frisson of closeness between Marlowe and Poley, just as the Sidney letter itself reveals a closeness between Marlowe and Baines. This world of spies contracts and constricts: a dangerous intimacy. Like Baines, Poley surfaces again in the story of Christopher Marlowe. He was one of the three men present on the night Marlowe was fatally stabbed at Mrs Bull's house in Deptford. This was in 1593, just a year after we find them linked in this context of Low Countries intelligence. Poley had in fact just returned from the Hague, having been employed there (in the words of his warrant) on 'Her Majesty's secret and special affairs' (PRO, E351/542, fo.182 v.).

Some of this is highly speculative, but I would say that a genuinely Dutch first edition of the *Epigrams and Elegies* is plausible in itself, and plausible in its connection to the political undertones of Marlowe's visit to the Low Countries. It can be linked both to the conspiratorial circles around Lord Strange, and to the smuggling of subversive books from the Netherlands, both of which were the targets of English intelligence activity in the early 1590s. In the puzzle of the Middleborough imprint, as elsewhere in Marlowe's career, I discern that rather disturbing closeness, that sense of collusion, between his work as a poet and his work as – for want of a better word – a spy.

Notes

1. Middlesex County Records, Session Roll 309/13, 9 May 1592.

2. PRO, Privy Council Register, Vol 6, No 381b, 29 June 1587.

3. Principally Thomas Kyd's letter to Sir John Puckering, mid 1593 (BM Harley MS 6849, fo.218), which refers to Marlowe 'bearing name to serve my Lord' and 'writing for his players' in c. 1591. The Sidney letter confirmed what was already supposed, that this unnamed patron is Lord Strange.

4. On the textual history of the book, see Gill and Krueger, 1971, 242–9; and Bowers, 1972, 149–72. The first two editions collate identically, and contain only minor variants. They are generally known as the 'Isham' and the 'Bindley' texts (referring to their previous owners). The 'Isham' survives in a unique copy (Huntington Library) and the 'Bindley' in two copies (Pforzheimer Collection, British Museum). There is some disagreement about their sequence, but Bowers's arguments in favour of 'Isham' as the first edition are more persuasive than Gill and Krueger's in favour of 'Bindley'. He shows, for instance, that misprints in 'Bindley' derive from broken type in 'Isham'. The third, much enlarged edition can be dated 1602 or later because it includes Ben Jonson's translation of one of the *Elegies*, taken from the 1602 edition of Jonson's *Poetaster*.

5. Edward Arber, *Transcript of the Registers of the Company of Stationers*, London, 1875–94, vol.3, 677. Also banned were individual works by John Marston, Thomas Middleton, Joseph Hall and Everard Guilpin, and 'all Nashe's books and Dr Harvey's books'. The decree was issued on 1 June 1599. Three days later, various books 'presently thereupon were burnt' at Stationers' Hall.

6. There are six extant MS collections of Davies's epigrams: one is dated November 1594, another 1595; see Gill and Krueger, 1971, 244. I see no real justification for their assertion that these MSS antedate the printed edition.

7. Sir John Harington, *Elegant and Witty Epigrams*, London, 1618, Bk 3, Epigram 21. Harington also refers to Davies's epigrams in his *Metamorphosis of Ajax*, London, 1596, 133: 'My good friend M[aster] Davies said of his epigrams that they were made like doublets in Birchin

Lane, for everyone whom they will serve'.

8. Bishop, 1972, 52–6.'Paulus' refers to the heretical Paulician sect, whose anti–Trinitarian views Raleigh was believed to share. On his affair with Miss Throckmorton, see Nicholl, 1995, 41–5.

9. *Works of Thomas Nashe*, ed. R. McKerrow and F. Wilson, Oxford, 1958, vol.3, 403–11. The poem survives in three MSS, one in cypher. On the identification of Strange as 'Lord S', see Nicholl, 1984, 293.

10. *Works of Gabriel Harvey*, ed. A. Grosart, London, 1884–5, vol. 2, 91. The comment occurs in *Pierce's Supererogation*, which Harvey completed in April 1593. Nashe was certainly part of Strange's circle by mid–1592, for in *Pierce Penniless* (published in September 1592) he speaks of his 'private experience' of Strange's generosity, and of 'benefits' he has received from 'this renowned Lord' (*Works*, vol.1, 242–5; Nicholl, 1984, 87–90, 293).

11. Eccles, 1982, 37. Letters from Davies to Cotton ('sweet Robyn') are extant. In early 1593 Nashe was a guest at Cotton's house at Conington, Huntingdonshire, where he wrote an early version of *Terrors of the Night* (1594); see Harlow, 1961, 7–21.

12. A pun on Strange's name is not impossible: there is certainly one in the preface to *Terrors of the Night* (Nashe, *Works*, vol.1, 341), which was dedicated to Strange's niece, Elizabeth Carey. Nashe may have been living *chez* Strange while writing *Strange News* in November–December 1592. He refers to a 'Lord' who is 'keeping' him, and in whose house he 'converses'. However, it is equally possible this is Archbishop Whitgift. Nashe had put on his play, *Summer's Last Will*, at Whitgift's palace in Croydon in early October.

13. See, for example, the interrogation of Henry Walpole, in September 1594, concerning the production and distribution of the *Advertisement* (printed in Pollen, 1908, 264–5). The full title, *An Advertisement written to a Secretary of my L. Treasurer of England concerning another Book newly written against Her Majesty's Late Proclamation*, is itself a spoof on the government's efforts to intercept these propagandist pamphlets.

14. On Poley and Moody, see Nicholl, 1992, 250–6, and sources there cited.

4. Visible Bullets: *Tamburlaine the Great* and Ivan the Terrible

RICHARD WILSON

On 18 March 1584 Tsar Ivan IV, Emperor and Great Duke of Vladimir, Moscow and of all Russia, King of Astrakhan, King of Kazan, and King of Siberia, was carried on a throne into his treasury, where (in the account of the English emissary Sir Jerome Horsey) he called for his jewels: the lodestone of the prophet Muhammed, 'without which the seas nor the bounds that circle the earth cannot be known'; the unicorn's horn encrusted with rubies and emeralds he had bought for 'seventy thousand marks sterling' from the Welsh wizard David Gower; the 'richest diamond of the orient,' which guaranteed chastity; a sapphire that 'cleared the sight, took away bloodshot, and strengthened muscles'; and an onyx that changed colour in the hand of vice. Armed with these charms, he summoned the 'Lapland witches' who had foretold his death, to tell them that 'The day was come; he was as heart whole as ever,' and that at sunset they would therefore be burned. Then he 'made merry with pleasant songs as he useth to [and] called his favourite to bring his chess board.' The opponent he chose was his rival, Boris Godunov; but the tsar set out his pieces confidently until he came to the king, which rolled onto the floor; whereupon 'the Emperor faints and falls backward. Great outcry and stir; one sends for his physicians, another for his ghostly father. In the meantime he was strangled and stark dead.'[1] Thus passed the tsar known as the Terrible: 'This Heliogabalus,' as Horsey reported him, who was 'A right Scythian; well favoured, high forehead, shrill voice; full of ready wisdom, cruel, bloody, merciless,' and whose Kremlin tomb, 'guarded day and night, remains a fearful spectacle to such as pass by or hear his name spoken, who are contented to cross and bless themselves from his resurrection.' But if there was jubilation in Moscow when the chancellor sarcastically announced that 'the English Emperor was dead,' there was consternation in London, where the Muscovy Company had built its fortune on Ivan's despotic word (Horsey, *Travels*, 313)

The Muscovy Company was England's first joint stock enterprise, floated in 1553 with 240 £25 shares, which members subdivided as the market value rose during Ivan's reign to £100 by 1557 and £450 in 1572: an exponential growth of 1,800 per cent (Willan, 1956, 41–3). The Company's success was thus the reverse of that to which the dying tsar had physically clung: the triumph of capital as an invisible power penetrating distant lands. For as Fernand Braudel explains, merchant companies were engines of a new global economy, pumping investment from an ever larger public through cycles of expanding trade (Braudel, 1982, 140–2). 'At the top of the world of commerce, the real big business' of the Renaissance was a fourfold operation (import–and–export and purchase–and–sale) by these international monopolists; and the Muscovy Company completed a classic circuit when they sold the English navy Russian cable bought with arms shipped to the tsar (Willan, 1956, 63–6, 91–2; Scott, 1912, I, 17–22).[2] Distance, volume, and demand made this semi–clandestine trade so lucrative that by the mid 1580s the Company was declaring goods worth £25,000 a year (£75,000 at market rates); but the stimulus for fresh capital on which its directors constantly called was the potential for new markets at each end of the line: in the Asian territories conquered by Ivan where, as Horsey wrote, 'great traffic is maintained with all nations for the commodities which each country yields'; and in the American colonies founded on the defeat of Spain (Braudel, 1982, 403–8, Horsey *Travels*, 311). From Virginia to Persia, the Muscovy Company straddled the shipping and caravan lanes of world trade; but the hub of its activity was its warehouse in Deptford, where up to £10,000–worth of cordage was stowed. That 'the fleet which defeated the Armada was rigged with Russian tackle and cable,' was due to the bills and invoices that meshed in this store, where the Company's London agent was charged with executing some of the most secret orders of the state (Willan, 1956, 185, 245–55; Wretts–Smith, 1914, 95). And this is significant, because from 1576 to 1599 the agent was Anthony Marlowe, long identified as a Crayford relative of Christopher Marlowe, and a cause, we may infer, of the dramatist's fatal connection with the Deptford docks.[3]

'For the silk of the Medes to come by Muscovy into England is a strange hearing,' exclaimed the English ambassador in Paris, when he learned of the new passage to Asia. It was such multilateralism, Braudel suggests, that destroyed the fair and elevated the warehouse into the key instrument of exchange; and Muscovy Company records reveal its Deptford depot as the nexus of communication between London and the tsar's domains (Braudel, 1982, 94–7; Willan, 1956, 58). With its accumulation of intelligence and stock, this was one room where 'infinite riches' were truly circumscribed in the Jew's audit that 'thus trawls our fortune in by land and sea, / And thus are we on every side enrich'd' (*Jew of Malta*, 1.1.105)[4] According to his predecessor, Anthony Marlowe had 'charge of all the business of the company,' including purchase of good reexported to Russia and was paid a bonus of £200 a year for 'executing the doings thereof quietly' (Willan, 1956, 28). In 1587, when the dramatist arrived in London, such discretion was at a premium, because the stores were at the centre of a gigantic fraud devised by the Company governor, George Barne, a Woolwich broker, with his brother–in–law, the spymaster, Francis Walsingham. Their scam was made possible when Ivan's successor Theodor revoked the Company's monopoly and Horsey rigged a secret deal between Godunov and his 'good friends' in London. Since a turnover of a mere £13,500 was declared in 1587, we can guess that this 'very cunning scheme' cost the shareholders about half of their dividend; and historians surmise that because they employed Company ships, Barne and Walsingham must have colluded with Anthony, who was supposed 'to prevent private trade by numbering every truss of cloth and hogshead of brimstone'.[5] The agent was, in fact, himself related to both men; and their conspiracy was presumably sealed with the complicity of the local official responsible for receipt of goods into the royal household: the bailiff of the Clerk of the Greencloth, the very Richard Bull in whose offices on Deptford Strand, long mistaken for a tavern, Christopher Marlowe would eventually pay his own mysterious reckoning.[6]

Ivan's death precipitated a crisis in the Muscovy Company that had loomed since 1580, when the Turks cut the route from Russia to Persia. By 1586 its books were nominally in the red; so at the annual court shareholders moved to censure its board for 'disposing of trade to the discontent of the inferior brethren, by liberality of Mr Horsey towards some of the chief dealers.' The upshot, however, was that 'the whole court with one assent by erecting of hands' voted to write off seventy–five per cent of the debt, refloat the Company with a new share issue, and, as Barne assured Lord Burghley (a major promoter), vest control in just ten directors, to avoid future 'inconvenience of forward men's opinions' (Willan, 1956, 23, 208–160). By crushing this shareholders' revolt, the City of London was already displaying its genius for insider dealing; and the affair reveals the restrictive practices Anthony Marlowe might have mobilized on behalf of kin. For the Muscovy Company was in reality a cartel of Kent families, linking many of the factors in Russia, such as Walsingham's stepson, Alexander Carlyle, with naval commanders like Hawkins, who married Anthony Marlowe's cousin. Anthony Marlowe's ties with Bull typified this dynastic network: Richard Bull's father had worked as Deptford Master Shipwright for his grandfather and uncle, William and Benjamin Gonson, successive Navy Treasurers; whilst Bull's employer at the Greencloth, Christopher Browne of Sayes Court, married another of Marlowe's Gonson cousins.[7] Peter Clark comments that though Kent led foreign enterprise, with gentry 'busy sending home carpets and news from India,' this was always managed 'for the consolidation of its oligarchy,' and the Justices of the Peace who invested in Russia or America shared the moral horizons of the Faversham pirate, Jack Ward, who plundered the Caribbean and Mediterranean for Queen or Sultan 'with exemplary impartiality.'[8] Certainly, the reflotation of the Russia Company as what critics termed a 'monopoly in a monopoly,' suggests that if the poet was privy to its accounts, he would have had a sound initiation into the double entries and strange fellows of venture capitalism.[9]

'Give me a map, a let me see how much / Is left for me to conquer all the world, / That these boys may finish all my wants' (2 *Tamburlaine* 5.3.124–6):[10] it is a commonplace that, as Stephen Greenblatt says,

Tamburlaine personifies 'the acquisitive energy of merchants and adventurers, promoters alike of trading and theatrical companies,' and that the 'historical matrix' of Marlowe's drama was Elizabethan commerce, since 'it is his countrymen that he depicts' (Greenblatt, 1992, 58). Ivan's deathbed endgame and the career of the Muscovy agent (who did indeed sponsor a playhouse in Finsbury)[11] point to a yet more specific context for what critics have described as the compulsion to repetition of 'the great Tartarian thief' (*1 Tamburlaine*, 3.3.171), in the relaunch of Asian trade by Marlowe's patrons: 'Upon a new and clear ground,' as they claimed, 'we having nothing to do with the former reckoning.' Stock in the Russia Company, as it was now called, was subscribed in April 1587: Part Two of *Tamburlaine* was acted by November; so it cannot be chance that Marlowe's epic of 'the rogue of Volga' (*2 Tamburlaine*, 4.1.4) should project what Burghley described as 'the great end of dealing with the Muscovite: discovery of a passage to Asia.'[12] For far from the aimlessness Greenblatt attributes to him, the hero's campaign 'to march toward Persia, / Along Armenia and the Caspian Sea' (*2 Tamburlaine*, 5.3.126–27), accords exactly with Company goals; while even his plan to circumnavigate 'along the oriental sea about the Indian continent ... from Persepolis to Mexico, / And thence unto the Straits of Jubalter [and] the British shore' (*1 Tamburlaine*, 3.3.253–590), simply retraces the Company's 1583 voyage to the Moluccas via South America.[13] If Marlowe's atlas was Ortelius's, Tamburlaine's map was actually the one surveyed for the cartographer in 1562 by the Company factor Antony Jenkinson and dedicated to its governor, Sir Henry Sidney of Penshurst (Willan, 1956, 282). And if his plan to 'sail to India ... along the Ethiopian sea' (*2 Tamburlaine*, 5.3.135–37) seems deluded for one 'paltry Scythian' (*1 Tamburlaine*, 1.1.54), its rationale lies in the Company's own charter to monopolize the entire orient beyond the northeast passage.[14]

Critics long ago decided that in *Tamburlaine* Marlowe 'was playing a great game of chess, with kings ... for pieces, and for chess–board the *Theatrum Orbis Terrarum*' (Seaton, 1924, 35), but they have been slow to historicize this *kriegspiel* in relation to the war–game waged by Elizabethan finance. Yet, as John Hale writes in his survey of *The Civilization of Europe in the Renaissance*, Ortelius's atlas charted 'one of the great sagas of sixteenth–century expansion ... when Muscovy exerted control southwards along the Don and Volga to the Asian trade routes.' Thus, at the very moment when new cartography supplied them with a key to self–orientation, Russian imperialism posed to the traders who made it possible to annihilate 'populations which had courage but no firearms,' the ethical problem of the frontier between civility and barbarism. Their doubt about whether Moscow stood in Europe or Asia signified the liminality of a terrain where nomenclature was ceaselessly revised (as it is by Tamburlaine), and 'the preparedness of maps to offer contexts for political developments broke down'(Hale, 1993, 24–45).[15] For as Philip II's ambassador reported in 1582, it was London merchants who hoped to gain most from the Russian dream of bathing in the warm waters of the Indian Ocean, since 'they calculated that by these means they might monopolize the drug and spice trades,' and by 'bringing goods from Persia to the Volga,' circumvent 'the territories of your Majesty and other Christian Princes.'[16] So, if Tamburlaine's *blitzkrieg* was projected from Ortelius's pages, one image would have illustrated the glittering commercial horizons of Elizabethan Londoners. There, bestriding the golden road to Samarkand (where the cartographer notes that 'great Tamber had his seat'), is a figure who seems by size and situation to dominate Asia. Like Tamburlaine, he is represented as a Tartar nomad, with tent and turban; but, as Hale infers, Ortelius thereby merely marks the deep conceptual ambivalence of sixteenth–century Russia (Hale, 1993, 26–7). For this Asiatic potentate is, in fact, the first Western portrait of 'John, Great King, Emperor of Russia, and Duke of Moscow,' who would soon be infamous as Ivan.

Greenblatt observes that while incessant movement in *Tamburlaine* does indeed 'reduce the universe to the coordinates of a map,' such dramaturgy makes 'all spaces curiously alike ... contriving to efface differences, as if to insist upon the essential meaninglessness of space ... Space is transformed into an abstraction.' For Greenblatt, this 'secularization of space' is the register of 'wants never finished and transcendental homelessness' (Greenblatt, 1992, 59–60); but Emily Bartels has recently keyed Marlowe's projective space more concretely to Elizabethan travel writing, and countered that 'the lack of differentiation between its worlds' should be viewed not as the sign of existential angst, but of a drive to 'break down the barriers of difference,' to 'show that the worlds out there are not so different from Europe. The point is not that space is meaningless, but that the differences assigned to it are empty, overdetermined, or arbitrary' (Bartels, 1993, 56–7). Bartels argues that when *Tamburlaine* is contextualized within the emerging discourses of ethnography and orientalism, its hero's contradictory mixture of the civilized and savage can be seen as admonitory for England's confrontation with Asia, 'where choosing sides became as difficult as defining them,' states were 'accorded both positive and negative attributes,' and their subjects were 'emulated *and* feared, not because civility would at any moment devolve into barbarism, but because that civility was coupled to barbarism.' 'East of England,' by this reading, Marlowe's game of empire deliberately deprived its players of moral bearings, and filled the Asian landscape with conflicting voices of nobility and savagery, to prove 'one man's hero another man's barbarian' (ibid., 60–61, 70–71). To Bartels, such moral neutrality 'undermines the agency of everyone involved'(ibid., 81); but this conclusion ignores the extent to which, as Thomas Cartelli remarks, 'Marlowe's discourse of mastery was apt to stir the emotions and fulfil the fantasies' of playgoers by projecting the very dreams to which they aspired (Cartelli, 1991, 80). It underestimates, that is to say, the material investment of Londoners in the Eastern ventures of their own exotic agents:

> Merchants of the Indian mines,
> That trade in metal of the purest mould;
> The wealthy Moor, that in the eastern rocks
> Without control can pick his riches up,
> And in his house heap pearl like pebble–stones,
> Receive them free, and sell them by the weight.
> (*Jew*, 1.1.19–24)

'Backwards and forwards near five thousand leagues' (*2 Tamburlaine*, 5.3.144), Tamburlaine's transit into Persia and Turkey recapitulates the expeditions that regularly earned Muscovy Company shareholders dividends of 400 per cent in the terrible years of Ivan. If Marlowe's hero is driven, as Greenblatt proposes, by a 'will to absolute play' (Greenblatt, 1992, 81–2), his Game is for real, since it is the Great one played from the sixteenth century between the European powers, with its prize of control of the passes into India. For though Greenblatt thinks that Tamburlaine pursues a mirage, the prospect he offers his army is precisely that from which London importers would generate their wealth: 'Men from the farthest equinoctial line, / [Who] swarmed in troops into the Eastern India: / Lading their shops with gold and precious stones' (*2 Tamburlaine*, 1.1.119–21). In her recent book on *Cultural Aesthetics*, Patricia Fumerton describes seventeenth–century East India trade as a 'perpetual motion machine of deferred expenditure and delayed profit,' whereby Spanish silver would be shipped from England to India to buy sugar and silk; which would be transported to the East Indies to exchange with spice; which would be carried back to England and sold for silver; which would then be reexported in a circle to the East (Fumerton, 1991, 180–85). The East India Company that perfected this multilateral system was founded in 1599 by the tycoons of the Russia Company, including Barne; so if Tamburlaine's loot of 'jewels and treasure' and 'golden wedges' is constantly 'reserved' for investment in 'East India and the late–discover'd Isles' (*1 Tamburlaine*, 1.2.2, 139, 166), this chimes with expectation in the City of attaining the jewel in the imperial crown: the 'diamonds, sapphires, rubies / And fairest pearl of wealthy India' (*2 Tamburlaine*, 3.2.120–21). His portfolio of ships and camels laden with gold, coral, slaves, carpets, cotton, silk, cassia, and myrrh, is shrewd enough; for when his joint–stock company divides 'the gold, silver, and pearl they got in equal shares' (*2 Tamburlaine*, 3.5.89–90), the dividend is an earnest of the interests that would drive the Raj.

In the context of the political economy of the great merchant empires, Marlowe's passage to India reads like a prospectus for the recapitalization of a Company that promised to 'open the golden road to Samarkand and make London the new Antwerp through which jewels, spices, silks, drugs, and metals would flow to Europe' (Willan, 1956, 152). The Prologue predicts that simply to 'hear the Scythian Tamburlaine / Threatening the world with high astounding terms' will make the public 'applaud his fortunes' (*1 Tamburlaine*, Prologue 4–8); and the arithmetic of this investment, from 'five hundred foot' and 'odds too great' at the outset (*1 Tamburlaine*, 1.2.121–22), to the 'millions of soldiers' he brings 'from Scythia to the oriental plage / Of India' (*2 Tamburlaine*, 1.1.28, 67–69), does seem pitched to tell Sidneys in Kent their prospects. Hakluyt's *Voyages* were doctored by Walsingham in 1589, we know, to promote investment in Russia (Crosskey, 1983, 546–64, esp. 563–4); and it is for calculating shorter odds on cards than on his father's 'shares' that the sceptical Calyphas is disowned. As Tamburlaine instructs the reckless son, Amyras, 'It is not chance' that wins this game, but 'greater numbers' (*2 Tamburlaine*, 4.1.47–81). 'Tempt not fortune' is therefore the prudent motto of this Tartar (*2 Tamburlaine*, 4.1.84), whose bookkeeping seems primed to Lombard Street. For if the scenario is in fact the blockade of the 1580s, when Turkish 'galleys and pilling brigandines' did 'yearly sail to the Venetian gulf' and 'cut the straits' to deny the 'argosies' of 'fair Europe the wealth and riches of the world' (*1 Tamburlaine*, 3.3.248–50; *2 Tamburlaine*, 1.1.39–41, 1.3.33), Tamburlaine's hyperbole works, Marjorie Garber notes, to minimize obstacles through the creative accountancy of writing (Garber, 1984, 302–3). Like the Company agent's, his pen is his sword as he deletes lines and multiplies figures with supreme indifference to actuality. Historians who view trading companies as states within states, which merged private profit into public priorities through the legerdemain of operators such as Walsingham, would find confirmation of their thesis, therefore, in the sleight of hand by which this projector maximizes markets, punctures frontiers, and redrafts the geopolitics of continents:[17]

> I will confute those blind geographers
> That make a triple region of the world,
> Excluding regions which I mean to trace,
> And with this pen reduce them to a map,
> Calling the provinces, cities and towns
> After my name and thine, Zenocrate.
> (*1 Tamburlaine*, 4.4.73–78)

Edward Said argues that Marlowe's 'oriental stage' helped fabricate the stereotype of Islam as Christendom's other (Said, 1991, 60–63); but what this

Scythian's breach of the continental blockade demonstrates is a refusal of binarism, a deconstruction of 'the confines and the bounds' of Europe (*1 Tamburlaine*, 1.6.80) that is dramatically enacted by third terms and intermediaries: the Persian defectors, Theridamas and Cosroe; Catholic Europe; India; Africa; America; even the 'land which never was descried' east of 'th'Antartic pole' – Australia (*2 Tamburlaine*, 5.3.154). Tamburlaine's subversion of polarity, his urge to 'leap from his hemisphere' (*2 Tamburlaine*, 1.3.51), shift 'the perpendicular' (*1 Tamburlaine*, 4.4.80), 'fix the meridian line' anew (*1 Tamburlaine*, 4.2.38), or 'travel to th'antartic pole, / Conquering the people underneath our feet' (*1 Tamburlaine*, 5.1.133), belongs, that is to say, precisely to the era of the chartered trading companies, when, as Jean–Christophe Agnew relates, long–distance transactions generated just such triangular relations as Marlowe stages (Agnew, 1986, 41–3). And if Tamburlaine's 'mighty line' expresses by its very attenuation the compound suspended payoff of those bills of exchange that connected the speculator in Canterbury with the cinnamon grower in Java, his characterization as a liminary neither Christian nor Muslim, Asian nor European, destines him to dominate a world dependent on the mediation of the arbitrageur and agent. For this 'Scythian slave' (*1 Tamburlaine*, 3.3.68) is the placeless New Man or *Conquistador* of the Renaissance; but he is also that most transgressive of all executants of commercial expansion, one of those 'vile outrageous men / That live by rapine and by lawless spoil' (*1 Tamburlaine*, 2.2.23–24), 'A monster... famous for nothing but theft' (*1 Tamburlaine*, 4.3.66), or pirate. Braudel reminds us that piracy is the term used by the waning power to stigmatize its rival; and when the Soldan calls Tamburlaine 'a base usurping vagabond' (*1 Tamburlaine*, 4.3.21), Marlowe's eastern world is a mirror that transcends mere orientalism. What we see reflected, of course, are English privateers such as Hawkins: the founders of the so–called Honourable Company.

With 'pillage and murder his usual trades' and 'a troop of thieves and vagabonds' (*1 Tamburlaine*, 4.1.66), the 'sturdy Scythian thief, / That robs your merchants of Persepolis / Treading by land unto the Western Isles' (*1 Tamburlaine*, 1.1.35–38), embodies the ambiguity of the freebooter for a culture in which raiding and trading were modes of the same enterprise.[18] An antique 'curtle–axe' in his belt, Tamburlaine begins as a Robin Hood, who vows, like Shakespeare's bandits, never to prosper 'by lawless rapine from a silly maid' (*1 Tamburlaine*, 1.2.9–10, 43); but his privateering promotes him into a blockade runner for England's eastern enterprise: 'The only fear and terror of the cruel pirates of Argier, / That damned train, the scum of Africa' (*1 Tamburlaine*, 3.3.55–56). From pillaging London merchants to policing Barbary corsairs, the whole history of buccaneering is thus figured when 'this thief of Scythia' becomes a 'proud King of Persia' (*2 Tamburlaine*,

3.1.14–15). Doubtless this is Marlowe's version of what the pirate said to Alexander when he objected, 'Because I do with a little ship, I am called a thief: thou doing it with a great navy, art called an emperor.'[19] But the gulf between pirate and emperor, we are constantly reminded, is technology. For if Marlowe's map is up–to–the–minute, so too is his analysis (confirmed by authorities such as Geoffrey Parker) that a prerequisite of modern hegemony was armament (Parker, 1988). Nothing remains, in any case, of Timur the Lame in this juggernaut who bombards and mines, editors notice, according to *The Practise of Fortification* by Paul Ive, a Kent aide to Walsingham (2 *Tamburlaine*, 3.2.62–90).[20] With 'great artillery / And store of ordnance' (2 *Tamburlaine*, 3.2.79–80), 'sulphur balls of fire' (2 *Tamburlaine*, 5.1.99), 'light artillery, / Minions, fale'nets, shakers' (2 *Tamburlaine*, 3.3.5–7), and even 'engines never exercised' (2 *Tamburlaine*, 4.1.190), Tamburlaine's pyrotechnics are a state–of–the–art display of early modern European ballistic supremacy. For though the tsar can muster one hundred and fifty thousand Tartars (so Horsey relayed), it is his 'warlike engines and munition' that suddenly 'exceed the force of mortal men' (*1 Tamburlaine*, 4.1.20–29), and he is 'termed the Scourge and Wrath of God' (*1 Tamburlaine*, 3.3.44) precisely because he has been equipped to actualize the Marlovian holocaust, and burn the topless towers of Asia:[21]

> So, burn the turrets of this cursed town,
> Flame to the highest region of the air:
> And kindle heaps of exhalations,
> That being fiery meteors, may presage,
> Death and destruction to th'inhabitants.
> Over my zenith hang a blazing star,
> That may endure till heaven be dissolved,
> Fed with the fresh supply of earthly dregs,
> Threatening a death and famine to this land.
> Flying dragons, lightning, fearful thunderclaps,
> Singe these fair plains, and make them seem as black
> As in the island where the Furies mask,
> Compassed with Lethe, Styx, and Phlegethon.
> (2 *Tamburlaine*, 3.2.1–13)

Editors have struggled to locate sources for Tamburlaine's weapons of mass destruction in Byzantine chronicles of the Mongolian Khan, but overlook obvious analogues for 'the flames the cursed Scythian sets on all the towns... bordering on the [Black] sea' (2 *Tamburlaine*, 3.2.51–55), in the arsenal of Ivan.[22] Yet if Marlowe was under the patronage of Walsingham, Horsey's despatches would have provided gruesome illustration of both the lethal efficiency of modern armaments and the seriousness of Tamburlaine's threat to 'raise cavalieros higher than the clouds, / And with the cannon break the frame of heaven' (2 *Tamburlaine*, 2.4.103–4). In 1569 Sigismund of Poland had warned the English government that 'the Muscovite, made more perfect in warlike affairs with engines of war and ships, will make assault on Christendom, to slay and bind all that withstand him'; and Horsey confirmed how in 1577 'the emperor and his cruel and hellish Tartars set forward with cannon and artillery, munitions, and ten thousand to draw his ordnance over rivers,' to 'batter' Reval with 'twenty thousand cannon shot,' leaving 'streets lying full of carcasses of aged men, women, and infants.'[23] Observers attributed Ivan's savagery to the death of the tsarina Anastasia (who was then sanctified, like Zenocrate); and Tamburlaine's mania to 'consume with fire' the 'cursed town [that] bereft me of my love' (2 *Tamburlaine*, 2.4.137–38), has its precedent in the razing of Novgorod in 1570, when the tsar pitched his pavilion to spectate as 'thirty thousand Tartars...ravished, ransacked, and murdered... burned all merchandizes and warehouses... and set all on fire with wax, together with the blood of seven hundred thousand men, women and children,' in an atrocity of which Horsey wrote, 'No history maketh mention of so horrible a massacre.'[24] When Marlowe's warlord pledges, therefore, to 'fill all the air with fiery meteors,' so 'it shall be said, I made it red myself' (1 *Tamburlaine*, 4.2.51–52), audiences at the Rose would have had no doubt of the real perpetrator of such conflagrations, even though he had smuggled his demand for explosives to Elizabeth in a vodka bottle (Horsey, *Travels*, Berry and Crummey, 1968, 294–8).

'Hang him up in chains upon the city walls, / And let my soldiers shoot the slave to death' (1 *Tamburlaine*, 5.1.108–9): it was during the performance of the 'firing squad' of the governor of Babylon in November 1587 that a 'player's hand swerved, his calliver being charged with bullets, missed the fellow he aimed at, and killed a child and a woman great with child, and hurt another man very sore in the head.'[25] Calyphas had warned how 'bullets fly at random where they list' (2 *Tamburlaine*, 4.1.52); and like the 'accidental' slaying of Olympia (2 *Tamburlaine*, 4.2.80), the incident reminds us of the materiality of Marlovian culture, with its 'deadly bullet gliding through the side' (2 *Tamburlaine*, 3.4.4.). It is by his homicidal staging of the victim 'having as many bullets in his flesh, / As there be breaches in the wall' (2 *Tamburlaine*, 5.1.158–59), that Marlowe discloses the covert cycle that links the joint–stock company with the tsar's bloodthirsty mafia, the *oprichnina*. All those commodities transported from Persepolis to Deptford are traded, we grasp, for these 'bullets like Jove's thunderbolts, / Enrolled in flames and fiery mists' (1 *Tamburlaine*, 21.3.19–20); and the poet's pyromania has its genesis in that warehouse where a kinsman 'quietly' consigned munitions to the arsonist of Moscow. Elizabeth always denied rumours of arms for Russia 'on her royal word'; but Marlowe's incendiary imagination gives away the game.[26] For if Tamburlaine's 'volleys of shot, bullets dipped in poison [and] roaring cannons' are a scourge, that is because they work, as he boasts, like a *pharmakon*, 'as baneful / As Thessalian drugs or mithridate' (*1 Tamburlaine*, 5.2.69–70, 159), or fire with fire. Set a thief to catch one, was the Queen's reasoning, at any rate, in secretly agreeing to 'let the Tsar have out of England all kinds of artillery and things necessary for war' (Willan, 1956, 91; Grey, 1962, 648–51, Stuart, 1917, 281–7). Thereafter, 'Christian merchants that with Russian stems / Plough up huge furrows in the Caspian Sea,' were happy to vail to Ivan, as the text records, in return for passage 'on the fifty–headed Volga's waves' (*1 Tamburlaine*, 1.2.103, 194–96); and the Kremlin Nero was satisfied with his cargo of invisible 'lead, copper, powder, saltpeter, and brimstone.'[27]

'He is advised by no council, but governeth altogether like a tyrant,' wrote Francis Bacon of Ivan the Terrible in 1582, and behind this remark it is possible to detect the equivocalness towards absolutism that made Tamburlaine the barnstormer of Bankside.[28] For though Philip Sidney scorned the 'slave–born Muscovite' who 'calls it praise to suffer tyranny,' what impressed investors like his own father was that this ogre 'whose name was synonymous with cruelty' should have waged his wars 'for the right of free trade.'[29] Thus, in spite of atrocities, reported Samuel Purchas, 'his memory is savoury to the Russians, who either of their servile disposition, or for his long and prosperous reign, hold him in no less reputation than a saint.'[30] It was the paradox that Marlowe made the crux of his play, and one that stockbrokers could appreciate, since out of a race of 'false truce–breakers, subtle foxes and ravenous wolves, barbarous, yet cunning and unfaithful,' the impaler had proved to be the one Russian whose word was his bond.[31] Whether licensing Christian traders or slaughtering the virgins of Damascus, Tamburlaine likewise resolved never to break a promise 'if I have sworn' (*1 Tamburlaine*, 4.3.125), since 'that which mine honour swears shall be performed' (*1 Tamburlaine*, 5.2.44); and his purge of silk roads and shipping lanes had shown how money knows neither morality nor margins. Marlowe's distant mirror had revealed to Kentish shareholders, indeed, not their polar other, but their mutual interest in a world apart. It had even imaged a Suez canal, cut 'whereas the Terrene and the Red Sea meet... That men might quickly sail to India' (*2 Tamburlaine*, 5.3.132–35); and if this was literally far fetched, it was no more so than the project that would preoccupy the Company in 1613, to secure 'the Persian trade by way of the Caspian Sea and Volga, to Archangel and England', by annexing Russia to the Crown.[32] 'Some of the nobility of Muscovy having offered to put themselves under King James,' the Privy Council noted, 'he is full of a scheme to send an army there, and rule that country by a viceroy, and is sanguine of success':

> In this project there is no injustice nor any breach or straining of treaties concluded with any other prince or state. Contrariwise, there is in it much glory to His Majesty, much charity towards those oppressed people with whom we have had long commerce, much policy in regard of the increase of our shipping and trade, which must needs augment both our strength and wealth, and much happiness promised thereby to His Majesty and this whole Kingdom.[33]

'The God of heaven and earth would not that all things should be found in one region, to the end that one should have need of another,' proclaimed the letter from Edward VI flourished by the first Muscovy merchants when they left Deptford in 1553; so 'All kings in all places under the universal heaven' should give 'aid and help' to such as 'carry good and profitable things as are found in their countries to remote regions... and bring from the same things they find commodious for their own' (Willan, 1956, 4–5). It was under this gospel of free trade that Marlowe could promote his terrible tsar as an instrument of Hermes, the god of universal commerce (*1 Tamburlaine*, 1.2.120): 'He that sits on high and never sleeps, / Nor in one place is circumscriptible' (*2 Tamburlaine*, 2.2.50). For as Greenblatt observes, by constituting 'desire of gold' as 'the wind that bloweth all the world' (*Jew*, 3.5.3–4), Marlowe's work familiarizes what Christian culture finds terrifying, installing outsiders (such as the Jewish broker) at the epicentre of power (Greenblatt, 1992, 66–7). Here, then, in the universalist ideology of the chartered company, and what Immanuel Wallerstein calls its 'inter–state system ... to encompass as many links in the commodity chain as possible' (Wallerstein, 1983, 30–31, 56–7), lies the market logic that explains why, in Simon Shepherd's reading, *Tamburlaine* 'traps the audience between the success and cruelty of the hero'(Shepherd, 1986, 241). To Shepherd, such an irony produces only 'a sense of powerlessness' in spectators (ibid., 151); but this is to undervalue the monetary interest of London's over–horizons *speculators* in breaching any arms embargo. For if Tamburlaine's God, 'Full of revenging wrath' (*2 Tamburlaine*, 5.1.181), is 'strikingly Protestant,' as Alan Sinfield finds (Sinfield, 1992, 241), this is because he is as much a deity of contract law as Faustus's. It is when Tamburlaine burns his universal 'writ' that 'the Scourge of God must die' (*2 Tamburlaine*, 5.1.188, 5.2.248); but while he observes those 'solemn oaths, / Signed with our hands' which Catholics break (*2 Tamburlaine*, 1.2.66–67), the alien thrives. Marlowe, who was born just as the doctrine of consideration emerged in English law to legitimate exchange, made contract the basis of his plots; and however great or small the sums in that final reckoning in the customs house at Deptford, it would determine his own hour of 'crisis' (*2 Tamburlaine*, 5.3.91), when he met with the assassin who had arrived by ferry that very morning hot from the Bourse at Amsterdam.[34]

The day after being pardoned for the murder of Christopher Marlowe, his killers were busy selling 'a number of guns and great iron pieces' on behalf of the Walsinghams (Bakeless, 1942, vol. 1, 167–8). Whatever the deceased's part in the contraband from which his backers profited, the fortunes he predicted in his play had not materialized under Ivan's heirs, and the Company was engaged in disposing of army surplus and settling accounts with the Clerk of the Greencloth at Sayes Court.[35] So, if *Tamburlaine* does dramatize despatches Horsey sent the Company during the Reign of Terror, their contents would confirm the mutuality of all who make a killing out of war.[36] It might have been news of how the barbarous Scythian struck his heir dead for commiserating with his victims that suggested Tamburlaine's (otherwise unsourced) murder of his pacifist son Calyphas; as it may have been the tsar's tragicomic marriage proposals to Elizabeth that inspired his devotion to the moon as Cynthia. It is possible that Marlowe was himself drawn by stories of Ivan's homosexuality;[37] but, as his ambivalence hints, this monster who was the prototypical outsider inside Europe – Uncle Joe, or The Russian with whom the West can do Business – was always threatening to become overfamiliar. Shakespeare's joke about the arrival of the 'frozen Muscovite' in the West (*Love's Labour's Lost*, 5.2.265) was very nearly realized in 1580, when Ivan 'prepared many boats and brought his treasure to be embarked, to pass down the river and so into England upon a sudden, leaving the tsarevich to pacify his troubled land'(Horsey, *Travels*, Berry and Crummey, 1968, 280). Though Tamburlaine is heroized by merchants of the Western Isles as the one Russian whose word is good, it is doubtful whether Elizabeth would have honoured her own secret promise to grant her 'cousin' asylum. Marlowe, however, recognized the identity trade imposed on both shareholder and savage; and so it was apt that when in 1698 a tsar did visit London to study shipbuilding, it was at Sayes Court in Deptford that Peter the Great encamped. The havoc he wrought there, 'As if a regiment of cossacks in iron shoes had drilled' through John Evelyn's house and precious hedge, might have been intended as a salute to Marlowe's epic of the Scythian who tramples every barrier, with snow on his boots (Massie, 1981, 209).

Notes

1. Jerome Horsey, *Travels*, BL Harleian MS 1813, in Berry and Crummey, 1968, 304–6.

2. For arms shipments from England to Ivan, and the opposition from other European governments, see especially Fuhrmann, 1972, 42–7. For Company profits, see Quinn and Ryan, 1983, 147.

3. For Anthony Marlowe, see Bakeless, 1942, vol. 1, 89, 141–2; *Harleian Society Publications*, 25, 1887; *Calendar of State Papers, Foreign, 1584–5*, 132–3; *Calendar of State Papers, Domestic*, 1591–4, 396–7, 408; Willan 1956, 27–8, 254, 259, 287; Edward Hasted, *History of Kent*, 1797, Canterbury, II, 280. Anthony's uncle, Walter Marlowe, was a charter member of the Muscovy Company, whose son, also named Walter, married the daughter of its governor, George Barne, brother–in–law of Sir Francis Walsingham; see Willan, 1953, 111. Thomas Barne had been sponsored as a haberdasher by one John Marlowe as early as 1535, and the possibility of family ties has been strengthened by the discovery that the dramatist's family originated not in Canterbury, but came from Faversham, which had strong commercial links with London. Christopher Marlowe's father, John, arrived in Canterbury only about 1556, aged twenty; see Urry, 1988, 12–13, 149–50.

4. References are to the edition of the *Jew of Malta* by N. Bawcutt, 1978.

5. Willan, 1956, 27, 202–5. The embezzlement perpetrated by Barne, Walsingham and Horsey apparently occurred with the collusion of the Moscow agent, Anthony Marsh, while the Company was officially represented in negotiations with Tsar Theodor by the ineffectual Sir Jerome Bowes. For this murky but immensely lucrative double dealing, see 165–72; and Berry and Crummey, 1968, 319–21.

6. For Richard Bull and the office of the Greencloth, see Urry, 1988, 84–5. Bull died in 1590, but his widow Eleanor was herself connected with the Cecils, so may have retained some of his perquisites. In any event, the idea that Marlowe died in a tavern 'is now utterly dissipated [and] what can be concluded is that the supposed ale–wife or bawdy–house keeper of Deptford came of an ancient armorial family with members close about the Queen' (ibid., 85).

7. For Richard Bull the elder, Master Shipwright at Deptford from 1550 to 1572, see *The Autobiography of Phineas Pett*, ed. W. Perrin, London, Navy Record Society, 1918, xxi–xxiii; *Acts of the Privy Council* I (1544) 233, II (1548) 186, V (1555) 189. This Bull was possibly the son of Thomas, Mayor of Plymouth and erstwhile adversary of the Hawkins family: see Williamson, 1969, 21. For the Gonsons, see Williamson 242–6, 314–5. Anthony Marlowe's mother was sister to Benjamin Gonson senior, Navy Treasurer from 1549 to 1577, when he was succeeded by his son–in–law, John Hawkins. Christopher Browne married the daughter of Benjamin Gonson junior, Clerk of Ships from 1589.

8. Clark, 1977, 207–9, 302. In 1608 twenty six of ninety six Kent Justices were investors in one or more trading company; and of the pioneers of the Russia trade, Richard Chancellor and Henry Sidney were Kent gentry, Barne, Carlyle and Thomas Randolphe were Walsingham's relatives, and Giles Fletcher, George Turbeville, and Horsey were under his patronage (Horsey's *Travels* were dedicated to him); see Berry and Crummey, 1968, 3, 61, 88, 253, 262, 320–21. For Jack Ward, the subject of a 1612 play by Robert Osborne, *A Christian Turn'd Turk*, see the *Dictionary of National Biography* and Lloyd, 1981, 48–53.

9. *Journal of the House of Commons* 1:220 (debate on monopolies, May 1604): 'The Muscovy Company has fifteen directors, who manage the whole trade ... and consign it into the hands of ... one Agent, and give it such account as they please. This is a strong and shameful monopoly; a monopoly in a monopoly; both at home and abroad a whole company has become by this means as one man, who alone hath the uttering of all the commodities of so great a country.'

10. The edition of *Tamburlaine the Great* referred to is that of Cunningham, 1981.

11. For Anthony Marlowe's sponsorship of a playhouse, see *Henslowe Papers* ed. W. Greg, London, 1907; Greenblatt, 1992, 64; Willan, 1956, 211–2.

12. *Calendar of State Papers, Domestic* XXIII (March 1589) 287.

13. Andrews, 1964, 203–4; *Calendar of State Papers, Colonial East Indies, 1513–1616*, 73–4.

14. Willan, 1948, 308–9; Willan, 1955, 399–400. Tamburlaine's naval ambitions may also reflect the fact that in 1585 a Russian fleet of twenty ships was constructed by shipbuilders from Deptford, and by 1587 there were preparations to build twenty more; see Fuhrmann, 1972, 46–7.

15. See Nick de Somogyi's discussion of maps in the present volume.

16. *Calendar of State Papers, Spanish, 1580–86*, 15 May 1582, 366–7.

17. For a monumental exposition of this thesis, see Brenner, 1993. On the Muscovy Company and its influence 'at the core of the eastward thrust during the second half of the sixteenth century', see especially 13–14, 20–21, 78–9.

18. For the coexistence of trading and raiding, see Andrews, 1964, 229–38, and Pérotin–Dumon, 1991, 196–227. See also Thornton Burnett, 1987, 308–23.

19. Michel de Montaigne, *Essays*, tr. G. Ives, New York, bk.3, ch.13, 1464.

20. Kocher, 1942, 207–45. In 1567 Elizabeth sent Ivan two dozen architects and craftsmen to 'make castles, towers, and palaces' for his fortification programme; see Wretts–Smith, 1914, 99.

21. Marlowe's estimates for Tamburlaine's armies follow the exaggerated reports of Ivan's forces by observers such as Horsey: 'He having strengthened himself by an invincible power of these Tartars ... sets forward with an army of an hundred thousand horse and fifty thousand foot, cannon, and all artillery, munition and provisions, towards Livonia' (*Travels*, Berry and Crummy, 1986, 266).

22. See, for example, Una Ellis–Fermor's introduction to *The Life and Works of Christopher Marlowe, Tamburlaine the Great*, 1930, 23–30. The single exception to the neglect of Marlowe's Muscovy is A. L. Rowse, who thirty years ago wondered 'that people have not thought of the parallel between Tamburlaine's personality and career, the savagery and barbaric splendour, blood–lust and mania, and that of the contemporary ruler of Russia, who was a figure well–known to the Elizabethans'(1964, 69).

23. Sigismund, quoted in Fuhrmann, 1992, 43–4. See also Kirchner, 1956, 250–51, and Esper, 1967, 180–96; Willan, 1956, 64–6, Horsey, *Travels*, Berry and Crummey, 1968, 267–8. It was during the Livonian War that Ivan slaughtered prisoners who had surrendered under a 'dejective flag of truce' (Horsey, 266), a crime that might have suggested Tamburlaine's tactics.

24. Horsey, *Travels*, Berry and Crummey, 1968, 269, and Graham, 1968, 216–20. Modern estimates of the number of Ivan's victims at Novgorod range from 40,000 to 60,000.

25. The link with *Tamburlaine* (and its implications for dating) was suggested in Chambers, 1923, vol.2, 135, and *The Times Literary Supplement*, 28 August, 1930, 684.

26. Willan, 1956, 64. Full details of the secret treaty (PRO State Papers. 193/161/fos. 9–12) which was signed in 1569 and renewed in 1577 and 1582, were printed for the first time in Huttenbach, 1971, 535–49. Item 3 states that each ruler will 'aid and assist the other with men, treasure, munition, and all things necessary for war' (546).

27. Horsey, *Travels*, Berry and Crummey, 1968, 298. In 1581 Horsey valued a consignment of armaments, carried in 'thirteen tall ships', at £9000, which suggests that they made up as much as ninety per cent of exports to Russia in the period. See also Yakobson, 1935, 597–610, esp. 602.

28. Francis Bacon, *The Works of Francis Bacon*, ed. J. Spedding, 14 vols., London, 1857–74, vol.8, 30; quoted in Anderson, 1955, 143.

29. Philip Sidney, 'Astrophil and Stella', sonnet 2, lines 10–11, in *The Poems of Sir Philip Sidney*, ed. W. Ringler, Oxford, 1962, 166. See Perrie, 1978, 275, and Baron, 1978, 568–9. Significantly, in the only other English Renaissance play set in Russia, *The Loyal Subject*, 1616, Giles Fletcher's nephew John drew a coded analogy between his hero, an old general of the reign of Ivan, and Raleigh, as a tribute to a dying breed of privateers.

30. Samuel Purchas, *Hakluytus Posthumus, or Purchas his Pilgrims*, 20 vols., Glasgow, 1905–7; quoted in Anderson, 1955, 143.

31. J. Barclay, *The Mirror of Minds, or Icon Animarum*, London, 1631, 125–8; quoted in Anderson, 1955, 145. For the conceptual confusion into which capitalism was thrown by the Muscovite state, with its 'mixture of Tartar and Byzantine elements' and 'extreme barbarity', see Besançon, 1988, 160–63.

32. The idea of linking the Mediterranean with the Indian Ocean across the Suez isthmus was, in fact, a project of the Levant merchants from the 1570's; see Hale, 1993, 147.

33. *Calendar of State Papers, Domestic, James I, 9, 1611–18*, 29 April 1613, 181–2 and 27 October 1613, 208; see Lubimenko, 1914, 246–56; Dunning, 1989(1), 94–108; Dunning, 1989(2), 206–26; also letter by J. Chamberlain, 29 April 1613: 'The King doth so apprehend the matter that he saith he never affected anything more than this, so that he doth not doubt of success, and makes account of sending ten or twelve thousand men' (*The Chamberlain Letters*, ed. E. Thomson, London, 1965, 210). Chamberlain believed that only the death of Prince Henry prevented the project, for otherwise James 'would send them his second son to be their Emperor' (which may explain why Russia reacted so strongly to the execution of Charles I that relations with England were frozen for half a century).

34. The earliest formulation of the concept of consideration (which shifted contract law from a gift– to an exchange–economy) was in 1549, and it was in the 1560s that accountability of agreements came to depend on the presence of consideration. The principle was affirmed in *Golding's Case*, 1586; see Simpson, 1987, 318–9. Robert Poley, a business agent of the Walsinghams, returned from The Hague on the morning of Marlowe's murder, to meet with the victim and two other of Walsingham's agents, Ingram Frizer and Nicholas Skeres; see Bakeless, 1942, vol. 1, 178.

35. Ironically, considering Marlowe's identification with Icarus, the outstanding account concerned payment for wax delivered to the royal household since 1587. After cordage, wax was the most important commodity supplied by the Company; see Willan, 1956, 183–4.

36. Willan, 1956, 249–61. Horsey began to collate his diplomatic memoirs sometime before the death of Walsingham, their dedicatee, in 1590. They exist in a single manuscript in the British Museum, Harleian MS 1813, and were first published by Edward Bond in *Russia at the Close*

of the Sixteenth Century, London, 1856. The archives of the Russia Company were destroyed in the Great Fire, but would have contained all letters sent from Moscow to the Company's board of directors. In their absence, Horsey's *Travels* must stand as an approximation of the information available to Marlowe's Kent patrons about their Asian investments.

37. Ivan was reported by contemporaries to have had a homosexual relationship with his favourite, Theodor Basmanov; see Von Staden, 1967, 35 and Graham, 1975, 216. For a psychosexual biography, see Crummey, 1987, 68–9.

5. Marlowe's *Massacre at Paris* and the Reputation of Henri III of France

DAVID POTTER

The intertwining of the literary career of Christopher Marlowe and Henri III's life is in some ways arresting. There is at least the possibility that Marlowe was in France in 1587, two years before the climactic scenes of his play. This would have been his only foreign journey other than the Dutch episode of 1592.[1] *The Massacre at Paris*, provided in effect an outline history of the king's reign which showed an evolution of his character but one which left him in a sort of limbo, neither hero nor villain. Shortly before the king's death, one of Henri's most dangerous and venomous enemies in Paris, the preacher Jean Boucher, at the height of the crisis of the League in July 1588, with the king a fugitive from his capital, published his *Histoire tragique et mémorable de Gaverston* (Paris, 1589) to draw the obvious parallels between Henri III and Edward II 'skewered alive with red hot iron.' This was a translation of Thomas Walsingham's *Historia Anglicana* and, whether Marlowe read it or not, the parallels between the two monarchs were all too plain by the late 1580s and still in evidence when Marlowe wrote *Edward II* in 1592–3. One of the most scurrilous attacks on the king in 1589 drew attention to Boucher's History 'which last year was shown (*représenté*) in our language' of a king (Edward II) 'who was too besotted with a Gascon and had him so close to his heart that, to put it briefly, he gave him everything he could.' A contemporary chronicler, Palma Cayet, noted the comparison between Henri III and a king, Edward II, who was 'a bloody, hypocritical and tyrannical prince.'[2] Those who accused the king of satanism and depravity were not slow to point out the bad auguries of the king's own name, Alexandre Edouard. The current obsession with anagrams produced not only, from 'Henry de Valois', 'Vilain Herodes' and 'O crudelis hyena', but also (found in Boucher's insolent epistle dedicatory of May 1588 addressed to Epernon, Henri III's most unpopular *mignon*), the phrase 'periure de Nogarets' from 'Pierre de Gaverston', Nogaret being the family name of the duc d'Epernon.[3]

The Massacre at Paris was probably not published until after 1600 and the surviving undated published text of the play as it stands seems to be a botched one, which may represent only part of the original.[4] The most convincing explanation is that it is a surreptitious transcription of a stage production, though there are signs of Marlowe's characteristic style throughout and there were numerous ways in which a stage version could end up in print. The one surviving possible autograph fragment does at least show that the printed text bears a reasonable resemblance to what Marlowe might have written.[5] As there is no dated early edition, we cannot establish any more secure a date than some time between August 1589 and 1593 for its writing, though 1592 seems as convincing as any. It was probably recorded by Henslowe as a newly licensed production, then called the 'tragedy of the gvyes', done by Lord Strange's men at the Rose on 30 January 1593, five months before Marlowe's death, with receipts that were the largest of the season.[6] Thereafter, the play was performed several times by the Admiral's men, to whom the work was brought from Lord Stranges' by Edward Alleyn, Henslowe's son–in–law, in 1594 and there were a number of performances in 1598–1601. In January 1602 Alleyn sold the rights to the company but, after that year, there was no recorded performance until 1940 (*Henslowe's Diary*, 22–5; Bakeless, 1942, II, 90–91; Wraight, 1993, 381–2).

Despite a certain popularity at the time, most critical opinion has tended to agree that, even taking account of the way in which the text has come down to us, the play as drama is pretty poor stuff, little more than crude propaganda. However, scholars in the last generation have seen more in it. Judith Weil, in a work that unusually places the play at the centre of Marlowe's *oeuvre*, has stressed 'the unusual blend of ironic detachment and moral outrage' of a play she sees as a *speculum principis* turned upside down (1977, 82–104). Julia Briggs's sensitive reevaluation of the drama as an extended tract on the futility of religious violence goes a long way to rehabilitating it. She shows convincingly how the violence of 1572 is matched and echoed by that of 1588 in a way that is totally at odds with crude propaganda (1983, 257–78). Marlowe attempted in the portrayal of the massacre a fast–moving series of tableaux intended to recreate the turmoil of the event. Oliver argued for the sophistication of the theatrical technique in this late play while a number of scholars have taken this up, arguing that the play's structure, however mutilated, reveals the work of a mature dramatist (1942, lxxiii; see also Wraight, 1965, 335, 338). Roy Eriksen has pointed up the extensive use of analogies and inversions conveying the idea that history repeats itself; he sees the play as a work in two movements, hingeing on the coronation in scene 14.[7] On the page the action might teeter on the brink of farce, though no more perhaps than some passages in *1 & 2 Henry VI*, between which and Marlowe's play there are definite echoes. In fact, the few productions of the play that have been attempted this century have been greeted enthusiastically and suggest that it can be made to work.[8]

In *The Massacre* we see Marlowe confronting one of the great political events of his time, one that could not be distanced by place or time. The conventions for representing contemporaries on the stage were not, of course, very clear. An English agent in Paris, protesting in 1602 against the mocking of Queen Elizabeth on the stage, was told in response that 'the Massacre of St. Bartholomews hath ben publickly acted, and this king represented upon the stage.' By the time of its production, the duke of Guise and Henri III were, of course, dead and could be attacked (Chambers, 1923, I, 323, n.l; Bakeless, 1942, II, 95–6). Henry of Navarre was a different matter and the treatment of him more circumspect. In fact, most critical opinion would view the portrayal of the Béarnais as dull and lifeless. It is not surprising, then, that the first mention of the play in 1593 refers to it as 'the tragedy of the gvyes.' The wicked duke is portrayed ostensibly in a strictly Protestant view as the arch villain but it is also clear that, for Marlowe, his character was pivotal. For this reason, he gets all the best lines. The great soliloquy in Scene 2, with the lines:

> What glory is there in a common good
> That hangs for every peasant to achieve?
> That like I best that flies beyond my reach.
> Set me to scale the high Pyramides,
> And thereon set the diadem of France,
> I'll either rend it with my nails to naught
> Or mount the top with my aspiring wings,
> Although my downfall be the deepest hell.
> (37–44)

is surely among the most impressive that Marlowe ever wrote and, though in some ways the oration of a conventional Elizabethan hero–villain, also betrays the Machiavellism which we know Marlowe attributed to the character.[9] A duke of Guise who aimed at the French throne was not an extravagant notion, though. It is certainly the case that a Guise claim was suspected by Protestants from 1560 onwards and canvassed and widely known among Catholics from 1576.[10]

The text tells us a great deal about how Marlowe shaped the sources for his drama. These sources have attracted some attention since Bullen in the 1884 edition pointed out the similarities between some passages of the play and sections of *The Three Partes of the Commentaries ... of the Ciuill warres in Fraunce* by Jean de Serres, published in 1574, and the case was also argued by John Bakeless (1937, 18–22). The evidence was fully deployed by Paul Kocher in 1941, with a thorough concordance between scenes 1–8 and the *The Three Partes*, and it was Kocher who pointed out that the section of the work that was used by Marlowe, book x, was no more than a copy of a work called *A true and plain report of the Furious outrages in Fraunce* (1573), ostensibly by one Ernest Varamund but in effect a translation of François Hotman's *De Furoribus Gallicis*.[11] This was by far the most widely read account of the Massacre in England then and in the following generation. Other sources, such as the *Tocsin contre les Massacreurs* (1579), give details, used by Marlowe, of the killing of the scholar Ramus which are not known elsewhere, while Simon Goulart's *Mémoires* (1576) have now also been revealed as a source from which many scenes of planning for the massacre may have been derived.[12]

However, Marlowe does not follow these sources slavishly since he has his own agenda. He might be putting forward the stock Protestant view of Guise, particularly in the last scenes, but it is modified. As Charles Nicholl has pointed out, it shaded into a 'general dark comment about the cynical pragmatism of the religious wars' (1992, 170). Julia Briggs, in emphasizing the dramatic polarity of the two 'massacres', of the Protestants and of the Guise, has usefully drawn attention to the sense in which Marlowe may have fully grasped the 'gruesome aspect of the psychology of violence' (1983, 277). Paola Bono has underlined that there are no heroes in the play, that all characters are ambiguous and that the total effect is 'una rappresentatione esasperata dei meccanismi del potere' (1979–81, 45). Within the constraints of his sources, then, Marlowe shaped his own interpretation. The duke of Guise is plainly the central villain and the most substantially delineated character for whom a fully fledged English Protestant view is clear as early as the 1576 edition of Foxe. Catherine de Medici is clearly also a villain, though more crudely presented. The idea of Catherine's ruthless Machiavellism may well derive from a reading of Henri Estienne's *Merveylous discourse* of 1575–6 but her passionate pursuit of Guise interests, however false it may seem in historical perspective, is less surprising when seen in the context of her policy of forcing the king to accept the League in 1588. Catherine was consistently reported to England by ambassador Stafford in 1585–8 as a ruthless schemer and for the last year of her life she was indeed very close to the Guise.[13] For Hotman, the hero and central character was the Admiral Coligny but Coligny has a relatively slight part in the play and excites little interest, despite the availability of Jean de Serres's *Lyfe* of 1576.[14] A.G. Dickens has pointed out the abundance of available literature in English on French affairs during the wars of religion and has indicated some other possible sources for Marlowe's characterization (1974, 52–70).

The argument of the play is concerned not so much with the Massacre alone. This occupies fewer than half the lines and scenes. The greater part of it covers the reign of Henri III from 1574 to 1589 (scenes 13–24), starting with Henri's coronation at Rheims after his flight from Poland, a scene viewed by recent commentators as a key turning point in the dramatic structure. After that, emphasis is placed on events following the battle of Coutras in 1587. The sources for this later part of the play must remain far more conjectural and certainly have no equivalent for Hotman on the Massacre. However, it is no longer so easy to assume that Marlowe is simply deploying a stage tradition of Machiavellism. Since the work of Kocher in 1947, it is clear that, lying behind much of the detail of these scenes, is the vast outpouring of polemical literature in France occasioned by the rise of the Catholic League in the 1570s and 1580s (1947, 151–73, 309–18). These provided a far more varied and contradictory series of sources that gave ample scope for Marlowe's invention. Kocher argues closely that the last four scenes, covering the period 1588–89 and the murders of the duke of Guise, the cardinal of Lorraine and then Henri III himself, stuck quite closely to the Protestant viewpoint deployed by Antony Colynet's *The True History of the Ciuil Warres of France*.[15] However, Kocher does not see the force of his own argument in drawing attention to Marlowe's use of Catholic literature as source material. The influence of such Catholic League polemic is to be found throughout. An example is the way in which the king tries to allay Guise's suspicions just before he is about to be murdered (21.40–46) and the lines: 'Mon cousin, croyez vous que i'aye l'ame si meschante de vous vouloir mal?' supposedly spoken to him by the king in *La vie et faits notables de Henry de Valois* (Paris, 1589) 93–4. This, and other works like Charles Pinselet's *Le martyre des deux freres* can now no longer be ignored as a source for the final scenes. Indeed, Julia Briggs has forcefully argued that, not only is League material behind these scenes but that Marlowe strikingly amplifies and shapes it in order to show the murdered Guise in a light of some sympathy (1983, 265–7). Scenes 12–19 in any case allowed Marlowe a much broader degree of creative licence and there is certainly more freedom with chronology and personalities, including the conflation of the *mignons* Saint–Mégrin and Maugiron.

Much of the play is structured simply around the struggle for power between the Machiavellian duke of Guise and a godly Henry of Navarre, the ultimate winner. But, as has been noted, Navarre is an uninteresting character. The centrality of Guise is indicated by the fact that he has 307 lines to speak (24.82%) and is on stage for 578 (44.83%). Between Guise and Navarre hovers the undecided figure of the king himself, who follows Guise in the number of lines (280 or 22.71%) but is on stage for longer (610 lines, 48.7%) (see Bono, 1979–81, 45, 48). An integral part of the story is the personality of Henri III, which emerges from that of Anjou ('Anjoy'), a stage villain of the Massacre itself, eagerly participating, with his monstrous mother, in the bloodletting of 1572, through the foppish mignon–obsessed monarch who returns from Poland in 1574, finally to the dignified ally of Henry of Navarre who hands the succession willingly to him, recommending him to Elizabeth and cursing the Pope and the Catholics. There is a real problem here. For Kocher, Henry III is a 'chameleon–like being who changes during the course of the play from something very black to something extraordinarily white' (1947, 316). Charles Nicholl finds it an 'unexpectedly sympathetic portrait' (1992, 342). However, Oliver has argued that Marlowe has not weakened Coligny's role or been inconsistent in the portrayal of Henri III. It is certainly the case that, in the scene during the Massacre in which Ramus is killed, we cannot assume that Anjou alone kills the scholar, as has sometimes been the case. Nor does Oliver find the portrayal of Henri III in the later scenes particularly sympathetic, seeing in it that of a clear Machiavellian who is punished for his cruelties. The sympathy for the murdered is no more than what is due to a man betrayed by one he trusts (1968, lxii, lxx–xxi, 119n.).

However, as ostensibly an English Protestant spectator on French affairs who may even have spoken to some witness of the events he portrays, it is difficult to see how Marlowe could have viewed Henri III as anything but a profoundly ambiguous character. The interesting point here is that this would have been in common with practically every other account of the king's public reputation. The remainder of this study will consider the ambiguity of that reputation in order to provide the context for Marlowe's understanding of the character, by comparing the virulent outpourings of the contemporary printed propaganda with other sources in order to show how Marlowe's ambiguity was rooted in the perceptions of most of his contemporaries.[16] Nor should it be assumed that all Marlowe's sources of information were printed. It must be reasonable to assume that his personal contacts were wide enough for him to have absorbed information and ideas from diplomats like Walsingham, Stafford and Cobham, soldiers and courtiers like Raleigh as well as merchants who knew France. Thus, Kocher's puzzlement at the absence of any pamphlet evidence for the scene of Henri's dismissal of his ministers in 1588 (19.78–91) is rendered pointless in the light of the very full contemporary diplomatic reports of the matter.[17]

Among contemporary writers who were capable of taking a measured view, Brantôme is perhaps characteristic. It is significant that, though he promised a biography of the king in the course of his *Hommes Illustres*, Brantôme was never able to pull one together. His opinions do emerge from many references and we can see how ambiguous his view was. The monarch's disreputable acts as heir to the throne are fully detailed (e.g. his participation in the murder of the first prince of Condé at Jarnac) but he goes on to praise his diligent attention to affairs of state and at one point sums him up as 'un très bon Roi s'il eût rencontré un bon siècle' (Cocula, 1992, 39–46). From another angle, the Parisian lawyer Pierre de l'Estoile, normally a loyalist, could never refrain from recording any gossip, however adverse, about the king (L'Estoile, *Journal*, 610, 625–6, 655). The distorted picture of the king that emerges from Agrippa d'Aubigné's *Les Tragiques* was born in the Protestant vituperation of the monarchomach era, itself a source of impetus in the process of discrediting Henri III. His lines:

Unlucky he who lives his slavish span
'Neath manlike woman and a female man

> (Mais malheureux celui qui vit esclave infame
> Sous une femme hommace et sous un homme femme
> (*Tragiques* bk. II, ll.759–60)

proved particularly influential.

Despite the lingering loyalty of figures like Villeroy and Brantôme, few had anything good to say about the king by the end of his reign and the critical tradition remained central in the historiography down to Gaston Dodu's *Les Valois* of 1934 (Dodu, 1930, 1–42; Dodu, 1934). The work of the last generation of historians on the period have revealed Henri III to be one of the more interesting rulers of the sixteenth century. Pierre Chevallier's biography with its subtitle 'Roi Shakespearien' gives us the picture of a cultivated, intelligent and at times energetic monarch with fatal flaws to his political personality. Jacqueline Boucher's massive study of the court life of the period reveals among other things the immense innovative energies of the period (Chevallier, 1985; Boucher, 1981; Boucher, 1986). This is the monarch, as he puts it to the envoys of Poland in the play:

> As hath sufficient counsel in himself
> To lighten doubts and frustrate subtle foes.
> (10.6–7)

His problem, though, was one of the relation between appearance and reality. Arlette Lebigre's work on the League tells us that the Louvre 'rather than being a glass palace ... is a distorting mirror sending back to the city a grimacing caricature of its king.'(1980, 49) Robert Descimon's and Eli Barnavi's work on the League reveals the role of Guise partisans in constructing the 'black legend' about the king and that of Keith Cameron on the satirical propaganda of the League has shown how reputations could be torn apart in the course of the political and religious struggles of the 1580s (Barnavi, 1980; Descimon, 1983; Cameron, 1978; Cameron, 1974, 152–63).

If the views of contemporary literary figures are somewhat divided it is also vital to remember, for the purpose of placing Marlowe's narrative in context, that the late 1580s saw a virulent and deliberate campaign of vilification directed against the king. Though Marlowe evidently accepted some features of the picture created by that campaign, it is interesting that his Henri III in the later scenes could be said, despite Oliver's scepticism on this point, to attain a stature that sets him apart from his earlier self, much as Brantôme's king is a more worthy figure than his earlier incarnation as duke of Anjou. Such a paradox is characteristic of the sources for the reign in general.

As Arlette Jouanna has shown, the years after Henri III's accession and especially of the Fifth War of Religion saw a polemical debate on the very nature of monarchical power and an upsurge of criticism both from the Protestants and the Catholics (1993, 39–52). As early as 1576, L'Estoile had recorded the posting of a joke titulary which began: 'Henry, by the grace of his mother, uncertain king of France and imaginary king of Poland, doorkeeper of the Louvre, churchwarden of Sant–Germain L'Auxerrois ... visitor of brothels, guardian of the mendicants' (*Journal*, 125). The Protestant Nicolas Barnaud's *Le cabinet du Roy de France* of 1582, with its image of the king as Heliogabalus and Sardanapalus as well as the attacks on the mignons, displayed most of the features of the distorted image of the king that were to become frequent by 1588. But it was the vituperative propaganda of the Parisian league, and especially that born in the aftermath of the king's summary execution of the duke of Guise and his brother the cardinal of Lorraine in December 1588, that set the tone.

A few representative examples of this propaganda in 1588–9, to which Kocher drew attention in 1947, will be used to illustrate the point. The first, André de Rossant's *Meurs, humeurs et comportemens de Henry de Valois* (Paris, 1589) is marked by extreme virulence of language; the other, *La vie et faits notables de Henry de Valois* is a more measured and systematic analysis of the king's policies. Once attributed to Boucher (also author the History of Gaverston and work on the reasons for deposing the king), this now seems more debatable.[18]

Rossant's work accuses the king of Machiavellism, of a secret plan to overthrow the kingdom and rebuild it as a tyranny. His wickedness is a sign that the people would be punished by God if they continued to endure his reign. His only positive quality is that 'he is the best son in the world'. The work ends with a clarion call for his deposition (*Meurs et humeurs*, 27–8, 91, 122–3). *La Vie et faits notables* accuses the king of a well laid plan to introduce two religions into his kingdom, sympathizing in secret with the Protestants and, in the end, 'living by his sensuality' like Caligula, Nero or Heliogabalus. The second edition accuses him of a desire to introduce 'atheism in the guise of a new religion' (*La vie et faits*, 130, 437, 450–477, 482, postscript).

For these accusations to have any effect, they needed to respond to notions that were already common currency. It is certainly the case that the king was widely accused of falling down in his duty to suppress heresy from the late 1570s. Rossant's accusation that 'he is changeable, without pause, without stability' is certainly given colour by the widespread reports of the fads indulged in by the king: anything from drinking spa water sent from Bourbon–Lancy to a passion for exotic animals (his parrots from the West Indies had been taught to say rude things about the Pope by the sailors of Dieppe) and the notorious cup and ball game about which he briefly became passionate in 1585 and which thereafter often appeared in satirical pictures of him. Thus whims become distorted into vices (*Meurs et humeurs*, 90; Boucher, 1981, I, 9–11, 22).

The king's supposed debauches with nuns and excessive indulgence in flagellation were widely discussed in polemical literature and ambassadors' reports. We know, in fact, that in 1580–81 the king's increasing anxiety about his failure to beget an heir led to a startling increase in his religious devotions but his enemies, as ever, saw only evil in this (Lynn Martin, 1973, 35–8). The most scurrilous attack on him in 1589, the one by Rossant, declared his religion to be a fraud 'an opinion of irreligion wallowing in his heart'; his priests 'serve him as jesters' and are 'a school of Bacchus or Epicurus' and he had practised 'the prostitution of sacred virgins ... in several convents.' Even the calmer and more measured attack of *La vie et faits notables* repeats this charge, in even greater detail: his favourite Nogaret (Epernon) had taken him to Poissy where:

> at the convent of St Louis there was a fair professed virgin whom, by force and in spite of her protests that she was dedicated to God, Henri de Valois, no Scipio in continence but really a sacrilegious against everything offered to God, violated. And afterwards, going often to St. Germain for this reason, he took such pleasure as he wished in Nogaret's company.
>
> (*Meurs et humeurs*, 76, 81; *La vie et faits*, 452)

It may perhaps be worth pausing over the essence of this accusation. That there was in 1580 and 1581 much talk about the king's monastic debauches is undeniable. In August 1579, Pierre de l'Estoile collected for his journal a verse of extreme obscenity concerning the king's visits to the nuns and affixed to the gates of the convent of Poissy. In 1580 he testily remarked that 'despite plague and war which burdened his people on all sides, he never stopped going to see nuns and stayed in their convents to make love to them' [nb. faire l'amour – an equivocal term – could mean courteous relations] (*Journal*, 238, 255). The English envoy Cobham reported in January 1580: 'the Kinge hathe bene at Saint Germans [and] at Poyse with those devout nunnes' and in March 'when he is at St Germaynes, his pleasure is sometymes to goe on pilgrimage to the holye nunnes of Poisy.' Not until October, however, does he send the ciphered – and startling – message:

> The kinges sickenes is happenid through wantones yoused among the nunnes having shed blood at his privie partes, which may become more dangerus.[19]

Lorenzo Priuli, the Venetian envoy, reported the view that the king's physical weakness stemmed from venereal disease contracted with prostitutes in his youth – a diagnosis widely discussed in the period.[20] It was the Papal nuncio, Dandino, who got near the truth through his contacts with the king's confessor. In February he reported:

> For many days it has been rumoured secretly in the court that the king has an intrigue at Poissy, near St Germain, with a nun' and that the Queen Mother had reproached the king, who blamed Saint–Luc for letting the story get out. He persuaded a chaplain who had the king's confidence to put the matter before him in the confessional without letting him know that the Pope was involved.

Having contacted the king's confessors, he found from one that:

> The king had not had his way with the nun, though he had tried. He had advised the king and admonished him, and the latter replied and swore that he had not come to any act ['non esser venunto con lei ad atto alcuno']. He believes that he had tried in every way but that the girl constantly remained steadfast in her refusal and the abbess is most careful in guarding her. And since, he has told me that he has found no truth in the matter. The chaplain also confirmed the same, adding that he had questioned the king in the confessional diligently without H.M. saying anything about it and believes that, as the king is accustomed to confess things scarcely less grave, he would have done the same with this. All in all, I do not know what to think, in view of the fact that the best hold it for true ... and blame the king.[21]

Here, then, we have the king's dilemma since not even those with access to the most privileged information could seem to withstand the power of rumour. The extent of such privileged information is indicated by the report of the next nuncio, Castelli, (1582) that the king, in asking for a Jesuit confessor, 'had confessed his whole life' to the general of the Jesuits, Claude Mathieu (*Acta Nuntiaturae Gallicae*, VII, 294).

Even in 1585 we find the Florentine envoy Busini reporting that 'there is here a nun of sixteen, fair of visage and manner, who 18 days ago was with the king the whole day in the house of his doctor, Miron'. But the origins of the scandal immediately became apparent 'the same evening the story was told to Mme de Montpensier who passed it on to me'. Mme de Montpensier was, of course, the king's sworn enemy who went around with a pair of golden scissors with which she declared she would tonsure the king like the last of the Merovingians.[22]

An important feature of the king's religiosity was his founding of new penitent orders. A. Lynn Martin has argued that the phases of the king's piety were dictated by his contacts with the Jesuit Edmond Auger, though this is perhaps too straightforward a view (1973, 88–120 *passim*). On his arrival in France in 1574, his strenuous activities in processions had seen off the ailing cardinal of Lorraine, who could not stand the pace, and thereafter such exertions came in spasms, with frequent pilgrimages to Chartres on foot in the early 1580s. The congregation of Penitents was founded in March 1583. At the foundation, the king was rumoured to have paraded anonymously in a Penitent sack. Another order founded was the Brothers of the Passion and Death of Jesus Christ even more devoted to flagellation (1585). In the summer of 1583, he installed the new order of Hieronymites (later Minims) and in December gave them their home at bois de Vincennes (Chevallier, 1985, 543–7). All the foreign envoys noted his new frantic access of devotion and many, like Sir Edward Stafford, were alarmed at his supposed neglect of state business while he participated in the services (*Négociations* IV, 467; *Acta Nuntiaturae* XVI, 330).

These devotions came in for some of the most venomous attacks against him. Even in 1583, Pierre de L'Estoile recorded a verse ridiculing him:

> He has chosen Our Good Lady
> As patron of his vows,
> But, on my soul, he prefers
> A young boy with blond hair
> (*Journal*, 345)

The pamphleteers of 1588–9 were particularly harsh about all this since, of course, they needed to dispose of any idea that the king was a truly pious catholic. How could Catholics reject a monarch so given to extravagant devotion? The answer, of course, was that it was all a show and dissimulation, as should have been expected in a Machiavellian ruler.

La vie et faits implies that the new religious orders were 'only hypocrisy and to make plots against the Catholic princes'. Rossant is quite specific here, building on the king's well known public devotions to distort the meaning. Starting with his inconsistency in building now in one place, now in another, now one rule now another, chanting the antiphons 'not without laughter sometimes' and taking the sacraments, standing up with his dogs on a leash. The first cloister, at Saint–Catherine in Paris, he had built 'to ensnare the princes and transfer them to the neighbouring Bastille', while another house at Bois de Boulogne was to get others imprisoned at the château de Madrid or massacre them in the woods. But in the end he chose Vincennes as nearer to the great keep there:

> There he wore a whip hanging from his waist but, however, kept
> his own shoulders from bearing it; he left that duty to the poor
> religious who, with that aim, he brought from various orders and
> his pastime was to bring ladies there to laugh and, sometimes, after
> the candle had been extinguished, he tested their shoulders to see
> if they had been whipping themselves lustily. ... Talking of the
> Catholics, he brandished his strap and said: here's what I whip
> them with. Why, asked the writer, was he involved so often in
> flagellation 'If not to get pleasure out of it or mock them behind
> their backs since he brought ladies and girls and others to see
> them.'
> (*La vie et faits*, 167–8; *Meurs et humeurs*, 17–21)

We have of course, seen that the king's religious devotions were regarded
with some confusion and puzzlement by contemporaries. Not even the papal
nuncios were quite sure how to respond to them and it was widely thought
that the king was spending too much time on his knees. However, The king
was quite capable of keeping his religious observances in control. Edward
Stafford reported from Paris in January 1585 that he would not 'make a color
of a devotion slacke the lookynge into a matter of so great a weight' –
negotiations with the Dutch – 'especiallie his devotion beinge so fewe
howeres in the daye'. This is how Stafford described the king's routine at this
time:

> He hathe never missed everie daye sence he went into Boys de
> Vincennes to come hether to dynner to gooe all the after noone
> into companyes in the towne that are assembled together to mak
> merie and gooe so from one to an other tyll eleven o clock att
> night or myd night and then lye at Zamettis and rise at six againe
> in the morninge [to] goo to Boys de Vincennes and att none be
> heere againe.
> (PRO SP 78/13, no.7)

It has sometimes been assumed that this means the king had resumed contact
with prostitutes, though the meaning here is far from clear. The Florentine
envoy at the same time talks of the king going 'continually to disport himself
at fêtes and "mascherate" trying but failing to seduce a beautiful widow'.
Certainly we have the extraordinary testimony of the Cardinal d'Este's agent
in Paris (now in the Vatican archives) that the king and Joyeuse went through
a paroxysm of fornication with 14 prostitutes ('puttane') in August 1585 – to

be followed in September by excessive devotionalism (*Négociations* IV, 546; Chevallier, 1985, 438).

It has been reasonably argued that Henri III used his devotionalism to some extent for political purposes. The summer of 1585 was one of growing crisis with the Catholic League increasingly active and opinion in Paris increasingly hostile to his policies. The autumn of 1585 saw another bout of red hot piety; the reason may well have been a desire to place his religious credentials before the public at a time when he was anxious to minimize League power (Lynn Martin, 1973, 149–50; L'Estoile, *Journal*, 124). Nevertheless, the effect is real enough and the nuncio Raggazoni reported in October that he had heard from a capucin friar close to the king:

> that his Majesty has been much inflamed for some days in his spiritual exercises, and particularly that he strips and flagellates himself, which has been further confirmed by one who has seen his shirt well blooded, and I understand that this new and great heat of devotion has come to his mind by the work and preaching of a French Jesuit named father Edmond Auger.
> (*Acta Nuntiaturae*, II, 457)

There seems no reason to doubt that the king was capable of inflicting such punishment on himself – a point usually left in obscurity by his enemies in 1588–9. The enemies of 1589 had the last word: 'What fruit has France gathered from all his parades of devotion and papalries: much money lost through many holes and curiosities ill–employed and lost' (*Meurs et humeurs*, 112).

Not only was the king accused of hypocrisy in religion, however. He was thought to have gone all the way to diabolism and the occult, the latter, of course, a preoccupation of the late Valois court. In 1589 a pamphlet called *Les Sorcelleries de Henry de Valois* accused the king of maintaining a diabolic cult at Vincennes and adduced as evidence the finding of two figures of satyrs in silver gilt supporting crystal bowls. The description is a convincing one but the conclusion is not: 'in these vases there were unknown drugs he used as oblations and what is more detestable, they stood before a gold cross holding a fragment of the true cross.' Some might say they were candle holders but there was no sign of this and – furthermore – the satyrs had their backsides turned towards the cross.[23] Who had instructed the king in these black arts? Sorcery, it claimed, was little known in France until the present reign but Epernon and others had brought 'magicians' from all over the world while, even before the king went to Poland 'he was already quite inclined to atheism', that is, in this case, occultism. There is also a hint of the kind of accusation of atheism discussed by Nicholas Davidson elsewhere in this volume. Rossant adds:

> One day, talking with some religious who were speaking of the punishments of Hell, his doctor Miron said to him 'Do you think there is a hell, Sir?' To this he remained silent. A propos of diabolic possession 'he said aloud that he did not believe that Devils could possess men and come to torment them'. It is sure that he uses the magic arts, which can only be done by the work of Devils.

Rossant adds the story of the man possessed by a devil at Meaux which, when exorcised, claimed he had been besetting the king for eleven years to murder the great enemy of the Huguenots (*Meurs et humeurs*, 73–4).

The accusation of diabolic possession as political attack has a long tradition behind it going back to the early fourteenth century and, of course, was potentially devastating. Frances Yates argued that the items found at Vincennes are fully explained by mystic reference to pagan sacrifice as prefiguring the mass and related to a reliquary given by St. Carlo Borromeo to the king (Yardeni, 1992 57–68; Yates, 1947, 172). This was well over the head of public opinion, more represented by the wildly extravagant satire *Les choses horribles contenues en une lettre envoyée a Henry de Valois* (Paris, 1589) in which the king is reminded that Nogaret d'Espernon was none other than an evil spirit Teragon, who had possessed the king while in bed with him.

Perhaps more serious for the king's reputation was the accusation of sodomy since it then carried the penalty of death by burning at the stake. The accusations here are often vague and the evidence usually difficult to interpret. Certainly the king's enemies saw nothing surprising in the coupling of accusations of misconduct with nuns and women of low repute and the 'abominable vice', as it was called, of acts with men. Rossant brings his castigations to a crescendo when he says:

> Do you not see that he is utterly negligent, fearful, effeminate, heliogabalised and completely lured to his pleasures and so many kinds of debauch that the earth vomits them up and heaven has them in horror? Nor even the one the page recounted one day crossing the river near the Louvre, that the king loved his master well, to whom he came often alone to *foitter* in his bed, the page being commanded to make himself scarce. ... And many times this same inverted lover has been seen kissing and rekissing his mignons, even in a place that should have been respected. It is no marvel that he has the bed of his heart Epernon placed next to his

in his *cabinet* at Vincennes or if he had to hide some young nuns
in the cellar when he went on pilgrimage to Maubuisson.
(*Meurs et humeurs*, 89)

It is well known that mockery of the so–called effeminacy of the courtiers
was rife in the late 1570s judging only by the satires and verses collected by
Pierre de l'Estoile for the period 1577–79 (*Journal*, 232–8). It is also certain
that the fashions of the court became more extravagant in the period. The
conclusions which may be drawn are, however, questionable. Pierre de
l'Estoile is often used to confirm that fact that Henri III dressed in women's
clothes. This and other comments led G. Robin to construct a zany
interpretation of Henri III as a man of undecided sexuality, psychologically
castrated by Catherine de Medici's excessive and possessive love. Though his
love of women was 'normal', his other characteristics made him 'une femme
manquée.' What is more, this bisexuality is supposed to have made him an
indecisive ruler (1964, 153, 192–3).[24]

Nothing illustrates more clearly the tendency of certain 'historians' to
copy each other or to use primary sources uncritically. Robin lists Henri's
dressing as a woman at Navarre's marriage in 1572, his use of make–up, a
comment of the Spanish ambassador that he had earrings so heavy 'that an
African moor could not have had bigger,' an isolated comment that 'the duke
of Anjou is a young girl,' and his dressing as a woman at a banquet at
Plessis–les–Tours in 1577 (ibid., 116–18).[25]

Needless to say Pierre Champion, who began the work of assembling the
king's correspondence, was quite certain that it contained no hint of
homosexuality (1939, 494–528; 1941–2, II, 331). This is a view confirmed by
the four volumes of his letters published so far, though the king's letters to
his 'troupe' indicate great intimacy and friendship. Phrases addressed to
favourites in letters like 'I kiss your hands' are stereotypes transferred from
formal Italian usage of the period, though Montaigne attacked them as part of
his general disapproval of innovations in manners.[26] Certainly the king gave
his enemies ammunition by his extreme generosity to his friends and he
himself admitted, in writing to Secretary Villeroy in 1579: 'We know each
other well ... when I love it is to extremes,' while Etienne Pasquier wrote in
1589: 'He loved those he favoured without measure and without knowing
why.' Among foreign envoys, only the prejudiced and hostile Savoyard
Lucinge relates the accusation.[27]

What, in fact, is the evidence for the King's transvestism? Largely,
again, the fact that at the *magnificence* of Bayonne in 1565 he accompanied
his brother Charles IX at the quintain dressed as an Amazon – a role he
played again in Paris, in Sept 1576 according to L'Estoile. L'Estoile again in
February 1577:

The king held tourneys, jousts and ballets and many masquerades where he was usually dressed as a woman, opening his doublet to show his throat, wearing a collar of pearls and three of linen, two frilled and one reversed like those then worn by women of the court.

So – in the course of what is currently a masquerade, the king is just wearing a woman's collar for the ballet. In fact, such disguise was very popular among the court aristocracy – even the model seducer Nemours dressed as a bourgeoise for one masquerade. The point made clearly by Jacqueline Boucher in her study of the court is that such masquerades have to be placed in their cultural context and simply cannot be lifted as stray pieces of evidence for perversion (*Journal*, 142; J. Boucher, 1986, 26).

Jacqueline Boucher followed by Pierre Chevallier categorically rejects the case for the king's sexual deviance (Boucher, 1986, 165–70; Chevallier, 1985, 435–7), though an intriguing side issue indicates the way evidence can be distorted even by the most scholarly of historians. In the course of her argument, she throws out the confirmed opinion that the king's younger brother François d'Alençon–Anjou was certainly homosexual, though in fact here too the evidence is highly ambiguous (1981, I, 136 *passim*; *Négociations*, IV, 465, 474–5). It is notable that he plays virtually no part in Marlowe's play (in fact is only mentioned, by Catherine, in passing)[28] and it may well be concluded that the subject was far too sensitive while Elizabeth (who had, after all, come near to marrying him in 1579) was still alive. The fate of John Stubbs, author of the anti–Anjou pamphlet, *The Discovery of a Gaping Gulf*, stood as a warning.

Everyone knows about Henri III and his *mignons*. In the coronation scene, Catherine says:

My Lord cardinal of Lorraine, tell me,
How likes your Grace my son's pleasantness?
His mind, you see, runs on his minions,
And all his heaven is to delight himself.
(14.43–5)

Just as in *Edward II* the Queen says:

Look, Lancaster, how passionate he is,
And still his mind runs on his minions
(2.2.3–4)

The scene is a key one in that it is usually interpreted as the moment at which

85

Marlowe points to the king's harbouring sexual love for his intimates:

> What says our minions ? Think they Henry's heart
> Will not both harbour love and majesty?
> (14.16–17)[29]

or:

> So kindly cousin of Guise, you and your wife
> Do both salute our lovely minions
> (17.7–11)

which is both doting and ironic, the duchess's intrigue with Maugiron thrown in the duke's face.

In fact, the word *mignon* began life in fifteenth–century France as signifying an aristocratic servitor. In the sixteenth century it could just mean 'favourite' – as in 1516 when Francis I, with 'some young gentlemen of his mignons and intimates,' scoured the streets of Paris in disguise. The English courtiers Nicolas Carewe and Francis Bryan had joined the French court in 1518 and took to disguising themselves in the same way and joined the king in his games of pelting the canaille. Edward Hall records of their subsequent expulsion from the king's privy chamber, that:

> These yong minions which was thus severed from the kyng, had bene in Fraunce, and so highly praised of the Frenche kyng and his courte that in a maner ... they were so high in love with the Frenche court, wherefore their fall was litle moned emong wise men.[30]

Early in the sixteenth century, then, a *mignon* could be viewed as a high spirited intimate of the prince, though in England a certain derogatory connotation was beginning to creep in. In France, only early in the reign of Henri III did it take on a derogatory meaning when applied to royal favourites and then because of the special conditions of civil war. The point is confirmed by Pierre de L'Estoile (Champion, 1939, 497–8; see *Journal*, 122).

The *mignons* became a byword for effeminacy and wickedness from the time of d'Aubigné's *Tragiques*. Another source for this was the sort of remark made by Pierre de L'Estoile when in October 1577 the king returned to Paris

> with a troop of his young *mignons* frilled and frizzed with raised crests, wigs on their heads, a manner *fardé* with similar ostentation, well groomed, speckled and sprayed with violet powder and

odoriferous scents perfuming all the places they went.
(*Journal*, 154)

The interesting word here is *fardé*: now it might mean 'made up' but then it often signified the sort of dissimulation that was a key Machiavellian characteristic.[31] L'Estoile also disapproved of new fashions. We should not assume from all this that the king's minions were feeble; as Brantôme insisted, some were tough fighters and there was a streak of violence in many of them. Both the sixteenth–century minion and the Restoration fop have been played excessively limply by modern actors.

Minions also served a serious political purpose. The pamphleteers of 1588–9 spent much time castigating the king's promotion of favourites and drew out several instances. Rossant declared that 'he studies to raise up little companions in great credit and honour so as to obtain greater obedience, so it seemed to him, for *caresse* and surety, than from his princes.' Epernon is accused of accumulating so many governments 'that he seemed ready to put in his possession, for his life time, the total government of the kingdom.' *La vie et faits* asserts that taxes went to nourish his '*mignons* and court harpies' and that they were 'so proud and arrogant that in particular they did not even respect him' (*Meurs et humeurs*, 21, 27; *La vie et faits*, 438–9). Most sources mention the famous duel of 1578 which grew out of court faction and led to the deaths of the two favourites Quélus and Maugiron, the latter being one of Marlowe's main examples of a *mignon*. As has been known since Kocher's work, Marlowe conflated the figure of Maugiron with that of another of Henri III's favourites, the comte de Saint–Mégrin, who was indeed killed on Guise's orders because he had become amorously involved with the duke's wife (Kocher, 1947, 169–70). In scene 19 it is Maugiron ('Mugeron') who is shot by an assassin. What Kocher missed was that it was natural for Marlowe to make this conflation in view of the widespread reporting of the duel fought in April 1578 between some followers of the duke of Guise and Quélus and Maugiron. Maugiron was accused in the pamphlet literature of crying out at the moment of death: 'I reject God, I die.' Above all, they blamed the king for erecting a sumptuous funeral monument to his friends 'because of their rare and detestable debauches and blasphemies' in the church of St. Paul at Paris – monuments smashed at Christmas 1588 (*La vie et faits*, 439–43; *Journal*, 187).

For the customers of these pamphlets, Epernon was the great bogeyman after the king and massive calumny was heaped up on him including the delighted assertion that he had had to retire to St Germain in May 1585 to be cured of syphilis, though in fact L'Estoile described it as a cancerous growth. The Parisians were amused that the king – supposedly the ruler miraculous whose touch could cure scrofula – was thus confounded. They chanted: 'He loves and cherishes only one cancer' (*Journal*, 380). Epernon had, in fact, been in semi–disgrace since the Spring of 1588 and only returned to favour in April 1589, after the assassinations of Blois. That in *The Massacre* it is Epernon who plays the role of the king's leading *mignon* and accompanies the king in every scene after his accession, is hardly surprising given the mass of printed venom directed against him in 1589.

Discussion of the *mignons*, and an awareness that the assemblage of a band of favourites by a monarch in Henri III's position was his only available answer to the crumbling of royal authority,[32] lead us back to Marlowe's picture of the king as one obsessed by favourites. Any familiarity with public discourse in France in the late 1580s would have made him aware of this. Without embarking on the difficult question of how much time, if any, Marlowe spent in France as a spy in the 1580s, it is improbable that he was unaware of the explosion of polemic and sheer vituperation aimed at the king. No one would argue that Marlowe's portrait of Henri III is other than a sketch. That his picture of the king is in the end an unsatisfactory and contradictory one is exactly what we should expect given the way in which the king's reputation was built up out of misunderstandings and distortions by his own subjects, but Marlowe saw and heard enough to realize that Henri III was a victim of circumstance as well as a participant in massacre. We should see Marlowe's portrayal as part of the polemical literature of the time on contemporary politics.

While noting Marlowe's emphasis on royal favouritism, which is certainly rooted in contemporary polemic, we should also note what is absent from Marlowe's view: the accusations of occultism, the fornication with nuns and others. Added to this must be the ambiguity of Marlowe's religious and aesthetic sensibility.[33] There are enough pointers to his religious unorthodoxy to call into question the idea that he was writing a straightforward English Protestant view of the French Wars of Religion, as is argued by Paul Kocher, even though there are moments in the play at which Catholic doctrine is held up to scorn by some characters (Kocher, 1946, 134–5, 208–9).[34] Simon Shepherd has argued, in fact, that a positive way of interpreting the play would be to see in it 'the suppression of the coherent sense of nation and of moral order' (1986, 123). Hence the apparently perfunctory treatment of the massacre itself and the lukewarm portrayal of Admiral Coligny, the great Protestant hero, should not surprise us. The words Marlowe puts into the mouth of his arch–villain, the duke of Guise, in describing the French Huguenots:

> I mean to muster all the power I can
> To overthrow those sectious Puritans
> (19.45–6)[35]

assimilated French religious divisions to a contemporary English category that could hardly have been seen sympathetically by the playwright.

In the final scene, the king calls in 'the English Agent' to express hope that he might live and denounce the wickedness of Rome:

> Agent for England, send they mistress word
> What this detested Jacobin hath done.
> Tell her, for all this, that I hope to live.
> (24, 55–7)

The then ambassador in France, Sir Edward Stafford, was absent and was represented by his *chargé d'affaires*, William Lyly, who had been in trouble in 1585–6 over his alleged involvement with the satirical tract of 1584, subsequently known as 'Leicester's Commonwealth'. In his moving report, made on the day of the attack to Elizabeth I, Lyly confirms the detail, used in the play, that Henri III had contributed to the death of his assassin by warding off the blow. He had, he said, been called in shortly afterwards:

> Amongst the rest which desired to see His Majeste, I was one, to whom he sayd: 'I am sure the Quene your mistres wilbe sory for this, but I hope yt shall quickly be healed and so I pray wryte unto her from me.'[36]

Seldom does the text of the play and contemporary diplomatic evidence overlap so closely. But Marlowe's aim is not just reportage. The king's closing lines, spoken to his faithful and tearful *mignon*, the duke of Epernon:

> Henry thy king wipes off these childish tears
> And bids thee whet they sword in Sixtus' bones
> That may keenly slice the Catholics...
> Salute the queen of England in my name,
> And tell her, Henry dies her faithful friend
> (24.97–105)[37]

provide an artificial conclusion likely to please the audience. However, it is surely the strangest invention of all by Marlowe in the portrayal of a king who, in reality, combined intense Catholic devotionalism with an inability to convince his strongly Catholic subjects that he was other than a secret sympathiser with heresy. Thus, paradoxically and indirectly, Marlowe reinforced the worst of anti–henrician Catholic polemic.

Notes

1. Nicholl, 1992, 94 and 234–9 (on 1592). A.D. Wraight is categorical that Marlowe had been to Rheims in 1587 (1965, 88–90). See also Wernham, 1976, 344–5. The putative visit to France early in 1592, carrying letters from Rouen to Dieppe and thence to England, suggested in Henderson, 1953, must remain conjectural.

2. A. de Rossant, *Les meurs et humeurs de Henry de Valois*, Paris, 1589, 115–16. This playing on the theme of Edward II and Gaveston in 1588 was noted by Pierre de l'Estoile, *Journal pour le règne de Henri III*, ed. L.R. Lefebvre, Paris, 1943, 569, and the theme was taken up by the chronicler Palma Cayet, *Chronologie novenaire*, vols. 38–43 of Petitot, *Collection des mémoires*, Paris, 1818–29, vol. 38, 414. The parallel between Epernon and Gaveston provoked the favourite's publication of the *Antigaverston*, entitled *Lettres d'un gentilhomme C. A. et R. et vrai français et fidèle serviteur du roi à un sien ami sur l'histoire de Pierre de Gaverston*, Paris, 1588.

3. L'Estoile in 1588 noted the currency of another typical anagram for Epernon: 'Jean Louis Naugarets duc d'Esparnon/Ung ladre punais de sot roi est advancé' (*Journal*, 587). Rossant, author of *Les Meurs*, had written a treatise on anagrams called *Onomastrophie*.

4. The text was published by Edward White 'as it was plaide by the right honourable the Lord *Admirall* his servants.' J. Bakeless, suggests a date before 1600 (1942, II, 69). One of the most commonly adduced arguments for a date slightly after 1600 is 21.67 spoken by Guise when warned of his murder: 'Yet Caesar shall go forth' found also in *Julius Caesar*, 1.2.28, though the priority is not clear. That Guise was referred to as a Caesar by his followers is established. Guise, whom 'the League called her Caezar, and made goodly comparisons betwene them' (*The Firste Booke*, bound with *An Historicall Collection* of Jean de Serres, 1598, 203, 207 *et passim*). However, Shakespeare could have been copying Marlowe here.

5. For this, see the Oliver, 1968, edition, 165–6, (Sc.19). Wraight, following Adams, de Ricci and Boas, gives approbation to this fragment, though that it is in the same hand as Marlowe's one known signature seems highly dubious (1965, 226–32).

6. J. Bakeless suggests some time 1590–93 for the writing, listing the wide variations of date that have been offered (1942, II, 72–3); Oliver, suggests 1592 'as the natural assumption' (1942, lii). The date of the first production raises a problem as a result of the chaotic dating of Henslowe's diary. Thus he interprets it as 30 January 1593/4 'exactly six months after Marlowe's death' (1942, II, 71–2). E.K. Chambers, gives 26 January 1593, an old correction given by Greg's edition of Henslowe (1923, III, 426). Nicholl gives just 'January 1593' (1992, 170). In *Henslowe's Diary*, ed. R. Foakes and R. Rickert, Cambridge, 1961, 20, we find the entry as '30 [January]' in a sequence of productions by Lord Strange's men that had begun in 'December 1592' and then been corrected to '1593' and in which there was a change in year date from 1592 to 1593 in the course of January. Henslowe was very irregular in his start of year date, sometimes putting it in mid–January, sometimes at Easter (the French custom abandoned in the 1560s) and never in the old English style on 25 March. Though Bakeless interpets the date as 'by modern reckoning this is 1594' (1942, II, 89), this ignores Henslowe's irregularity and, in the context of the series in which it occurs, 1593 is the best presumption, bearing in mind there must always be a doubt on the matter.

7. Erikson, 1981, 41–54; for his conclusions on the structure, see 51–2. P. Bono makes a similar argument but in much more complex form (1979–81, 11–52).

8. Roy Eriksen points out, for instance, the parallel between the openings of *The Massacre* and *Henry VI part 2*, and notes the lines of Coligny: 'O fatal this marriage to us all' and Gloucester: '... Fatal this marriage/ Undoing all, as all had never been' (1981, 42). Paola Bono examines the problems of the *mise–en–scène* in detail, including the problem of 'doubling' (1979–81, 13–20).

9. C.V. Boyer, argues that the soliloquy is the means Marlowe uses to reveal the duke's deception (1914, 53ff.), E. Meyer, that there is no trace of Machiavellism (1897, 56). The Prologue of *The Jew of Malta* makes clear that Marlowe thought of Guise as a Machiavel. Beyond this, though, D. Cole denies that we should see the portrayal of Guise as 'a spiritual quest for self–fulfillment' (1962, 157).

10. E.g. in Jean David's 'Mémoire', in *Mémoires de la Ligue*, Amsterdam, 1758, I, 2–7.

11. Kocher, 1941, 349–68, especially 366–7. *De Furoribis Gallicis, horrenda & indigna Admirallii Castillionei, Nobilium atq: illustrium caede ... Vera et simplex Narratio* Hotman (Varamund), London, 1573. Some of the most important texts in the background to the play are printed in Thomas and Tydeman, 1994, 249–92.

12. Scene 9.15: 'Come Ramus, more gold, or thou shalt have the stab'; *Tocsin*, 130–31: 'aiant r'achepté sa vie de grande somme de deniers' (Ramel, 1979, 5–18).

13. *Acts and Monuments*, J. Foxe, 1576, 2001. H. Estienne, *A merveylous discourse upon the lyfe, deedes and behaviours of Katherine de Medicis, Queen Mother* 'Heidelberg/Cracow', 1575; for examples of Stafford's reports in 1586: PRO SP78/15 passim and esp. BL Harleian 288, fo.159: warning 'of a dangerous practyse of *the queen mother* to sowe a greatt sedition...'

14. *The Lyfe of the most godly, valeant and noble capteine ... Iasper Colignie Shatilion*, Jean de Serres, London, 1576.

15. London, 1591. Covering the period from 1585.

16. For a more detailed examination of Henri III's historical personality, see Potter, 1995, 485–527.

17. The point was made in Bakeless, 1942, II, 77–8; see also Briggs, 1983, 259, 261–2. Stafford to Walsingham, 1 Sept.1588, PRO SP 78/18, no.158, fo.326: 'Strange newes was brought thatt a greatt soudden change was att the cowrt ... Theie give owte att Paris thatt theie be chassez becawse the K: hathe fownde them halte and to looke uppon other favours then his.' For Stafford's report on the executions at Blois, 15 Dec.1588, see B[ritish] L[ibrary], Cotton, Caligula D III, fo.321: Henri's words to Catherine: 'Madame, I am now come to tell you that I am K: without companion and that the d: of Guise thenemy of all my proceedinges is dispatched. Whereunto she answered, that he had given a great blowe, so all the rest might succeed accordingly.' See *Massacre*, 21.135–9.

18. (Paris, 1589), 2nd. ed. repr. in L.Cimber et F. Danjou, *Archives curieuses de l'Histoire de France*, 30 vols. (Paris, 1834–49), vol.12. On the authorship of Boucher, see the denial in Baumgartner, 1973, 108–9, n.38. J. Boucher argues that Boucher was the author (1985, 341).

19. *Calendar of State Papers, Foreign, of the Reign of Elizabeth* (hereafter *CSPF*), 1580, 142, 177, PRO SP 78/4A, no.10, no.25; 4B, fo.309.

20. E. Alberi, *Le relazioni degli ambasciatori veneziani al Senato* (Florence, 1839–62), ser. 1, vol.iv, 423–4.

21. *Acta Nuntiaturae Gallicae, correspondance des nonces en France*, VIII (Rome, 1970), 595, 646–7.

22. A. Desjardins, *Négociations diplomatiques de la France avec la Toscane* 6 vols. (Paris, 1859–86), IV, 581.

23. *Les sorcelleries de Henri de Valois* (1589), repr. in *Archives curieuses*, 12, 487–91, esp. 488–90.

24. The same sort of idea is present in Shepherd, 1986, 199, where it is argued that Marlowe's Henri III's obsession with his minions leads him to ignore his public responsibilities and is part of a 'questioning' of his values in sodomy.

25. On contemporary fashion, see Chevallier, 1985, 414–18.

26. A key passage here is Montaigne's essay, published in 1588, 'Des loix somptuaires' (book I, ch.xliii), translated by Florio: 'These long effeminate, and dangling locks: That fond custome to kiss what we present to others, and *Beso las manos* in saluting our friends' (*Montaignes Essayes*, 1634 ed., 146).

27. Examples: *Lettres d'Henri III* ed. M. François, 4 vols. (Paris, 1959–84) II, 331, 386, IV, 201; E. Pasquier, *Lettres historiques*, ed. D. Thickett (Geneva, 1966), 447–8; Lucinge, *Le miroir des princes*, ed. A. Dufour, *Ann.–bull. de la Soc. de l'Hist. de France*, 1954–5, 95–6 and 104–5.

28. 14.62–4: 'And if he do deny what I do say,/ I'll despatch him with his brother presently,/ And then shall Monsieur wear the diadem.' Catherine is referring to Guise as 'Monsieur' though that was always the title by which the king's eldest brother was known. Briggs suggests that the omission of Alençon–Anjou is a dramatic device to concentrate attention on 1572 and 1588 (1983, 269).

29. H.S. Bennett, in his edition of *The Massacre at Paris*, 1931, pointed out that the reference here seems to be Ovid's *Metamorphoses*, II, 846: 'Majesty and love do not go well together, nor tarry long in the same dwelling–place' ('Non bene conveniunt, nec in una sede morantur, maiestas et amor').

30. *Journal d'un bourgeois de Paris* ed. L. Lalanne, Paris, 1854, 55; Hall, *Henry VIII* ed. C. Whibley, 2 vols., London, 1904, I, 178.

31. This point was discussed in Thomas Sorge, 'The Theatricality of Jacobean Discomfort', paper presented during the conference on Marlowe at the University of Kent, Canterbury, July 1993.

32. This is the argument advanced in Jouanna, 1992, 155–66.

33. The problem is too complex to go into here, except to indicate the pattern by which, from 1587, Marlowe seems to have been subject to rumour about his religious views. The Baines note, with its accusations of atheism and fondness for Catholic ceremonies: 'That if there be any god of any good Religion, then it is in the papistes' (BL Harley 6848, fo.185–6, printed in Wraight, 1965, 308–9 and Kocher, 1946, 34–6) cannot, obviously, be regarded as proof in isolation (see Nicholls, 1992, 308–13). However, set in the context of other contemporary references it points at least to unorthodoxy. For the argument that atheism was an intellectual possibility at the time, see Nicholas Davidson's essay in the present volume.

34. A similar point is made by C. Cole: 'a work shaped principally around the historical conflict between Protestantism and Catholicism, as seen from the contemporary English Protestant viewpoint' (1962, 150).

35. Also the words of Lorraine in 14.54–5: 'My brother Guise hath gather'd a power of men/ Which, as he saith, to kill the Puritans', looks like a doubling of this line.

36. PRO SP 78/19, fo.199, Saint–Cloud, 22 July/1 Aug.1589: on the king's reaction to the blow: 'with great courage and force gate the knife from him and therwith gave the Jacobin two blowes, thone on the face, thother in the brest, with which and the servantz assistans the felon was presently slayne.' On Lyly's response to the king: 'I told him that no prince in the world wold so muche sorow yt, nor none more joy that His Majeste did comfort yt with so muche magnanimytie and with that told

him that all the world might see and testyfie with what reason your Majeste punisshed that race...' On Lyly himself, see Peck, 1985, 10, 290–91.

37. Henri is certainly alleged to be partial to England in *La vie et faits*, 106. The most reliable account of the king's last hours is to be found in *Mémoires du duc d'Angoulême sous Henri IV, en 1589*, ed. La Pijardière, Montpellier, 1879, 7–11 and contains only expressions of the king's piety. All accounts speak of the copious tears of the king's servants. For an example of contemporary comment: *Discours véritable des derniers propos qu'a tenus Henry de Valois à Jean d'Espernon*, in Michaud and Poujoulat, *Archives curieuses*, ser.I, xii (1836), 391–5. The only example of the king's call for vengeance I have found is in the words Henri spoke to Epernon, as recorded by the latter's secretary, G. Girard, *Histoire de la vie du duc d'Espernon*, Paris, 1655, 109: 'I hope God will soon give me the grace to be revenged on them.'

6. Marlowe's Maps of War

NICK DE SOMOGYI

There was a map of Vietnam on the wall of my apartment in Saigon... That map was a marvel, especially now that it wasn't real any more. For one thing, it was very old... Vietnam was divided into its older territories... to the west past Laos and Cambodge sat Siam, a kingdom. That's old, I'd tell visitors, that's a really old map.' – Michael Herr, *Dispatches*.

By opening his *Dispatches* from Vietnam with this 'really old map', the war–reporter Michael Herr rooted them in the oldest traditions of war journalism. 'War news', writes a historian of the sixteenth century, 'is one of the first kinds to appear' (Shaaber, 1929, 121). By the 1570s, such reportage was often supplemented by the narrative aid provided by a new map. George Gascoigne, for example, promises news 'of *Hollandes* state' in one poem, 'the which I will present, / In Cartes, in Mappes, and eke in Modells made'.[1] That promise seems to have been fulfilled in his prose account of *The Spoyle of Antwerp* in 1576, a work originally supplemented by a 'Model of the whole place... annexed to thend' (A7v). Its absence from all extant copies perhaps corroborates John Dee's remarks in his preface to Billingsley's *Euclide* in 1570, as to how 'manifolde commodities' of geography 'do come unto us, daily and hourely', and how some use maps 'to beautifie their Halls, Parlers, Chambers, Galeries, Studies, or Libraries' since they illustrate 'battels fought... & such like occurrentes'.[2] Certainly, as Richard Willes's preface to Richard Eden's *History of Travayl* (1577) insists, the decade witnessed a thoroughgoing vogue for cartography: 'Al studies have theyr special tymes', it reads, and while grammar, logic or philosophy have waned in 'theyr singuler seasons', 'of late who taketh not uppon him to discourse of the whole worlde, and eche province thereof particulerly?'(fos.ii r–ii v) .

Among such popular 'commodities' must be counted Ortelius's world atlas, the *Theatrum Orbis Terrarum*, and its sister–publication, Braun and Hogenberg's collection of cityscapes, *Civitates Orbis Terrarum*, which first appeared in Antwerp in the early part of the 1570s, and both of which were regularly reprinted, translated and augmented well into the seventeenth century. Such works magnificently exploited the greater sophistication of copperplate engraving over woodcuts, allowing maps of unprecedented detail and compactness to be affordably printed. The Netherlands became the centre of cartographic expertise because they boasted the most skilful engravers. Maps of the four continents stand at the beginning of the *Theatrum*, underlining its decisive break from mediaeval representations of the world, the so–called T–in–O maps in which the three continents of Asia, Africa and

Europe are formed by the spaces marked off by the Don, Nile and Mediterranean, the crux of the T marking Jerusalem. 'Some, for one purpose', wrote Dee, 'and some for an other, liketh, loveth, getteth, and useth, Mappes, Chartes, & Geographicall Globes' (Preface, *Euclide*, a iiii r).

But not everyone loved the fruits of this study: 'The worlde was merier', bemoans a speaker in Edward Worsop's 1582 surveyance manual, 'before mesurings were used then it hath beene since'.[3] His grudge is that 'a tenant in these daies must pay for every foote', but his anxieties also resonate with the fable of the Golden Age, when (according to Ovid) 'Men knew none other countries yet, than where themselves did keepe', and before 'men began to bound, / With dowles and diches drawen in length the free and fertile ground'.[4] Such an anticipation of Xanadu's 'twice five miles of fertile ground / With walls and towers... girdled round', and the 'Ancestral voices prophesying war' that Kubla Khan 'heard from far', serves to emphasize the widely perceived link between the genesis of war and the demarcation of land. That mythic equation was renewed in the crucial military applications of advanced geometric surveyance in the sixteenth century, and confirmed in the singular historical coincidence of the centre of cartographic excellence in the period being also the cockpit of its wars.

Robert Greene's Marlovian *Selimus the Turk* paraphrases Ovid in remembering an age when 'the earth knew not the share, nor seas the barke, / The souldiers entred not the battred breach'.[5] Greene's exactly contemporary military authority, Helenus in *Euphues his Censure* (1587), lists the benefit of such skills to the renewed Iron Age:

What captayne shall be able to make choice of his ground to fight with his enemy to intrench, to imbattayle, to leguer, to pitch his Pavilions at advantage, unlesse skilfull in Geography, to know the Nature and plott of the Countrey so lately discovered...How shall he order his men, or devide them in companyes: how shall hee bring them into square... or any other forme, unlesse instructed in Arithmetike and Geometry[?]
(*Works*, VI, 207)

'Geography... so lately discovered': Thomas Digges had indeed lately uncovered such expertise in his *Arithmeticall Militare Treatise, Named STRATIOTICOS* (1579), a work whose 'chiefe intention' was 'to shew how *Arithmetike* maye stand a Souldioure in steade' (31). Digges's father Leonard had begun this work, as a natural successor to his earlier geometrical treatises, *TECTONICON* (1562) and *PANTO–METRIA* (1571). *STRATIOTICOS* fulfils its intention to 'employ... *Mathematicall Muses* upon this *Militare Argument*' (A2v) by couching a course in Euclidean geometry in terms, for example, of the necessary proportion of soldiers' pay to the length of a campaign (67), of gunpowder to a cannon's firing rate (31), or of pikemen to halberdiers in an optimum formation (48). Although it has been observed that in one such equation, 9416 and two thirds of a pioneer were required (Cruickshank, 1966, 197), *STRATIOTICOS* was emulated by the flood of military treatises that followed it.

Thomas Digges was later appointed the supervisor of England's coastal fortifications, since the angular deflections of such constructions demanded his geometrical expertise. Such expertise was also essential to the converse art of siege. The act of surveying a town in order to draw a map of it is of the same order as the calculation of diagrams for the purposes of its assault, for an optimum ballistic trajectory. Our own Ordnance Survey maps tell the same story. *'The Generall'*, reads *STRATIOTICOS*, 'is by good, especial and perfite *Plattes*, *Mappes*, and *Models*, to know the *Scituation*, Nature, and propertie of the Countrey' (143). Digges singles out the Prince of Orange 'in these late *Flemishe* warres', as an exemplary soldier who 'greatly aided himselfe: For havyng of *Hollande*, *Zelande*, and all other partes of the lowe Countries verie perfite and exquisite *Mappes* & *Plattes*' (148). It seems likely that these would have been from Ortelius's collection. A letter dated May 1586 certainly survives, written by a Dutch soldier requesting from a friend 'a cheap set of Ortelius's maps for the summer campaign' (Van Dorsten, 1962, 131). So geographic methods and commodities proved essential in waging sixteenth–century war, while war sponsored the advances in surveyance–techniques that revolutionized the period. Moreover, the reporting of these wars increasingly employed cheaply produced maps. And while European cities for the first time achieved a graphically distinct representation, those cities were themselves being girdled by fortifications deriving from an identical expertise. Maps were essential in war, and served to represent war. The finest examples derived from a group of states racked by war. It has been claimed that the European wars of the period deserve to be considered as a first First World War, due to expanding colonization:[6] it was certainly the first time that war had been waged and visualized in terms of an accurate description of the world.

Such a lengthy preamble renders it reasonable, I hope, to envisage certain of Marlowe's Renaissance heroes in the context of this newly limpid world at war. The merchant Barabas 'in his Counting–house', the scholar Faustus, 'the man that in his study sits', and the soldier–king Tamburlaine in his 'stately tent of War' (*The Jew of Malta*, 1.1.1SD; *Doctor Faustus*, Prologue, 28; *1 Tamburlaine*, Prologue, 3)[7], comprise the very customers to which the first English translation of Mercator's *Atlas or a Geographicke Description of the... World* (London, 1636) was aimed. Its preface, written by the war veteran and erstwhile war reporter Henry Hexham, meditates on the power of the map in a manner strongly reminiscent of Marlowe's heroes, from a time when (as Richard Willes's 1577 preface to Eden's *History of Travayl* puts it) 'all Christians, Jewes, Turkes... be this day in love with Geographie' (fo. iii v). 'Here then', writes Hexham:

> the great Monarches, Kings and Princes of this Universe, may representively in their Cabinets take a view of the extention, and limits of their owne Kingdomes, and Dominions... Here the Noble–man and Gentle–man by speculation in his closset, may travell through every Province of the whole world... Here the Souldier hath matter of delight ministred unto him, in beholding the place, & reading the storie, where many bloodie Battles have beene fought, and many famous seiges performed... Here the Marchant sitting in his counting–house, may know what Marchandises every Countrie affordeth, what commodities it wanteth, and whither he may transport, and vent those which are most vendible, to returne gaine and profite into his purse.
> (fo. 1 v – 2 r)

To an extent, such quotation speaks for itself. Part of the effect of Barabas's opening soliloquy resides in his precise knowledge of 'what Marchandises every Countrie affordeth... and whither he may transport':

> East and by South: why then I hope my ships
> I sent for *Egypt* and the bordering Iles
> Are gotten up by *Nilus* winding bankes:
> Mine Argosie from *Alexandria*,
> Loaden with Spice and Silkes, now under saile,
> Are smoothly gliding downe by *Candie* shoare
> To *Malta*, through our Mediterranean sea.
> (*The Jew* 1.1.41–7)

Barabas's mercantile worth is measured 'In *Florence, Venice, Antwerpe, London, Civill, / Frankeford, Lubecke*, and where not' (4.1.71–2), but the financial world he exploits is also a world at war, and one in which Barabas is also expert. 'I was', he gloats, 'an Engineere, / And in the warres 'twixt *France* and *Germanie*, / Under pretence of helping *Charles* the fifth, / Slew friend and enemy with my stratagems' (2.3.186–9). Likewise prominent amongst Doctor Faustus's necromantic aspirations is a more partisan but no less military imperative. 'I'le leavy souldiers with the coyne they bring', he speculates, 'And chase the Prince of *Parma* from our Land... Yea stranger engines for the brunt of warre / Then was the fiery keele at *Antwerpe* bridge,

/ I'le make my servile spirits to invent' (1.1.119–24). *'Our* land': Faustus identifies himself as a fellow countryman to Ortelius and Mercator. Charles V is their common patron (we later learn), as he is Barabas's, their common home the centre of cartographic endeavour. Marlowe's earliest hero Aeneas means to 'build a statelier *Troy*' (5.1.2) by recourse to resonantly modern methods, entering Act V 'with a paper in his hand, drawing the platforme of the citie'. So Faustus's vow to 'wall all *Germany* with Brasse' (1.1.114) opulently reflects the newly geometric systems of fortification that were even then girdling European cities.

'How wonderful a good map is', wrote a later connoisseur in 1678, 'in which one views the world as from another world'.[8] Faustus's astronautical flight aboard the dragon's back 'to prove *Cosmography*' (2.3.773) is infused with the same rich wonder. With an atlas in front of him, Hexham claimed, a 'Gentle–man by speculation in his closset, may travell through every Province of the whole world'. By speculation in his theatre, Marlowe's play does similar work:

> So high our Dragons soar'd into the aire,
> That looking downe the earth appear'd to me,
> No bigger then my hand in quantity.
> There did we view the Kingdomes of the world,
> And what might please mine eye, I there beheld.[9]

Such a telescoping of space is the very basis upon which Mercator's Atlas was subsequently presented to its potential readership – its counting–house, closet and cabinets containing 'the whole world'. And the basis, I want to argue, upon which Marlowe's theatre represents that world. Barabas's cartographic survey of his fleet famously turns 'to inclose/ Infinite riches in a little roome' (*Jew*, 1.1.36–7). That phrase came to be echoed in Francis Bacon's Essay 'Of Travaile', which recommends a thorough preparation:

> If you will have a Young Man, to put his *Travaile*, into a little Roome, and in short time, to gather much, this you must doe. First... he must have some Entrance into the language... Then... Let him carry with him also some Card or Booke describing the Country, where he travelleth.[10]

It is on both the 'Language' and the 'Card' of war that I should now like to concentrate, on Tamburlaine's 'representative' view of the extension, and limits of his kingdoms and dominions.

In his first play, Cosroe deprecates Tamburlaine's 'Giantly presumption', 'to cast up hils against the face of heaven' (*1 Tamburlaine*, 2.6.2–3). The reference is unambiguous: the rise of this 'man, or rather god of war' (*1 Tamburlaine*, 5.1.1) is associated with the advent of the Iron Age, when (as Ovid again summarises) 'Giantes went about the Realme of Heaven... to place themselves to raigne as Gods... and hill on hill they heaped aloft' (B3v). Marlowe consolidates the reference in the following scene by having Tamburlaine cite Jove's usurpation of Saturn as a mighty precedent to his own career (*1 Tamburlaine*, 2.7.12–17). The lines are accompanied by a paean to those 'faculties [that] can comprehend/The wondrous Architecture of the world' (2.7.21–2). What faculties are these if not geographic ones? 'I will confute those blind Geographers', he later declares,

> That make a triple region in the world,
> Excluding Regions which I meane to trace,
> And with this pen reduce them to a Map,
> Calling the Provinces, Citties and townes
> After my name and thine *Zenocrate*:
> Here at *Damascus* will I make the Point
> That shall begin the Perpendicular
> (*1 Tamburlaine*, 4.4.75–82)

These lines conflate a number of the contexts I have sketched. Most obviously they allude to the ascendance of modern maps over mediaeval representations of the world, the T–in–O *mappae mundi* that divided it into a 'triple region'.[11] But, crucially, Tamburlaine's words occur in the context of a siege. Damascus's fall will provide the co–ordinates by which Tamburlaine's own map may be drawn with his pen–as–sword. The same geometric constructions necessary to survey a town are those required to open up a breach in its defences. In the strictest contrast to 'those blind Geographers', Menaphon had described Tamburlaine's eyes as 'piercing instruments of sight' (*1 Tamburlaine*, 2.1.14). That startling phrase insists upon the inscriptive nature of the art of describing. The earth 'knows the share' in terms both of Iron Age mythology and of fully contemporary military science.

The same equation is made at an equivalent moment in *2 Tamburlaine*, this time when Tamburlaine's lieutenants besiege Balsera: 'Pioners away', orders Theridamas, 'and where I stuck the stake,/Intrench with those dimensions I prescribed'. Techelles obeys his orders:

> Both we (*Theridamas*) wil intrench our men,
> And with the Jacobs staffe measure the height
> And distance of the castle from the trench,
> That we may know if our artillery
> Will carie full point blancke unto their wals.

(3.3.41–53)

The 'Geometricall Instrument of wood called Jacobs staffe' (as a contemporary military architect called it) was an early form of theodolite.[12] It is surely significant that George Peele, in a siege–scene from *David and Bethsabe* (1590), substitutes 'Jacob's God' for 'Jacobs staffe': It is 'Jacobs God', says King David there, 'That guides your weapons to their conquering strokes'.[13] The quibble seeks to reign back the autonomous techno–military power of Tamburlaine, the Scourge of God, to the subservience of God. For the point about Tamburlaine's championship of the rudiments of arithmetical soldiership is the freedom it affords him from the traditional, chivalric forms of the Just War. As the Soldan complains in the first play, 'The slave usurps the glorious name of war' (*1 Tamburlaine*, 4.1.67).

In *2 Tamburlaine*, the siege of Balsera is dramatized immediately after Tamburlaine's lengthily technical lecture to his sons on the 'rudiments of war', a passage often cited as evidence of Marlowe's waning imagination in the sequel. As is well known, the speech derives, almost slavishly, from a treatise on fortification by Marlowe's Corpus Christi contemporary Paul Ive. The overtly practical tone of Ive's work ('where you determine to place a Bulwarke, there set downe a stake, and stretch a lyne betwixt stake and stake...')[14] is duplicated in Marlowe's paraphrase.

> Then next, the way to fortify your men,
> In champion grounds, what figure serves you best,
> For which the *quinque*–angle fourme is meet:
> Because the corners there may fall more flat,
> Whereas the Fort may fittest be assailde,
> And sharpest where th'assault is desperate.
> (*2 Tamburlaine*, 3.2.62–7)

We must take care however not to mistake the technical for the prosaic, since it is here that Marlowe's mighty line most aligns with Tamburlaine's 'Perpendicular'. The basis of Tamburlaine's absolute rule is his championship (as it were) of the slide–rule. And his lecture, first delivered from his stately tent of war in 1588 or 1589, was topical in the extreme. For just across the river from the Rose on 4 November 1588, Thomas Hood delivered his inaugural address as mathematical lecturer of the City of London, intended for the captains of the city's militia which sought to demystify for them the 'Mathematicall science... most convenient for militarie men' (Johnson, 1942, 99, 100).

Let Geographie witnesse in universall Mappes [he declared] let

Topographie witnesse in several Cardes... you your selves may
witness in Martiall affaires, let the Gunner witnesse in planting his
shot, witnesse the Surveior in measuring land, witnesse all those...
whose skill being tolde us, we would scarcely beleeve it, were it
not lying at our doores.
(Johnson, 1942, 105)

In the urgent days of 1588, when danger indeed lay at our doors,
Tamburlaine's lecture duplicated for a broader audience the technicalities of
modern war. William Garrard's 1591 *The Arte of Warre* was to recommend
to its officer class readership that 'both what is written before, and shalbe
written after in this booke... may ever [be] read as a lecture to their soldiers'
(22). Tamburlaine anticipates such practical advice, as well as anticipating
Clausewitz's resonant summation of the Napoleonic Wars: 'It was as if war
itself had given a lecture' (Earle, Craig and Gilbert, 1944, 96). The parallel
struck Coleridge too, noting in 1818 that 'to power in itself, without reference
to any moral end, an inevitable admiration and complacency appertains,
whether it be displayed in the conquests of a Buonaparte or Tamerlane, or in
the foam and thunder of a cataract' (Ashe, 1907, 334). Napoleon, like Hitler
after him and Marlowe's Tamburlaine before him, was particularly absorbed
by maps: it is not too fanciful to imagine Tamburlaine humming along to a
later soldier's tune:

I'm very well acquainted too with matters mathematical,
I understand equations, both the simple and quadratical...
I am the very model of a modern major–general.[15]

England being England, there were many voices that agreed with the Soldan's
cry of foul, that Tamburlaine 'usurps the glorious name of war'. Sir John
Smythe, for one, sarcastically rebuked men like Hood, Digges, and Garrard
in 1590, the year that saw Tamburlaine's lecture printed. 'Are they newlie
fallen from heaven with some divine instinct and gift, to teach us the Art
Militarie?'[16] Smythe's objections centre, crucially, on language, complaining
– in the Blimpish manner of countless other retired experts – that English
ideals of chivalry, bows–and–arrows, and fair play were ill–served by an
obsequious adoption of what Paul Jorgensen has called 'the cosmopolitan
stream of military science' (1956, 49). 'These our such men of warre',
continues Smythe:

have procured to innovate, or rather subvert all our ancient
proceedings in matters Militarie... as for example; They will not
vouchsafe in their speeches or writings to use our ancient termes

103

> belonging to matters of warre, but doo call a campe by the Dutch name of *Legar*; nor will affoord to say, that such a Towne, or such a Fort is besieged, but that it is *belegard*... as though our language were so barren, that it were not able of it selfe, or by derivation to affoord convenient words.
>
> (*Certain Discourses* B2r–B2v)

But England's insularity from European advances in military science is testified to by the fact that most of our military vocabulary derives from this very period. Such words as *ambush, alarm, squadron, infantry, cavalry* and *artillery* constituted a linguistic invasion altogether more successful than any of Philip of Spain's attempts. And just as jeeps, the Blitz, Molotov cocktails and Scuds have entered the language in our own times, so Robert Barret prefaced a lengthy glossary of terms in his *Theorike and Practike of Modern Warres* (1598) by stating that 'most of our termes now used in warres are derived from straungers; as the French, the Italian, the Spaniard and the Dutch' (248).

Contemporary military service indeed seems to have constituted a grounding in a sort of Esperanto of War, not least since the armies ranged against each other across Marlowe's Europe comprised multinational units. William Blandy described Parma's army of Spaniards, Walloons, Italians, Germans and others as the 'froth and scomme of many nations'.[17] Likewise, English troops fighting for the Protestant cause found themselves rubbing shoulders with Dutch, Swiss, Scottish or French soldiers. It is for this reason that the Earl of Leicester issued a warning to his troops in 1586 that 'whereas sundrie nations are to serve with us in these warres, so as through diversitie of languages occasion of many controversies may arise'.[18] It is against this specific background that we should view the tense negotiations that open *2 Tamburlaine*. Sigismund's Christian force of 'Hungarians,/ Sclavonians, Almain Rutters, Muffes, and Danes' (1.1.21–2) is to form an alliance with Orcanes's confederation of:

> revolted Grecians, Albanees,
> Cicilians, Jewes, Arabians, Turks, and Moors,
> Natolians, Sorians, blacke Egyptians,
> Illirians, Thracians, and Bythinians.
> (1.1.61–4)

This United Nations force is to counter the 'world of people' (67) that Tamburlaine brings to the field. If the Elizabethan context of European wars is discernible in this fragile and exotic military coalition, the broader and enduring relevance of Marlowe's representation of war should be immediately

104

clear to those with memories of the Middle Eastern campaign waged four centuries later, known as Desert Storm.

In 1607 Thomas Dekker memorably described a band of English war–veterans as a 'mingle mangle of countries, a confusion of languages, yet all understanding one another'.[19] Just as the armies that Tamburlaine mobilizes comprise a 'mingle mangle of countries', so his lecture on the 'rudiments of war' constitutes a 'confusion of languages':

> The ditches must be deepe, the Counterscarps
> Narrow and steepe, the wals made high and broad,
> The Bulwarks and the rampiers large and strong,
> With Cavalieros and thicke counterforts,
> And roome within to lodge sixe thousand men.
> It must have privy ditches, countermines,
> And secret issuings to defend the ditch.
> It must have high Argins and covered waies
> To keep the bulwark fronts from battery,
> And Parapets to hide the Muscatters:
> Casemates to place the great Artillery,
> And store of ordinance that from every flanke
> May scoure the outward curtaines of the Fort,
> Dismount the Cannon of the adverse part,
> Murther the Foe and save the walles from breach.
> (2 Tamburlaine II, 3.2.68–82)

Of course these lines are stiff with jargon, but what modern editors fail to note is the foreign extraction of the technical terms, the fact that they needed glossing at the time, a service provided by Robert Barret's *Theorike and Practike*: '*Rampier*, a French word, and is a fortification or wall of earth' (252); '*Cavaglere*, an Italian word... in fortifications, a Cavaliere is a mount or platform of earth, built or raised high, either within or without the wall for to plant great Ordinance upon' (249); '*Casamatta*, a Spanish word, and doth signifie a slaughter–house, and is a place built low under the wall or bulwarke, not arriving unto the height of the ditch, serving to scoure the ditch, annoying the enemy when he entreth into the ditch to skale the wal' (249); '*Curtine*, a French word, is the long wall running levell from bulwarke to bulwarke' (250); '*Parapet*, an Italian word, is the upper part of the wall, which shadoweth the souldiers from the sight and annoyances of the enemy' (251). Tamburlaine's words must have sounded as strange to his original audience as the litany of geographic and military exotica that constitutes his progress.

This warrior, in Bacon's words, has 'some Entrance into the Language', and later he also carries 'some Card or Booke describing the Country, where he travelleth', namely the map he calls for at the end of *2 Tamburlaine*. 'Give me a Map, then let me see how much/ Is left for me to conquer all the world' (*2 Tamburlaine*, 5.3.123–4). With this command, his intentions in *1 Tamburlaine* to render obsolete the *mappae mundi* of 'blind Geographers' are graphically fulfilled. As long ago as 1924, a direct correlation was established between Marlowe's *Tamburlaine* and Ortelius's *Theatrum Orbis Terrarum*. So overwhelming is the similarity between Ortelius's map of Africa and Marlowe's description of one particular campaign (described at *2 Tamburlaine*, 1.3.186–205), that, as Ethel Seaton put it, 'one can almost follow Marlowe's finger travelling down the page as he plans the campaign' (1924, 18). Her research goes some way to counter T.S. Eliot's lament in 1919 over Marlowe's 'facile use of resonant names' (1932, 121). 'Here I began to martch towards *Persea*,|Along *Armenia* and the Caspian sea', says Tamburlaine before his map, 'And thence unto *Bithynia*... From thence to *Nubia* neere *Borno* Lake|And so along the Ethiopian sea...'. It is not that these names prompt specific associations, over and above their foreignness (such resonances, for example, as Eliot himself provokes throughout *The Waste Land*). Rather that their deployment sustains the 'aura of knowledge and prestige' that surrounded maps in this period (Alpers, 1983, 133).

The irony of this last request, and one that is secured by the subsequent stage–directions '*They crowne him*' and '*They bring in the hearse*', is that this aura of militant and military subjection surrounding maps, finally enclose Tamburlaine's own failure, his own subjection to human limit: 'For *Tamburlaine*, the Scourge of God must die' (*2 Tamburlaine*, 5.3.248). There is a mighty precedent in history for the map that appears on stage in his dying moments, whose symbolism indeed measures the 'extention, and limits' by which Mercator's Atlas was to be recommended to kings and princes. The Emperor Charles V, the fictive patron of Faustus, and of Barabas, had recognised the symbolism of conquest provided by a map. Guillaume du Bellay, the French sixteenth–century statesman, records that Charles was so absorbed by a map of the Alps and Low Countries of Provence which he acquired in 1536, 'que désjà il presumoit d'avoir le païs en son bandon, ainsi comme il en avoit la carte' – he convinced himself he owned the country as absolutely as he owned its map (Bourilly, and Vindry, 1908–19, III, 118–19). Such apparently deranged behaviour is not the exclusive preserve of the Renaissance. In October 1990, Saddam Hussein issued a new map of Iraq, incorporating Kuwait, to his schools at home and embassies abroad. Charles V was so pleased with a terrestrial globe fashioned for him by Mercator, that he commissioned from him a set of surveyors' instruments which he took with him on his campaigns (Brown, 1951, 159). But the symbolism of such a crowning achievement, embodied in a map, can swiftly do more funereal service. How redolent of Tamburlaine's final survey that at Charles's abdication in 1555/56, the emperor should have recalled his travels, through the Netherlands, Germany, Italy, Spain, France, England, and Africa, asserting (as Roy Strong puts it) 'the geographic extent of his universal monarchy' even as it ebbs (1973, 83). The abdication came to take its place in the symbolism of the *memento mori* tradition. The Spanish painter Antonio de Pereda portrays amongst the skulls, hourglass and snuffed candle of *Vanitas* (c.1634) a miniature of Charles V, held above a terrestial globe (Jordan and Cherry, 1995, 81). Such ironies persist. Five months after Saddam Hussein's distribution of his new world map, the forces of the new world order were burying the Iraqi dead on the road to Basra. Each corpse's location was logged in a satellite computer's micro coordinates.

The great mapmaker Ortelius claimed that knowledge of geography was 'The eye of History'.[20] In 1589 Thomas Blundeville agreed. His *Brief Description of Universal Maps and Cards* is prefaced by the observation that 'I Daylie see many that delight to looke on Mappes', and that without geography, 'the necessarie reading of Histories is halfe lame' (A2v). Marlowe's history of Timur the Lame is poignantly rooted in this notion, as he fuses the military hi–tech of the map with its newly narrative function, and exploits the aesthetics and linguistics of violence it embodies. When Gascoigne's piece of prose journalism *The Spoyle of Antwerp* was dramatized as *A Larum for London* in the 1590s, the anonymous playwright converted Gascoigne's 'Model of the whole place... annexed to thend' into a dynamic image of violent conquest: 'This Cittie... now remaines the Map / Of sad destruction and perpetuall ruyne', gloats its conqueror, 'Her streetes lie thwackt with slaughtered carkasses'.[21] The map annexed to the end of *Tamburlaine* measures how much the soldier has conquered, and how much is left for him to conquer. 'The great Monarches', as Mercator's *Atlas* was to say, 'may representively in their Cabinets take a view of the extention, *and limits* of their owne Kingdomes, and Dominions'. So here, Tamburlaine's map 'representively' recapitulates the events of his military history.

> Here I began to martch towards *Persea*,
> Along *Armenia* and the Caspian sea,
> And thence unto *Bythinia*, where I tooke
> The Turke and his great Empresse prisoners,
> Then marcht I into Egypt and *Arabia*....

The telescoping of space that encloses Marlowe's 'infinite riches' in the 'little roome' of his stage is a feature of his topical writing of place. In *Tamburlaine the Great*, Marlowe provides a linguistic topography of war, at once a *mappa mundi*, a *memento mori*, and a *theatrum belli*.

Notes

1. George Gascoigne, 'Gascoignes voyage into *Hollande. An.* 1572' in *The Complete Works of George Gascoigne*, ed. J. Cunliffe, 2 vols, Cambridge, 1907–10., I, 363.

2. *The Elements of the Most Auncient Philosopher EUCLIDE of Megara*, tr. H. Billingsley, London, 1570, a iiii r.

3. Edward Worsop, *A Discoverie of Sundrie Errours and Faults Daily Committed by Landemeaters, Ignorant of Arithmetike and Geometrie*, London, 1582., I2v.

4. *The .xv. Bookes of P. Ovidius Naso, entytuled Metamorphosis*, tr. Arthur Golding, London, 1567, B2v–B3r.

5. *The Works of Robert Greene*, ed. A. Grosart, 15 vols (repr. New York, 1964), XIV, 204.

6. C.R. Boxer, quoted in Parker, 1975, 49.

7. Quotation is from the Bowers, 1981, edition, unless otherwise stated.

8. Samuel van Hoogstraten, quoted in Alpers, 1983, 141.

9. *Doctor Faustus*, ed. W. Greg, 1950, 217, ll. 872–6. The lines are unique to the 1616 B–Text.

10. Sir Francis Bacon, *The Essayes or Counsels, Civill and Morall*, ed. Michael Kiernan, Oxford, 1985, 57.

11. Marjorie Garber discusses the 'displaced metonymic alternative to the...world–as–stage' presented in these lines, but overlooks the specifically military contemporaneity of the image (1984, 302).

12. The architect in question is John Symonds, who bequeathed the instrument in his will (P.C.C. 1597 Cobham 61); see Summerson, 1967–68, 220.

13. *David and Bathsabe, 1599*, ed. W. Greg, Malone Society Reprints, Oxford, 1912, 171–3.

14. Paul Ive, *Practise of Fortification*, London, 1589.

15. W.S. Gilbert, *The Savoy Operas*, London, 1962, 458.

16. Sir John Smythe, *Certain Discourses Military*, London, 1590, fo.2v.

17. William Blandy, *The Castle, or Picture of Pollicy shewing forth most lively, the Face, Body and Partes of a Commonwealth, the Duety, Quality, Profession of a...Souldiar*, London, 1581, G2r.

18. *Lawes and Ordinances, set downe by Robert, Earle of Leycester, the Queenes Majesties Lieutenant and Captaine Generall of her Armie and Forces in the Lowe Countries*, London, 1586, B1r.

19. Thomas Dekker, *Worke for Armorours: Or, The Peace is Broken*, London, 1609, in *Dekker: Non–Dramatic Works*, ed. A. Grosart, 5 vols, London, 1884–6, repr. New York, 1963, IV, 103.

20. Preface: Abraham Ortelius, *The Theatre of the Whole World: Set Forth by That Excellent Geographer Abraham Ortelius*, tr. W. B., London, 1606.

21. G. Gascoigne, *A Larum for London, or the Siedge of Antwerp, 1602*, ed. W.W. Greg, Malone Society Reprints, Oxford, 1913, lines 1614–17.

7. Marlowe and the New World

THOMAS CARTELLI

The majority of the eight direct references Marlowe makes to the New World primarily identify it with boundless wealth, particularly gold, and usually associate that wealth with Spanish possession. For example, in *1 Tamburlaine* Callapine attempts to win his release from captivity by bribing his jailer, Almeda, with the offer of 'a thousand galleys,' which shall 'bring armadoes from the coasts of Spain, / Fraughted with gold of rich America' (1.3.32-35).[1] In *The Massacre at Paris*, the Guise twice remarks that his anti–Protestant crusade is financed by the 'stately Catholics' of Spain (2.60-61), in one instance asserting that 'the Catholic Philip, king of Spain, / Ere I shall want, will cause his Indians, / To rip the golden bowels of America' (18.63–5). In *Doctor Faustus*, Valdes promises that spirits shall 'drag huge argosies' from Venice and 'from America the golden fleece / That yearly stuffs old Philip's treasury, / If learned Faustus will be resolute' (1.1.131–4). Valdes also draws a suggestive connection between these servile spirits and Philip's Indians when he remarks that 'As Indian Moors obey their Spanish lords, / So shall the spirits of every element / Be always serviceable to us three' (1.1.122-4). Like the Guise, Valdes envisions the getting of gold as a procedure that depends on the ready labour of unresisting servants who will do all that their masters bid them do. Indeed, the fantasy of effortless acquisition that Valdes associates with necromancy seems imaginatively rooted in Spain's absolute control of Indians whose subjection makes them seem as magically obedient as spirits.

In an earlier anticipation of Valdes's promise, Faustus envisions spirits flying 'to India for gold' and searching 'all corners of the new-found world / For pleasant fruites, and princely delicates' (1.1.95-96). The marvellous prospects of the 'new-found world' make a more sustained appearance in the dying Tamburlaine's vision of conquests he will never achieve as he traces on a map an unnamed 'world of ground' that '[l]ies westward from the midst of Cancer's line / Unto the rising of this earthly globe'(*2 Tamburlaine*, 5.3.145–47):

> Lo, here, my sons, are all the golden mines,
> Inestimable drugs and precious stones,
> More worth than Asia and the world beside;
> And from th'Antarctic Pole eastward behold
> As much more land, which never was descried,
> Wherein are rocks of pearl that shine as bright
> As all the lamps that beautify the sky.
> And shall I die, and this unconquered?

110

(5.3.151–58)

While this passage arguably constitutes Marlowe's most wide-ranging appraisal of the prospects of exploration, it characteristically inscribes the marvellous in a language of desire and possession. Like 'the lamps that beautify the sky' which exist in balanced relation to 'rocks of pearl,' all that might make the mere experience of discovery momentous is made to correspond to expressly material standards of value and measurement, with Tamburlaine's inability to possess so 'much more land' operating as the driving force of the passage as a whole.[2]

In *The Jew of Malta*, a play deeply invested in the cultural capital of early modern politics and trade, the Maltese Governor, Ferneze, consolidates these inscriptions of the New World as a space of desire and possession in his response to the Turkish ambassador's explanation that it is 'the wind that bloweth all the world besides, / Desire of gold' which has driven him 'into Malta rhode':

> Desire of gold, great sir?
> That's to be gotten in the Western Inde:
> In Malta are no golden minerals.
> (3.5.1–6)

Indicating that it is not merely gold that's 'to be gotten in the Western Inde' but 'Desire of gold,' the entire complex of gold and the drive to possess it, Ferneze's words help bring into focus Marlowe's construction of the New World as both an object and medium of distinctly material desire.

It is, I would submit, no coincidence that most of Marlowe's direct references to the New World specifically associate it with Spain, and that the most sardonic of them is made by the Machiavellian Governor of Malta, ally of Spain and Spaniards. Like Hakluyt in his *Discourse of Western Planting* (1584), Marlowe identifies America as an open field of gold slavishly mined by Indians who are nakedly submissive to the 'will' and 'shall' of Spanish desire. And though he chooses neither to stage, nor to elaborate on, the operation of Spanish desire in the New World, the singleminded and arrogantly self–assured nature of the Spanish approach to conquest and plunder has particularly suggestive analogues in Marlowe's construction of the drive for power and possession in the Tamburlaine plays.

Prior to Marlowe's composition of *1 Tamburlaine*, at least nine works treating Spanish efforts at navigation, mapping, conquest, medical and botanical investigations had been translated into English.[3] Excerpts from several of these would have been available to him in Hakluyt's *Divers Voyages Touching the Discoverie of America* (1582), and he might well have had access to others in French, Latin, Spanish, Italian, and Portugese. Marlowe would have had readier access to Richard Eden's translation of Peter Martyr's *Decades of the newe world or west India* (1555) and, presumably, to Hakluyt's *Discourse of Western Planting*. Of these works, Hakluyt's *Discourse* and Thomas Nicholas's translation of Lopez de Gómara's *Pleasant Historie of the Conquest of the Weast India* (1578) could have served as formative influences on his repeated identification of the New World with Spanish conquest and possession. Both texts certainly influenced Raleigh's plans and efforts to exploit Spain's weakening hold on its Caribbean possessions in the 1580s and 1590s, as well as Raleigh's increasingly perceptible modelling of himself on the example of free-ranging Spanish adventurers and opportunists like Cortés and Lope de Aguirre. As Kenneth Andrews observes:

> The kind of trade [Raleigh] valued most was 'forcible trade' and the kind of expansion he called for and attempted was militant and acquisitively imperialistic. He admired Spain's colonial achievement and urged his countrymen to emulate the courage and endurance of the *conquistadores*.
> (Andrews, 1984, 9)

The suspicions of both Elizabeth and James regarding Raleigh's intentions had precedents in the Spanish Crown's anxieties about the freebooting activities of *conquistadores* like Cortés, whose conquest of New Spain was effectively undertaken on his own authority and in flagrant disregard of official demands that he return to Cuba. Indeed, in 1553 the Spanish Crown officially prohibited further export to the Indies of 'all the histories of the conquest' and specifically 'placed a ban on the works of Lopez de Gómara' (Cortés, 1986, lviii), publication of Cortés's own letters from Mexico having been suppressed as early as 1527.[4]

I stress this connection because it is particularly the example of Cortés that English New World promoters like Hakluyt and Nicholas were advancing as a precedent for the emulative efforts of English New World explorers. For example, in his 'Epistle Dedicatory to Sir Walter Raleigh' of 1587, which prefaces his re–publication of Peter Martyr's *Decades*, Hakluyt writes:

> Go on, I say, follow the path on which you have already set foot, seize Fortune's lucky jowl, spurn not the immortal fame which is here offered you, but let the doughty deeds of Ferdinand Cortés, the Castilian, the stout conqueror of New Spain, here beautifully described, resound ever in your ears and let them make your nights not less sleepless than did those of Themistocles the glorious

triumphs of Miltiades.
(Taylor, 1935, II, 368–69)

In Hakluyt's *Discourse* of 1584, Spain is spoken of in an ostensibly more ambivalent manner, with its 'monarchie' in one instance likened to the 'Empire of Alexander the grate' and at another represented (in a manner Marlowe might well have remarked) as 'the scourge of the worlde' (Taylor, 1935, II, 264). Drawing a direct correlation between Spain's commitment to its New World projects and its current enjoyment of European domination, Hakluyt presents Spain as a model for the development of an imperial England. But in demonizing the ruthless and predatory activities by which Spain had enriched itself, Hakluyt opens up an alternative space for England to fill in the future history of New World colonization, one characterized by more pious aims and more enlightened colonial practices. However, even Hakluyt's demonization of the Spanish – which he supplements with relevant quotations from Las Casas on Spanish outrages (ibid., 259-61) – maintains an emulative component. In representing Spain as 'the scourge of the worlde' in formulations like the following – 'And to say the truthe what nation I pray you of all Christendome loveth the Spaniarde the scourge of the worlde, but from the teethe forward and for advantage' (ibid., 264) – Hakluyt implicitly betrays an admiration for Spanish arrogance and presumption that his 1587 celebration of Cortés explicitly confirms. While England might *prefer* worldly pride of place premised on the more pacific accomplishments of trade and good government, respect enforced on an international scale by awe and fear does not seem entirely undesirable.

We find a similarly pragmatic balancing of contempt and admiration for Spain in an earlier section of the *Discourse* where Hakluyt describes 'howe Charles the Emperor employed his treasure to the afflictinge and oppressinge of moste of the greatest estates of Christendome'; quotes Peter Martyr's injunction to Spain's 'most noble younge Prince' to 'embrace this newe worlde' 'whereby all the world shalbe under your obeysaunce'; and concludes that 'in very deed it is most apparaunte that riches are the fittest instruments of conqueste' (ibid., 244–45). At this early, and generally unfocussed, stage in the English colonial enterprise, the association of wealth with conquest appears to have particularly aroused the interest of that relatively small group of English adventurers who 'came mostly from the court and received little merchant support' for their exploits. As Carole Shammas writes 'To these court gentlemen'– whose number included Walter Raleigh, Humphrey Gilbert, and Richard Grenville – 'the western hemisphere was primarily a place where one created dominions built on the gold and silver tributes of conquered Indians' (Shammas, 1978, 174):

> Any reader of the histories of the Spanish in America translated into English at this time might conclude that a small band of valiant white men could with relative ease seize Indian cities and collect princely tributes of gold, silver, and jewels from the awed inhabitants in exchange for a promise of protection.
> (Shammas, 1978, 157)

Shammas also notes that 'The adventurers were encouraged to think that new lands in America, unlike other places, were in the reach of "pryvat men" because of the example of the *conquistadores*' (ibid., 154, n.7) and that 'In an age when the Crown had control over so many offices and privileges, the comparable patronage that would flow from the claiming of New World territories was supremely attractive to private gentlemen' (ibid., 157).

I cite these remarks in order to underwrite the connection I am trying to draw between the admiration for Spanish imperial resolve shared by Hakluyt and Raleigh, and Marlowe's sympathetic representation of the drive for power in the Tamburlaine plays. Although both parts of *Tamburlaine* are historically and geographically rooted in the East, the impetus to draw on this material might well have come from the contemporary pressure of Spain's Western conquests which were already arousing the efforts at plunder and privateering of such forward English spirits as Drake and Raleigh. It has, of course, often been maintained that contemporary developments in conquest, trade, and exploration establish an important context for understanding Tamburlaine's will to worldly power and possession. In my own earlier work on *Tamburlaine*, I took general account of the possible impact of these developments on Marlowe's representation of Tamburlaine's transformation from aspiring commoner to scourge of God. However, I positioned Tamburlaine's radical exercise in social mobility in relation to the specifically English phenomenon of the masterless man, drawing support from the repeated representation of Tamburlaine and his cohorts in terms employed elsewhere in the period in descriptions of popular risings and rebellions (see Cartelli, 1991, 67-93). It now seems to me that Tamburlaine may also be modelling the exploits of another kind of masterless man, particularly, the opportunistic conquests of the *conquistador*, and doing so at least in part to suggest what similarly motivated 'pryvat men' of England might do for themselves by operating outside the pale of officially constituted constraints and controls.

I am moved to broach these considerations not only by the affinities between Marlowe's references to the Spanish conquest and Hakluyt's promotional agenda, but by their capacity to explain some of the more controversial aspects of the Tamburlaine plays. For instance, should we conclude that Marlowe was directly influenced by accounts of the Spanish conquest like that of Lopez de Gómara, and by the exemplary representations of Cortés purveyed by Hakluyt and Nicholas – who describes Lopez de Gómara's book as 'a Mirrour and an excellent president, for all such as shall take in hande to gouerne newe Discoueries; for here they shall behold, how Glorie, Renowne, and perfite Felicitie, is not gotten but with great paines, trauaile, perill and daunger of life' (*Pleasant Historie*, A2) – we will have identified specific contemporary precedents for Marlowe's unqualified approval of Tamburlaine's conquests and provocative equation of self-realization with the most extreme forms of self assertion. Indeed, it is hard to ignore the pointed echoing of Nicholas's formula for 'perfite Felicitie' in Tamburlaine's 'earthly crown' speech which calls for the similarly tenacious pursuit of 'the ripest fruit of all, / That perfect bliss and sole felicity, / The sweet fruition of an earthly crown' (*1 Tamburlaine*, 2.7.27-29) and whose materialist orientation has long unsettled critics in search of a more idealized resolution.[5]

Sixteenth–century representations of an inexplicably confident and self-possessed Cortés, carving his way back and forth through the heart of Mexico at the head of a small band of white men, are, in fact, remarkably consistent with Marlowe's representation of Tamburlaine and his loyal confederates. Equally remarkable is Tamburlaine's supersession of the precedent for what Hakluyt terms 'moste outragious and more then Turkishe cruelties' (Taylor, 1935, II, 257) that Cortés and his fellow *conquistadores* established in the minds of their contemporaries. Although the official English view of these cruelties was decidedly censorious, with the cruelties themselves often justifying planned or actual interventions in the Spanish colonial enterprise, they could also be construed as symptomatic of the resolve that was necessary to effect such conquests and, hence, as worthy of at least forced admiration.[6] It is from such a vantage point that we may remark the affinities of Marlowe's depiction of Tamburlaine's wholesale destruction of Babylon in *2 Tamburlaine* with Lopez de Gómara's account of Cortés's destruction of Tenochtitlan.

Most of us will recall the onstage execution of the Governor of Babylon; Tamburlaine's commission of the holy books of Islam to a bonfire; his order that every surviving man, woman and child be drowned; and Techelles's subsequent description of that order's fulfilment:

> I have fulfilled your highness' will, my lord,
> Thousands of men, drowned in Asphaltis' lake,
> Have made the water swell above the banks,
> And fishes, fed by human carcasses,
> Amazed, swim up and down upon the waves,
> As when they swallow asafoetida,

Which makes them fleet aloft and gasp for air.
(5.1.201–7)

Most of us are, however, probably less conversant with Lopez de·Gómara's descriptions of the destruction of another city of temples built upon a lake, two of which read as follows:

the houses that were beaten downe could scarcely hold the people [that] were alive, the streates also being so full of dead carcasses and sicke bodies, that our men could not passe but needes treade upon them.
(*Pleasant Historie*, 342)

as the Spaniardes wente walking in the cittie, they founde heapes of dead bodies in the houses, streates, and in the water: they found also the barke of trees and rootes gnawen by the hungry creatures, and the men so leane and yellow, that it was a pitifull sighte to behold.
(ibid., 341)

Although different in a great many ways, the three passages document a devastation as unprecedented as the completeness of the conquests they commemorate, and suggest the kind of connection that could be made between Cortés's arguably incidental engagement in mass destruction and Tamburlaine's deliberate cultivation of 'sights of power to grace [his] victor[ies]' (*1 Tamburlaine*, 5.2.411).[7] The singularity of Cortés's exploits in Mexico and Tamburlaine's conquests in far–flung quarters of a tripartite world is, in each instance, prominently inscribed in the very number and quality of deaths they are able to countenance in order to realize their aims.

In Stephen Greenblatt's influential construction of Tamburlaine's drive to conquer and possess, this kind of imperious self–assertion and Tamburlaine's energetic movement across the map of an ever-expanding world often appear to be ends themselves (1980, 194–95). In my provisional reading of Marlowe's displaced reckoning with the Spanish conquest, such actions are, instead, pointed manifestations of an imperial resolve that at least some of Marlowe's contemporaries thought they would do well to emulate before the new worlds of the West slipped permanently from their grasp.

Notes

1. All quotations from Marlowe's plays are drawn from the Irving Ribner (1977) edition of the complete plays.

2. Marlowe seems deeply attuned here to the motives that informed, at roughly the same time, Richard Hakluyt's compilation of his *Principal Voyages*. As Richard Helgerson observes: 'In its very form, its systematic representation of the whole of a hitherto unknown world, a book like Hakluyt's expresses and inspires similar dreams of universal dominance. Something of this sort had from the first been the effect of the new maps and globes that began appearing in the wake of Columbus's discoveries' (Helgerson, 1992, 184–5). See also Nicholas de Somogyi's essay in the present volume.

3. Of these works the most influential would have been Thomas Nicholas's translations of Francisco Lopez de Gómara's *Pleasant historie of the conquest of the the Weast India* (1578) and Augustin de Zarate's *Strange and delectable history of the Discoverie and Conquest of the Provinces of Peru* (1581), Bartolomé de Las Casas's *The Spanish Colonie, or Briefe Chronicle of the Acts and Gestes of the Spaniards in the West Indies* (1581), and Martin Cortés's *The Arte of Navigation* (1561), a volume translated more often than any other Spanish work of the period.

4. As Anthony Pagden observes, 'The crown ... found Cortés's mythologizing of the conquest, which had become a powerful ideological weapon in the hands of the rebellious *conquistador* élite, an obvious political embarrassment' (Cortés, 1986, lviii–lix).

5. We might also find precedents in this material for other unexplained liberties Marlowe took in modelling Tamburlaine on the historical Mongol warlord, Timur Khan. As Una Ellis-Fermor long ago noted, 'the "debt" of Marlowe to his sources is ... as small as any poet's' (Ellis–Fermor, 1930, 35). According to Ellis-Fermor, 'the likeness and the unlikeness ... of Timur Khan and Marlowe's Tamburlaine, lays an irresistible problem before us: how was this other glittering figure, so unlike in all detail, so like in a few essential qualities of the spirit, derived from the Mongolian despot?' (1930, 18). Ellis-Fermor effectively concludes her own effort to address this problem by assembling a composite portrait of what Marlowe 'would have learnt' about Timur Khan from 'practically all' of his sources, namely, that Timur Khan 'was distinguished for courage, energy, fixity of purpose,

117

for transcendent military genius and great administrative ability' (35). Although I am not specifically interested here in substituting one presumptive source for another, it goes without saying that Marlowe would have learned exactly the same things about Cortés by reading either Lopez de Gómara or Hakluyt.

6. This clearly appears to have been the position of Nicholas who continues his 'Epistle Dedicatory to Sir Francis Walsingham', which prefaces his translation of Lopez de Gómara, in the following vein: 'Here shall [all such as shall take in hande to gouerne newe Discoueries] see the wisedome, curtesie, valour and pollicie of worthy Captaynes, yea and the faithfull hartes which they ought to beare vnto their Princes seruice: here also is described how to vse and correct the stubbern & mutinous persons, & in what order to exalt the good, stoute and vertuous Souldiers, and chiefly, how to preserue and keepe that bewtifull Dame *Lady Victorie* when she is obtayned' (*Pleasant Historie*, A2-A2v).

7. One of the 'sights of power' to which Tamburlaine refers here, incidental to the destruction of the city of Damascus, bears a close resemblance to the scenes described by Lopez de Gómara: 'Wretched Zenocrate, that livest to see/Damascus' walls dyed with Egyptian blood,/Thy father's subjects and thy countrymen;/Thy streets strowed with dissevered joints of men,/And wounded bodies gasping yet for life' (*1 Tamburlaine*, 5.2.256-60).

8. The Stage, the Scaffold and the Spectators: The Struggle for Power in Marlowe's *Jew of Malta*

ROGER SALES

This is an exploration of relationships between the stage and the stage–play world of Elizabethan society. It considers, more particularly, links between the drama of the stage and the drama of the scaffold. The argument is divided into two main parts. There is, first of all, a study of Elizabethan public punishments and executions that concentrates on the way in which they attempted to choreograph power. The main examples are the punishment of John Stubbes in 1579 and the execution of the Babington conspirators in 1586. These are followed by a brief discussion of the merits of applying Michel Foucault's general thesis about public spectacles of suffering and their decline in the nineteenth century to the Renaissance period in particular. Secondly, there is a reasonably detailed reading of the ending of *The Jew of Malta*, where Barabas is publicly executed before both an onstage audience and the spectators in the theatre itself. It is argued that on the Elizabethan stage this ending may have been provocative, and therefore potentially subversive, because it encouraged spectators both to recognize and to question the ways in which power was choreographed on the Elizabethan scaffold. It is suggested that the executions that were staged by Marlowe and other Elizabethan dramatists in the public theatres always ran the risk of disturbing and possibly disrupting what has been called the royal monopoly in violence. The scaffold inevitably lost some of its majesty and mystique when playwrights repositioned it on the stage.

Although *The Jew of Malta* is then the main text, it may still be worth noticing that all of Marlowe's major plays also contain execution scenes. *2 Tamburlaine* represents the execution of Calyphas, Tamburlaine's effeminate son, in front of an onstage audience that includes a defeated army and its generals. *Edward II* contains Marlowe's best–known execution scene in which it is the King himself who is executed. Although this takes place in a dungeon, it becomes a form of public execution when it is staged in the theatre. The play as a whole shows other executions and is full of references to various kinds of punishment. One of the available versions of *Doctor Faustus* ends with Faustus himself being executed and dismembered, after Lucifer and the Devils have formally processed or progressed onto the stage to take up their positions as onstage spectators for this spectacle of suffering.[1]

It would be possible to use these and other examples to argue that Marlowe's theatre was often a theatre of physical cruelty. This would, however, risk ignoring the possibility that for Elizabethan audiences these execution scenes were more shocking for their savage irony rather than for the ways in which bodies themselves were savaged. Tamburlaine the rebel executes his son to prevent a rebellion. Edward is both a monarch whose power is based around the control and use of the scaffold and what Elizabethans would have referred to as an 'alien stranger' who had to be executed for the safety of the state. Lucifer's stage presence and position, together with his speeches, suggest unsettling similarities between his power and that of the Renaissance prince just before, in most productions of this version of the text, Faustus's offstage execution; the stage, or scaffold, is usually strewn with Faustus's torn and mangled limbs. When Marlowe transforms his stage into a scaffold it is certainly the ironies, as much as the cruelty itself, which have the power to shock.

John Stubbes was publicly punished in 1579 for writing (in *The Discoverie of a Gaping Gulf Whereinto England is like to be Swallowed by Another French Marriage*) against Queen Elizabeth's proposed marriage to the Catholic Duke of Anjou. He fulminated against what he saw as being a contrary coupling between good and evil. A proclamation was issued on 27 September that all copies of the book should be destroyed in the presence, or open sight, of a public official (Hughes and Larkin, 1969, vol. 2, no.642). William Camden, the historian, was one of the spectators on 3 November when Stubbes was brought to the scaffold for punishment:

> Not long after upon a Stage set up in the Market–place at *Westminster*, *Stubbes* and *Page* had their right hands cut off by the blow of a Butcher's knife, with a mallet struck through their wrists ... I can remember that, standing by *John Stubbes*, so soon as his right hand was off, put off his hat with his left, and cried aloud, *God Save the Queen*. The people round him stood mute, whether stricken with fear at the first sight of this strange kind of punishment, or for commiseration for the man whom they reputed honest, or out of a secret inward repining they had at this marriage, which they suspected would be dangerous to Religion.[2]

Camden (or at least his translator) indicates that stage and scaffold could be inter–changeable terms. The scaffold is described here as a stage and Elizabethans quite often referred to theatrical stages as scaffolds. Stubbes's punishment was indeed a theatrical performance, a carefully choreographed display of power, and yet like all performances there was a risk that different spectators would interpret it in very different ways. At one level, Stubbes might have appeared to be playing the part that had been written for him. He endured his punishment and then thanked the absent, but nevertheless omnipresent, Queen for inflicting it upon him. At another level, however, the act of immediately doffing his hat with his left hand, while his right lay before him on the scaffold, might have been seen as a gesture of defiance rather than of deference. The performance of the spectators is just as difficult to interpret as that of the leading actor. Although their silence could certainly be read as an act of deference, Camden himself suggests reasons why it could also be seen as being much more defiant.

Renaissance executions and punishments inevitably contained much improvisation. Stubbes's hand was not, for instance, severed cleanly at the first attempt. Three blows were needed before it finally came off, the same number incidentally as were required to sever completely the heads of Mary, Queen of Scots in 1586, and the Earl of Essex in 1601. It is nevertheless still possible to identify a theatrical script that had to try to contain these sorts of improvised moments. The choreography of power often began with a ceremonial procession of privy councillors and other dignitaries to the place of execution. This was followed by the more grotesque procession that brought the condemned man or woman to the scaffold, usually after symbolic stops had been made along the way at locations that had some association with the crime. The soldiers who guarded the scaffold probably made their way there with some ceremony. After the various participants had made their entrances, it was time for a number of plays within the play. It was always possible that there might be a last minute reprieve while one of these plays was in performance. They might take the form of confessions, or sometimes the re–enactment of the crime itself. Although the practice in France was for those deemed to be heretics to be gagged, such victims were usually given every opportunity in England to make as full a confession as possible of what were taken to be their errors. Executions were in danger of losing their theatrical power if a prisoner who had promised to recant either religious or political views then refused to do so, as appears to have happened when Dr William Parry was brought to the scaffold in 1585 to be executed for allegedly plotting to kill Elizabeth.[3]

Although there was a general script for executions, their improvised moments always had the potential to disrupt the spectacle. The executioner was meant to be a sacrificer rather than a butcher who attacked those parts of the body, such as the bowels and 'privities', that were specifically associated with Satan and rebellion. His job was to display such grotesque parts of the body before they were eventually burnt. As Stubbes's punishment indicates, however, the executioner's own poor performance could put the preferred message of the play as a whole at risk. This is by no means an isolated example. Dr Roderigo Lopez and his accomplices were executed in 1594 for yet another alleged plot to kill Elizabeth.[4] As Lopez himself was Jewish by birth if not always by outward profession, it appeared that nothing could possibly go wrong with an execution that was staged in London at a time when there was intense hostility towards all those who could be demonized as 'alien strangers'. One of Lopez's alleged accomplices, Manuel Tinoco, managed to free himself from the gallows. He eventually had to be caught and held down so that his 'privities' could be attacked by the executioner. It seems that this muddle and incompetence, momentarily at least, turned the spectators against the spectacle.

A very similar moment occurred during the execution of the Babington conspirators in 1586. This was a more familiar Elizabethan dramatic script in which Catholics rather than Jews were cast as 'alien strangers'. Like Tinoco, John Savage attempted to escape from the incompetent clutches of his executioners: 'Savage broke the rope, and fell down from the gallows, and was presently seized on by the executioner, his privities cut off, and his bowels taken out while he was alive'.[5] More generally, the execution of the Babington conspirators illustrates the way in which the necessarily improvised parts of the play must have given at least some spectators the opportunity to resist the official messages of the play. John Ballard, a Catholic priest, and then Edward Abington both refused, like Dr Parry, to play the parts that had been written for them:

> [Ballard] craved pardon and forgiveness of all persons, to whom his doing had been any scandal, and so made an end; making his prayers to himself in Latin, not asking her majesty forgiveness, otherwise than 'if he had offended' ... And being urged by Dr White to be of a lively faith he [Abington] answered, he believed stedfastly in the catholic faith. The Doctor asked him, how he meant, for I fear me, said he, thou deceivest thyself: he answered, That faith and religion which is holden almost in all Christendom, except here in England. This done, he willed them not to trouble him any longer with any more questions, but made his prayers to himself in Latin ... Ballard was first executed. He was cut down and bowelled with great cruelty while he was alive. Babington beheld Ballard's Execution without being in the least daunted: whilst the rest turned away their faces, and fell to prayers upon their knees. Babington being taken down from the gallows alive too, and ready to be cut up, he cried aloud several times in Latin, *Parce mihi, Domine Jesu!* Spare me, O Lord Jesus![6]

Ballard only gestured towards the expected confession of guilt, preferring instead to say his own prayers in Latin. Abington had no interest in participating in a play within the play, which was meant to allow the member of the state church to be seen to win a theological dispute or dialogue. He too openly performed Catholic rituals rather than allowing himself to get drawn into the part that he was expected to perform. Babington also used the scaffold as a stage on which Catholic prayers and rituals could be performed.

Although the hostility of the spectators to such performances was almost inevitably commented on in the surviving contemporary accounts of these executions, this should not necessarily be seen as being the only response that they were capable of evoking. The incompetence of the executioner, together with the way in which Dr White failed to have the last word in his dispute, may have undermined the effectiveness of the official script. As almost all executions were public spectacles, there was always the danger that they were open to carnivalesque forms of reception. More specifically, the need to produce and display a demonic Catholicism in the open sight of spectators before it was then destroyed always ran the very real risk that it might in fact acquire a certain dignity in extreme adversity.

Recent historicist accounts of Renaissance punishment have been much influenced by Foucault's *Discipline and Punish: The Birth of the Prison*, first published in English in 1977.[7] Foucault highlights the precariousness of performance in order to suggest that public executions were phased out in the nineteenth century not for humanitarian reasons, but rather because they could not be relied upon to coerce all of the spectators all of the time. He shows, very productively, that this precariousness was in part the result of the ambiguous status of the executioner. This goes beyond simply a view of the executioner's almost proverbial incompetence and bad timing, towards seeing him as a figure who had the impossible theatrical role of impersonating both the monarch and the Devil. For Foucault, an execution was a play that was staged in a theatre of Hell. Agony had to be prolonged for as long as possible so that both the victim and the spectators were given a glimpse of the everlasting torments of Hell. The point that an execution represented not an end, but merely the prelude to endless torture, was reinforced by the way in which the spectacle continued after death. Dismemberment of the corpse, followed either by the burning or the display of its fragments, showed that death itself offered no release from punishment. The contradiction that interests Foucault here concerns the way in which this theatre of Hell was written and staged by the monarch. This meant that the executioner, while licensed to play the part of the Devil or Lucifer when he burnt and dismembered bodies, was still one of the monarch's representatives on the scaffold. The performance as a whole was precarious because a figure of rule could also be seen by spectators as embodying demonic misrule. As already implied, this potential for a dangerous confusion of categories is exploited at the end of one version of *Doctor Faustus* by allowing Lucifer's entrance, stage presence and speeches to be uncannily like those of a Renaissance prince. Lightborn, the executioner in *Edward II*, has a demonic name as well as a repertoire of diabolical methods and yet is employed by those who claim to be on the side of rule. As will become apparent, such categories also become badly confused during the execution of Barabas at the end of *The Jew of Malta.*

Although Foucault's work has been widely used in recent reconstructions of Renaissance executions, it should be emphasized that he himself does not deal with the punishments of this period. The snapshot, or vignette, that is used to establish the idea of bodily suffering as spectacle is taken from the eighteenth century. It is then juxtaposed with a series of longer vignettes about the birth of the Benthamite prison or penitentiary in which punishment takes the form of mental torture produced by both surveillance and self–surveillance. Foucault produces sharp and startling contrasts between one world which is quite literally dominated by theatricalized spectacle and another, more modern, world which is governed through surveillance. This means that he tends to ignore the evidence that suggests that spectacle and surveillance reinforced each other during the nineteenth century itself, and earlier periods. To take just one example, Elizabethan prisons were not always just used as lockups for those waiting to make their grotesque progress to the scaffold. Sir Francis Walsingham's spies or eyes, such as Robert Poley, kept long–stay 'political prisoners' under a form of close surveillance by contriving to share their cells and therefore their thoughts (compare Nicholl, 1992, 113, 135–7, 163–4, 336–7). Marlowe's own representation of the way in which Edward II is subjected to the psychological torture of depersonalization, disorientation and deprivation may have been based on practices that were common in some Elizabethan prisons. Although Foucault's thesis requires a great deal more of this kind of historical qualification, it is still valuable for the way in which it highlights the precariousness of performance.[8]

The execution of Barabas, like the punishment of Stubbes and the executions of the Babington conspirators, is open to different interpretations. Ferneze, the Governor of Malta, is a representation of a Renaissance prince who follows the official script of the theatre of rule as far as execution and punishment are concerned. As soon as he has Barabas in his power, thanks to the mercenary machinations of underworld characters rather than to his own effectiveness as a ruler, he gives orders for the prisoner to be tortured: 'Make fires, heat irons, let the rack be fetched' (5.1.23).[9] The rack was another stage or scaffold on which the theatre of Hell was played out: those who were deemed to have grotesque opinions were provided with bodies to match them. Barabas is not in fact tortured as Ferneze is persuaded, uncharacteristically, to wait and see whether there might be a voluntary confession. When the unexpected news arrives moments later that Barabas is dead, Ferneze orders the outcast to be cast out quite literally: 'For the Jew's body, throw that o'er the walls, / To be a prey for vultures and wild beasts' (5.1.55–6). Ferneze may have been deprived of the spectacle of Barabas's death but, in keeping with the official script for the theatre of Hell, he tries to make sure that punishment continues even after death itself.

Ferneze believes that divine intervention has been responsible for Barabas's capture and death: 'Wonder not at it, sir; the heavens are just' (5.1.52). Spectators are unlikely to accept this official script, which is then almost immediately made to look ridiculous anyway by the revelation that Barabas has in fact only been shamming death. He rises again from the dead and does not need anything like three days to do so. He and Ferneze therefore still have to resolve their struggle for power. This final conflict between them is given specifically theatrical dimensions. Barabas's overflowing rhetoric, reconstruction of the stage itself and ability to cue entrances at will all signify his power. It is a power that closely resembles that of the dramatist. Barabas and Ferneze need to be seen as rival playwrights who compete with each other for the authorship of the play in general and its final scene in particular. Spectators have a choice between supporting Barabas's improvised theatre of misrule and Ferneze's carefully choreographed theatre of rule. Such a choice would have been available to Elizabethan spectators, even when the play was revived during the period of anti–semitic hysteria that was generated by the trial and execution of Lopez and his alleged accomplices (see Dimock, 1813, 440–72; Wolf, 1924–7). Barabas's improvisations and frolics are capable of providing theatrical pleasure particularly when the only alternative that is offered to them is Ferneze's cold, formal and processional style of theatre. Marlowe often places his spectators in a difficult and perhaps an impossible position by seeming to ask them to applaud the death of the playwright, or entertainer, figure. Both Faustus and Gaveston in *Edward II* stage plays and shows within the plays themselves before they are executed. Applause is certainly sought by their executioners, but may not necessarily be given by spectators who have gained pleasure from their entertainments.

Ferneze's theatrical script calls for the public execution of an 'alien stranger'. Thanks to his careful rehearsal of some complicated stage business, it is Barabas rather than Calymath who falls through the trapdoor in the gallery into the cauldron below. Ironically, Barabas turns out to have built his own scaffold on the stage. The Knights of Saint John have recaptured the stage and therefore their power. Ferneze, who was forced to kneel before the Turks earlier on, is now able to command them to form an onstage audience for the spectacle of Barabas's suffering: 'See his end first' (5.5.71). Barabas himself tries to appeal to the spectators who are grouping themselves on stage to watch his execution: 'Governor, why stand you all so pitiless?' (5.5.73). Ferneze's orthodox script allows no pity for the condemned man and insists that there should be a spectacle of suffering in a theatre of Hell. Barabas then tries to subvert this spectacle by refusing to beg for forgiveness in his dying speech. His earlier control of the stage was characterized by the sheer speed of the events brought about by his improvisations. Now the tempo has changed dramatically: there is as suggested time for an audience to group itself selfconsciously on stage. Ferneze has always been a dramatist who writes scenes in which stage entrances and groupings are designed to display his power. Barabas is expected to make a confession to the spectators who are on the stage, or scaffold, as well as to those who surround it. However, he is defiant rather than deferential. He emphatically rejects the official script with its trite acknowledgements of divine intervention, blaming only his bad luck or fortune for his downfall:

> And had I but escap'd this stratagem,
> I would have brought confusion on you all,
> Damn'd Christians, dogs, and Turkish infidels!
> (5.5.86–8)

It is only the increasing 'extremity of heat' (5.5.89) that stops his mouth and therefore puts a stop to this subversion of the part that Ferneze has written for him.

Ferneze, the Renaissance ruler, readily supplies an orthodox conclusion to the spectacle of Barabas's suffering: 'So march away; and let due praise be given, / Neither to Fate nor Fortune, but to Heaven' (5.5.125–6). The Knights slowly and deliberately process off the stage or scaffold. Some Elizabethan spectators may certainly have marched away from the stage accepting such a resolution, just as others clearly left the scaffold feeling that Stubbes and the Babington conspirators had been justly punished. Spectators are nevertheless given some encouragement to question this resolution. There is a problem about the way in which Ferneze so openly commands and controls the onstage spectators. The Turks are in fact quite literally a captive audience. Perhaps Ferneze also wishes to enslave the paying customers. The mention of money complicates matters even more. Ferneze pockets the money extorted from the Jews at the beginning of the play. He probably takes a substantial cut from the profits of the slave market. It seems highly likely that he will keep the bag containing the 'hundred thousand pounds' (5.5.21) which he raised to pay Barabas for changing sides. Perhaps he is still carrying it when he delivers the orthodox resolution. He will almost certainly get a good ransom for Calymath. His final couplet is a terse and trite monologue of power which may nevertheless provoke, rather than suppress, dialogue and debate. He may not personally execute Barabas and yet, as he clearly enjoys presiding over the proceedings, it is possible that some of the contradictions that clung to the executioner become associated with him. His praise for 'Heaven' may not convince some of the spectators who have just seen him revel in a theatre of Hell.

Notes

1. My interest in representations of punishment in Marlowe's plays is shared by Karen Cunningham, (1990, 209–221), which I was not able to consult before the publication of my *Christopher Marlowe* (1991), which also deals extensively with forms of punishment. See especially Cunningham, 1990, 214 for a summary of the different kinds of punishment in Marlowe's plays.

2. William Camden, *Annales, The True and Royall History of the Famous Empresse Elizabeth Queene of England* ... (Benjamin Fisher, London, 1625 edn.), Bk.3, 16. Part one of the work appeared in Latin in 1615 (the spelling in this extract from the first published translation has been slightly modernized). In the English edition of 1688 the structure is described as 'a Scaffold:' *The History of the Most Renowned and Victorious Princess Elizabeth, late Queen of England: Selected Chapters*, ed. W. MacCaffrey, Chicago, 1970, 138–9.

3. See Smith, 1986, 11–19, for a good account of Parry's career as a government agent who may have become a double–agent. As I understand it, Smith's compelling thesis is that, given the mentality of the period, any agent had almost by definition to be at least a double–agent and yet was incapable of rationalizing such a necessity.

4. For more details of the Lopez scandal, see Gwyer, 1952, 163–84. For references to the revival of *The Jew of Malta* during this period, see *Henslowe's Diary*, ed. R. Foakes and R. Rickert, Cambridge, 1961.

5. *Cobbett's Complete Collection of State Trials and Proceedings for High Treason and Misdemeanors from the Earliest Period to the Present Time*, Hansard et al., London, 1809–26, 33, I, 1158.

6. Ibid., 1156–8.

7. For examples of such studies see Rebhorn, 1988 and Tennenhouse, 1986.

8. For an example of the way in which historians caution against applications of Foucault's thesis to the early modern period see Spierenburg, 1984. Other informative historical accounts include Nicolls, 1988, 49–73 and Sharpe, 1985, 144–67.

9. All quotations are from the Gill, 1971, edition.

9. Christopher Marlowe and Atheism

NICHOLAS DAVIDSON

Marlowe was well aware of his reputation for atheism. In 1592, when Henry Chettle published Robert Greene's description of him as one 'who hath said ... like the foole in his heart, There is no God', Marlowe reportedly took offence.[1] But more detailed charges were made against him the following year. On 18 May, 1593, a warrant for his apprehension was issued by the Privy Council, and two days later, he was brought to appear before the Council in person. On 27 May – just three days before his death – a 'Note' of his religious opinions was delivered, apparently to Sir John Puckering, Lord Keeper of the Great Seal and a member of the Queen's Privy Council, by Richard Baines. This document asserted that Marlowe had denied the divinity of Christ and the authority of the Scriptures; Moses was a 'juggler', Christ a sodomite, and religion nothing more than a means of social control. '[T]his Marlow doth not only hould [these opinions] himself but, almost into every company he cometh, he perswades men to atheism, willing them not to be afeard of bugbeares and hobgoblins, and utterly scorning both God and his ministers.' At about the same time, Baines's charge that Marlowe was an active proselytizer for atheism was corroborated by another informer in a document listing the beliefs of Richard Cholmeley, supposedly one of his 'converts'.[2]

Marlowe's reputation for atheism survived his death on 30 May 1593. Within a few weeks, Thomas Kyd had produced a further list of his opinions for Puckering, which confirmed some of the charges in the earlier documents, and added to them his hostility to prayers, his rejection of miracles, and his addition of St Paul to the ranks of 'jugglers'.[3] Four years later, Thomas Beard wrote that Marlowe was 'not inferiour' to any other sixteenth–century atheist: 'he denied God and his Sonne Christ, and not only in word blasphemed the trinitie, but also (as it is credibly reported) wrote bookes against it, affirming our Saviour to be but a deceiver, and Moses to be but a coniurer and seducer of the people, and the holy Bible to be but vaine and idle stories, and all religion but a device of pollicie'.[4] Many modern critics have concurred with such a judgement: Paul Kocher, for instance, describes Marlowe as 'a man of violently anti–Christian beliefs' (Bevington and Rasmussen, 1993, 23; Kocher, 1974, 68).

But how reliable is this contemporary evidence against Marlowe? Robert Greene, Richard Baines and Thomas Kyd certainly knew him personally, but their evidence cannot be accepted uncritically. Greene's account was written on his deathbed, and was designed more to justify his own recent conversion to religious faith than to document the beliefs of his acquaintances. Baines was a professional informer, and his charges were never tested in court. Kyd wrote his document against Marlowe while in prison, probably as part of an attempt to buy his own release. The anonymous denunciation of Richard Cholmeley deals with Marlowe only indirectly; Beard's later report is no more decisive, since there is no evidence that he had previously even met Marlowe. It is hardly surprising, then, that these statements about Marlowe have failed to find universal acceptance among recent scholars. Indeed, Charles Nicholl has argued that many of the documents used by historians as evidence of Marlowe's religious beliefs were produced to order as part of a campaign to discredit both Marlowe and Sir Walter Raleigh. If this is true, then we must obviously be doubly wary of placing any faith in their contents (see Kocher, 1974, 23–4; Nicholl, 1992, 44–6, 122–31, 236–9, 277–83, 288–90, 295–7, 308–9; Dutton, 1993, 3–4, 19–20).

So can we use Marlowe's plays and poems as more trustworthy evidence of his opinions? It is certainly tempting to assume that a writer's work must reflect his life, and that Marlowe's beliefs can therefore be identified among the statements he gave to his characters on stage.[5] There are, however, a number of good reasons for rejecting this assumption in Marlowe's case. Firstly, he wrote some of his plays in collaboration with other authors. *Dido Queen of Carthage* was written with Thomas Nashe, and work on *1 Tamburlaine the Great* and *Doctor Faustus* may also have been shared. Scholars have tried to determine which sections of these plays were written by which writer, but we can never be entirely sure that any one statement was Marlowe's own (see Bevington and Rasmussen, 1993, 19, 63–4, 70–1; Pendry and Maxwell, 1976, 191). Secondly, with the exception of *Tamburlaine*, which was published in 1590, our sources for the texts of the plays all post–date Marlowe's death. *Edward II* and *Dido* were published in 1594, *The Massacre at Paris* a little later, and *The Jew of Malta* not until 1633. *Doctor Faustus* survives in two different versions, published in 1604 and 1616 (see Pendry and Maxwell, 1993, xxxvi–xxxvii, 271). It is therefore impossible to exclude the possibility that what we read today may be the work of a later reviser rather than of Marlowe himself. In the case of *Doctor Faustus*, for instance, we know that Philip Henslowe paid William Bird and Samuel Rowley to make extensive additions in 1602, and it seems likely that the texts as printed incorporate further changes introduced by the acting companies that performed the play to great acclaim for many years after Marlowe's death. The same process of textual development may have helped to shape the surviving versions of Marlowe's other plays as well.[6]

Thirdly, we have to remember that Marlowe, his collaborators and revisers were all restricted to some degree by the terms of government censorship. As early as May 1559, a royal proclamation had required local officials to ensure that no plays were performed, in public or private, which dealt with 'matters of religion or of the governaunce of the estate of the common weale'; in the following month, another injunction prohibited the publication of plays which contained anything heretical, seditious, or 'unseemely for Christian eares'. In the 1570s and 1580s, the Common Council of London sought to establish even stricter controls over performances on the local stage, and in 1586, the government introduced a new licensing system for publications, requiring authors and printers to secure the approval of the archbishop of Canterbury or the bishop of London before printing any text (Chambers, 1923, IV, 263–5, 269–89, 303).

Marlowe's early plays were probably first performed in the later 1580s; but the failure of the existing licensing system to prevent the publication of the Marprelate Tracts in 1588 and 1589 seems to have provoked a further review of the regulations. On 12 December 1589, concerned that some acting companies had taken it 'upon themselves to handle in their plaies certen matters of Divinytie and of State unfitt to be suffred', the Privy Council proposed yet another new procedure. In future, all texts of plays for public performance were to be reviewed by representatives of the Lord Mayor of London and the Archbishop of Canterbury, and by the Master of the Revels, who were instructed to 'stryke oute or reforme suche partes and matters as they shall fynd unfytt and undecent to be handled in playes, both for Divinitie and State' (Chambers, 1923, IV, 305–6).[7] Further legislation in 1606 banned the use on stage (though not in publications) of the name of God, Christ, the Holy Ghost or the Trinity (Clare, 1990, 103; Dutton, 1993, 28–9).

It is impossible to calculate the exact impact of such censorship on the surviving texts of Marlowe's plays. The frequent repetition and revision of the relevant legislation might suggest an uneasy awareness among the authorities that its provisions were not being strictly enforced; and we know that in 1592, the Lord Mayor and aldermen of London sent complaints to Archbishop John Whitgift about the relatively tolerant attitude of one of the censors appointed in 1589, the Master of the Revels, Edmund Tilney (Chambers, 1923, IV, 307–9; Dutton, 1993, 15–19, 21–2, 26). But even if the censors intervened only rarely to alter the text of a play or publication, writers may well have moderated their expression in advance of the licensing process in order to avoid the need for later alterations. The works attributed to Christopher Marlowe which we read now may thus have been affected not just by the official censorship of the authorities, but also by the self–censorship of the author, his collaborators and revisers. We cannot therefore regard them as unambiguous evidence of Marlowe's own opinions.

Taken together, then, the sources available do not enable us to say that Marlowe was definitely an atheist – or that he was not. The 'problem' of his religious position can therefore never be finally resolved. At one level, of course, this conclusion can hardly surprise us. Religious dissent of any kind was dangerous in Tudor England, and men and women who did not believe in any God were unlikely to have seen much long–term benefit in suffering in this world for their opinions. We cannot therefore expect them to have revealed themselves readily at the time, and in such circumstances it is bound to be difficult for us to identify them convincingly now (compare Hill, 1984, 208). Many historians, however, have gone one step beyond these considerations of evidence and method to argue, not only that atheism is difficult to uncover, but that it could not have existed at all in the sixteenth century. The leading proponent of this view has been Lucien Febvre, whose *Problem of Unbelief in the Sixteenth Century* was first published in French in 1942. This book seeks to demonstrate that the period lacked the mental equipment to reject the Christian religion: that intellectual unbelief was actually impossible in the sixteenth century. Its conclusion, indeed, is entitled 'A Century that Wanted to Believe' (Febvre, 1982, 131–41, 455–64; compare Wootton, 1985, 83; Wootton, 1988, 695–730; Wootton, 1992, 16–17.).

This is not to deny, of course, that terms such as 'atheism' were used before 1600. There are plenty of references to 'atheists' in the records of the time – including the intriguing spelling out of the word 'atheo' by Robin in the B text of *Doctor Faustus* (2.2.8). But these words were, it is argued, used very loosely. Often, they served only as a smear against a personal enemy. In 1572, for example, creditors of the poet George Gascoigne sent a petition to the Privy Council, requesting that he be excluded from his seat as member of Parliament for Midhurst in Sussex. Their main argument was that he was using his elected position to avoid paying his debts; but, to add strength to their case, they also claimed that he was 'noted as well for manslaughter as for other greate crymes .... a notorious ruffianne and especiallie noted to be bothe a spie, an Atheist and godlesse personne'.[8] Contemporaries often linked immorality with atheism in this way, and we should obviously therefore beware of taking such references too literally. Gascoigne had certainly had a colourful life before this date, but there is no corroborative evidence to suggest that he had adopted any serious intellectual unbelief. We should be equally suspicious when we find Marlowe's critics resorting to the same tactic – as in 1598, when Francis Meres used Marlowe's murder to make the moral point that 'our tragicall poet Marlow for his Epicurisme and Atheisme had a tragicall death'.[9]

The conclusion of Lucien Febvre, then, is that in the sixteenth century, words such as 'atheist' and 'atheism' had no precise intellectual connotation, and were used mainly as terms of abuse or as a literary device on which to hang more orthodox arguments. Febvre's thinking has had a significant influence on students of Marlowe. Gordon Campbell, for instance, has used Febvre to support his suggestion that 'Marlowe could not have been an atheist because that way of thinking was not available to anyone, however radical and intelligent' in the sixteenth century; Marlowe was 'irrevocably locked in the mental world of the Renaissance' (1992, 518–20). Stephen Greenblatt has made the same point a little more hesitantly: 'the stance that seems to come naturally to the greenest college freshman in late twentieth–century America seems to have been almost unthinkable to the most daring philosophical minds of late sixteenth–century England' (1981, 43).

The key to Febvre's argument is the assumption that an atheistic understanding of the world became possible only in the later seventeenth century, once the impact of natural science had made possible the rejection of inherited Christian teaching. When Febvre mentioned science, he was thinking particularly of Descartes; yet natural science predated Descartes, and the impact of scientific thought on religious debates can be traced well before the later seventeenth century. In 1592, for example, Thomas Nashe referred in his *Pierce Penilesse* to recent mathematical calculations that had cast doubt on the chronology and historical accuracy of the scriptures.[10]

Throughout the Renaissance, though, the work of ancient scientists also helped to shape contemporary thought. The most influential ancient author in this context was probably Aristotle. Since the Middle Ages, his works had provided many of the compulsory texts on university syllabuses, and his arguments about God, the world, and the soul were therefore familiar to all educated men. It is interesting to note, for example, that at the celebrated discussion over dinner at Sir George Trenchard's house in the summer of 1593 in which Raleigh was involved, Raphe Ironside began his defence of Christian teaching on the soul by citing Aristotle's *De Anima*, a text all graduates would have known intimately. When the discussion moved on to the nature of God, Mr. John Fitjames quoted Aristotle once again.[11] But everyone knew that Aristotle's opinions could be meshed with Christianity only after a struggle. The detail of his teaching was subject to continual debate, but many Renaissance writers argued that Aristotle and his followers had believed in the eternity of the world and the natural mortality of the human soul: beliefs directly at odds with orthodox Christian doctrine, which insists that the world was created by God and that the soul survives the death of the body (Febvre, 1982, 207, 272). A document of 1571 in the Public Record Office, for example, is entitled a 'confutation of the atheists opynyon as Aristotle etc: who foleshely doeth affyrme the world to be wythout begynnyng'. The work of Aristotle could therefore serve to feed unorthodox beliefs long before the Scientific Revolution highlighted by Febvre (Hunter, 1985, 140).

Among other ancient authors credited with a dangerous influence, we might also consider Epicurus and his followers who, it was believed, had denied the providence of God as well as the immortality of the soul and the afterlife; Cicero, whose *De divinatione* rejects belief in prophecy; and Lucretius, whose *De rerum natura* discounts the possibility of divine

133

providence and the afterlife, as well as the divine creation and miracles.[12] Another important figure was Lucian, who made fun of the gods. Gabriel Harvey called Marlowe 'a Lucian', and Lucian's *Dialogues* were available in the huge private library of John Gresshop, Marlowe's former headmaster at the King's School in Canterbury (Bakeless, 1942, 127; Urry, 1988, 116–17). There were many others. These texts, these ideas, were therefore readily available in the sixteenth century. The point is that pagan writings from the ancient world provided many powerful arguments against orthodox Christian teaching, quite independent of, and much earlier than, seventeenth–century science. The Renaissance interest in the classics could thus have provided the starting point for a number of potentially dangerous religious speculations.

Not surprisingly, worries about the possible influence of Greek and Roman writers appear regularly in Renaissance authors. But travellers outside England had access to an even wider range of sources for unbelief. In 1570, for instance, Roger Ascham deplored the effect of study in Italy, where, he believed, dangerous intellectual speculation went unchecked. According to Ascham, Italian books 'shall easily corrupt the mynde with ill opinions, and false iudgement in doctrine: first, to thinke ill of all trewe Religion, and at last to thinke nothyng of God hym selfe, one speciall pointe that is to be learned in Italie and Italian bookes'. Englishmen who have lived in Italy, he says, are 'Epicures in living, and αθεοι in doctrine'; they come to reject the Bible and religion altogether as instruments of 'Civill policie'.[13] A number of Italian authors were thought to foster unbelief, including Boccaccio, whose book on the generation of the gods was also held in Gresshop's library in Canterbury, and Giordano Bruno, who lectured in Oxford in 1583 and lived in London for two years after that.[14]

Ascham's last point, about religion as an instrument of civil policy, recalls the most celebrated Italian author of them all, Machiavelli. Despite regular prohibitions on his works in Italy, manuscript and printed versions of *Il principe* and *I discorsi* continued to circulate in Tudor England. William Harrison, for example, referred to Machiavelli in his 'Chronology' in the early 1530s: 'of whom I stand in doubt whether he were indeed with most worldlie witte or less relligion of any man living in his time'.[15] By the 1580s, both of Machiavelli's best known works had been translated into English, and by the last years of the century, his thought was quite familiar among educated Englishmen (Raab, 1964, 30, 52–3, 274). Indeed, John Dove's *Atheism Defined and Confronted*, published in 1605, makes special mention of the 'Englishmen Italianat' who, following Machiavelli, profess religion only for political advantage (Aylmer, 1978, 33). Machiavelli's views were not all original, of course; but his influence was often blamed for introducing the idea that religion was invented to maintain public order. Robert Greene certainly claimed that Marlowe had been influenced by Machiavelli, and the

Italian makes a personal appearance at the beginning of *The Jew of Malta* to assert that:

> I count religion but a childish toy,
> And hold there is no sin but ignorance.
> (Prologue 14–15)[16]

Other characters in the plays are deliberately associated with Italy or use Italian words in their speech: Gaveston and Lightborn in *Edward II*, and Guise in *The Massacre at Paris*, who confesses, again in Machiavellian fashion, that 'My policy hath fram'd religion' (*Massacre*, 2.65–9; *Edward II*, 1.1.22, 1.4.412–13, 2.5.5, 5.4.31).

Given the availability of so many dangerous ideas, derived particularly from the ancient world or modern Italy, it is perhaps not surprising that books, sermons, and even plays against alternative beliefs were so common in Tudor England, whether written in English or translated from other languages. Such apologias followed a long tradition, of course: Christians had written in defence of their faith throughout the Middle Ages.[17] But they had become especially numerous by the 1580s and early 1590s, when anxiety about atheism in England seems to have been on the increase. In 1591, for instance, William Lambarde told Sir John Leveson that, when selecting military commissioners for Kent, he should take care that 'they ought to be, not only no papistes, but no Libertines, or Atheists, whoe are (next to the papistes) the most daungerous' (quoted in Aylmer, 1978, 24). These late sixteenth–century texts deal explicitly with a number of the arguments we have already touched on: the existence of God, the origin of the world, the extent of divine providence, the immortality of the soul, the authority of scripture, the role of reason and morality. They make a fascinating study, for they provide us with an image of what the 'atheist' was deemed to believe. In 1593, for example, Thomas Nashe characterized two types of atheists in his *Christs Teares over Ierusalem*, the careless and the deliberate. The first, he wrote, forget God and heaven as a result of too great a preoccupation with life in this world; the second come to believe by reasoning that 'there is no God' and no resurrection, no divine providence and no creator. These intellectual atheists, he insists, 'followe the Pironicks, whose position and opinion it is that there is no Hel or misery but opinion'; they deny the accuracy of the scriptures and call Moses a magician.[18]

But such texts also reveal the enormous effort which orthodox writers devoted to the task of blocking the growth of 'atheism', and it is hard to believe that so many people thought it worth their while to attack so often and so thoroughly something that did not exist, or that could not have existed. And their efforts may have been ultimately counterproductive, for they guaranteed that the arguments against orthodox Christianity which they were attacking remained permanently in circulation. During the Cerne Abbas investigation of 1594, for example, Robert Hyde reported that his brother had learned of a 'sect' that denied the existence of hell, heaven, God, the devil and the immortal soul from an orthodox sermon against it.[19] Another telling example is the summary of unitarian arguments derived from John Procter's *Fal of the Late Arrian*, published in London in 1549, which turned up among the papers of Thomas Kyd over forty years later. The precise origin of the document found in Kyd's possession remains unknown, but it is clear that in this case, Procter's refutation had served as much to foster his opponent's arguments against the divinity of Christ as to undermine them.[20]

But merely to point to some ready sources of unbelief and atheism does not in itself demonstrate that unbelief and atheism existed in sixteenth–century England. What we know of the cultural life of the late Renaissance, however, suggests that such ideas did in fact play a part in contemporary intellectual debate. The Cerne Abbas investigation of 1594 provides evidence of the sort of open speculation that could take place on fundamental religious and philosophical matters. And religious doubt was certainly no unfamiliar experience in this period. In March 1519, for example, Elizabeth Sculthorp told the court of the Bishop of Lincoln 'that since Whitsunday last she has not had perfect nor steadfast belief in God' (Wootton, 1985, 82). Such private uncertainties appear also in the autobiographical writings of later Protestant writers, which frequently record their doubts about the existence of God, heaven or hell. In some cases, of course, uncertainty could turn to conviction, and Protestant groups such as the Socinians turned extreme unorthodoxy into their own orthodoxy in the seventeenth century (Thomas, 1971, 199–202; Hunter, 1985, 154).

So we have, then, a period in which ancient ideas, stimulus from abroad, and the arguments of anti–atheist writers could feed private speculation, religious doubt and doctrinal heterodoxy: a ferment of debate long before the seventeenth century, in which the most dangerous theories could develop. And in recent years a number of historians have begun to uncover information about some of the individuals who contributed to this debate – figures such as the 'Athiest' John Minet, a lay reader at East Drayton in Nottinghamshire, who, it was claimed in the Court of High Commission at York in 1589, 'hath openlie and manifestlie reported that ther is no god, no devill, no heaven, no hell, no lyf after this lyf, no iudgment to come'; or John Baldwin, who in a Star Chamber case of 1595 'questioned whether there were a god; if there were, howe he showld be knowne; if by his worde, who wrote the same; if the prophets and the Apostles, they were but men, *et humanum est errare*' (Aylmer, 1978, 31–2; O'Mara, 1987, 183–4; Hunter, 1985, 137). Another example, not previously noted, is the case of Christopher Stremar, a Protestant born in England, who in 1610 made a public confession in Livorno, Italy, that he had previously denied the existence of God, the devil, heaven and hell; everything was governed by nature, and only fools would believe otherwise, for religion was invented to coerce and govern men.[21]

The beliefs associated with such individuals is very wide ranging. Many of them rejected the doctrine of creation, believing, with the Aristotelians, that the world had no beginning or end. In 1573, for example, Robert Master at Woodchurch in Kent was reported 'for that he denyeth that god made the Sune, the Moone, the earth, the water' (Jenkins, 1911, 314). Associated with this was often a denial of the authority of the Bible which reports the divine act of creation. In December 1584, a priest called John Hilton confessed at Westminster that he had preached a sermon at St Martin–in–the–Fields in which he had claimed 'that the Old and New Testaments are but Fables'. And if the Gospels were the work of human imagination, then Christ's divinity was cast in doubt too: Hilton also confessed that he had denied the doctrine of the Trinity.[22] Several individuals were executed for such unitarian beliefs in the 1570s and 1580s, though not all cases were necessarily punished so severely: in 1579, John Boyce of Stock, Essex, was merely assigned a penance 'for lykening the Trinitie to a foote ball playe' (Hale, 1847, 173; compare also Hale, 175–6; Emmison, 1973, 110; Buckley, 1932, 56–8.). Some went further, however, calling Christ an impostor. This accusation can be traced at least as early as the thirteenth century, and it was sometimes extended to cover Moses and Mohammed as well. The religions associated with them – Christianity, Judaism, and Islam – had, it was occasionally suggested, all been invented for political purposes only, to aggrandize their founders and to secure the power of secular rulers. In 1581, for example, the Earl of Oxford was accused of asserting that the Trinity was a fable and the Scriptures just for 'policy'.[23] Similar doubts were associated with church teaching on the afterlife: in 1587, it was reported of Augustine Draper of Leigh 'that he doth not acknowledge the immortalitie of the sowle; and by his owne speches he hath affirmed the same' (Hale, 1847, 193–4; Emmison, 1973, 110; compare Aylmer, 1978, 31).[24]

The 'atheistic' beliefs attributed to Marlowe were therefore by no means exceptional. It might be argued, however, that much of this information is taken from trial documents, and that it is consequently inherently unreliable. It is certainly true that we cannot assume that all accusations or depositions in all trials are necessarily accurate; but we cannot assume either that they are all necessarily false (compare Wootton, 1992, 18–21, 30–1). And the very fact that such charges were made so often surely indicates that they were a familiar feature of contemporary patterns of thought. If atheism were not an intellectual possibility in the sixteenth and early seventeenth centuries, not even the most malevolent of informers could have invented it. It is also worth noting that in a number of these cases, the 'atheist' elements emerged only by chance. Many suspects had initially been investigated for other matters entirely, and reports of their unbelief refer back to events some weeks or months earlier (compare Hunter, 1985, 137, 151–3). A good deal of atheistic speculation might therefore have gone unnoticed and unprosecuted, and the courts are not likely to have investigated every suspect 'atheist' in the kingdom. Incredulity may in fact have been quite common.[25] Of course, we cannot put any figures on its frequency; nor can we always say how carefully constructed such beliefs might have been. But some contemporary writers thought that the authorities' response to it was much too lax, and it was not perhaps always seen as a very serious offence (Hunter, 1985, 138).

And it is in this context, perhaps, of extensive religious doubt and occasional orthodox investigation, that the charges against Raleigh and Marlowe should be considered. Raleigh's reputation certainly survived him: Christopher Stremar, the Englishman investigated at Livorno in 1610, told his interrogator 'that in England there was a man called Sir Walter Raleigh who used to say that everything was governed by nature ... and that all [religions] were invented for the benefit of civil government'.[26] In the light of the other cases we have examined, the beliefs attributed to Raleigh and his associates do not really seem so unusual. Witnesses in the Cerne Abbas investigation suggested a denial of the existence of God and the authority of scripture, a mockery of Moses and Christ, and a rejection of immortality, Heaven and Hell. Much of this evidence came from men who had been present at the discussions reported. It is nonetheless difficult to construct a coherent 'philosophy' for Raleigh's group as a whole. They seem to have picked up a variety of ideas already in circulation, and to have discussed them together long before the official investigation. Raleigh's statements on the soul, for example, had been made openly some nine months before the trial; but nobody had thought to denounce him earlier.[27]

The charges laid against Marlowe are, for the most part, equally familiar. He was not by any means the only person charged in Tudor England with denying the existence of God, Heaven and Hell, for asserting that the Bible was false, for insulting Christ and Moses, or for insisting that religion was invented to keep men in awe. He had had access, in Canterbury and Cambridge, to many of the ancient and modern sources of alternative ideas – his scholarship has never been in doubt – and his reputation for atheism was established well before the formal accusations of 1593, as Robert Greene's reference in the previous year demonstrates. And some of the assertions associated with 'atheism' in the contemporary literature can be found in the texts of his plays. In *1 Tamburlaine*, Techelles refers to 'Nature', not God, as creating form out of 'eternal chaos' (3.4.75–6), and Tamburlaine himself slips a sly note of doubt into his exhortation to Muslims to:

Seek out another godhead to adore:
The God that sits in heaven, if any god,
For he is God alone, and none but he.
(5.1.198–200)

Faustus argues that the notions of the afterlife are but 'trifles and mere old wives' tales'.[28] He similarly scorns the Bible (A–text, 1.1.38–50), while the Evil Angel tells him (at 2.1.18–19) that prayer and other religious practices are:

Rather illusions, fruits of lunacy,
That makes men foolish that do trust them most.

Barabas likewise warns his daughter in *The Jew of Malta* that religion 'Hides many mischiefs from suspicion' (1.2.281; compare also 1.2.96, 161–2).

Of course, in all the plays, such subversive arguments are overcome by a dominant Christian orthodoxy: Tamburlaine, Faustus and Barabas do not die happy or at peace. It is difficult to imagine the Elizabethan censors tolerating anything less. But what is important from our point of view is that these lines (and many others that are similar) were nonetheless included in the printed versions of the plays (Greenblatt, 1980, 293, n. 31; Greenblatt, 1981, 44; Dutton, 1993, 20, 27).[29] They thus helped to keep alternative ideas in circulation. At times, indeed, they are accorded almost equal status with more conventional statements. In *Doctor Faustus*, for instance, the traditional condemnation of Faustus's actions is taken over from the play's chief source, *The Historie of the damnable life, and deserved death of Doctor Iohn Faustus*, published for the first time possibly in 1588;[30] but several less traditional elements were added to it, including Faustus's rejection of theology as 'Unpleasant, harsh, contemptible, and vile' (A–text, 1.1.111). And throughout the play, the Good Angel and the Evil Angel are given the same number of lines to present their rival positions. The use of a formal literary debate to advance unorthodox ideas is well attested in the sixteenth century; but what matters here is not just the intention of the dramatist, but also the potential reaction of the audience. Readers and viewers will have recognized the 'dominant ideology' of the plays; but they might have remembered the subversive arguments embedded within them, too (compare Marcus, 1989, 22; Bevington and Rasmussen, 1993, 6–7, 23–6, 37; Greenblatt, 1981, 42; Davidson, 1992, 72).

If the charges made against Marlowe by Baines and Kyd were neither exceptional nor new, however, we need to ask why they were presented to the authorities only in the spring of 1593. The explanation seems to be related to contemporary political preoccupations. The threat to the Crown from Catholic

Europe had not been destroyed by the defeat of the Armada in 1588, and the established Church was still vulnerable to the influence of determined Protestant reformers at home. As a result, the government became increasingly nervous of religious dissent of any kind in the later 1580s and early 1590s (for background, see Outhwaite, 1985, 23–43; Neale, 1957, 241–2, 244–5, 260, 280–1, 291; and compare Buckley, 1932, 92–4). As we have seen, censorship was reformed in the wake of the Marprelate Tracts of 1588–9, and action against puritans and separatists was stepped up at the same time. Many Protestant dissenters were imprisoned; some were executed. Persecution of Catholics was also intensified, and observers from both sides of the religious divide claimed by 1593 that the government was seeking to introduce a new 'Inquisition' into England.[31]

In February of that year, bills were introduced in Parliament to stiffen the penalties imposed on anyone who failed to attend the local parish church. The extraordinarily wide scope of these bills raised alarm among some MPs (including Sir Walter Raleigh), and it was clear from the debates that the government did intend to use the new legislation to prosecute all dissenters, whatever their private religious opinion.[32] It certainly allowed for the examination of those who avoided the Church because they rejected its teaching, and the following months saw continued government action against dissenters who were labelled neither Catholic nor Protestant. On 20 May, for instance, the Privy Council wrote to Whitgift, ordering him to investigate the 'very blasphemous, disobedient, and unreverent speeches uttered by Mr Richard Danvers [of Reading] upon small occasion (as yt seemeth)'.[33]

It is interesting to note that this letter was dated on the same day that Marlowe appeared before the Privy Council in answer to the warrant of 18 May (Dasent, 1901, XXIV, 244). It may also be significant that Baines's and Kyd's documents on his religious opinions were delivered to Sir John Puckering, who was responsible at the time for collecting information about Protestant and Catholic dissenters and recusants.[34] It seems, then, as if Marlowe's case became involved in a much wider official campaign against religious dissent; the investigation of Raleigh in 1594 formed part of the same campaign (BL, Harleian MS 7042, fo. 206r).

The immediate cause of Marlowe's apprehension remains unclear, however. Richard Baines's 'Note' of his religious opinions was delivered to the Privy Council on 27 May, almost ten days after the warrant for his arrest – by which time the Council had already released him on condition that he report to them daily. It is thus impossible to be sure that the Council's initial interest in him sprang from any concern about his 'atheism'. Some scholars have recently preferred to link his arrest to the 'Dutch Church Libel', a document affixed to the wall of the Dutch churchyard in Broad Street, London, on 5 May 1593, which threatened a massacre of foreign residents in the city, and which made explicit reference to Tamburlaine, though not to Marlowe. Others have suggested that the Council saw Marlowe more as a potential informant than as a suspect. In either case, the Baines 'Note' might have been put together by men fearful of what he could reveal in order to discredit him before the Council (see Freeman, 1973, 44–52; Dutton, 1993, 4–5, 26–7; Marcus, 1989, 16; Bartels, 1993, 16). It is obviously impossible now to unravel the full story. What does seem clear, though, is that, as in many other cases of 'atheism', details of Marlowe's religious opinions became of interest to the authorities only after his arrest.

Those opinions, as we have seen, were not exceptional. The only unusual feature of the documents against Marlowe is the reference in Baines's 'Note' to his opinion 'That St John the Evangelist was bed–fellow to Christ and leaned alwaies in his bosome, that he used him as the sinners of Sodoma' (compare n. 2 above). Kyd's evidence seemed to corroborate this charge: 'He wold report St John to be our saviour Christes Alexis I cover it with reverence and trembling that is that Christ did love him with an extraordinary love' (compare n. 3 above). The nature of the relationship between Christ and 'the disciple whom Jesus loved', traditionally identified as John the son of Zebedee and the author of the Fourth Gospel, had long been a matter for speculation. In the twelfth century, for example, St Aelred of Rievaulx had discussed the 'special love' of Christ and St John; but he had emphasized very strongly that it was a spiritual love only, 'with no hint in it of the pleasures of the flesh'.[35] The suggestion that Christ and St John were sodomites, and the likening of their relationship to that of Alexis and Corydon, which is depicted in Virgil's *Eclogues* as explicitly homosexual, is remarkably daring.[36] Sodomy and homosexuality both appear in Marlowe's writings; but there seems to be no precedent for such a startling assertion in any other English trial records, nor in the anti–atheist literature.

It does, however, appear occasionally in cases in Italy. In 1550, for instance, fra Francesco Calcagno was denounced in Brescia for saying that Christ 'was merely human, and that he often had carnal knowledge of St John, whom he used as his minion (*cinedo*)'. In fact, the documents listing Marlowe's beliefs echo several of the charges against Calcagno: it was alleged, for example, that Calcagno had said 'that God does not exist ... and that when the body dies, the soul dies also', that he gave more faith to Ovid than the Gospels, that the Bible had been written to frighten its readers so that its authors could rule the world – and 'that he would rather worship a pretty little boy in the flesh than God'.[37]

So while most of the charges contained in the documents presented by Baines and Kyd can be explained away as nothing more than the usual 'atheistic' smears and insults familiar from many other cases, the origin of the charge about Christ and St John is more difficult to trace. It is possible that

Baines and Kyd just invented it, or that they picked it up from some Italian source. Baines was certainly well travelled. But, given the long list of standard opinions they already wanted to attribute to Marlowe, it is difficult to see what advantage they foresaw in adding such a bizarre novelty to their accusations. In a sense, then, the very rarity of this charge in other English records is an indication of its authenticity: Baines and Kyd could only have recorded such an unusual charge because they really had heard Marlowe talk in such terms about Christ and St John. If this is so, its inclusion in their documents increases the likelihood that the other charges against Marlowe were also accurate. Nobody who claimed that Christ and St John were sodomites is likely to have believed at the same time in the doctrine of the Trinity, the authority of scripture, or even the existence of the Christian God.

– – –

When Lucien Febvre insisted that 'it is absurd and puerile ... to think that the unbelief of men in the sixteenth century, insofar as it was a reality, was in any way comparable to our own', he was clearly correct. We should not expect sixteenth–century 'atheism' to be exactly the same as twentieth–century atheism: 'unbelief changes with the period' (Febvre, 1982, 460). But we should not conclude from this that the word 'atheism' had no meaning before the seventeenth century. Contemporaries repeatedly associated it with a limited set of non–Christian beliefs that were entirely consistent with each other. And there is plenty of evidence that these beliefs were regularly discussed and sometimes accepted by individuals before and during Marlowe's lifetime. Thus, while it is true that the records available will never allow us to conclude with confidence that Marlowe was an atheist, the opinions attributed to him in the documents produced in and before 1593 are certainly plausible. And even if the charges against him were produced by his enemies, we need not on that account reject them as necessarily false. The Baines 'Note', and Kyd's later accusations, merely added detail to Marlowe's existing reputation.

Marlowe's case was therefore not aberrant: he can be placed within a documented tradition of anti–Christian thought. So can his plays, which present many of the arguments characteristic of that tradition, and whose texts were repeatedly revised after his death to keep them profitable (Marcus, 1989, 13–14, 22–4). The scandalous reputation of their first author may well, indeed, have helped to maintain their appeal in the seventeenth century. In this way, Marlowe's contribution to the history of unbelief survived his death. The dominant Christian ideology of the early–modern period was by no means able to secure an absolute monopoly.

Notes

For generous advice and assistance when preparing this essay, I am grateful to Dr Terry Hartley, Dr Richard Palmer, Professor Adriano Prosperi and Dr Peter Roberts, and especially to Dr Shearer West. References to Marlowe's works are taken from Pendry and Maxwell, 1976, except for quotations from *Doctor Faustus*, which come from Bevington and Rasmussen, 1993.

1. Robert Greene, *Groats–worth of Witte, bought with a million of Repentance*, London, 1592, E4v–F1r; for Marlowe's reaction, see Henry Chettle, *Kind Heartes Dreame*, 1592, ed. G. B. Harrison, London, 1923, 5–6. The 'fool' appears in Psalms 14.1 and 53.1.

2. Baines's 'Note' appears in British Library (BL), Harleian MS 6848, fos. 185r–6v; it is printed in Kocher, 1974, 34–6, and in Pendry and Maxwell, 1976, 513–14. An edited version, sent to the Queen, is in Harleian MS 6853, fos. 307r–8v; compare also Harleian MS 7042, fo. 206r. The warrant for Marlowe's arrest, and the report of his appearance before the Privy Council, are printed in Dasent, 1901, 244. The charges against Cholmeley are in Harleian MS 6848, fo. 190r–v; compare Harleian MS 7002, fo. 10r–11v, and Harleian MS 7042, fo. 206r.

3. Kyd's undated evidence is in BL, Harleian MS 6848, fo. 154r; it is printed in Tucker Brooke, 1930, 107–8. Compare also Harleian MS 6849, fos. 218r–19v.

4. Thomas Beard, *The Theatre of Gods Iudgments*, London, 1597, 147–8.

5. Compare, however, the warnings in Dutton, 1993, 1, and Bevington and Rasmussen, 1993, 23.

6. For the texts of *Doctor Faustus*, see especially Marcus, 1990, 3–24; Bevington and Rasmussen, *Doctor Faustus*, 49–51, 63–4, 71–6; Dutton, 1993, 11. These authors' interpretations of the differences between the A– and B–texts are not always consistent with each other.

7.   The Queen was always nervous about the public discussion of matters of Church and State: compare Lambeth Palace Library (LP), MS 2019, fo. 5r, a report of the speech from the Queen read in Parliament on 28 February 1593.

8.   Public Record Office, SP Dom 12/86/59; this is printed in Prouty, 1942, 61. I am grateful to Peter Roberts for drawing Gascoigne's case to my attention.

9.   *Francis Meres's Treatise 'Poetrie'*, ed. D. Allen, Urbana, 1933, 84; the authority for Meres' view was Thomas Beard.

10. *The Works of Thomas Nashe*, ed. R. McKerrow, London, 1910, 5 vols, vol. 1, 172.

11. *Willobie His Avisa*, 1594, ed. G. Harrison, London, 1926, 266–8; compare *Edward II*, 4.6.17–19.

12. See for example Beard, *Theatre of Gods Iudgments*, 139; Febvre, 1982, 227–8, 271.

13. *Roger Ascham: English Works*, ed. W. A. Wright, Cambridge, 1904, 229–33; compare *Sir Thomas Browne: Selected Writings*, ed. G. Keynes, London, 1968, 27, for Browne's reference to an Italian physician who doubted the immortality of the soul.

14. For Boccaccio, see Urry, 1988, 119; for Bruno, see the letter of Sir Henry Cobham to Sir Francis Walsingham dated 28 March 1583 in Spampanato, 1921, 329, n. 4. Bruno's speculations on the eternity of the world appear in his *De l'infinito, universo e mondi*, first published in 1584 when he was resident in London. See also Bossy, 1991, 149.

15. BL, Add. MS 70984, fo. 236v. I am again indebted to Peter Roberts for informing me of this recent acquisition.

16. See Greene, *Groats–worth*, E4v–F1r; compare also Hunter, 1985, 141.

17. See for example the arguments for the existence of God presented by the *Proslogion* of St Anselm of Canterbury (c.1077–8), especially caps 2–5; or by the *Speculum caritatis* of St Aelred of Rievaulx (c.1142–3), lib. 1, cap. 6. Both authors pick up the psalmist's reference to the 'fool'.

18. Nashe, *Works*, ed. McKerrow I, 114–29; see also for example, Lyly, *Euphues*, part I, of 1578; Philip of Mornay, *A Woorke concerning the trewnesse of the Christian Religion, written in French: Against Atheists, Epicures, Paynims, Iewes, Mahumetists, and other Infidels,* London, 1587; and Cyril Tourneur's *Atheist's Tragedy*, published in 1611. Compare Buckley, 1932; Aylmer, 1978, 22, 30; Hunter, 1985, 139–41, 144–7.

19. *Willobie*, ed. Harrison, 269–70. Compare also Hunter, 1985, 149–50.

20. A copy of Procter's *Arrian* was held in Gresshop's library in Canterbury. See Kocher, 1974, 24; Urry, 1988, 116.

21. Pisa, Archivio Arcivescovile, *Inquisizione*, b. 4, letter of R. Sherwood to the archbishop, Livorno, 31 March 1610. I am most grateful to Adriano Prosperi for providing me with copies of documents from this trial.

22. BL, Lansdowne MS 982, fos. 46r–7r; compare John Strype, *The Life and Acts of the Most Reverend Father in God, John Whitgift*, London, 1718, 210; Thomas, 1971, 201–4; Hunter, 1985, 149–50.

23. Hunter, 1985, 149. The Earl of Oxford had been in Venice in 1575–6: see Venice, Archivio di Stato, *Santo Uffizio*, b. 41, 'Cocco Orazio'; Brown and Cavendish Bentinck, 1890, 527, 548. Professor Alan Nelson is completing a new study of Oxford. For the 'three impostors', see Buckley, 1932, 131; Nicholl, 1992, 56, 353.

24. The Familists believed that the notion of hell was allegorical: John Strype, *The Life and Acts of Matthew Parker*, London, 1711, 437.

25. Compare Hill, 1984, 210. Incredulity in the fifteenth century is discussed in Thomas, 1971, 199–200.

26. Pisa, Archivio Arcivescovile, *Inquisizione*, b. 4, interrogation of 3 April 1610. Raleigh's name appears as 'Ser Vueart Rale'; he died in 1618. For his continued reputation, see Nicholl, 1992, 298–9, and compare the allegations of the Jesuit Robert Parsons in 'Andreas Philopater', *Elizabethae, Angliae Reginae haeresim Calvinianam propugnantis, saevissimum in Catholicos sui Regni edictum*, Augsburg, 1592, 36; and the English version, *An Advertisement written to a secretarie of my L. Treasurers of Ingland*, 1592, 18. The *Advertisement* was probably

compiled by Richard Verstegan.

27. *Willobie His Avisa*, ed. Harrison, 255–71. One of the commissioners hearing the evidence had himself been present at the dinner with Raleigh and Ironside the previous summer: 211–13. Compare also Kocher, 1974, 12–13. Aylmer calls Raleigh 'more ... an intermittent patron of heterodox ideas than ... an unbeliever himself' (1978, 23).

28. *Doctor Faustus*, A–text, 2.1.138; compare 2.1.130, 2.3.6–7; and Greenblatt, 1980, 210 on Tamburlaine's 'anti–transcendentalism'.

29. Compare Bartels, 1993, 12.

30. *The English Faust Book: A Critical Edition based on the Text of 1592*, ed. J. James, Cambridge, 1994.

31. The same image is used by the Catholic Richard Verstegan in a letter to Robert Parsons, dated 5 March 1592 (printed in Petti, 1959, 39), and by the Protestant James Morice in the House of Commons on 27 February 1593 (LP, MS 2019, fo. 3r; a transcription of parts of this document will appear in Hartley, 1995). Morice was arrested on 28 February: Neale, 1957, 275–6.

32. Reports of the debates appear in LP, MS 2019, fos. 3r–4v; compare Neale, 1957, 267–76, 280–96.

33. LP, MS 2008, fo. 50r; compare Dasent, 1901, vol. 24, 250, who prints the letter among the documents for the Council meeting of 23 May 1593. For further examples, see LP, Register of Archbishop Whitgift, Vol. 2, fo. 113r; BL, Harleian MS 7042, fo. 78r.

34. Compare the copies from Puckering's manuscripts in BL, Harleian MS 7042, fos. 70r–105v, 142r–236v; Hunter, 1985, 136–7.

35. *Speculum caritatis*, lib. 3, cap. 39; for 'the disciple whom Jesus loved', see John 13.23; 19.26; 20.2; 21.7, 20, 24.

36. The appeal of Corydon to Alexis is in *Eclogue II*; compare also the reference to Alexis in the *Greek Anthology*, XII.127, a poem by Meleager.

37. Venice, Archivio di Stato, *Santo Uffizio*, b. 8, 'fra Francesco Calcagno'. Calcagno confessed to all these charges, without torture. Compare Davidson, 1992, 80.

10. Necromantic Books: Christopher Marlowe, *Doctor Faustus* and Agrippa of Nettesheim

GARETH ROBERTS

The name of Heinrich Cornelius Agrippa of Nettesheim was literally one to conjure with in the sixteenth century. It is rivalled in its polysyllabic perversity only by the name of another German suspected of magic, the dedicatee of Agrippa's book on occult philosophy and the authority for one of the earliest references to Faustus, the Abbot Johannes Trithemius of Sponheim (Palmer and More, 1966, 83–6). Agrippa's name sometimes appears briefly (like 'dragon' in the middle of the B text's conjuration in *Faustus*) in introductions to Marlowe's *Doctor Faustus*, in articles on it (e.g. Hattaway, 1970, 51–78; Keefer, 1983, 324–46), and inevitably in any edition's note on the play's one explicit allusion to Agrippa: Faustus's resolve that he:

> Will be as cunning as Agrippa was,
> Whose shadows made all Europe honour him.
> (A text 1.1.119–20)[1]

Roma Gill's note in her Mermaid edition provides a typical annotation:

> The magician and necromancer Henry Cornelius Agrippa von Nettesheim (1486–1535) was famous for his reputed power of invoking the shades of the dead.
> (Gill, 1989, 11)

Now actually Agrippa, as far as I know, is *not* famous for invoking the shades of the dead. Although Gill's note, and others like it, imply something of a contemporary historical reputation, this idea is found only, or at least mainly in three works of sixteenth–century English fiction: Lyly's *Campaspe*, Nashe's *Unfortunate Traveller* and Marlowe's *Doctor Faustus*.[2]

Lyly refers to Agrippa's necromantic powers in 'The Prologue at the Court' to his *Campaspe* (played before the Queen, New Year 1584), where the playwright contemplates his play's raising of Alexander the Great from his grave:

> *Appion* raising *Homere* from hell, demanded onely who was his father, and we calling *Alexander* from his grave, seeke onely who was his love. Whatsoever we present, we wish it may be thought the daunsing of *Agrippa* his shadowes, who in the moment they were seene, were of any shape one woulde conceive.[3]

In Nashe's *The Unfortunate Traveller* (printed 1594 and finished ?1593[4]) Jack Wilton meets Agrippa at the court of the Duke of Saxony in Wittenberg, where Agrippa raises Cicero for Erasmus, and they then travel with Agrippa. Then, at the court of the Emperor, courtiers tell Jack and the Earl of Surrey tales of Agrippa having shown Thomas More the destruction of Troy in a dream and of his having shown Thomas Cromwell Henry VIII hunting at Windsor. Nashe's Agrippa also outdid the lords in *Love's Labours Lost*, as he presented to the Emperor Charles V the Nine Worthies 'in that similitude and likeness that they lived upon earth'. Agrippa is credited by Lyly and Nashe with shows, some of them literally evocations of the notable past (Nashe, *Works* ii 252–5; see Crewe, 1982, 77–80). Marlowe's allusion to Agrippa ('Whose shadows made all Europe honour him') seems close to Lyly's, 'the daunsing of *Agrippa* his shadowes', and it may be significant that in both Lyly's *Campaspe* and Marlowe's *Faustus* Alexander the Great is 'raised'.

In these instances the interplay between history and fiction is complex as it always is in texts representing magic in the Renaissance, as magic itself constitutes a very particular series of Renaissance fictions. For example, as the *Unfortunate Traveller* reports, Agrippa *did* know Erasmus and corresponded with him (Nauert, 1965, 109–10), even if he did not raise Cicero for him (as far as we know), and Agrippa really *did* have some connection with Charles V (he wrote an account of his double coronation in 1530).[5] No-one apart from Nashe tells the tale of Agrippa raising the Nine Worthies, but Agrippa's pupil the German doctor Johann Wier tells a similar story in his sceptical demonological treatise *De Praestigiis Daemonum* where we find the story of a conjuror who raised Hector, Achilles and David at the court of the Emperor Maximilian I.[6] Even closer to Nashe's narrative is a report, in the *Tischreden* of Martin Luther, of the abbot Trithemius of Sponheim raising the Nine Worthies for the emperor Maximilian.[7]

This essay tries to address two large questions about Marlowe and Agrippa. Firstly, is it likely that Marlowe knew of Agrippa or had read any of Agrippa's works? Some might argue that the lines in *Campaspe* provide all the information contained in Marlowe's allusion in *Faustus*. Secondly, what might be gained from thinking of Agrippa and Faustus and even Marlowe together, and also of thinking together of their writings, and their representation *in* writings of the late sixteenth century?

II

Many people in late sixteenth–century England did of course know of and read Agrippa. His two best known works were published within a few years of each other. His declamation against all human learning and science *De Incertitudine et Vanitate Scientiarum et Artium* (Antwerp 1530) appeared later in an English translation, James Sanford's *Of the Vanitie and uncertaintie of*

Artes and Sciences (1569). Agrippa's compendious work on magic, *De Occulta Philosophia Libri Tres*, the work that we suppose aroused the curiosity of Frankenstein,[8] was printed in its final three–book form at Cologne 1533. The *De Vanitate*, which was seen as Agrippa's retraction of his thoughts on the occult sciences, thus confusingly appeared in print *before* his three books on occult philosophy which gave those thoughts their widest currency.

Probably the most familiar reference in sixteenth–century English literature to the *De Vanitate*, the most frequently printed of Agrippa's books, is in Sidney's *Apology*: 'Agrippa will be as merry in showing the vanity of science as Erasmus was in commending of folly'.[9] A remark of Barnabe Riche in 1578 suggests *De Vanitate* may have been particularly popular as a mine for witty opinions and *sententiae*, as does a manuscript note of Gabriel Harvey's which refers to Agrippa's *De Vanitate* as 'Doctor Fulkes Cournu–copia for Table philosophie: & one of Sir Philip Sidney's storehouses, for common discourse'.[10] In the case of the *De Vanitate*, Agrippa's common talk became sound aphorisms. Thomas Nashe borrowed from it in several of his works,[11] and in twenty passages of *Summer's Last Will and Testament* (*Works*, v 121). Ben Jonson drew on it in *Volpone*, and Lodge versified part of Agrippa's attack on alchemists.[12] In the seventeenth century Thomas and Henry Vaughan were influenced by Agrippa's writings, and Agrippa's effect on Thomas, who under the pseudonym 'Eugenius Philalethes' wrote the encomiastic verses prefatory to the 1651 English translation of *De Occulta*, was profound.[13]

As one would have expected, works on magic attributed to Agrippa were in John Dee's library: he possessed a 1550 edition of *De Occulta* and an edition [?1559] of the pseudo–Agrippan *Liber Quartus*, which he presumably thought was also by Agrippa as his library catalogue describes 'Agrippae de occulta philosophia, libri tres ... Eiusdem de occulta philosophia liber quartus ...'.[14] Dee used Agrippa during his experiments (French, 1972, 113).[15] The physician Richard Napier owned Agrippa's book and prescribed the sigil of Jupiter for one patient (Macdonald, 1981, 255, n. 10).[16] Perhaps a more surprising sixteenth–century owner of *De Occulta* was Archbishop Cranmer whose autograph is on the title–page of a 1533 edition in the British Library (BL pressmark 719.k.3). Another English Archbishop of Canterbury owned a copy of this work of Agrippa's. Matthew Parker's copy of *De Occulta Philosophia* (Lyons, 1550) was part of the library he left on his death in 1576 to Corpus Christi College, Cambridge, of which he was sometime Master and Christopher Marlowe was sometime a scholar.[17]

The bibliography of Agrippa's works is extremely complicated and confused, especially as the magical works were usually published under fictitious imprints (see Ferguson, 1924, 12). Agrippa had completed a first version of *De Occulta* as early as 1510 and it seems to have circulated in manuscript well before being printed (Nauert, 1965, 32–3). The first book of Agrippa's *De Occulta* was printed by itself in 1531. It seems to have reached England almost immediately for in 1532 the confession of William Neville, who had ambitions to be Earl of Warwick, reveals that the conjuror 'Jonys of Oxford', who raised devils for him, talked to Neville of Agrippa's *De Occulta Philosophia*.[18] All three books of occult philosophy were printed together at Cologne in 1533 as *De Occulta Philosophia Libri Tres*, and a pseudo–Agrippan *Liber Quartus*,[19] giving even more detailed and practical instructions for conjuring soon circulated under his name. Johann Wier, Agrippa's pupil, was defending Agrippa from attribution to him of that 'detestable little book which has recently seen the light of day [ie recently published]'[20] in the 1566 edition of *De Praestigiis*. Wier, in *De Praestigiis* II v, gives a long, detailed and accurate description of the contents of the *Liber Quartus*, followed by a similarly detailed description of Peter of Abano's *Heptameron*. Clearly, from the almost verbatim echoes of the *Liber Quartus*, Wier wrote his description with the book or very detailed notes from it before him.[21] My inference from the sentence in which Wier moves from describing the spurious *Liber Quartus* to the *Heptameron* is that he read them both in a volume where they were printed together: 'Annexed [*subjungitur*] after that [i.e. the *Liber Quartus*] is that absolutely noxious little book entitled the *Heptameron* or *Magical First Principles* of Peter of Abano'.[22]

From 1567 onwards the *Liber Quartus* was included in a volume comprising the *De Occulta*, the *Liber Quartus*, the *Heptameron* of Peter of Abano and a collection of small works on magic by other authors, originally assembled by Walther Hermann Ryff, who was an enterprising sixteenth–century German compiler of works likely to appeal to readers with a taste in occult arts (see Nauert, 1979, 282–6). This collection was printed at Paris, 'Parisiis, Ex Officina Iacobi Dupuys 1567', when this group of works was apparently brought together for the first time. This 1567 imprint is apparently genuine, but the collection also appeared later, almost always undated, and with the fictitious imprint of the Beringi brothers, Lyons,[23] sometimes as part of the *Opera* of Agrippa. There are copies of the 1567 volume in the Bodleian Library and some college libraries in Oxford and Cambridge.[24]

III

I want to suggest not only that Marlowe had read Agrippa's works on magic, but that it is likely that it was in a volume of this kind. Marlowe's play demands commentary on its representation of magic, which is detailed and precise. It is difficult to think of any other printed text in the sixteenth century which could have provided Marlowe with such detailed and copious information. Other English dramatists also drew on these works. The 'names of those mercurial spirits / That do fright flies from boxes' (i.e. Malthai, Tarmiel, Baraborat, Rael, Velel and Thiel) which Subtle knows in Jonson's *Alchemist* are indeed the names of mercurial spirits and Jonson found them in Peter of Abano's *Heptameron*.[25] And since Barnabe Barnes's play about the magician Pope Alexander VI, *The Devil's Charter* (played before King James on Candlemas Night, 1607)[26] draws on *De Occulta*, the pseudo–Agrippan *Liber Quartus* and the *Heptameron* (see Roberts, 1976, 210–2), it is reasonable to assume that it was in the 1567 Paris edition of Agrippa or one of its reprints that he found the works collected together.

Indeed, a search in some early modern English magical manuscripts in the hope of finding alternative sources of detailed magical operations actually reveals that many of the conjuring books themselves copy from Agrippa, or construct their magical practices according to instructions in Agrippa's books, thus also providing evidence that Agrippa's works were actually read for practical instructions on how to conjure. BL Additional MS 36,674, arts. 1–4 were at one time in the possession of Gabriel Harvey, who was a great admirer of Agrippa, whom he termed 'a demi–god in omnisufficiency of knowledge' and 'the omniscious doctor', for which he was mocked by Nashe,[27] and Harvey annotated them throughout, perhaps in 1577 (see Moore Smith, 1913, 80, and Stern, 1972, 1–62, especially 15–16, 50–1). Article 2 is described by Harvey's annotation (fo.23) as having been found among the papers of Dr John Caius, who refounded Gonville Hall as Gonville and Caius College, Cambridge in 1557 and was subsequently its Master from 1559 to 1568 when he was dismissed for recusancy. The manuscript was therefore presumably written before Caius's death in 1573, after which it passed, according to Harvey's note, to the next Master, Dr Thomas Legge (Caius's nominee) and from him to a fellow of Gonville and Caius, Mr Fletcher. Half of article 2 (fos.23–36ʳ) is a compilation in Latin from the *Liber Quartus* and the *Heptameron*, and Harvey commented on a fragmentary leaf (fo. 45):

> The best skill, that Mʳ Butler / physician had in Nigromancie, /
> with Agrippas Occulta / Philosophia: as his coosen / Ponder upon
> his Oathe / often repeated, / seriously intimated unto mee.

This comment again provides evidence that Agrippa's books of occult philosophy (whether the *De Occulta* or *Liber Quartus* or both is not entirely clear, but then neither can we be sure a sharp distinction was made between the two in the sixteenth century) were used to provide instructions for actual conjuring. The combination in article 2 of material from the *Liber Quartus* and *Heptameron*, again suggests that they were read together and probably printed together in the same volume. Wier's detailed discussion of the two of them in *De Praestigiis* II v pointed in the same direction.

BL Harley MS 2267 is a conjuring book made on 13 February 1600, at an astrologically appropriate time, as on fo.1 is affixed a strip of paper reading:

> Golde hill in ['hampsher' deleted] Sussex. / Owin Lordinge of Boxgrove / discringe [ie writing] it. ffebrarij. 13, 1600 / at the howre of 4 a clocke in / the afternoone beinge friday / George Stent. present

It is a compilation of extracts from the *De Occulta*, the *Liber Quartus* and the *Heptameron*. On fo.1ᵛ there is a magic circle enclosing a square containing a rather crude representation of Christ, drawn from the Apocalypse (Vulgate Revelation I, xii–xvi), among seven candlesticks and with a sword proceeding from his mouth, which was made following the instructions from the *Liber Quartus* for making a pentacle containing 'figura majestatis Dei sedentis in throno, habentis in ore gladium bis acutum'. Fos.2–2ᵛ present a number–square,[28] characters of the moon, and the appropriate Hebrew names of God from *De Occulta*, II xxii, but the character of the angel Gabriel on fo.2 comes from the *Heptameron*. The following pages contain similar compilations of characters, divine names and number squares for the other planets. Clearly, this conjuring book was made on the instructions of and collated material from 'Agrippan' books and the *Heptameron*, I assume as collected together in the one printed volume. It was presumably also used in the practice of actual magic along lines described in such a volume.

An extract from BL Sloane MS 3851, fo.30 clearly shows that Agrippa's works were regarded as giving practical instructions for magic:

> Morneing and evenning read the prayers appoin= / ted for the day together with the psalmes for / the day and the lettany. / Call the common invocation in Agrippa / for each day of the weeke and the Angel / appropriated to that day.

And in a series of visions on 25 February 1567 Agrippa appeared to John Davis and an 'H G', after red, blue and green dragons and in the rather mixed company of 'Assasel' [presumably the demon Azazel], Solomon, Job, Adam and Bacon (BL Additional MS 36,674, fo.59ᵛ).

IV

Many moments in *Faustus* suggest Marlowe had been reading Agrippa. The scope of this essay does not allow the presentation of all the detailed evidence, but will focus on one small detail and then sketch in large areas of similarity.

Part of Valdes' advice to Faustus on conjuration is:

> Then haste thee to some solitary grove,
> And bear wise Bacon's and Albanus' works.
> (A text: 1.1.155–6)

Since a reviewer of an edition of Marlowe's works in the *Gentleman's Magazine* in 1841 made the tersely imperious emendation 'Read, "Albertus"',[29] editors have worried over the minor crux in the A and B texts' unanimous reading 'Albanus' wondering whether Peter of Abano or Albert the Great is meant, and whether to emend to 'Abanus', the more normal form of the name.[30] One minor feature of the 1567 edition of Agrippa is the form on the title page of the name of Peter of Abano, to whom the magical work the *Heptameron* is regularly attributed. The list of contents on the title page of the 1567 collection and also its later reprintings reads 'Heptameron Petri de Albano'. This oddity,[31] 'Albano' rather than 'Abano', is explicitly remarked upon in a manuscript annotation on the form 'Albano' on the title–page of the Bodley copy of the 1567 collection: 'l(ege) Abano. pag(ina) 556'. And, although as Ward's edition of Faustus (1878) notes, Bacon and Abano occur together in a sentence in Agrippa's *De Vanitate*, they are also in a list of magicians in *De Occulta*: 'ego vidi, Rogerium Bachonem, Robertum Anglicanum, Petrum Apponum...' (*De Occulta*, α4ᵛ–5).

Marlowe's play will bear, indeed demands, commentary on its representation of magic, which is more detailed than any other sixteenth–century English play. Its depiction of magic is far more technically precise than that of the *English Faust Book* which can offer very little as the basis for the play's detailed imagination of the contents of books of magic, the technicalities of conjuration and magical practice in general. We read in the *English Faust Book* only that Faustus's advisers used:

> figures, characters, conjurations, incantations, with many other ceremonies belonging to these infernal arts, as necromancy, charms, soothsaying, witchcraft, enchantment[32]

This is a rather imprecise and indiscriminate jumble of magical categories, techniques and practices, rather than the difficult, technical and specialized business of invoking spirits and magic in *Faustus*.

A specific instance, the first conjuration (A and B I iii), will make the difference clear. In the *English Faust Book*, Faustus becomes skilled in using his '*vocabula*, figures, characters, conjurations, and other ceremonial actions,' but in Spissers' Wood he only 'made with a wand a circle in the dust, and within that many more circles and characters' and called for Mephostophiles, charging him in the name of Beelzebub to come (*English Faust Book*, ll. 74–85). However, in Marlowe's *Faustus*, the conjuration scene is full of specific magical practices and theories which can be paralleled and therefore explained by Agrippa's books:

> Within this circle is Jehovah's name,
> Forward and backward anagrammatised,
> The breviated[33] names of holy saints,
> Figures of every adjunct to the heavens,
> And characters of signs and erring stars
> (A–text 1.3.8–12)

In Agrippa's scale of the number twelve can be found a table containing twelve cabalistic anagrammatizations (gematria) of the Hebrew Tetragrammaton IHVH ('Jehovah's name forward and backward anagrammatized') to produce new names of power. The rubric to the table notes 'The great name is unrolled [*revolutum*] into twelve banners'.[34] 'The breviated names of holy saints', which has never been satisfactorily explained, may be glossed by one of Agrippa's methods of producing magical *characteres*, by contraction of words into a sort of magical monogram containing all the letters. He gives as an example the 'abbreviating' of the name of the archangel Michael.[35] Agrippa constantly talks about and sometimes illustrates magical *characteres*[36] and *signa* and *signacula* and Hebrew letters, like the 'Lines, circles, signs, letters and characters' Faustus finds in his magic book and the 'characters of signs and erring stars' he inscribes in his circle. The Latin conjuration invokes the gods of the underworld, and addresses elemental spirits, uses the name of God, and ends by sprinkling holy water and using the sign of the cross. Agrippa says we must beseech spirits by the stars, infernal deities and by the natural elements,[37] that evil spirits are overcome when the petitioner sings forth sacred words, conjuring by divine names (*De Occulta*, III, xxxii, 397), and recommends the magical virtues of the sign of the cross, especially as it frightens demons (ibid., II xxiii, 226; III xii, 344–5). The *Liber Quartus* recommends the sprinkling of the circle with holy water.[38]

More generally, Agrippa's books on magic can again and again provide such close glosses on and explications of the magic in *Faustus* – its aspirations, theories, practices and detailed techniques – that it is difficult not to suppose its influence on the play. For example, like the spirits in Faustus's imaginative rhapsodies in I ii, those allotted to the seven days of the week in the *Heptameron* have the ability to find [*impetrare*] gold and jewels, tell secrets, cause and fight wars and provide soldiers, teach experiments and purvey knowledge.[39] And if the magic in *Faustus* may be characterised as Agrippan, then we might conversely characterize the mode of hyperbolic magical aspiration in Agrippa as 'Marlovian'. Indeed, in Leah Marcus's terms, Agrippa too must produce the 'Marlowe effect' of 'simultaneous exaltation and undermining of official ideology' (1989, 22). The exclamatory characterization of Agrippa in the preface of the English translation of the *Liber Quartus* (1655) sounds rather like bits of *Tamburlaine*:

> Behold *Agrippa* mounting th'lofty skies,
> Talking with gods;...

In terms of magical aspiration, Agrippa too can provide the powers of magic to effect things 'against nature'. One passage recounts the ability of art to produce effects like those imagined severally by Faustus and Cornelius: redirecting rivers, drying the seas, searching the bottom of the sea, making new lands and joining them to continents (*De Occulta*, II i). Another passage, in typically hyperbolic and exalted style, speaks of man dominating nature and producing wonderful effects, and of men who:

> raised up by theological virtues, command the elements, drive away clouds, raise the winds, drive down the clouds in rain, cure the sick and raise the dead.[40]

This is close particularly to

>   Emperors and kings
> Are but obeyed in their several provinces,
> Nor can they raise the wind or rend the clouds;
> (A–text 1.1.59–61)

and

> Be thou on earth as Jove is in the sky,
> Lord and commander of these elements.
> (A–text 1.1.78–9)

In the light of these considerations, what are we to make of the status of the magic in Marlowe's *Faustus*? It has been suggested that the detailed magical practices represented in Marlowe's play are likely to have come from Agrippa. So for example, there is no part of Faustus's conjuration that does not have explicit sanction, as it were, for its details, formulations and rituals in some chapter of Agrippa. But on the evidence of many English

Renaissance magical manuscripts, some 'real' magical practices in early modern England also drew on Agrippa's books. How does this affect our understanding of what was understood to be happening on stage in the 1590s when Faustus conjured, especially if one believed that some words could have automatic magical efficacy? Samuel Rowlands has a famous recollection of Edward Alleyn's performance as Faustus: a credulous gull is tricked into attempting to conjure and 'gets on a surplis / With a crosse upon his brest / Like *Allen* playing *Faustus*'.[41] How is our understanding of Edward Alleyn's performance and our understanding of the contemporary audience's understanding, affected when we (and Marlowe?) read in instructions for conjuring in the pseudo–Agrippan *Liber Quartus* that the magician's garment should be a priest's if possible, and that the magic circle should be sprinkled with holy water?[42] This must surely add to Leah Marcus's sense of the 'Marlowe effect' in performance, and of a moment of performance, as well as a magician, 'at the extreme edge of transgression' (Marcus, 1989, 5).

V

Agrippa's two best known works appeared within a few years of each other. The problematic relationship between the *De Vanitate* (Antwerp 1530) and *De Occulta* (Cologne 1533), particularly the seeming paradox of their quite different attitudes to magic, still exercises scholars (see Keefer, 1988, 614–51; Bowen, 1972, 249–56; Korkowski, 1976, 594–607; Zambelli, 1960, 166–80). 'Why did he publish, within a few years of each other, a textbook of magic and occult philosophy ... and a condemnation of all philosophy and learning' (Bowen, 1972, 249) and 'How, having published *De vanitate* in 1530, could Agrippa go on to publish a greatly enlarged version of his *De occulta philosophia*' (Keefer, 1988, 618)? Whatever interpretation we may now offer of the *De Vanitate*, it was commonly seen in the Renaissance as Agrippa's retraction or recantation of his views on magic.[43] Printers of Agrippa's works presented their original readers in a particularly acute form the problem of Agrippa's magical aspirations juxtaposed to his rejection of magic as vanity when they printed the 'retraction' of magic from the *De Vanitate* immediately after the *De Occulta*. Thus, readers glancing through one volume could have experienced almost simultaneously both Agrippa's enthusiastic elaboration of magical arts and his declamation against them. In the 1567 compilation printed at Paris by Duphys, the relevant chapters from *De Vanitate* are printed immediately after the text of the *De Occulta* (505–20) and before that of the *Liber Quartus* and are entitled 'Henrici Cornelii Agrippae Censura, sive Retractio de Magia, ex sua declamatione de Vanitate scientarum [sic] & excellentia verbi Dei'. Other editions of the *De Occulta* and the 1651 English translation by J. F. of the *De Occulta* adopt the same procedure.[44] In addition, readers of the 1567 edition and other editions of the *De Occulta* would have found the statement by Agrippa that he retracted many opinions in this work in the *De Vantitate* and that he wrote the three books of occult philosophy hoping later to include retractions and enlargements (α3). The same volume thus often contained both Agrippa's praise and condemnation, his enthusiastic advocacy *and* retraction of magic.

The question of the interrelationship of these two Agrippan works, and the difficulty of finding a consistent reading of Agrippa, when these two important works seem to gesture in opposite directions, is illuminatingly analogous to the balance of two antithetical critical views of Marlowe's *Faustus*. This balance, whose fulcrum is the question of the play's attitude to magic, has a substantial critical history in the nineteenth and twentieth centuries and is still present in critical debate. It is one of readings of the play as either orthodox or subversive; or as two juxtaposed sections in the critical introduction in the Bevington–Rasmussen edition summarize them, 'The Orthodox Framework' and 'Humanist Aspiration' (1993, 15–31). Indeed, this problematic conjunction of Agrippa's two most famous works and Agrippa's intellectual dilemmas that may have informed this conjunction, invite more general reflection not only on *Faustus* but on those 'particular conjunctions of contradictory impulses in Marlowe's works' as a whole (Hattaway, 1970, 51).

And if we listen to Marlowe's play hearing the echoes of these Agrippan 'two voices', we may hear the opening scene of *Faustus* (which is not in the *English Faust Book* at all) and its declamation of the emptiness of traditional kinds of orthodox knowledge following the radical programme of most of the *De Vanitate*. However, at that moment when Faustus bids divinity adieu and picks up a book of magic, as it were turns from the *De Vanitate* to the *De Occulta*, Agrippa's *De Vanitate* (its full title ends, after all, '*& excellentia verbi Dei*') turns aside at the last moment from its sceptical course to take refuge in an idea of Christian simplicity in its final chapter, the digression in praise of the ass. The early part of *Faustus* then continues in the spirit of aspiration and learned magic of the *De Occulta*. The end of the play might return us to a reading of the representation of the perilous vanity of magic in the sceptical spirit of *De Vanitate*, and a consequent assessment of Faustus's career through the perspective on Agrippa's work and career provided by a reading of Agrippa's *De Vanitate* as a retraction. This reading gives us a retrospect on Marlowe's play and its protagonist from the viewpoint of the Englished *De Vanitate*'s construction of Agrippa's life as a tragedy, that is of a man:

> whose knowledge, although it were great, yet greatly he erred, and
> no merveil, for he gave his minde to unleeful Artes, contrarie to
> the Lawes of God and man: for it is saide, and his workes testifie

the same, that he exercised the Arte Magicke, and therein farre
excelled all other of his time, but in the ende, his wicked
knowledge was the cause of his miserable deathe ... [45]

VI

There are similarities in the careers of Agrippa and Faustus, and also and
more importantly in the tales that circulated about both. Both were wanderers.
Agrippa visited France, Spain, England (which he visited in 1510, the *De
Occulta* contains a description of Stonehenge) Italy, Switzerland, the Low
Countries and Germany. Like Agrippa, Marlowe's Faustus was a great
scholar, whereas the protagonist of the *English Faust Book* is not always
represented unambiguously as such. Although both the *English Faust Book*
and Marlowe's play agree in a depiction of Faustus that 'none for his time
were able to argue with him in divinity', the former also seems to say that
Faustus wasted his time at university, 'Faustus being of a naughty mind and
otherwise addicted, applied not his studies, but took himself to other
exercises' (lines 40–1, 26–8). Agrippa certainly had a licentiate in arts (1502)
and claimed to have doctorates in both canon and civil law and in medicine.
Like Marlowe's Faustus, Agrippa was 'a new Trismegistus in the three higher
faculties of Law, Theology and Medicine'.[46]

There is good reason to think that late sixteenth–century representations
of Agrippa contributed to the formation of the figure of Faustus, as later they
were to contribute details to incidents in Goethe's *Faust*.[47] Indeed, the most
recent edition of the *English Faust Book* claims that one passage in it echoes
Agrippa.[48] Already by 1599 the Jesuit demonologist Martin Del Rio is
connecting the names of Faustus and Agrippa, and reporting the same sort of
stories about them as tricksters as those in the *English Faust Book* and the
texts of Marlowe's *Faustus*:

> Rumour has it of the magicians Faustus and Agrippa, that when
> they went on their travels, they paid innkeepers with the usual
> coins, which looked genuine enough to the eye, but which their
> recipients discovered after a few days to be scraps of horn or the
> most filthy rubbish.[49]

Del Rio too tells of Agrippa's boarder [*commensalem*] who (like Robin) stole
his magic book and conjured devils (*Disquisitionum*, II, quaestio 29, i, 360–1).
As Faustus imagines military uses for his magic (A–text: 1.1.94–9), so, at
least according to Nashe, Agrippa offered Charles V to blow up Tunis 'by Art
Magicke' (*Terrors of the Night*, *Works*, i, 371–2). Like Marlowe's Faustus,
and Marlowe himself according to Thomas Beard,[50] Agrippa died cursing.
Many sixteenth–century authors repeat the story of how Agrippa died cursing

the demon who had destroyed him and who attended him in the shape of a black dog. Paolo Giovio seems to have been the main source for this tale.[51] In his unpublished manuscript 'Chronology' the Elizabethan antiquary William Harrison, who died in the same year as Marlowe, noted 1486 as the year of Agrippa's birth. The succeeding entry gives a fascinating epitome of Agrippa's career, fame and popular reputation and how that mixture might have been perceived at the end of the sixteenth century:

> Henricus Cornelius Agrippa is borne at Nettesheym upon the 14 of September & for his lerning & wisdomes / sake became afterward counsellor to Maximilian themperour & Charles the 5 who succeded him in that throne / somewhat was he geven also to magike & sorcery as it is thought wherof at his death he repented but as I gesse / to late. for taking a coller from his necke as he laie in his death bed, curiosuly fretted with stone & graven / with sondry Characters he threw it as it is said unto his spaniell saying avoide thou wicked best & get thee hens / for thou by sutlety hast brought me to destruction. wherupon the dogge departed & was after never herd of, some sup / posing that he drowned himself in the Araris but other avouching rather that he died in prison wherunto the emperour / Charles did cast him because he held with the divorse betweene Henry the 8 & quene Catherine his first wife / he wrate 3 bokes de occulta philosophia or the hidden philosophy with the foureth which he intituled the kaie unto the other & now also in printe he had moreover divers enemies who wrate very sharpely against him because of / his declamation made against the vanity of friers & for other his treatizes of which there is in truth no one / that in some thinges deserveth not reprehension but when I see that same confuted with so moche skill as he hath penned / them then will I saie that his bokes are to be destroied & yet in the meane time I advouche not that they are toller / able. he died at Lions in a pore victualling house. P. Jovius in Eulogiis.[52]

Agrippa contributed to the construction of the figure of Faustus and Faustus of Agrippa. William Godwin's account of Agrippa in his *Lives of the necromancers* (1834) is a good example of how a 'life' of a figure like Agrippa or Faust – and in Godwin the life of Agrippa is followed by that of Faustus – may be constructed and how 'history' and 'fiction' commingle in such a 'life'. A couple of pages of history tracing Agrippa's birth, attainments and career is followed by the first of the 'stories' Godwin gives, one 'connected with the history of one of the most illustrious ornaments of our early English poetry, Henry Howard earl of Surrey' (*Lives of the necromancers*, 323). Godwin then gives a paraphrase of the Agrippa section in Nashe's *Unfortunate Traveller*, acknowledging Nashe as the 'sole authority for this tale'. The rest of the section on Agrippa is taken from what we might want to consider as more 'factual' sixteenth– and seventeenth–century reports: Paolo Giovio, Martin Del Rio, Johann Wier and Gabriel Naudé.

VII

I would like finally to isolate one very particular way that representations of Agrippa in the sixteenth century can shed light on both the protagonist of Marlowe's play and on representations of Marlowe himself. In late sixteenth–century reactions to Agrippa, in Marlowe's play and in late sixteenth–century representations of Marlowe, it is possible to detect ideas of magic as conspiracy, the construction of supposed occult fraternities, and an equation between occult books and subversion. Such a nexus of ideas should not surprise us if we reflect even for a moment on the Latin *coniuro* and *coniuratio* and the English *conjure* and *conjuration*. In all cases 'swearing together' and 'conspiracy' are the primary meanings, with *coniuratio* meaning also 'a band of conspirators', 'a plot'.[53] Renaissance readers of Roman history turning to Sallust's account of the conspiracy of Catiline would read *De Coniuratione Catilinae*. The sense of 'conjure' as 'to constrain a spirit to appear by invocation' is later than and derived from this primary sense. A nice instance of the verb in which conspiracy, brotherhoods, sedition and magic are all present occurs when Death confronts Milton's Satan at the gates of Hell:

> Art thou that traitor angel, art thou he,
> Who first broke peace in heaven and faith, till then
> Unbroken, and in proud rebellious arms
> Drew after him the third part of heaven's sons
> Conjured against the highest ...?
> (*Paradise Lost*, II, 689–93)

The reaction of the orthodox to Agrippa after his death (1535) is partly one of anxiety about his seditious influence. For the demonologist and political philosopher Jean Bodin, Agrippa was 'le maistre Sorcier' who had left behind disciples, and his books with their magic characters were among the most dangerous plagues of the commonwealth (*Démonomanie*, fos.19^v–20). In 1584 André Thevet, sounding unnervingly like Thomas Beard,[54] exclaimed on Agrippa's death:

> And would to God that he had drowned alone in this gulf of impiety: today we would not have had a multitude of atheists,

blasphemers and mockers as this century has produced.[55]

Thevet talks darkly too of groups and classes of atheist, just as there are classes of magicians.[56]

An idea of conspiracy and sedition by occult fraternities (and sororities) is of course one of the staple anxieties about magic in medieval and Renaissance Europe. The accusation in Scotland in the early 1590s against the Earl of Bothwell of witchcraft and conspiracy with witches provides a precisely contemporary conjunction of magic and conspiracy. He was indicted for dealing with the necromancer Ritchie Grahame for the destruction of James VI, and of 'conspyracies, conventions and conjurations' against his Majesty.[57] The Elizabethan government too was sensitive about magical conspiracies against the Queen. In September 1578, the Spanish ambassador Mendoza wrote home about the discovery of three wax images in a stable, pierced with hog's bristles, one of them with 'Elizabeth' inscribed on the forehead. The Privy Council were still worried about the incident in January 1579, when they made enquiries about witches apprehended at Windsor. Jean Bodin too mentions the affair.[58] Stephen Mullaney has powerfully suggested some interesting elisions between anxieties about the power of ambiguous words, the 'preternatural', conspiracy and treason (Mullaney, 1988, 16–34).

Ideas of magical conspiracy and sedition are ones which Marlowe has incorporated into his play. Faustus's preceptors in magic, Valdes and Cornelius – and given the argument of this essay that latter name may be significant – are Marlowe's addition to the story of the *English Faust Book*, where we learn only that Faustus 'accompanied himself with divers that were seen in those devilish arts' (lines 50–1). With Faustus they form a small occult community with particular magical theories, practices and aspirations. Faustus wants the 'conference' ('meeting', 'rendezvous' as well as 'conversation') of Valdes and Cornelius (A–text: 1.1.70, 101). Clearly, these two, according to the First Scholar long notorious for magic (A–text: 1.2.33–4), have finally and painstakingly, as we would now say 'recruited' Faustus to magic: 'Know that your words have *won me at the last* [my italics]/ To practise magic and concealed arts' (A–text: 1.1.103–4). Concealed within the variety of desires for power, pleasure and knowledge through magic, and behind easy appeals to a 1590s audience's chauvinism in expelling the Spanish governor of the Netherlands (A–text: 1.1.94–5) and stealing gold from Spanish ships returning from the Americas (A–text: 1.1.133–4), there is the politically subversive side of magical aspirations. This is most intense in the section beginning 'By him I'll be great emperor of the world' (A–text: 1.3.106): it also includes telling the secrets of all foreign kings (1.1.89) and making engines of war (1.1.87–9). And, extraordinarily, Faustus's first response to Mephostophiles's offer of service is a moment of literally subversive desire, 'To do whatever Faustus shall command, /Be it to make the moon drop from her sphere / Or the ocean to overwhelm the world' (A–text: 1.3.38–40). Although these lines are in part coloured by details from the doings of witches from classical literature (e.g. Virgil, *Eclogues*, VIII 69), they also recall standard Renaissance images of subversive disordering and collapse into watery chaos, which reverse God's divine ordering in his separation of the created world from the waters in Genesis.[59]

Allusion may serve to sketch in these same features: magic, secret books and subversion, conspiracy, supposed occult fraternities, in early representations of Marlowe: Greene's 'Mad and scoffing poets, that have propheticall spirits as bold as Merlins race' and his elision of Marlowe with his first hubristic and atheist protagonist: 'daring God out of heaven with that Atheist Tamburlan'.[60] In spring 1593 the authorities were anxious to find persons suspected of a 'libell that concerned the state', that seditious little book for which the Privy Council tried to arrest Kyd and Marlowe and about which Kyd wrote to Puckering: 'that libell that concerned the state, amongst those waste and idle papers which I carde / not for & which unaskt I did deliver up ...'.[61] Beard reported that Marlowe wrote a book against the Trinity. Kyd wrote to Puckering protesting against a charge of atheism and hinting that information might be got from those Marlowe conversed with – 'Harriot, Warner, Royden and some stationers in Paules churchyard'. These names of course lead one to, as it were, the full anxiety, in Robert Persons's account of Raleigh's School of Atheism, complete with its master conjurer, its jesting at Christ, recruiting of young gentlemen, and cabalistic practices of spelling God backwards:

> Of Sir Walter Rauleys schoole of Atheisme by the waye, and of the Conjurer that is M(aster) thereof, and of the diligence used to get young gentlemen to this schoole, where in both Moyses, and our Savio'; the olde, and the new Testamente are jested at, and the schollers taught amonge other thinges, to spell God backwarde.[62]

I suggested earlier that the interplay between history and fiction is particularly complex in texts representing magic in the Renaissance, and that magic itself is arguably a very particular series of fictions. This essay may have moments, especially at its end, which seem rather like those in Umberto Eco's novel, *Foucault's Pendulum*, in which events are called into being and shaped by apocryphal magical fictions. But in dealing with magic in Renaissance texts and Renaissance society we may have ultimately to acknowledge the power of magic words to form actual practice and to construct events.

Notes

1. Unless otherwise indicated all references to *Doctor Faustus* are to the Bevington and Rasmussen, 1993, edition.

2. I have only come across two reports of anything like necromancy attributed to Agrippa. Martin Del Rio says that Agrippa was credited with the temporary reanimation by a demon of the body of a young man it had killed (*Disquisitionum Magicarum Libri Sex* 3 vols. Louvain, 1599, 1600, bk. 2, quaestio 29, vol. 2, 360–1); in 1532 a majordomo of cardinal Campeggio alluded to a mirror that Agrippa once showed him in which the dead seemed alive (Thorndike, 1923–58, vol 5, 132).

3. John Lyly, *The Complete Works of John Lyly* ed. R. Bond, 3 vols., Oxford, 1902, vol. 2, 316. As Bond notes in vol. 2, 541, the allusion here is to Pliny's *Historia naturalis*, 30, vi where Apion, a teacher of rhetoric, claimed to have raised the ghosts of the dead [*umbras*] to ask the names of Homer's parents.

4. Thomas Nashe, *The Works of Thomas Nashe*, ed. R. B. McKerrow, 5 vols., London, 1904–1910, vol. 4, 252.

5. *Caroli Quinti ... Coronationis Historia*, Antwerp, 1530; see also Nauert, 1965, 105–111. André Thevet reports that Agrippa was a counsellor at the court of Charles V, that Charles took him into his service and that some atttributed the Emperor's victories to Agrippa's magic, *Pourtraits et vies des Hommes illustres*, 2 vols., Paris, 1584, vol.2, fos. 542^v–3.

6. Wier, *De Praestigiis Daemonum*, Basle, 1583, bk. 1, xvi, 79–80. This is the expanded version of the *De Praestigiis* and the story is not in the earlier and shorter edition of 1563. McKerrow thought the tales about Agrippa in the *Unfortunate Traveller* Nashe's invention, but perhaps suggested by Wier's description of the conjuror at the court of the Emperor Maximilian I (*Works*, vol. 2, 276).

7. Johannes Aurifaber, *Tischreden oder Colloquia Doct. Martin Luthers*, Eisleben, 1566, fos. 301–301^v. The passage is reprinted in *Historia von Dr Johann Fausten: Text des Druckes von 1587, kritische Ausgabe*, ed. S. Füssel and H. Kreutzer, Stuttgart, 1988, 254. I am grateful to Mike Pincombe for drawing my attention to this passage.

8.   Mary Shelley, *Frankenstein, or the Modern Prometheus*, ed M. Hindle, Harmondsworth, 1985, 83, 85, 92, 94.

9.   Sidney, *Apology for Poetry*, ed. G. Shepherd, Manchester, 1973, 121.19–21. A. C. Hamilton argued for the 'thorough and even formative' influence of *De Vanitate* on Sidney's *Apology* (1956, 151–7).

10. Barnaby Rich, *Allarme to England*, 1578, G2; see Stern, 1972, 56.

11. For Nashe's use of *De Vanitate* and other references to Agrippa in his works see *Works*, vol. 1, 191, 320, 324, 328, 371–2; vol. 2, 132, 252–5; vol. 3, 16, 111, 221 and also McKerrow's notes on these passages as well as his section on Nashe's reading, especially vol. 5, 115, 118–9, 121; '[*De Vanitate* was] a work of which Nashe seems to have been very fond and of which he made constant use' (vol. 5, 118).

12. See Jonson, *Volpone* ed. P. Brockbank, London and New York, 1988, xxi and Brockbank's notes on *Volpone*, 1.3.51–5, 1.4.20–5; Thomas Lodge, 'The Anatomie of Alchymie' in *A fig for Momus* (1595), Epistle vii, I^v–I3^v. See also Duncan, 1942, 626. John Davies of Hereford quotes the 1569 English translation of Agrippa's *De Vanitate* [cap vii fos.21–21^v] in *Microcosmos* (1603); see Kocher, 1953, 56.

13. For Agrippa and Henry Vaughan see Judson, 1926, 178–81, but also Allen, 1943, 612–4. Agrippa's pervasive influence on Thomas Vaughan may be traced in *The Works of Thomas Vaughan*, ed. A. Rudrum, Oxford, 1984, through the index *sv* Agrippa, *Three Books, De Vanitate*. For the prefatory verses, see *Three Books of Occult Philosophy* tr. J. F., 1651, a2.

14. Items 742 and 743 of the facsimile of the 1583 MS catalogue in *John Dee's Library Catalogue* ed. J. Roberts and A. Watson, The Bibliographical Society, London, 1990; see Clulee, 1988, 37.

15. For a more cautious view of the indebtedness of Dee's operations to Agrippa, see Clulee, 1988, 135, 136, 139, 141, 161, 205, 206–7, 211–12, 214, 218–19, 236.

16. Napier also prescribed the sigil 'that hath the planet Jupiter and his characters [presumably from Agrippa, *De Occulta*, bk. 2, xxii]', which he thought potent if used with good prayer (ibid, 214).

17. This book (Adams A387) is still in the Matthew Parker library at Corpus (Corpus SP 96). It has the initials 'J K' stamped on the binding. It is among those books listed in the Parker Register (Corpus Christi CCCC MS 75, fo. 99) which was drawn up at the time of Parker's bequest to the college. The date of its arrival there is uncertain, as is that of the arrival of many of the Matthew Parker books. On the Parker books see Page, 1990, 17–39 and on the Parker Register, Vaughan and Fines, 1960, 119.

18. *Letters and Papers Foreign and Domestic of the Reign of Henry VIII, 1531–2*, London, vol. 5, 1880, 694–5.

19. Lynn Thorndike considered the *Liber Quartus* to have been added to the other three in 1565 or 1567 (1923–58, vol. 5, 136).

20. 'abominabilis libellus nuper in lucem ... emissus' (Wier, *De Praestigiis*, bk. 2, v, 141).

21. Compare, for example, Wier's description of the section on 'pentacles and sacred figures' with the *Liber Quartus*:

'Pentacula describuntur quoque tanquam figura quaedam sacra, à malis eventibus nos praeservantia, & ad malorum daemonum constrictionem, & exterminationem adiuvantia: malos etiam spiritus allicentia, nobisque conciliantia, que ex characteribus ...' (*De Praestigiis*, bk. 2, iv, 142)

'Sunt autem ipsa Pentacula tanquam signa quaedam sacra, à malis eventibus nos praeservantia, & ad malorum daemonum constrictionem, & exterminationem adiuvantia, bonosque spiritus allicentia, nobisque conciliantia, ...' (*Liber Quartus*, Paris, 1567, 535)

(All references to the *De Occulta Philosophia*, the *Liber Quartus* and the *Heptameron* are to the edition of *De Occulta* containing also these other works and printed at Paris 1567.) Presumably the difference of Wier's 'malos etiam spiritus allicentia' from 'bonosque spiritus allicentia' in the *Liber Quartus* is explained by Wier's wish to blacken the character of the latter as much as possible.

22. 'Inde pestilentissimus subjungitur libellus, Heptameron inscriptus sive elementa Magica Petri de Abano' (*De Praestigiis*, bk. 2, v, 144). Shea's translation at this point is misleading, 'Then there is the pestilential little book...', [Johann Weyer] *Witches, devils and doctors in the Renaissance: Johann Weyer, De Praestigiis daemonum*, general editor George Mora, tr. John Shea, Medieval and Renaissance texts and studies (Center for Medieval and early Renaissance studies: Binghampton, New York 1991), 112. Mora (612 n.) says that the first edition of the *Heptameron* was published in Paris 1559 with the *Liber Quartus*.

23. See, for example, the undated copy 'Lugduni, Per Beringos fratres', BL 232.1.5.

24. At Cambridge in Caius (see Adams, 1967, A389); at Oxford in Corpus Christi, Christ Church and St John's.

25. *The Alchemist*, ed. F. Mares, Revels Plays, London, 1967, 1.3.65–8; see also *Ben Jonson* ed. C. Herford and P. Simpson, 11 vols., Oxford, 1925–52, vol. 10, 66.

26. Barnes, *The Devil's Charter*, ed R. B. McKerrow in W. Bang, *Materialen zur Kunde des älteren englischen Dramas*, Louvain, 1904.

27. Harvey, *Pierce's Supererogation* in *The Works of Gabriel Harvey*, ed. A. Grosart, 3 vols., The Huth Library, 1884–5, vol. 2, 46, 70. For Harvey's enthusiasm for the *De Vanitate* see *Three Proper, and wittie familiar Letters* in Spenser, *Poetical Works*, ed. J. Smith and E. de Selincourt, Oxford, 1912, 624. For Nashe's mockery, see *Have with you to Saffron Walden*, in *Works*, vol. 3, 16.

28. On Agrippa's number–squares, seals and 'characters' see Nowotny, 1949, 46–57, and Calder, 1949, 196–9.

29. *The Gentleman's Magazine*, January 1841, 46.

30. Johann Wier, who like Agrippa also mentions Bacon and Peter of Abano as it were in the same breath in a list of magicians, calls him 'Petrus Aponensis' or in another chapter 'Petri de Abano'(*De Praestigiis*, bk. 2, iv and v, 136 and 144).

31. Instances of the form of Peter of Abano's name as 'Albano' would seem to be very rare, at least on the evidence of the forms of his name in the early manuscripts and printed editions of his works as listed in Thorndike, 1923–58, vol. 2, 917–26. Thorndike notes 'de Albano' in a 14th century MS of Abano's translations of Galen now in Vienna (ibid., vol. 2, 919). This, I think, is the only instance in Thorndike's lists, whereas 'de Abbano', 'de Abano', 'de Appono' and 'de Ebano' are far more frequent. On Peter of Abano, or Peter of Padua as he was often called, see Thorndike, ibid., vol. 2, 875–947, and also Thorndike, 1919, 317–26.

32. *The English Faust Book: A Critical Edition based on the text of 1592*, ed. J. Jones, Cambridge, 1994, lines 52–5.

33. 'Th'abbreviated', B–text, 1.3.10.

34. 'Nomen magnum in duodecim vexilla revolutum', *De Occulta*, bk. 2, xiii, 198–200.

35. 'qui fit per literarum colligantiam', *De Occulta*, bk. 3, xxx, 393.

36. It was these 'caracteres' that, among other features, excited the indignation of Jean Bodin against Agrippa, *De la Démonomanie des Sorciers*, Paris, 1580, bk. 1, iii, fo.19^v. Johnstone Parr turns to Agrippa for an explanation of Faustus's 'characters' (1971, 32–7), and Michael Hattaway also noted that characters are to be found in Agrippa's, *De Occulta* (1970, 62).

37. 'per coelestia sidera, per inferna numina, per naturalia elementa' *De Occulta*, bk. 3, xxxii, 396.

38. 'aspergat circulum aqua benedicta', 562.

39. Compare *Faustus*, A–text: 1.2.84–5 with *Heptameron*, 571; and 1.2.89 with *Heptameron*, 573; 1.2.94–5, 127–8 with *Heptameron*, 575.

40. '... theologicis istis virtutibus elevati, imperant elementis, pellunt nebulas, citant ventos, cogunt nubes in pluvias, curant morbos, suscitant mortuos', *De Occulta*, bk. 3, vi, 321.

41. Samuel Rowland, *The Knave of Clubs*, ?1615, D2^v.

42. 'Vestis sit sacerdotalis, si fieri potest'; 'aspergat circulum aqua benedicta', *Liber Quartus*, 560, 562.

43. John Cotta, *A short Discoverie of the Unobserved Dangers of severall sorts of ignorant and unconsiderate Practisers of Physicke in England*, 1612, bk. 2, iv, 109; Alexander Roberts, *A Treatise of Witchcraft*, 1616, 79.

44. e.g. Lyons 1550, 568–86; *Three Books of Occult Philosophy*, 1651, 567–83.

45. *Henrie Cornelius Agrippa, of the Vanitie and uncertaintie of Artes and Sciences*, tr. James Sanford, 1569, 'To the Reader', iii^v.

46. 'un nouveau Trismegiste és trois facultez superieures de la Theologie, Jurisprudence & Medecine', Gabriel Naudé, *Apologie*, Paris, 1625, cited Keefer, 1988, 614.

47. The influence of stories about Agrippa on Goethe's Faust has been detected in the appearance of the black poodle who appears and fawns on Faust before the first entry of Mephistophiles (see n. 51 below).

48. *English Faust Book*, ed. Jones, 772–84 and notes 203–4; see also lines 803–5 and note 205, although the latter passage is a commonplace about the four elements.

49. 'Sic fert fama Faustum & Agrippam Magos, cum iter facerent, solitos nummos ad oculum sinceros in diversoriis numerare, quos qui receperant, post pauculos dies cornuum frusta vel scruta vilissima reperiebant' (Del Rio, *Disquisitionum*, bk. 2, quaestio 12, vol. 1, 167–8).

50. Thomas Beard says that Marlowe blasphemed against the Trinity, and died cursing and blaspheming to his last gasp (*The Theatre of God's Judgements*, 1597, 147–8). On Beard's account of Marlowe see Nicholl, 1992, 65–8, 70–2, 77–8.

51. Paolo Giovio, *Elogia Doctorum Virorum*, first printed 1548 (Antwerp 1557), cap xci, 223–4. Keefer, citing Paola Zambelli, says that the first slander printed against Agrippa is in Gratius, *Lamentationes Obscurorum Virorum*, 1518 (1988, 616 n.7). Agrippa's pupil, Johann Wier, protested that Agrippa's black dog was simply a black dog: Agrippa named it 'Monsieur' and gave it a mate called 'Mademoiselle'. He was very

affectionate towards it and would kiss it, so affectionate indeed that after rejecting his third wife (Wier doesn't tell us what happened to Mademoiselle), Agrippa used to let it sleep in bed under the covers with him (*De Praestigiis*, bk. 2, v, 165–6). Francis Coxe has the black dog story and hints that Agrippa very likely 'endid after some straunge sorte'(*A short treatise declaringe the detestable wickednesse, of magicall sciences*, 1561, B4). The preface to Sanford's 1569 translation of the *De Vanitate* also tells the story (fo. 3ᵛ). For a useful seventeenth–century summary and survey of stories about Agrippa, and the defence by Thomas Vaughan of 'my Author' against them, see *Anima Magica Abscondita*, 'Preface to the Reader' in *Works*, 99–103.

52. BL Additional MS 70,984, fo. 214. I am grateful to Peter Roberts for drawing my attention to this manuscript.

53. For the association of the secret meetings of a *coniuratio* and ritual practices see Henrichs, 1970, vol. 1, 18–35, especially 33.

54. 'I would to God (and I pray it from my heart) that all Atheists in this realme, and in all the world beside, would ... forsake their horrible impietie' (*Theatre of God's Judgements*, 148).

55. 'Et, pleut à Dieu, que tout seul il se fust noyé en ce goulphre d'impieté, aujourd'huy nous n'aurions un tas d'Athees, de mesdisans & brocadeurs, comme ce siecle les nous a produict' (Thevet, *Pourtraits*, ii, fo. 543ᵛ). I am grateful to Christopher Gold for taking me through Thevet's difficult French.

56. For Agrippa's place among sixteenth–century 'libertins' see Wirth, 1977, 601–27. The penultimate paragraph (627) on 'cadres historiques' offers a suggestive analogy between 'libertinage' and 'sorcellerie'.

57. *The Warrender Papers*, ed. A. Cameron, 2 vols., Publications of the Scottish Historical Society, Edinburgh, 1931, vol. 2, 159.

58. *Calendar of Letters and State Papers Relating to English Affairs, 1568–1579*, 1894, 611; *Acts of the Privy Council*, ns. X, 309, 322, 326; *A Rehearsall both straung and true, of hainous and horrible actes committed by Elizabeth Stile*, 1579, in *Witchcraft in England, 1558–1618*, ed. B. Rosen, Amherst, 1991, 83–91; *Démonomanie*, é4ᵛ.

59. The most obvious example is *King Lear*, 3.2.1–9, but see also *The Winter's Tale*, 3.3.91–4, *The Tempest*, 1.2.3–5, and *2 Henry IV*, 1.1.153–4.

60. Robert Greene, *Perimides the Blacksmith*, printed in Maclure, 1979, 29–30.

61. Kyd, writing to Lord Keeper Puckering, BL Harley MS 6849, fo. 218. 'Libel' in the sixteenth century still has as its primary meaning 'little book', 'writing', 'pamphlet' rather than seditious or damaging statement, which seems to have become more current in the seventeenth century, see OED *sv* 'libel'.

62. Joseph Cresswell, *An Advertisement written to a Secretary of my Lord Treasurers of England by an English Intelligencer as he passed through Germany towards Italy*, Antwerp?, 1592, 18. See also *Elizabethae Angliae Reginae Haeresim Calvinianam Propugnantis, Saevissimum in Catholicos sui Regni edictum ... Cum Responsio*, 1592, 36, and Nicholas Davidson's essay in this volume.

11. 'What passions call you these?': *Edward II* and James VI

LAWRENCE NORMAND

In a now familiar formulation, Alan Bray argued that sodomy was conceived in the sixteenth century to be subversive of the entire order of creation; it was 'not ... part of the created order at all; it was part of its dissolution' (1982, 25). Actual cases of sodomy rarely appeared in the English or Scottish courts, yet sodomy was a developed concept in religious, legal and moral ideology. Bray suggests that in the minds of men who had sex with other men there may have been a mental gap between this idea of sodomy as heinous and the actual sexual acts which they enjoyed, a gap which prevented their sexual actions being identified by themselves as sodomy (ibid., 43). When Marlowe wrote *Edward II* in 1592, then, he may have been writing in a context which, on the one hand, fiercely repressed the possibility of sexual acts between men by the fearful idea of sodomy, and yet, on the other hand, was generally indifferent to most same–sex eroticism among men and boys. Bray's understanding of sodomy as an ideological notion is confirmed by evidence from Scotland, where, in 1570, during the civil war between Mary, Queen of Scots and the Protestant party, two men in Edinburgh were executed for the crime of sodomy. The account in *The Historie of James the Sext* interprets the men's actions as being political in intent, a political intervention by Satan to undermine the established order of state by the use of sodomy:

> Thir enormiteis in the cuntrie [i.e. of civil war], as thay war aganis policie and reasoun, sa Sathan had also possest the myndis of tua men to commit the abhominable syn of Sodomie within Edinburgh, for the whilk they war puneist on this maner: first, they were detenit in preasoun for the space of 8 dayis, upoun bread and watter; then thay were placit at the mercat place, with the inscriptioun of thair fault writtin on thair foreheid; efter that they war placit in the kirk, to repent befoir the people thrie severall sondayis; fourthlie, thay were dowkit [ducked] in a deap loch over the heid thrie several tymes; and last of all bund to a staik and fyre kendlit about them wher their bodeis wer brint [burned] to ashis to the death.[1]

The systematic punishments are ideological in the same way as the series of Edward's torments in Marlowe's play. The men's sexual acts were seen as subversive of the social order. The impulse to enact sodomy is not so much sexual as supernatural, since Satan is prompted by political strife (the 'enormiteis' that were 'aganis policie and reasoun') to put the idea of sodomy

172

into the men's heads. The sexual act signifies and enacts Satan's plot to intensify subversion in the country. The process of punishment – immurement followed by spectacular public display – stages sodomy as social subversion and shows it being overcome in a participatory social drama. 'Placit at the mercat place, with the inscriptioun of thair fault writtin on thair foreheid', the men are spectacular proof of Satan's hostility to the state. They are compelled to speak words of repentance in the kirk 'befoir the people thrie severall sondayis', thus affirming the truth of Christian judgement that defines their sexual acts as extreme sin, and proving Christ's power over Satan. Their immersion 'in a deap loch over the heid thrie severall tymes' is a violent, ritual reimposition of baptism's triple immersion, again demonstrating the church's power. The final burning at the stake publicizes the state's will to destroy utterly Satan's agents, as well as showing the repeated and extreme violence required to destroy Satanic power. As a scapegoating ritual, the whole process locates social subversion in the men's sexual acts, and then overcomes it by utterly destroying them, 'brint to ashes to the death'.

The *Historie* continues with another example of 'the bissines of Sathan' in which a minister murders his wife (*Historie*, 64–6). Significantly, though, this story produces a moral effect as the minister confesses and dies penitently 'to the great gude example and comfort of all the behalders' (*Historie*, 66). By contrast, the sodomy narrative effects a closure that blocks any possible moral effects; indeed, it is the story's insistence on absolute destruction as its ending that is its moral point. The men are subjects who are engulfed by their sodomitical acts, and for whom the only possible outcome is to be erased. The murdering minister, on the other hand, retains a subjectivity that allows him moral responses that are recognizable to the onlookers at his execution, even though the impulse to murder, like the impulse to commit sodomy, was planted in his mind by Satan. The idea of 'sodomy' precisely erases the subjectivities and moral capacities of the victims, and projects a simple, totalizing message: sodomy's only meaning is that of negativity, absolute destruction and blank meaninglessness.

Sodomy can be seen as an ideological formation latent in the culture, awaiting a moment of crisis to become activated in particular persons who might then be ritually destroyed. The story of the men executed for having sex with each other confirms Bray's thesis that sodomy was conceived of in the sixteenth century as something that could not be represented – since it was entirely negative. When James VI came to write *Basilicon Doron* in 1598 for Prince Henry, sodomy came to his mind as he wrote of the crimes that a prince might not pardon: 'Witch–craft, wilfull murther, Incest...Sodomie, poisoning, and false coin'.[2] James's words exemplify Bray's thesis that the same person could, apparently contradictorily, hate sodomy and at the same time enjoy homoerotic relations. This contradiction lies in the incommensurability of the sixteenth–century notion of 'sodomy' and the range of actual same–sex desire that might be imagined and experienced in the early modern period. The research done since Bray's pioneer work in 1982 has generally shown that, in Claude J. Summers's words, 'discourse about homosexuality in Renaissance England is more various than [Bray's sodomitical] construction can accommodate'(1994, 27).[3] Sodomy is only one way in which homoeroticism might be represented and imagined. If we want to recognize the range of sixteenth–century homoeroticism we have to look for terms and discourses in addition to that of sodomy.

This essay examines the discourses of homoeroticism in *Edward II* and in certain texts that were produced out of a particular historical episode concerning James VI and Esmé Stewart that bears a close resemblance to the central relationship in Marlowe's play.[4] I am not concerned with uncovering the truth of sexual relations in these texts (far less with the anachronistic notion of sexual identities), but rather with recognizing the available range of discourses in which same–sex eroticism might appear, and thereby reaching a more complex and subtle sense of homoeroticism both in the historical episode and in Marlowe's play. Is it appropriate, however, to compare a play–script with historical writings, since these are different kinds of discourse? Such a comparison may be useful and valid if the texts are read not for their referentiality, but rather for the ways in which they write same–sex desire. Clearly, Marlowe's play recalls real historical figures and depends on historical sources for evidence of Edward and Gaveston's sexuality. But Marlowe reshapes history and, crucially, reinterprets his protagonists' sexuality to suit his dramatic purposes. The play does not refer to real persons so much as to create the illusion of fictional beings. The writings on James VI and Esmé Stewart certainly refer to real people, but I wish to focus on the ways in which those people are represented, which is far from fixed and steady. The final truth of the James–Esmé Stewart affair is lost: its subjective intensity, sexual desire, sexual acts, or political intentions. All that remains of it are linguistic traces. But the shared relation of play–script and historical texts is their capacity to evidence the ways in which same–sex desire might be represented, imagined and brought into being. There is, as Gregory Bredbeck argues, 'a subjective potentiality to the rhetoric of homoeroticism' by which homoeroticism may become a part of who we are as readers (1991, 148). He continues that 'although this potentiality happens in a literary milieu that is patently *not* the same as the material consideration of social subjectivity, if we accept...that textual subjectivity and social subjectivity are engaged with each other, then we can also assume that the presence of the sodomite in literature indicates the *possibility* of the sodomite in society'(ibid.). Bredbeck uses the word 'sodomite' in contradistinction to Bray's usage to include varieties of homoerotic expression. His insistence on the mutual engagement of social and literary texts provides the justification for placing Marlowe's play alongside a moment in history and its textual representations (see also Normand, 1994, 53–68).

II

Marlowe would certainly have known something of Scottish politics. After Marlowe's death, Thomas Kyd wrote down what Marlowe supposedly told him: 'He wold perswade with men of quallitie to goe vnto the K(ing) of Scotts whether / J heare Royden is gon and where if he had liud he told me when J / sawe him last he meant to be' (quoted in Bakeless, 1942, vol.1, 137). This document provides evidence for Marlowe's indirect involvement in, and presumably knowledge of, Scottish affairs. Matthew Roydon was, as Charles Nicholl's investigations have shown, a law–student, writer, and close friend of Marlowe's, part of the intellectual coterie around Henry Percy, Earl of Northumberland, and someone who had been employed to carry letters and news from Burghley in England to Sir Edward Kelley in Prague as 'part of the Cecils' intelligence network' (Nicholl, 1992, 259). Roydon, like Marlowe, was involved in what Nicholl calls the 'cross–over between the poets and the shady servants of government' (ibid., 257). Kyd's statement carries opprobrious implications and is political: Marlowe and Roydon were involved in some way with the succession, in what Nicholl speculates was 'a drift towards James, propagandising for it, persuading wealthy "men of quality" to join a pro–Jacobean faction' (ibid., 261). All this points to certain tantalizing, if unverifiable, possibilities: that Marlowe was about to be employed as a courier to the Scottish Court, or, more generally, that he thought he might find favour there, or even that he was thinking of Scotland as a bolt–hole to escape imminent arrest. It looks as if Marlowe was watching the situation in Scotland with an eye to personal advancement. His friend Matthew Roydon seems to have found such advancement there, for in 1604 he is mentioned in a lawsuit as 'living in the house of James's favourite, William Hamilton, Earl of Haddington' (ibid., 334). Marlowe would also have acquired knowledge of Scottish affairs from Robert Poley, 'an old Scottish hand', in Nicholl's words (ibid., 261), who had been travelling to and from Scotland for many years. In 1583 information about the D'Aubigny affair would have reached England through no less a person than Sir Francis Walsingham, who travelled to Scotland that year to remonstrate with James once it was over; and it was around this time that Marlowe may have started work for the English government as a spy. It would have been easy for Marlowe to have learnt of the Scottish king, who was three years his junior, and his doings through these channels, and it is likely that he would have been drawn to historical events which displayed what Claude J. Summers calls his 'characteristic association of eroticism with issues of power and his equally characteristic resistance to his society's attitudes toward homoerotics' (1995, 465).

The events which took place in Scotland about twelve years before Marlowe wrote *Edward II* involved the fourteen year old King James and the Frenchman Esmé Stewart, sixth Sieur D'Aubigny.[5] I am proposing that the narrative outline of these events provided Marlowe with a way of organizing his diverse material from 'the cluttered narrative of Holinshed' and other materials into the spare and purposeful plot of *Edward II*.[6] In 1579 Esmé Stewart, 37 years old, a member of the Lennox branch of the Stewart family, left his wife and four children and travelled to Scotland. He was a first cousin to James's father, Henry Stewart, Lord Darnley, and in 1579 stood close to the Scottish throne. It seems likely that James wrote to him inviting him to Scotland, possibly at the suggestion of Catholics at court who would welcome a Catholic royal kinsman. D'Aubigny quickly found favour with the king. In March 1580 he was made Earl of Lennox after the existing Earl was persuaded to accept another title. By September 1580, and with a speed equal to that of Gaveston's advancement, he had been made a privy councillor, governor of Dumbarton castle, first gentleman of the bedchamber and, like Gaveston, Lord Chamberlain, an office specially revived for him that allowed him to accompany the King wherever he went. Lennox declared in a letter to the King that he had left his wife and children 'pour du tout me dédier à vous', and that he would die for him to prove 'la fidelité qu'ay engravée dedans mon coeur, laquelle me dura éternellement'.[7] Queen Elizabeth was alarmed at the sudden rise to power in the Scottish Court of a Catholic subject of a foreign power, but her ambassador failed to dissuade James from favouring Lennox. The King meanwhile was instructing his kinsman in Protestantism, as were some Edinburgh ministers, who were unconvinced of the Frenchman's sincerity. Lennox played a leading part in the downfall of the ex–Regent, the Earl of Morton, who had run the government for the last eight years and who was executed in 1581. The Earl of Lennox became Duke of Lennox, the second person in the realm and with a strengthening claim on the throne. He received Morton's castle and lordship of Dalkeith. During the autumn of 1581, two years after his arrival, he was involved in a plot hatched in France and Spain to invade England, overthrow Elizabeth and install Mary and James as joint sovereigns over England and Scotland. James was secretly informed; he allowed the plan to develop, and by early 1582 Lennox had won agreement from two Jesuit agents of France and Spain that he or the Duke of Guise should command a promised army of 20,000 that would be paid for by those two countries. While the plot remained secret, suspicion and hatred of Lennox grew in the Kirk and among a strongly Protestant faction at court. A plot to seize the King was hatched, and in August 1582, when he was travelling to Perth after hunting in the highlands, James was captured and held in a *coup d'état* in the castle of Ruthven, and forced to accede to the installation of a fiercely Protestant regime. James was separated from Lennox, and forced by his captors to declare himself to be free. Lennox meanwhile plotted to release James but failed, and finally left the country in December 1582. His attempts to win Elizabeth's support for a return to Scotland also failed, and in France in May 1593 he died, refusing on his death–bed the ministrations of priests and declaring himself to be a Protestant. James escaped from his captors in August 1583, three months after Lennox's death, and the new regime was overthrown. The Lennox affair was over. In the same month James Stewart, Earl of Arran, James's new favourite, reappeared on the Privy Council.

The episode provided Marlowe with the example of a Renaissance prince's passionate attachment to a favourite that in many ways resembled Edward II's passion for Gaveston in its combination of desire, power, and politics. A play representing obliquely an episode of King James's life would be of immediate interest to an English audience whose monarch he was likely to become. The focus of interest for this essay, however, is not to identify any precise (or vague) historical similarities (impressive though these are), but rather to analyse the different discourses in which the Lennox affair came to be represented. The eroticism of the James–Lennox affair is not co–extensive with the discursive boundaries of sodomy, and those who wrote about it represent its eroticism within a range of other discourses. As Valerie Traub has argued, 'the meanings of homoerotic desire during the early modern period seem to have been remarkably unfixed'; and she continues, the 'discourses of homoeroticism were neither monological nor monovocal'.[8] Homoeroticism, instead, since it has no identifiable social definition nor social discourse of its own, makes its appearance in discourses which seem to be other than erotic. Writers putting the James–Lennox affair into discourse employ a variety of rhetorical tactics that represents the dispersed, multivalent, and contradictory meanings of homoeroticism. Traub's aims, in her investigations of Shakespeare, are the same as those pursued here, 'to delineate not only those statements [describing the subjective erotic dramas of early modern people] that circulate throughout the social fabric, but also to "re–vision" and put into play those historical meanings that have been repressed, lost, or unspoken' (ibid., 114). In *Edward II* there are many discourses and social practices in which we can read a range of signs by which homoerotic desire might be recognized, imagined, and experienced. Even a king, it may be added, is a subject in relation to the forms of representation, both social and textual, in which his experience may find expression, though a king has more power than a subject to shape his actions and how they are represented. In this respect a king is both subject and sovereign; subject like everyone else in his culture to the prescribed forms of representation, but more empowered to attempt to shape those representations

177

to his will. Both James and Marlowe's Edward make this attempt. The stories of both seem to confirm Traub's contention that homoerotic desire is 'located within a matrix of gender and status relations', and is to be understood 'in relation to other modes of power'(ibid., 113). Lennox's sophisticated, courtly term of affection and respect for James was 'mon petit maistre' (Bingham, 1968, 144). The use of this term seems likely to have resulted from differences of age, sexual experience, political power, and nationality. How powerful are the locations that homoerotic desire may inhabit within the social and ideological fields when confronted by other configurations of power, such as ecclesiastical or political? The same problematic is evident in the play and in the texts which record the homoeroticism of the Lennox affair: how does that which may only be indirectly nameable, thinkable or imaginable appear in discourse? Accounts of the James–Lennox relationship are heterogeneous and divergent, and attribute different valencies and meanings to the eroticism they recognize or deny there.

There is, of course, the discourse of gossip. If Marlowe did hear about the King of Scots, a likely way was through gossip. Most of this has vanished, and what scraps remain are as true as gossip ever is. What gossip may reveal are the ways people are thinking, and the implicit limits of respectable public statement beyond which unrespectable or unfounded gossip may flourish. It is in the gossip about James that sex is closest to the surface. The Englishman Sir Henry Widdrington reported that James was 'in such love with him as in the oppen sight of the people, oftentymes he will claspe him about the neck with his armes and kisse him'.[9] David Moysie, another observer of the scene, was clerk to the privy council and well placed to observe the Court's workings, and he kept a private memoir in the form of a chronicle of events. Moysie's writing is private (only being published in the nineteenth century) and so records events in ways that need only make sense to himself as he writes; it is not writing that is engaged with political or theological power seeking to produce certain ideological effects. For these reasons, Moysie's memoirs might be read as revealing a view of James and Lennox that is unremarkable to an educated man close to the heart of government. Interpretation or subjective comment on any matter in Moysie is rare, and appears only when it is needed to account for political events. It is significant, then, that Moysie mentions James's intimate emotional response to D'Aubigny to account for their extraordinary relationship: '...his Majestie, having conceavit ane inwaird affectioun to the said lord Obynnie, enterit in great familiaretie and quyet purpoisses with him'.[10] What 'quyet purpoisses' are it is impossible precisely to say. The personal and political in Moysie's words are not easily disentangled: James's unceremonious personal dealings with D'Aubigny extend to political intimacy. The power differential between king and courtier is the enabling condition which generates the king's 'affection', as well as that which enables that 'affection' to find expression in 'familiaretie and quyet purpoisses'. Moysie needs no special language to describe James's feelings; but it is the very absence of language specially marked by homophobia as 'homosexual' (which modern readers expect) that has allowed homoerotic desire to be repressed or ignored.

John Hacket, who became Bishop of Coventry and Lichfield, recorded years later (after James had become King of England) that the king's relationship with D'Aubigny was both emotionally and physically intense: '...from the time he was fourteen years old and no more, that is when the Lord D'Aubigny came into Scotland out of France to visit him, even then he began, and with that noble personage, to clasp someone gratioso in the embraces of his great love, above all others'.[11] D'Aubigny's arrival is the occasion, Hacket suggests, for James's first passionate attachment to a man, which is the first of a series of such attachments that delineate an aspect of James's erotic nature. There is sexual pleasure – and need – in the king's urge 'to clasp someone gratioso in the embraces of his great love'; although the word 'love' may contain James's passions, despite Hacket's sly knowingness, within the bounds of friendship. Hacket sees something like sexual desire, but names it love. The signs of male friendship in the sixteenth century, as Alan Bray has shown, were intense and physical: 'the embraces and the protestations of love, the common bed and the physical closeness, the physical and emotional intimacy', and yet they were not taken to be signs of illicit sexual desire (Bray, 1990, 7). James Melville, a minister who was to write about James and Lennox, illustrates Bray's thesis as he writes about his friend Thomas Seton, 'whom I was verie glad to accompanie, whylls to Sterling, and now and then to his kirk, for my instruction and comfort. He lovit me exceeding weill, and wald at parting thrust my head in his bosome and kis me'.[12] Male friendship encompassed a breadth of behaviours that to twentieth–century eyes seem sexual (and are now proscribed); and yet were not then so interpreted. Within the broad compass of physical intimacy and emotional response that constituted friendship, then, both James's attachment to D'Aubigny and Edward's to Gaveston might be acceptably represented. But, as Bray argues, 'the signs of [friendship] were sometimes also the signs of [sodomy]', and the distinction between them was 'neither as sharp nor as clearly marked as the Elizabethans would have us believe'; there was therefore an 'unacknowledged connection between the unmentionable vice of Sodom and the friendship which all accounted commendable' (1990, 8). Same–sex attachments that seem to exceed friendship's broad limits problematize their own representation, and create the opportunity to be represented in the hostile discourse of sodomy. For a king to be a sodomite is a contradiction in terms since sodomy implies the overthrow of the established order. It is, in Edward Coke's words, '*crimen laesae majestatis,* a sin horrible committed against the king: and this is either against the king celestial or terrestrial'.[13] But if 'sodomy' is an impossible definition for a king's enacted desires, its discourse is nevertheless potentially present in the acceptable discourse of friendship. James's enemies were slow to approach sodomitical suggestion in their writing, so fearful and dangerous were its ideological and political implications, but eventually they did so. Edward II too is eventually in the play cast as a sodomite.

The ministers of the reformed, Calvinist church of Scotland were particularly hostile to Lennox. In their sermons they attacked Lennox on several fronts as a source of sexual and social disorder: for his 'prodigalitie and vanitie in apparrell', like Gaveston being attacked for his 'short Italian hooded cloak / Larded with pearl' (1.4.412–3). Lennox is also attacked for his 'superfluitie of banquetting and delicat cheere', his 'deflowering of dames and virgins' (the harlots 'Fawcon and Armstrong' in particular), for abusing 'his Majestie's chaste ears...with unknowne Italian and Frenche formes of oaths'(quoted in Bingham, 1968, 161), as well as provoking the King 'to the pleasures of the flesh' (Calderwood, 1843, 649). The last comment comes close to naming a sexual relation between king and favourite. For the ministers, Lennox was a sodomite in the sense of one who subverts sexual, social and political boundaries. Accusations of Lennox's heterosexual excesses ran alongside rumours of his sexual feebleness: the presbyterian historian David Calderwood reports how 'libells were spread in the king's chamber, and other places, wherin Lennox was called a feeble sow, that saw his wife deflowred before his eyes' (Calderwood, 1843, 487). Suspicions that Lennox's desire for the King was sodomitical come close to being directly asserted in a sermon of Walter Balcanquhall in St Giles Kirk in Edinburgh in December 1580, which condemned:

> the whoordoms and adultereis of your courts; the murthers, the oppressiouns, the cruelteis, and all the rest of the vices that are into your courts. But rather by the contrare, with Christ, I pronounce this against you, and against all courts, that except yee doe repent, it sall be easier for Sodome and Gomorrha in the day of the Lord's judgements, than it sall be for you. And, therefore, my lords, the exhortatioun that I give unto you in the name of the Lord is this, That everie one of you be carefull, first, to beginne to reforme your owne persons, to reforme your owne housses and courts; to travel and see that the king's hous be weill reformed, that no profane nor mischant persons be found there, but suche as feare the name of God.[14]

The letter that Queen Elizabeth's ambassador read to the Convention of the

Estates on 20 February 1581 also represented Lennox as intent on corrupting the King, though emphasizing less his moral and sexual corruption than his religious and political perversion: '...it had beene discovered by sindrie meanes unto her Majestie,' Elizabeth wrote:

> that the Pope and his adherents have concluded...to attempt the recovering of Scotland to his obedience...by sending Monsieur D'Aubigney, a profest Papist, into Scotland, under colour of his kinred to the king...partlie by dissimulatioun and courting with the king, being young, and of a noble and gentle nature, and partlie by nourishing and making factiouns among the nobilitie...to bring strangers, being Romanists, into the realme, for his partie, and, consequentlie, by degrees, to alter religioun, yea, in the end, to bring the person of the young king in danger; which is seene verie easie to be done, by colour of his office, being now...made his principall chamberlan, and possessor of his person: and so to make himself,...speciallie by pretence of his neerenesse in blood to the king, to gett the crown also, in the end, to himself.
> (ibid., 491)

In this scenario, religious subversion and political ambition are imagined as happening under cover of Lennox's gradually coming to dominate and direct, with the King's compliance and pleasure, his affections and possibly his very body. The personal and political are conjoined in an enterprise, directed by the Pope, that threatens the person of the King, the realm's religion, and the crown's succession, and that therefore might be called, in its potential for subversion, sodomitical. Elizabeth's letter represents the affection or eroticism in the James–Lennox affair as resulting from Lennox's politically subversive intentions (like Satan's with the executed sodomites) and James's youthful good nature, and gives a sinister reading of the James–Lennox relationship that in its thoroughgoing politicization might be called political sodomy.

Some religious ministers did not see things as simply either sexual corruption or political threat. James Melville, nephew and supporter of the leading presbyterian Andrew Melville, hardly sees sex at all in the King's attachment to Lennox, though his autobiography shows him conscious of the dangers of his own heterosexual desires.[15] He, like Elizabeth, sees in Lennox primarily the threat of Catholic ascendancy, complaining of the 'Papists that haid flocked hame with and efter Monsieur d'Obignie, wha haid presence and credit at Court' (*Autobiography and Diary*, 80), noting that the Negative Confession of Faith of 1581 was meant 'for removing suspition of Papistrie from the Court' (ibid., 87), and that the Ruthven raiders who held the King in August 1582 claimed they wanted to 'schew his majestie whow all things

181

went wrang be the misgoverning of that new Counsall com latlie from France', and that, like Edward favouring Gaveston at the expense of long established nobles, James ought to banish his present counsellors and 'tak him[self] to be counsallit be his auld Nobilitie' (ibid., 133–4). Although Melville's stated intention in writing was to trace God's involvement in events, 'to haiff recordit the wark of God, quhilk I saw with my eis, and hard with my eares'(ibid., 118), something else appears in his writing that registers Lennox as more than just a corrupting Catholic counsellor. Melville does indeed register Lennox as corrupting James's whole political outlook, describing the King as being 'sa miserablie corrupted' at the 'wrong' time, at the start of his youth, and so unnaturally and perhaps radically, with false accounts of what happened in his minority, and dangerous political ideas about governing church and state (ibid., 119). But quite unexpectedly, a sentence appears in a different register when Melville describes James's separation from Lennox: 'And sa the King and the Duc war dissivered [dissevered], and never saw uther againe'(ibid., 134). This is not the language of politics but rather of medieval or Renaissance romance, and it unsettles the surrounding discourse, emerging to represent the James–Lennox affair as a love story rather than a political conspiracy.[16] Melville returns to providential, political analysis when he records how the Kirk did 'rejoise in God, and thank him for delyvering King, Kirk, and Commoun–weill of sic cownsall, as sett tham selves plainlie to pervert all' (ibid., 134); and he sees the Duke's downfall as demonstrating harsh, retributive justice:

> ...[before] he gatt passage [to sea], he was put to als hard a dyet as he causit the Erle of Morton till use ther, yea, evin to the tother extremitie that he haid usit at Court: For, wheras his kitching was sa sumptuus that lumpes of butter was cast in the fyre when it soked [smouldered]...he was fean till eat of a magre [lean] goose, skowdrit with bar stra [scorched with barley straw].'
> (ibid., 134)

Just as the fallen Edward's deprivation is made to contrast with his previous material comfort, so Lennox's fall from power and his personal humiliation become to his enemies a narrative of poetic justice. This similarity, along with others that are noted, suggests that in *Edward II* Marlowe was tracing the congruence of the James–Lennox and Edward–Gaveston stories.

Another version of the James–Lennox relationship emerges from inside the court in the account of Sir James Melville, courtier, diplomat, loyalist and confidant of the King, whose *Memoirs* recognize nothing unusual in James's favouring Lennox. Melville responds to the affair with no anxiety, much as Mortimer Senior does in Marlowe's play: for them it is a familiar aspect of courtly government. Melville recognizes the strong feelings between James and Lennox, but sees their relation simply as part of the political scene, subsuming the personal into the political, and representing personal feelings as a function of state. He attributes the dangerous intrigues in Court leading to the Earl of Morton's fall to the influence of 'thir twa yong men [Lennox and James Stewart] about [the king], wha knew of na parelis [perils]'.[17] Lennox, he writes, who 'was cheiffest about His Maieste', was 'of nature vpricht, just and gentill, laking the experience of the estait of the contre...Bot his cheiffest falt was, that he being trew to the King, he was thocht vnwonnable [unwinable] to ther [James Stewart (the 'English party' in Scotland) and the English ambassador] behoue, as he wes indeed' (*Memoirs* 275). Melville sees no international conspiracy nor sodomitical subversion; but merely Lennox's inexperience and susceptibility to intrigue: he 'wes led be euell consellours...wherby he wes moued to medle in sic hurtfull and dangerous courses, that the rest of the nobilite tok suspition' (ibid., 275). With suave confidence in his judgement, Melville passes judgement on Lennox: 'He louit baith the King and the commown weall, bot he wantit experience' (ibid., 281); love is directed unproblematically to the person and the state in a familiar formulation. Melville calmly records the feelings of king and favourite after their enforced separation, though noting the surprising intensity of James's reaction: 'his Maieste tok the matter farther till hart then any man wald haue beleuit' (ibid., 281). James's personal loss is indivisible from his political humiliation in Melville's account, as James 'lamentit his mishandling to sindre noblemen...[and said] that he intendid to releaue him self with tym of ther handis who held him as captyue', as he suffered what Melville calls 'inwart greif for his [own] taking and retenying' (ibid., 283). Melville registers James's strong feelings but he does not note them as exceptional. The way he accounts for Lennox's death from grief is also contained within the discourse of Court politics: '...the Duc of Lenox, wha wes past throw England to France, wher he died schortly efter of a seaknes contracted for displeasour' (ibid., 283). 'Displeasure' is grief or sorrow, but its cause is obscure: neither specifically sorrow for the king's love nor for political failure. The subjective responses that Melville identifies are contained within the discourse of state affairs; and although modern readers of his *Memoirs* might imagine they are glimpsing James's and Lennox's homoerotic love, what emerges from his discourse is an unproblematic blending of the personal and the political.

The historian John Spottiswoode's *History of the Church of Scotland* gives another articulation of the James–Lennox relationship which comes close to one version of the Edward–Gaveston relation as subjective desire. As a scrupulous historian, Spottiswoode voices the Kirk's opposition, but at the same time, surprisingly, he articulates a sympathetic subjectivity for the King that suggests something that is neither the political subversion of sodomy, nor sexual corruption, nor international Catholic machiavellianism, but rather the intensity of personal feeling. In his detailed account of events Spottiswoode, like Sir James Melville, locates Lennox within the matrix of politics, but sees the church–state conflict as the main engine of events. In his eyes, Lennox shows 'courteous and modest behavior' when he first arrives in Scotland, but is soon hated for his 'sudden and unexpected preferment' (Spottiswoode, 1847–51, vol.2, 266). The Kirk opposes Lennox on the grounds of his Catholicism, seconded by the English ambassador whose address to the Convention of Estates in 1581 objects that 'such a person...be tolerated to possess the King, him alone, and rule all things at his pleasure' (ibid., 275). But religious and personal corruption are barely separable in this discourse. In 1582 the Kirk ordered a fast day for, among other reasons, 'the aboundance of sin...and the danger wherein the king stood by the company of wicked persons, who did seek to corrupt him in manners and religion' (ibid., 288). Spottiswoode gives ample evidence of this familiar discourse of corruption by which the Kirk justified its hostility to Lennox, and its support for the *coup d'état* in which James was captured. The lords who held the King and separated him from his favourite parallel the rebel lords in *Edward II* who seize Edward. Lennox was banished to France, and James eventually escaped his captors. The Kirk approved the rebels' intention 'to guard and preserve the innocent person of the king his majesty and estate, being in no less hazard then the other, and to remove the corruptions and confusion entered into the body of the commonwealth' (ibid., 294). The double threat is to the person of the king and the state, and the state is threatened precisely by corruption directed at the king. This comes close to accusing the Duke of sodomy, and the language is charged with sodomitical suggestion: 'corruptions and confusion entered into the body of the commonwealth'. The language here expresses an image of physical invasion or even penetration of the body that epitomizes political sodomy. It is Edward's fate to suffer in his body the physical enactment of this discourse.

But Spottiswoode writes a counter–discourse to the Kirk's view of James and Lennox that presents the protagonists as having complex subjectivities. He notes that the duke was someone 'to whom the king could deny nothing' (ibid., 280). He records that when James was captured by the rebels, he burst into tears, prompting the contemptuous response from the Master of Glamis, '"It is no matter of his tears, better that bairns should weep then bearded men"'; and adds that these 'words entered so deeply into the king's heart, as he did never forget them' (ibid., 290). Spottiswoode suggests the king's concern for Lennox when he fell ill on his first attempt to leave Scotland: 'The king, advertised of his ill disposition, advised him to travel through England in regard of the winter season' (ibid., 297). When finally Lennox was ordered to leave Scotland, Spottiswoode writes that 'He craved to see the king and be permitted only to salute him; but this being denied, he departed in great heaviness.'(ibid., 297) This recalls Edward's plea to see Gaveston for the last time (*Edward II*, 2.5), and it creates a space of intense personal feeling in Spottiswoode's discourse. He suggests that sorrow might actually have contributed to the duke's death, who 'partly of grief, partly through the long and troublesome journey he made in that cold and rainy season, contracted a fever at his coming to Paris, whereof after a few days he died' (ibid., 298). James, he writes, was 'much perplexed...with the report of the duke of Lennox his death' (ibid., 298). Spottiswoode's narrative, however, has a happy ending, as he recounts James's calling Lennox's eldest son, the thirteen year old Lodowick, from France in 1583: 'The king receiving him with great expressions of love, did presently invest him in his father's lands and honours' (ibid., 306). 'Thus', Spottiswoode concludes the entire story, 'the untimely loss of their father did turn to the children's benefit, by the constant and unmatchable kindness of a loving king'(ibid.). The story finally resolves into a demonstration of James's royal grace and power.

The tenor of Spottiswoode's history owes much to the politics of establishment historiography in which he seeks to defend the royal, episcopalian view against the presbyterian outlook of the Kirk; and his sympathetic account of James and Lennox contributes to this overall aim. The accounts of the affair become a function of the wider ideological conflicts in late sixteenth–century Scotland. Spottiswoode's history is significant in that it allows two quite separate discourses to emerge, the Kirk's and Spottiswoode's own, which offer conflicting ways of understanding the relationship. *Edward II* contains broadly similar, conflicting accounts of its central relationship, which also spring from wider political difference. All these Scottish texts are not innocent of political purpose: they all have something at stake in their writing. The same can be said of the characters in Marlowe's *Edward II* who render versions of Edward's relation with Gaveston which suit their own political interests.

III

Two texts exist which might be expected to give us direct access to the subjective dimension of this relationship: a letter Lennox wrote to James on the day he died, and James's poem, 'Ane Metaphoricall Invention of a Tragedie called Phoenix', written after Lennox's death and published in 1584.[18] But neither in fact offers easy access to its writer's experience or self–consciousness. Lennox's letter asked James to protect his children, warned him against certain lords, and, what is startling, promised to send James his embalmed heart (Bingham, 1968, 184–5). This seems to promise the core of his being, a symbol of his love, giving James priority over his wife, but it is an uncertain, if excessive, sign pointing perhaps to the intimacy of lovers or friends. It seems to anticipate Edward's lines when he is recaptured, telling Leicester to 'rip up this panting breast of mine, / And take my heart in rescue of my friends' (*Edward II*, 4.7.66–7). Other reports described Lennox on his deathbed refusing the last rites of a Catholic priest, and professing to die as a Protestant. Both the profession and the letter might of course be the performance of a shrewdly political death; and illustrate what Bingham calls Lennox's 'duplicity of motive' (1968, 186). James's poem is no less ambiguous. It identifies the phoenix of its title as Esmé Stewart, and addresses it as 'she'. The wild beauty of this unique bird impressed all who saw her, but it was James who tamed her (presumably by D'Aubigny's religious conversion). But the 'rauening fowlis' (1.98)[19] came to hate the phoenix and drove it to its fiery destruction. James bemoans the loss of the phoenix's physical beauty, in the feathers whose 'heauenly hewes, whilkis loued / Were baith by men and fowlis that did them see'(ll.234–5), and the phoenix's 'rarenes (sen there was none of her kynde / But she alone'(ll.242–3). A moment of textual awkwardness may reveal a sexual fantasy or sexual memory: pursued by her enemies the phoenix flees to the speaker, 'yet they followed fast / Till she betuix my leggs her selfe did cast'(ll.165–6), and shortly after that the speaker's legs are bleeding, 'in stede of her, yea whyles they made to bleid / My leggs' (ll.171–2). But the poem is not evidence of the eroticism of the relationship, since it doubly displaces Lennox into a female figure, and a bird. Rather, it performs a refashioning and revaluation of the relationship destined for public consumption in a published volume. Like Spottiswoode, James provides a happy ending that overcomes the 'tragedy' of the phoenix's death, since the ashes in which the phoenix lies promises that it will rise again, unlike the ashes in which the sodomites were burned which signified their utter extinction. In the poem at least, James has power to shape and publish representations that can serve as an answer to his enemies' hostile representations.

The king's power to shape discourse took a directly political form when he issued three proclamations in 1583: one prohibiting men from speaking of Lennox as anything other than a true Christian, under pain of death; and another declaring that James had been detained in the Ruthven Raid against his will (Moysie, *Memoirs,* 46). Perhaps James's feelings are most evident in a poem written some time between June 1581 and June 1582, 'Since thought is free, thinke what thou will' (*Poems of James VI*, vol.2, 132), which enunciates the machiavellian political insight that a prince must 'Be cairefull' (1.5), and keep his thoughts and feelings to himself: 'pleas thy selfe with thy concaite / And lett none knowe what thou does meane' (ll. 7–8).[20] James, unlike Edward, turns away from tragedy and conforms himself to actual political conditions. He emerged from the affair as a redefined political agent who had learned how to manipulate the self in the exercise of power: he acquired a new technique of power, that of dissimulation. The idea of the phoenix may have occured to James as he sent for Lennox's thirteen year old son from France, the new Duke of Lennox, and welcomed him to Court.[21]

IV

Edward II presents a range of articulations of the central relationship similar to those that treat the James and Lennox affair; and, indeed, the play can be read as dramatizing a struggle of competing discourses over the subject of same–sex eroticism. But Marlowe does more than simply introduce into his play the range of same–sex discourses that were either conventionally or routinely available to him in his culture: he goes beyond those discourses to produce an articulation of same–sex desire which creates its own space of sexual self–consciousness and homoerotic subjectivity. The power of the play lies in its insistence on representing same–sex desire as something that exceeds and escapes the familiar same–sex articulations of the sort that emerge in the accounts of James and Lennox. *Edward II* gives value to same–sex desire as a form of passionate relationship and self–defining subjectivity, which exceeds the other representations of homoeroticism that run through it, and indeed may even provide the ground for, and ironize, other discourses of desire.

In Act 2 Scene 1, where Lady Margaret appears as a lover reading a letter from her beloved Gaveston, the familiar early modern social articulation of marriage is merely an echo of a moment of same–sex desire earlier articulated, for Lady Margaret's situation repeats that of Gaveston and Edward at the start of the play. Her first words, 'The grief for his exile was not so much / As is the joy of his returning home' (2.1.57–8), echo Edward's joy at Gaveston's return. There are even some verbal echoes from the first scene: the words of Gaveston's letter to her, 'I will not long be from thee, though I die' (2.1.63), echo Gaveston's sexually charged line, 'The king, upon whose bosom let me die' (1.1.13). Lady Margaret speaks from within the conventions of courtly heterosexual love, but her words and her situation are ironized in several ways: the intensity of feeling in this scene does not match that in the first, and the words seem by contrast conventional and empty; the voicing of heterosexual desire is surrounded by, and shot through with, signs of intense same–sex desire; and this moment follows immediately after that in which Spencer and Baldock initiate a strand of same–sex action by preparing to seek favour from Gaveston. Lady Margaret's courtly love discourse seems relatively powerless as a way of realizing her desires, even though, as Spencer comments, 'Our lady's first love is not wavering; / My life for thine, she will have Gaveston' (2.1.27–8). Her proposed marriage is itself a function of Edward's love for Gaveston, since it depends on it not only for its language but also for its social and political arrangement. It is intended to bring Gaveston into a kinship relation with the King: and in these ways it is entwined with political considerations. This brief dramatic moment raises the question of how much power inheres in Lady Margaret's heterosexual courtly discourse in the midst of conflicting political and erotic pressures; for in the answer to that depends her success in gaining the satisfaction of her desires. Edward is in an analogous position to Lady Margaret, since the satisfaction of his desires depends on how successfully they can be realised within the socially available discourses. The material practice of marriage is one such discourse. James could claim kinship as a basis for favouring Lennox, and that carried weight. In the play, Gaveston is not Edward's kin but this marriage will start to make him kin. It is Edward's sovereign power that wills Lady Margaret 'to repair unto the court / And meet [her] Gaveston' (2.1.67–8) in order to bind the King closer to his favourite, rather than to please Lady Margaret. The pathos of her situation lies in her apparently speaking the language of erotic freedom while being subject to the dictates of power politics.

Although the language and action of the play are fully sexualized, it is not the language of homosexual desire familiar to the twentieth century. And while characters in the play recognize sexuality in the relationship of the King and Gaveston, they do not have one single discourse in which to represent it. Like the accounts of James and Lennox, same–sex eroticism appears in several discourses which are not necessarily tabooed nor specifically marked as sexual: marriage, sodomy, neoplatonism, friendship, patronage. Marlowe dramatizes his characters attempting various ways adequately to represent the Edward–Gaveston relationship. Two utterly opposed versions of male same–sex eroticism frame the action of the play: Gaveston's fantasy scene involving 'nymphs', 'satyrs', and 'a lovely boy in Dian's shape' (1.1.57–60), and the squalid, humiliating murder of Edward, in which sodomy, understood as an extreme of subversive transgression, coincides with the crude notion of sodomy understood merely as anal intercourse. Gaveston's pageant represents homoerotic desire itself, arousing and offering the possibility of satisfying it as the boy teases and stimulates the onlooker: 'And in his sportful hands an olive tree / To hide those parts which men delight to see' (1.1.63–4). Although the hunt of Actaeon could be and was read moralistically, what Gaveston's speech emphasizes is pleasure, sensuousness, physical beauty, and sexual allure (see Woods, 1992, 69–84). Edward's murder, on the other hand, is the work of his enemies and is designed, like the execution of the Scottish sodomites, to impose on him their conception of sodomy that signifies the dissolution of the royal identity. Between these two extreme and conflicting representations, however, lies the rest of the play in which same–sex eroticism is located in various conflicting discourses.

It is the *excess*, in the eyes of the Court, in Edward's relation with Gaveston that problematizes it, and prompts others to try to give an account of it. The nobles see Edward's relation with Gaveston as a political problem, as it manifests itself in Gaveston's power, just as the Protestant Melville saw Lennox. Lancaster protests, '"My lord of Cornwall" now at every word; / And happy is the man whom he vouchsafes, / For vailing of his bonnet' (1.2.17–9). For others it is Gaveston's class that they detest: Mortimer is touchiest about this, calling Gaveston 'villain... / That hardly art a gentleman by birth' (1.4.27–8). James could claim royal kinship as a basis for favouring Lennox: Marlowe deliberately lowers Gaveston's social rank to emphasize class differences (see Forker, 1994, 52). Edward's marrying Gaveston to Lady Margaret has him introducing Gaveston into kinship relations among aristocratic and royal families, as a way of giving expression to, and naturalizing, his feelings for his favourite. If Gaveston were to be ensconced within the Gloucester family, then kinship and homoerotic relations might be reconcilable. But Edward's passion for Gaveston, and the political hostility it arouses, works against this solution, and keeps that passion problematical.

Insofar as Edward's desire for Gaveston in the play exceeds conventional early modern ways of representing and naturalizing it, either in social practices or discursive formations, the problem appears of knowing what it is and how to account for it. As Valerie Traub has commented, 'what is culturally specific is not the fact or presence of desire toward persons of the same gender, but the meanings that are attached to its expression'.[22] The signification of same–sex desire may barely be named, as when Edward appears grieving for his banished lover, and Lancaster cries '*Diablo*! What passions call you these?' (1.4.318). Having no name for what he is seeing he reaches for a language other than English, like the word 'gratioso' used of James's embraces by Hacket, the expletive '*Diablo!*' invoking Spain as a place of powerful, alien pleasures, but also suggesting the Christian horror of homoeroticism as manifesting the diabolic. Edward uses neoplatonic ideas to represent his and Gaveston's love. When Gaveston first returns from France Edward asks, 'Knowest thou not who I am? / Thy friend, thy self, another Gaveston' (1.1.141–2). In this version of male friendship two men are so similar that they effectively share a common soul and body. These fragments of conventional neoplatonic idealism are not, however, adequate to the sexual content of the relationship, nor strong enough to survive as a way of plausibly representing Edward's attachment to Gaveston in the face of hostile political pressures, and this language is abandoned.

Marlowe also inserts an account of homoeroticism which places it in terms of classical rhetoric and values. When Mortimer Senior advises his nephew to let Edward have his lover since 'riper years will wean him from such toys' (1.4.400), he provides a catalogue of rulers and heroes who had male lovers:

> The mightiest kings have had their minions:
> Great Alexander loved Hephestion;
> The conquering Hercules for Hylas wept;
> And for Patroclus stern Achilles droop'd.'
> (1.4.390–3)

Same–sex passions are transvalued here into a positive attribute of 'mightiest kings' and 'wisest men'. Marlowe shows Mortimer trying to identify Edward and Gaveston's mutual passion as a familiar characteristic throughout history of certain political leaders and, like Sir James Melville and John Spottiswoode, trying to subsume it within the familiar socio–political practices of court culture. Mortimer resists this reading, and insists on the immediate political effect on the nobles of the relationship. He dismisses Edward's feelings as a mere 'wanton humour' (1.4.401), and focuses on the financial and political effects of Edward's favouring Gaveston who, according to Mortimer, 'wears a lord's revenue on his back, / And, Midas–like, he jets it in the court' (1.4.406–7). What the barons see in Edward's relationship with Gaveston is not primarily a sexual relationship, but rather a distorted political relationship: it is the displacement of patronage from the nobility which traditionally received it to the upstart newcomer that enrages the barons, with the additional sting that it is a foreigner on whom the wealth is being heaped. Mortimer detests Edward's sexual attachment to Gaveston not for its sex in itself, but as the cause of redirected patronage and his own political disadvantage. Or, to reverse the explanation, they see political disadvantage as the outcome and effect of homoeroticism, and therefore hate that eroticism for its political effects. The inseparable fusion of erotic and political interests is evident in Mortimer's angry charge hurled at the King in Act 2, Scene 2: 'The idle triumphs, masques, lascivious shows, / And prodigal gifts bestowed on Gaveston', he claims, 'Have drawn thy treasure dry and made thee weak' (156–9); where 'treasure' may refer both to money in the exchequer and to Edward's store of semen.[23] Signs of political irresponsibility become readable as signs of sexual excess, with sexual and political meanings intermingled in the same discourse.

It is Edward who imagines a private discursive and geographical space where his relation with Gaveston might be realized, a politically impossible, utopian space that can exist only in discourse.[24] He agrees to Gaveston's banishment, 'So', he says, 'I may have some nook or corner left / To frolic with my dearest Gaveston' (1.4.72–3). He expresses his love for Gaveston as intense, private and separate from other areas of experience. His sense of himself only exists, he claims, when Gaveston is present: 'Ah, had some bloodless Fury rose from hell, / And with my kingly sceptre struck me dead / When I was forced to leave my Gaveston!' (1.4.315–7). When he is being tormented by his jailors he accepts responsiblity for the deaths of Gaveston and the Spencers, and sees that relation as purely interpersonal, not political: 'O Gaveston, it is for thee that I am wronged; / For me, both thou and both the Spencers died' (5.3.41–2). Edward's words, which resist the barons' definitions of him, insist on the value of his subjective, erotic and emotional experience. Unlike James, who was forced by aristocratic power to banish Lennox, to abandon his emotional attachment to him, and to accommodate himself to the imposed political situation, Edward insists (in the play as in English history) on having male intimates. And the play lends support to the protagonist's and Gaveston's intimacy in the unconscious linguistic echo between Edward's words on being captured – 'O day! The last of all my bliss on earth, / Centre of all misfortune' (4.7.61–2), and Gaveston's when he too is captured – 'O, must this day be period of my life, / Centre of all my bliss?' (2.6.4–5). In this verbal echo Marlowe seems to indicate an affinity between Edward and Gaveston that supports their relationship. It is especially in Edward that Marlowe dramatizes the will to assert a subjectivity involving homoeroticism; for Edward insists on exceeding the boundaries of the discourses which are acknowledged for realizing same–sex erotic energies. Neglecting the responsibilites of royal power in the early part of the play, when his attention is concentrated on Gaveston, he nevertheless reclaims a function of his sovereignty in the last act in seeking to define in his terms the meaning of his love for Gaveston. This belatedly takes up what other characters have been doing throughout the action. Like James using royal power and authority to fashion and fix a version of the Lennox episode in his subjects' minds, Edward attempts to articulate the elusive truth of his relation with Gaveston.

The last act dramatizes a conflict between two discourses of same–sex desire: Mortimer acts to impose on Edward the meanings of same–sex desire as sodomy; while Edward seeks to represent himself in a way that involves both his sovereignty and his homoeroticism. For Edward, unlike his courtiers, there is no disjunction between the two.

With Isabella's connivance, Mortimer arranges a death for Edward that seeks to define him as a sodomite. Once Edward yields his crown to the barons he is killed in stages in a way that is intended to destroy his identity, and that resembles the step–by–step degradation and deaths of the Edinburgh sodomites. Finally, Lightborn (whose name translates 'Lucifer') stage–manages a parody of anal intercourse that elides sex and death, and displaces all other possible representations of same–sex eroticism with sodomy, with its significances of Satanic, negative action undermining the created order. His ritualized death is his enemies' attempt to have the last

191

defining word: to impose on his body sodomy's ideological force. But ironically, in killing the king who sustains social and political order, it is Mortimer and Isabella who are the true sodomites.[25]

Edward, on the other hand, having no material power left, turns to the power of discourse to assert a newly self–aware subjectivity. At Killingworth Castle, he questions 'if gentle words might comfort me' (5.1.5), but just before he is murdered he tells Lightborn the story of his sufferings in the hope of winning his sympathy: 'List awhile to me, / And then thy heart... / ...will...melt ere I have done my tale' (5.5.51–4). He recognizes and accepts that his love for Gaveston and Spencer has brought him to ruin, 'O Gaveston, it is for thee that I am wronged' (5.3.41), and maintains that attachment, 'tush, for them I'll die' (5.3.45). Edward asserts that he will go to heaven after his death, because he recalls that he is an anointed king specially linked to God; his references to the Christian heaven recall the sacrament by which he was made king. As James wrote his relations with Lennox in a positive light as loving and taming the phoenix, so Edward represents himself positively as the anointed king suffering martyrdom. It is one of a sequence of self–representations that are attempted, prove inadequate and are replaced with others.

V

Early modern same–sex desire is not to be understood as being the same as modern homosexuality, for the common understanding of homosexuality is that it issues from someone's essential homosexual nature. But there is no such notion of homosexuality present in *Edward II*, and critics who approach the play with that notion in mind will inevitably misread it. When Bray points to sodomy as the ideological formation that is used in the sixteenth century to represent certain sexual acts between men, he is countering the unhistorical notion of homosexuality, and describing a specifically early modern concept. But this idea of sodomy in turn, historically accurate as it is, is inadequate in itself to encompass and account for the range of ways that homoeroticism in the sixteenth century is responded to, represented, and assigned value. The range of different responses to the James–Lennox affair attests to this. More importantly, it demonstrates that such different responses issue from differing accounts of the king and Gaveston's homoeroticism are prompted by different political and material interests: at one extreme, Mortimer Senior's catalogue of distinguished male lovers of antiquity is offered as a reason for ignoring the king's lover; while, at the other extreme, Mortimer's killing of Edward as a sodomite is designed to impose the most extreme devaluation on the king, subjecting him to an existential erasure that is intended to strengthen Mortimer's position as Protector. In a situation of political conflict, homoeroticism therefore appears in a multiplicity of discursive and ideological modes. Indeed, from certain positions it does not exist as a separate thing at all; in James Melville's account, desire between James and Lennox is merely a familiar aspect of how a court functions. But it is not the argument of this essay that homoeroticism as a mental category or range of emotions did not exist in the sixteenth century; rather, it is that early modern homoeroticism appears in a range of discourses each of which represents it as a differently delineated and differently valued phenomenon. It is therefore inaccurate to talk about 'it' at all; instead, one needs to talk of a plurality of representations which offer distinct, if related, formations of desire and behaviour: neo–platonic friendship, for instance, has very little in common with sodomy.

The claim that homoeroticism is only the effect of other discourses (such as politics) is, however, dangerous, for it allows the hostile claim to be made that homoeroticism does not really exist as something in itself at all; and, at the same time, it leaves it open for homoeroticism to be constructed merely and reductively as sodomy, which is what is attempted in the manner of Edward's death. In *Edward II* same–sex desire is expressed, and is therefore discernible, in a variety of discourses, but this does not imply that it is only constructed in and by them. On the other hand, the fact that same–sex desire does appear in different discourses does not imply it is merely polyonymous, one thing with a number of different names. This essay takes the view that different discourses representing same–sex desire refer to, and help to bring into being, same–sex desire which is real, plural and polymorphous. This view does not imply that any particular formation of same–sex desire is essential or transhistorical; but it does imply that different erotic formations carry different significations and values, and that the potential exists for realizing those erotic variations in subjective experience. Both James VI and Marlowe's Edward can be seen as attempting the various ways that their culture offers them of bringing same–sex desire into social and subjective reality. The meanings of homoeroticism are unfixed and open to redefinition and revaluation for both Marlowe and the writers of the James–Lennox affair; and the play, like the historical accounts, enmeshes same–sex desire into the political action as something over which struggles of definition, realization or suppression are taking place. But Marlowe shows Edward's desire for Gaveston as exceeding the familiar and often reductive ways of representing homoeroticism, as an insistent claim for the value of his emotional and erotic desire. It is this claim that may make twentieth–century audiences and readers seem to see in the relationship represented between Edward and Gaveston the familiar form of twentieth–century homosexuality, with its essentialist assumption that homosexuality is always already present in the subject. Edward's insistence in Act 5, scene 5 on his homoerotic attachments as well as his kingship shows him still attempting to generate moral and subjective meanings from his defeat and imminent death.

Homoerotic desire is least subject to fixed definition and most open to transformations in Gaveston's account at the start of the play of projected royal entertainments (1.1.50–71), in which indefinition, ambiguity and metamorphosis constitute sexual desire. Sodomy, on the other hand, is the ultimate reduction of sexual desire; it seeks to erase the subjectivities, and the emotional and moral responses of its victims. Mortimer employs his newly–gained power to try to impose a sodomitical death and meaning on Edward that is doubly reductive: the relationship between Edward and Gaveston is reduced merely to a sexual act, in which Edward as the passive partner becomes in his enemies' eyes more despicable; and Edward's penetration by the spit, as a parody of anal sex, reduces even further a crude understanding of a same–sex relationship. The manner of Edward's death fails to impose a sodomitical definition on the king; it does not produce the definitive account of Edward, any more than Barabas's fall into the cauldron summarizes him. Homophobic critics, however, have been only too ready to take up Mortimer's position, since his scenario has the attractions of dominant ideology and an attempt at closure; but a critical response which is horrified at the manner of Edward's death registers the inadequate reductiveness of the category of sodomy. The play returns finally to questions of power, specifically the power of discourses to impose their truth on subjects, and the power of subjects to produce power for themselves to represent themselves against or beyond those discourses. Edward's final subjective claims for identity can only be fragmentary, and are powerless to change events; yet they have moral authority in their attempt to speak the truth of his subjectivity. Edward insists to the last in voicing a subjectivity that involves sexual desire as one of its irreducible constituents.

Notes

I should like to thank, for their suggestions and advice, Gareth Roberts, Claude J. Summers, Susan Wiseman, Gordon Williams, Robert Mighall and Peter Mitchell.

1. *Historie and Life of King James the Sext being an Account of the Affairs of Scotland from the Year 1566*, ed. T. Thomson, Bannatyne Club, Edinburgh, 1825, 64.

2. King James VI and I, *Political Writings* ed. J. Sommerville, Cambridge Texts in the History of Political Thought, Cambridge, 1994, 23.

3. For other recent research on early modern same–sex desire, see Smith, 1991; Bredbeck, 1991; Summers, 1992; Goldberg, 1992; and Goldberg 1994.

4. Connections between *Edward II* and James VI's relation with D'Aubigny were first discussed by John M. Berdan, who believed the play defended the institution of monarchy, and James's claim to the English throne (1924, 197–207). C. B. Kuriyama draws parallels between Edward and James VI, though her view of James is prejudicial and historically ill–informed (1980, 209–11).

5. For accounts by modern historians of the Lennox episode, see Donaldson, 1965, 172–80; Bingham, 1968; Fraser, 1974, 36–9; and Willson, 1956, 32–47.

6. The phrase is Charles Forker's from the Introduction to his edition of *Edward II*, 45. All quotations are from this edition.

7. Manuscript letter, B.L. Add. MS 36,530, fo.1; quoted in Bingham, 1968, 152.

8. 1992, 111; Traub continues, 'Most importantly, homoerotic activity – for men or women – was not a primary means of identification of the self. Homoeroticism had little to do with any of the social roles, statuses, and hierarchies in which an early modern subject might be located and thereby define him or herself. Early moderns simply did not essentialize homoeroticism in quite the way we do.'

9. See *The Border Papers: Calendar of Letters and Papers Relating to the Affairs of the Borders of England and Scotland*, 2 vols, H.M. General Register House, Edinburgh, ed. Joseph Bain, Vol. 1, 1560–1603, 82; quoted in Bingham, 1968, 162.

10. *Memoirs of the Affairs of Scotland, 1577–1603, from Early Manuscripts*, D. Moysie, Maitland Club, Edinburgh, 1830, 27.

11. *Scrinia Reserata: A Memorial Offer'd to the Great Deservings of John Williams, D.D.*, John Hacket, London, 1692, 39; quoted in Bingham, 1968, 132. Bingham notes that the source for this piece of gossip was supposed by John Aubrey to be William Camden, who had 'Minutes of King James's life to a moneth and a day', and which John Hacket 'did filch ... from Mr. Camden as he lay a dyeing', and then passed to Sir William Dugdale (Bingham, 1968, 208).

12. *The Autobiography and Diary of Mr. James Melvill*, ed. R. Pitcairn, The Wodrow Society, Edinburgh, 1842, 75.

13. *Twelfth Part of the Reports*, Edward Coke, 1656, 37; quoted in Bray, 1990, 3.

14. Ibid., 776; Calderwood includes Balcanquhall's disingenuous disclaimer about the sermon 'whereof [Balcanquhall] supposeth, that ather the erle of Lennox, or anie of his dependers, may tak anie occasioun of offence' (772).

15. 'I was then [1579] in the floure of my age, about a twa and twentie and thrie and twentie yeirs; a young man nocht unlovlie, and of nature verie loving and amorus, quhilk was the proped schot of Sathan wharby to snare me, and spoill the haill wark of God in me. Manie lovers haid I, and sum loves also; monie occasiones, in dyvers places and sortes of persones, and nocht of inferior rank: Yit my guid God, of his frie grace and love towards me, a vean, vyll, corrupt youthe; partlie by his fear wrought in my heart, partlie by necessar occupation in my calling, and partlie be a certean schamfastnes of a bashfull nature, quhilk he pat in me, sa keipit me that I was nocht overcome nor miscaried be na woman, offensivlie to his Kirk, nor greivuslie to my conscience, in blotting of my bodie' (Melville, 1842, 79).

16. Cf. the parting of Lancelot and Guinevere, '"I requyre and beseche the hartily, for all the love that ever was betwyxt us, that thou never se me no more in the visayge . . ." And they departed; but there was never so harde an herted man but he wold have wepte to see the dolour that they made ...' *Works of Sir Thomas Malory*, ed. E. Vinaver, 3 vols., Oxford, 1947, vol. 3, 1252–3.

17. *Memoirs of His Own Life, 1549–1593, from the Original Manuscript*, Sir James Melville of Halhill, Edinburgh, The Bannatyne Club, 1827, 266.

18. Published in the volume *Essayes of a Prentise, in the Divine Art of Poesie*, Edinburgh, 1584.

19. The poem is quoted from *The Poems of James VI of Scotland*, ed J. Craigie, Edinburgh and London, Scottish Text Society, 1955–8, vol.1, 39–59.

20. The poem is discussed in Goldberg, 1983, 22, and Bingham, 1968, 153.

21. For discussions of James VI's literary writing, see McClure, 1990, 96–111, and Akrigg, 1975, 115–29.

22. 1992, 103; Traub refines her position, one shared by this essay, when she writes, 'I reject the dominant constructivist trend that sees specific desires as being *produced* independently by discursive practices, and return to Freud's assertion of the polymorphous perversity and nondifferentiated nature of the infant's earliest desire ... [and] like the social constructivists, emphasize the ideological character of the process of subjectification, by which the various modalities of desire are manipulated and disciplined ...'(ibid).

23. See Williams, 1994, vol.3, 1419 *sv* 'treasure'. 'Treasury' also has sexual and political senses in Isabella's words to Edward as she kisses him: 'nor let me have more wealth/ Than I may fetch from this rich treasury'(1.4.330-1). Compare also Shakespeare, Sonnet 20, 'Mine be thy love, and thy love's use their treasure', l.14.

24. I am grateful to Gareth Roberts for this insight.

25. Compare the discussion of *Edward II* in Goldberg, 1992, 114–26, which concludes by defining Isabella as a sodomite for 'refusing the limits of marriage' (126).

12. Christopher Marlowe: Ideology and Subversion[1]

MICHAEL HATTAWAY

In Elizabethan and Jacobean drama ... there is almost no analysis
of the particular society of the times ... [the dramatists] believed in
their own age... And, accepting their age, they were in a position
to concentrate their attention ... upon the common characteristics
of humanity in all ages, rather than upon the differences.
(T. S. Eliot[2])

1. Subversion and Representation.

To begin from a moment in *1 Tamburlaine* when Tamburlaine spectacularly
violates an Egyptian and, presumably, an Elizabethan cultural practice or
ideological code. A Messenger describes to the Soldan of Egypt the quaint
and very theatrical device of Tamburlaine's white, red, and black tents. The
Soldan retorts:

Merciless villain, peasant ignorant
Of lawful arms or martial discipline!
Pillage and murder are his usual trades –
The slave usurps the glorious name of war.
(*1 Tamburlaine*, 4.1.64–7)[3]

His outburst seems to be in excess of the facts until we reflect that, by
constituting a new set of martial signals and abrogating to himself the
meaning of language (usurping the 'name of war'), Tamburlaine is in fact
re–constituting the state, what the Elizabethans termed the 'nation'.[4] This
immodest, audacious upstart is enhancing his absolute military authority over
Asia by a process of totalisation, and the Soldan is offering a description not
only of sedition but of subjection.[5] (Tamburlaine, at this moment, is more
revolutionary than, say, the Giant with the balances in *The Faerie Queene*
(5.2.30–5) who has simply *usurped* the divine scales of justice.)

From the obverse perspective, it is also a moment of social realism: the
Soldan may be regarded as an analogue of the nobility of England, and
Tamburlaine as a nightmare figure, one of the Elizabethan bogymen, this one
emblematized in the cruel Turk or Tartar.[6] The old order dominated by the
nobility has been subverted or 'problematized'[7] by what is not only a
physical but a cultural invasion by Tamburlaine. Codes of war had once been
chivalric honour codes, but more lately, of course, they had been used (as in
Elizabeth's Accession Day Tilts) (Yates, 1975, 88–111) to sustain an
aristocratic group which, as the quotation suggests, were no longer self
evidently the only hegemonic class. Tamburlaine's new signs proclaim, in

fact, a crisis for aristocracy, a triumph of absolutism over constitutionalism, the destruction of hereditary monarchy, and the destabilizing of a stratified order of privilege by a new order of status based upon the personality or charisma of a buccaneer.

The moment is related to a sequence near the beginning of the play, the famous stage image, or 'Gestus' as Brecht termed such a device, wherein Tamburlaine laid down his shepherd's weeds:

Lie here, ye weeds that I disdain to wear!
This complete armour and this curtle–axe
Are adjuncts more beseeming Tamburlaine.
(*1 Tamburlaine*, 1.1.41–3)

That too is an image not just of bravado but of political challenge: by his self–fashioning the shepherd Tamburlaine defies the sumptuary laws which maintained what Shakespeare called 'degree' and we would call a status system.[8] That was the theory. The fact that these laws existed at all suggests how much the reach of the Elizabethan state exceeded its grasp. Repeated attempts by the Tudors to control the dress of their subjects suggest some degree of phobia on part of the political elite (Harte, 1976, 132–165). Well might they fear: some of the most notorious transgressors of the sumptuary code were the players themselves, their own licensed servants.[9] Tamburlaine's dressing up draws attention to the ease and dangers of self–fashioning and social climbing, for both of which the stage provided a model. Moreover, he dreams of and creates an order where monarchical authority is sustained by no title, mystic corporation, or king's 'second body', but solely by sagacity and material power: the nation and the prince become one.[10] 'But what are kings, when regiment is gone, But perfect shadows in a sunshine day' (*Edward II*, 5.1.26–7).

Tamburlaine, in fact, displays within the playhouse what had been carefully kept offstage elsewhere, in that theatre of power that we know as the Elizabethan court, where elaborate rituals were deployed in order to imply that far more than might was needed to create right.[11] Marlowe, as we know, is rudely demystificatory: even Tamburlaine's lieutenant Theridamas can, with no ceremony, take the crown from the regal Zabina and hand it to Zenocrate: 'Here, madam, you are empress; she is none' (3.3.227). Crowns are no longer sacral 'ceremonies' (objects) but, like the papier mâché circlets that rounded the temples of the common players, merely indices of power.[12]

It might, however, be claimed that Tamburlaine's eponymous role as scourge or flail of God[13], *flagellum dei, does* make him, like Shakespeare's kings, 'twin–born with greatness'. However, a theatre audience, denied a coronation sequence, would be keenly aware that he makes his way to power not by undergoing ritual sanctification or by the divine right of the Pope[14] but simply by killing kings. Therein lies a political challenge.

Not only tyrants were associated with flails: theatre clowns probably bore them too, as we see in various engravings of the time. Marlowe himself was a man possessed of a dark *élan*, a savage jester who, as his table talk reveals, scourged his auditors with outrageous aphorisms; in the texts he wrote, he was a mannerist who, in his prologues, drew attention to his outlandish and astounding rhetorical play. He adopts a position of sardonic detachment – bordering on contempt – from his creations, a stance which is like the position of a jester vis–à–vis his subjects (Weil, 1977, 3): his co–author, Thomas Nashe, certainly occupied that role. In another play, *The Jew of Malta*, Barabas also functions as both jester and scourge.[15] His role is as much that of the playhouse clown as the moral vice, wearing a bottle nose and red beard (see 3.3.9–10 and 4.2.99), confiding in his audience, adopting outrageous roles, plaguing and exposing the hypocrisy of the Christians. Like all scourges of God, Barabas must die at the end, but in a manner that is both frightening and ghoulishly amusing. Indeed many of the most serious moments in the plays seem to be rendered within the conventions of clownery. At the beginning of *Doctor Faustus*, after the climax of the Latin spell – '*nunc surgat nobis dicatus Mephistophilis!*' – a devil appears, only to be rudely dismissed by Faustus:

> I charge thee to return and change thy shape,
> Thou art too ugly to attend on me.
> Go, and return an old Franciscan friar,
> That holy shape becomes a devil best.
> (1.3.23–6)

The hero and the devils seem to be playing out a clowns' double–act. Returning to the earlier play, we reflect that Tamburlaine's role shares some characteristics with that of Barabas. The Scythian shepherd is not only Herculean (Waith, 1962) but Gargantuan, and by this I refer not only to his stature but his wit. For him, seizing the crown from Cosroe is 'a pretty jest' (*1 Tamburlaine*, 2.5.90), and there is something of Groucho Marx in his most serious moments: after wooing Zenocrate with a great *suasio*, Techelles retorts 'What now! In love?' To which Tamburlaine replies:

> Techelles, women must be flatterèd:
> But this is she with whom I am in love.
> (1.2.106–8)

Moreover, just as the theatre clown or stage vice could, by speaking more than was set down for him or upsetting decorum, usurp the authority of both player–king and author, so, by the simplest of tricks or by main force, might the determined man with what Barabas calls 'a reaching thought' (1.2.220) displace the monarch and *his* authority. Comedy is no laughing matter, and, as we shall see, understanding this comic detachment is crucial to the understanding of Christopher Marlowe.

Marlowe's political plays, *Tamburlaine, Edward II, The Jew of Malta*, and *The Massacre at Paris*, are therefore, as I have inferred, pointedly secular. They generally demand the use of only one level of the Elizabethan playhouse[16], suggest no necessary pattern of divine retribution, and, as in Machiavelli, their imagery is often drawn from struggles for survival in the animal kingdom.[17] The fate of Greek tragedy, Napoleon told Goethe, had been replaced by politics. Marlowe anticipated this world and wrote plays whose theme is the gaining, maintaining, and losing of power. This power is, as Barabas boasts, gained by policy (5.2.26–47) and is never a function of moral or divine supremacy. Politicians cultivate fear rather than love (*Edward II*, 5.4.52), operate by martial rather than by civil law (*Edward II*, 5.4.88), and win or lose not so much by main strength as by politic contrivance: the very stuff of the theatrical improvisation of which I have just spoken. Indeed this combination of the themes of theatricality and absolutism,[18] 'theatrocracy', is one of the main topics of this essay.

These two moments from *Tamburlaine*, in short, serve two functions: Tamburlaine is insinuating into the Elizabethan consciousness the nightmare of class war, demonstrating that a peasant's revolt[19] could turn into rebellion or even revolution. As they watched the creation of this type of Asiatic absolutism, Marlowe's audiences were being offered an ironic analysis of the culture they themselves inhabited. A shepherd has, as it were, stepped out of the pages of a pastoral romance into the political arena.[20] By setting aside the old rules of war, he exposes the realities – social and moral realities as I shall demonstrate – of the Elizabethan political order. War, it turns out, belongs not in the realm of theodicy, as a writer like Spenser would have us believe, but in the realm of strategy, an awareness which reached its apogee with the writings of Karl von Clausewitz in the nineteenth century. The Soldan's lines serve as a defamiliarizing device, which may lead us to ruminate, with St Augustine, that war is also a form of piracy: 'Set justice aside then', reflected Augustine, 'and what are kingdoms but fair thievish purchases [pursuits]? For what are thieves' purchases but little kingdoms? For in thefts, the hands of the underlings are directed by the commander, the confederacy of them is sworn together, and the pillage is shared by the law amongst them'.[21] Piracy, cynically legitimized by Cecil and the monarchy (Williams, 1979, 106–7; Andrews, 1964), was, for the Elizabethans, in reality the most notable form of war.

But we must pay attention not only to what is represented or signified here but to the manner of theatrical representation. We leap forward to another related moment, at the end of Part 1 when, having heard again of Tamburlaine's tents, the virgins of Damascus (played by children in Terry Hands's 1992 Royal Shakespeare Company production) remind the Governor how selfish have been his tactics. The amazing thing that we then hear is that Tamburlaine's blackness signifies not just 'slaughtering terror' (*1 Tamburlaine*, 5.1.72) but melancholy. In fact the scourge of God seems to be tilting towards madness as he threatens the Damascenes with his 'servant Death' (5.1.117).

A complete analysis of these three related moments must therefore include their mode of representation – spectacle is not just a way of making violence aesthetically intriguing, but serves both as a register of cultural change and an index of Tamburlaine's mind, an elaborate way of representing mood or fancy.

2. Shakespeare and the Truth of Fancy

It has long been realized that Marlowe's mode of characterization resembles that of Spenser. His personages are iconic, both real and ideal: in the case of all the plays, except perhaps *Edward II*, we speak of flesh and blood heroes only at our peril. The texts call for an acting style in which there is as much alienation as identification between player and role. They are strangely intellectual, and Marlowe's location of the discourse of religion within the discourse of power, for example, reveals that, like Machiavelli and others, he understood the workings of what we have come to call ideology (Dollimore, 1984, 17–28). It follows that his characters, their actions and utterances, are more culturally than psychologically significant. Indeed their power derives from their ideological locations more than their actions: Tamburlaine may be less of a 'Herculean hero' than the *type* of one who puts resistance theory into practice and then creates a tyranny as powerful as that which he overthrew. The emphasis is not really on the kind of physical action we find in Shakespeare's Henry VI plays and heroic romances like *Orlando Furioso* by Greene and others: in *Tamburlaine*, for example, battles tend to take place offstage, being generally signified in theatrical shorthand by drummers and trumpeters.[22] The hero seems to conquer by simple actions that transgress decorum rather than by main strength: picking up a crown, changing his costume, using an emperor for a footstool, serving a banquet of crowns. The 'tragical discourses', as the printer termed them, are essays not on acts of conquest but on the processes of subjection. They constitute a 'mirror for magistrates' that goes far beyond the kinds of moralizing analysis provided by the 1563 collection of that name in that Marlowe displaces the attention from the moral relationships between princes and the deity to the political relationships between princes and their states.

Shakespeare, in fact, gives us an epitome of Marlowe's art in the Pyrrhus speech in *Hamlet*.[23] Marlowe's drama, he reminds us, is drama of the mind's eye:

HAMLET   The rugged Pyrrhus, he whose sable arms,
          Black as his purpose, did the night resemble
          When he lay couchèd in the ominous horse,
          Hath now this dread and black complexion smeared
          With heraldry more dismal. Head to foot
          Now is he total gules, horridly tricked
          With blood of fathers, mothers, daughters, sons,
          Baked and impasted with the parching streets,
          That lend a tyrannous and damnèd light
          To their vile murders. Roasted in wrath and fire,
          And thus o'er–sizèd with coagulate gore,
          With eyes like carbuncles the hellish Pyrrhus
          Old grandsire Priam seeks...
FIRST PLAYER   Anon he finds him,
          Striking too short at Greeks. His antique sword,
          Rebellious to his arm, lies where it falls,
          Repugnant to command. Unequal matched,
          Pyrrhus at Priam drives, in rage strikes wide;
          But with the whiff and wind of his fell sword
          Th'unnervèd father falls. Then senseless Ilium,
          Seeming to feel his blow, with flaming top
          Stoops to his base, and with a hideous crash
          Takes prisoner Pyrrhus' ear. For lo, his sword,
          Which was declining on the milky head
          Of reverend Priam, seemed i'th'air to stick.
          So, as a painted tyrant, Pyrrhus stood,
          And, like a neutral to his will and matter,
          Did nothing.
          But as we often see against some storm
          A silence in the heavens, the rack stand still,
          The bold winds speechless, and the orb below
          As hush as death, anon the dreadful thunder
          Doth rend the region: so, after Pyrrhus' pause,
          A rousèd vengeance sets him new a–work;
          And never did the Cyclops' hammers fall
          On Mars his armour, forged for proof eterne,
          With less remorse than Pyrrhus' bleeding sword

> Now falls on Priam...
> But who, O who had seen the mobled queen ...
> (2.2.453–505)

This, of course, is no mere parody, for the figure of Pyrrhus besieges the mind of Hamlet – he is not sure why – and occupies a central position in Shakespeare's analysis of revenge (see Hattaway, 1987). Pyrrhus is an 'antic' or grotesque, both an old–fashioned avenger out of classical drama and a monster, an eidetic, obsessive image, a horrendous version of what a man who turns executioner – or obeys his father – might become. He, like Tamburlaine and Barabas, revels in excess; his violation of decorum, political and aesthetic, indicates that he is not bound by the rules of art — and must, paradoxically, be a creature from the 'real' world. 'Extravagance is a privilege of the real', as Gérard Genette wrote (Genette, 1969, 74). Shakespeare and Marlowe are exploring the 'truth' of fancy in a manner similar to that of François Rabelais – to whom I shall return. It was Rabelais who wrote of 'this imitation of the ancient Herculeses, Alexanders, Hannibals, Scipios ... and that which heretofore the Barbars and Saracens called prowess and valour we now do call robbing, thievery, and wickedness'.[24] Conversely, in his *Schoole of Abuse* (1579), Stephen Gosson concedes that the players have 'purged their comedies of wanton speeches', but then proceeds to inveigh against the abuses of plays which 'cannot be shown because they pass the degrees of the instrument, reach of the plummet, sight of the mind'[25] – implying that the liminal fancies that the theatre unfolds usurp the place of right reason. Plays are both demystificatory and the seedbeds for unimagined thoughts.

It is also that case that Pyrrhus stands at the undiscovered borders of Hamlet's consciousness: Tamburlaine operates at the threshold of Europe. *1 Tamburlaine* is contained within Asia; the second part of the play starts near Vienna, and moves through Christendom towards Germany and then towards Jerusalem and Babylon. Conversely, as Stephen Greenblatt notes, Marlowe's heroes are themselves outsiders and see the worlds they inhabit with the observant eyes of aliens (1980, 196).

This engagement with ideology and the creation of characters in this particular archetypal mode seem to me to constitute the manner of Marlowe's sedition: his texts do not depict 'life' but life as it is constructed in ideology or belief, conscious or unconscious. Characters in Marlowe are 'figures' in the technical hermeneutic sense, *figurae*, not likenesses of truth, plastic forms, but embodiments of ideas (see Auerbach, 1984, 11–78). He is not just the creator of outsize or outrageous personalities (that is the speciality of Robert Greene). I would go so far as to claim that the critical argument about whether Marlowe's heroes are Promethean rebels – or whether Marlowe himself is in fact reactionary, giving us a series of retellings of the myth of Icarus – is ultimately an arid one, for his plays do not really admit of simple moral readings. They deal rather with the power and the weakness of fancy. It can even be claimed that there is a measure of solipsism to be found throughout Marlowe: there is, I think, an analogy between Marlowe's art and a moment when Tamburlaine vaunts that he can subdue the world. To Zenocrate he addresses a witty conceit which expands the proverb 'Gentility sprang from the pen or pike' (Tilley, 1950, G61):

> I will confute those blind geographers
> That make a triple region in the world,
> Excluding regions which I mean to trace[26],
> And with this pen reduce them to a map,
> Calling the provinces, cities, and towns
> After my name and thine, Zenocrate.
> (*1 Tamburlaine*, 4.4.71–6)

The pen is a grim joke for Tamburlaine's sword – for a more ingenious critic than myself it is probably a phallus as well. The whole is a figure of what can be conceived but may not be realized. (This does not, however, prevent a kind of theatrical realism: Hands's Royal Shakespeare Tamburlaine was memorable not just as a Herculean monster but, late in the play, as a portly, uxorious, almost suburban figure, obsessed by the power that was available to him.) Machiavel, in the prologue to *The Jew of Malta*, presents himself as an idea: doubling the part with that of Ferneze, as is frequently done in the playhouse, makes the hero both an individual and a type.

Ideology, fancy, myth: these are the arenas in which this freethinker operates. Marlowe does not engage directly with the realities of court politics or the formation of class consciousness in the way Shakespeare does in his history plays, and his handling, in *Faustus* and *Jew*, of the relationship between the accumulation of wealth and actual structures of authority, the subject Ben Jonson made his own, is an incidental theme and not embedded in a world that offers *l'effet du réel* (Barthes, 1982, 16). Wealth for Marlowe is generally what comes from the rape of nature;[27] it is not displayed, as in Jonson, as an index of political change.

Ideology and representation are the focuses of recent theory–led criticism, and this has served, I think, to rehabilitate Marlowe. He suffers if we read him within the traditions of the nineteenth century: his 'characters', fancies as they are, will be found wanting compared with the 'rounded' personalities post–romantic criticism grafted on to Shakespeare, and his ideals – even if they can be determined – do not match those of a post–revolutionary period. The nineteenth century – and here I am thinking of Burckhardt in particular – constituted the 'Renaissance' as a revolution. But of the three great Burckhardtian concepts, the state as a work of art, a new subjectivity, and a new secularism (the rending apart of the veil of faith), only the first seems true of a cultural moment we now want to call not 'the Renaissance' but 'the early modern period'. Marlowe's texts do not dramatize a 'great refusal' (Foucault, 1978, 95): they do, however, offer a critique that is arguably pre–revolutionary.

Marlowe is, therefore, obviously a writer in what Gabriel Harvey, writing in 1592, calls 'the fantastical mould'[28], in which category he casts Robert Greene, Pietro Aretino, and François Rabelais.[29] It is an interesting group, and I want to argue that Marlowe belongs firmly within it, alongside Greene, who was a fellow 'university wit'. In order so to do, I want to leap to very different play by a third university wit, George Peele's *Old Wives Tale* of 1593, another kind of heroic romance, in order to complete my attempt to define the Marlovian mode. This play has an induction which Peele used to make his method clear. There we find three pages: Antic, Frolic, and Fantastic – all, incidentally, deconstructions of the subject. I have dealt with the antic and the fantastic. 'Frolic' is another key word in Marlowe:[30] in *Dido* Iarbas makes sacrifice to Jove – Jove is generally a figure of subversion in Marlowe – 'Father of gladness and all frolic thoughts' (*Dido*, 4.2.5), and Machiavel comes from France 'to frolic with his friends' (*Jew*, Prologue, 4). Queen Isabella says of her husband Edward II:

> I will endure a melancholy life,
> And let him frolic with his minions
> (1.2.66–7).

'Frolic': the word gives us a way of talking about sex in Marlowe. It is not just an obsessional topic in his texts. His depiction of the frolicsome suggests Marlowe's delight – *jouissance* – in the ludic, the way he and his characters are, as we have seen, clowns who follow their desires and explore and subvert élite groups within their societies. In *Edward II*, Gaveston's masque of the mind depicts the sports of love that might be deployed to draw the pliant king, and Tamburlaine plays the games of rhetoric[31] to win Theridamus over to his cause. He delivers a great and thundering speech, vaunting that he holds Fate bound fast in iron chains, to which Theridamus replies:

> Not Hermes, prolocutor to the gods,
> Could use persuasions more pathetical
> (*1 Tamburlaine* 1.2.210–11).

At Stratford in 1992 we watched the sports of politics when Antony Sher took one of Tamburlaine's tirades ('Now clear the triple region of the air', *1 Tamburlaine* 4.2.30ff.) as a circus performer, doing acrobatics up a rope. Indeed Marlowe's whole *aesthetic* is frolicsome – like Oscar Wilde's – at once indecorous, sensuous, outrageous, and serious. There may have been originally more jokes – or political scenes when the wily turn the powerful into gulls by acts of bravura outfacing. We remember how the printer of *Tamburlaine* cut out 'fond and frivolous jestures' (*sic*), a word that resonates, in the Marlovian context, with the Brechtian notion of the 'Gestus'. Marlowe is also like our contemporary Joe Orton: from one perspective his crazy but well–knit plots seem like farce, from another like tragedy. (Remember how Eliot called *The Jew of Malta* a tragic farce.)

It was easy for scholars of fifty years ago to describe what made Marlowe 'primitive': his use of the patterns of the morality play and his deployment of what has variously been called 'kitchen humour' (Curtius, 1953, 431–5), 'eldritch laughter' (Bradbrook, 1963, 83–90), or 'sacral parody' (Grotowski, 1969, 23) – of the kind we find in pieces like the *Secunda Pastorum*. Like so many of his contemporaries, he minds 'true things by what their mock'ries be' (*Henry V*, 4.1.52–3). But Marlowe also wanted to 'make it new', and to do this he operated a transgressive aesthetic, was a violator of decorum, valuing for little what the academic dramatists praised by Sidney and others were doing. His art of inversion, as at the moment quoted above when Faustus subverts the authority of the devil, questions values and social structures which we and his contemporaries might take as basic and secure.

This can make interpretation or theatrical realisation difficult in that there often seems to be no locating tone. The prologues: are they serious or sardonic? As Bruce Smith wrote, 'we can never quite tell whether Marlowe is *playing* the satirist or *taunting* the satirists' (Smith, 1991, 206). Audiences laughed at the slaughter of nuns in the 1964 Royal Shakespeare Company production of *The Jew of Malta*. Tamburlaine may have seemed to certain members of the audience as a threat and therefore as a horrifying monster. What about the supernatural machinery in *Faustus*, the mysterious 'dragon' that appeared, it would seem, in the middle of Faustus's great speech of conjuring? Was it carnivalized, equipped with squibs, as in *Friar Bacon and Friar Bungay* where a tree appears '*with the dragon shooting fire*'?[32] In *Faustus* Mephistophilis enters '*with a devil dressed like a woman, with fireworks*'. The moment is 'Rabelaisian' since the fireworks signify both Lucifer's hell and the vagina (Bakhtin, 1984, 377), as Faustus's retort, 'A plague on her for a hot whore' (2.1.144SD–146), makes us aware. It is significant that the theatrical history of *Faustus* registers a decline into clownery and pantomime (Hattaway, 1982, 165–7): there is no need to assume that Marlowe upheld decorum, the Renaissance hierarchy of genres which forced categorical differences on comedy and tragedy.

There is no such thing as society, said Mrs Thatcher: Marlowe's demolition, by his ludic artistry, of what she and her conservatizing forbears called a natural order, demonstrates that there is no such thing as nature. As in Rabelais we rejoice as the lowborn, be they shepherds, scholars, or Jews, lord it over the respectable and overthrow the traditional. Marlowe was using fancies or fantasies to displace myths, question traditional values.

3. Tacitus and the Political Moment

Post–romantic critical orthodoxy demands that we skip over the biography, the unorthodox opinions, and certainly do not identify the man with his heroes. And yet that table talk – if Baines and Kyd are to be believed – is unforgettable, and matches if not the sentiments at least the tone of bits of *The Jew of Malta*, *Dido*, and *Massacre*. What Hazlitt wrote of Wordsworth might be applied to Marlowe: his 'genius is a pure emanation of the spirit of the age. Had he lived in any other period of the world, he would never have been heard of ... The political changes of the day were the models on which he formed and conducted his poetical experiments' (Hazlitt, 1904, 151, 152). I do feel that Marlowe had something to say, that he occupies a distinctive marginal position that serves to experiment with and question much of the cultural practice of his time. Marlowe was obviously a man who was author of himself: in turn *we* need to fashion a Marlowe who was not just a picturesque 'individualist' but a keen and sardonic analyst of the forms and pressures of his time. It follows that we should not just consider his heroes as free spirits, authors of their destinies, but as personages brought into being by the heterocosms they inhabit. Their trade in violence was not inimical to their cultures but part of it. The nature of their being can be described in a phrase used by Marx when he wrote, concerning a stereotype that his century inherited from the age of Marlowe, 'It is from its own entrails that civil society ceaselessly engenders the Jew.'[33]

There are none of Hazlitt's major significant political changes or *events* during Marlowe's creative period, but there was a political *moment*: Marlowe's blasphemies and iconoclasm are in fact typical of his time. Just before Marlowe went up to Corpus Christi College, Gabriel Harvey noted that, in Cambridge, 'You cannot step into a scholar's study but (ten to one) you shall lightly find open either Bodin *De Republica* or Le Roy's exposition upon Aristotle's *Politics* or some other like French or Italian politic discourse'.[34] No exact dating is possible, but there is common ground occupied by, say, Kyd's *Spanish Tragedy* , Shakespeare's Henry VI trilogy, and Marlowe's *Massacre at Paris*. Let us date it the moment of politic history and locate it about the time of the composition of Marlowe's translation of Lucan's *Pharsalia* and the publication of Sir Henry Savile's translation of Tacitus's *Histories* in 1591[35] with an epistle that, according to Jonson, was written by the Earl of Essex himself (Tuck, 1993, 105).[36] Marlowe himself translated Lucan who, of course, took a very sceptical view of Julius Caesar's imperial ambitions, and Tacitus's view of history was likewise quizzical and secular: his emperors were, unlike some of Shakespeare's monarchs, scarcely possessed of a mystic as well as a natural body, and his great themes were ancient liberty,[37] what his translator, almost certainly invoking Tamburlaine, called 'higher aspiring minds',[38] and modern servitude.[39] Jonson was to get into trouble by writing Tacitean history plays in the next century and during the next reign. But Tacitean matter — it is not just a question of style — can be discerned earlier. Tacitus delighted in exposing the hypocrisy of courtiers: his target was absolutism and its handmaid, theatricality. His tone was sardonic and his characters could be theatricalized and fantastical.[40] Marlowe's politics, I believe, are in this mould: unlike Tacitus, however, he was constrained by the literary genres of comedy, romance, and tragedy. Perhaps deliberately he chose the outdated form of the morality play for his narrative of Faustus – 'We must perform The form of Faustus' fortunes good or bad' says the Chorus, almost as a complaint. In the case of The Jew of Malta he may have written a Christianized and grotesque variation of the revenge theme put into circulation by Thomas Kyd in The Spanish Tragedy. Overall, with the exception of Edward II, the emblematic endings of the plays – the Jew in his cauldron, the discovery of the mangled limbs of Faustus – have a sterile, antique, and unresonant quality to them.

4. Delinquency and Deviance

The question is, how far did Marlowe's political and moral scepticism go? In order to answer it I want to explore notions of delinquency and deviance or dissidence. I owe the resonance of these words to Foucault and Jonathan Dollimore, although I am not in agreement with all of what the latter has to say, and am in fact using the words to designate different categories.[41]

Dissidents are those who reject a whole political or theological order, delinquents those who violate its codes and, despite their appearance of being outsiders, have probably internalized its codes. Prisons produce, in the words of Foucault, pathologized subjects (Foucault, 1984, 231). Dissidents, or the modern ones we think of, tend to want relief from some totalizing political or metaphysical system. This definition of dissidence is encapsulated in 1 Samuel 15.23: 'For rebellion is as the sin of witchcraft, and transgression is wickedness and idolatry.' Definitions of crime are legitimated by invocations of sin – and vice versa. In order to explain what I mean by internalization I wish to turn to a famous formula of Ovid: video meliora proboque, deteriora sequor (Metamorphoses, vii, 21). Medea was thinking about her father's commands and part of her thought was translated thus by Golding:

> But now an uncouth malady perforce against my will
> Doth hale me. Love persuades me one, another thing my skill.
> The best I see and like: the worst I follow headlong still.
> (vii, 24–25)

Ovid's phrase became proverbial in the early modern period (Tilley, 1950, B325) and, when combined with aspects of Pauline moral theology, almost encapsulated Christian tragedy. Sidney gives us the combined formula when he writes of the way 'our erected wit maketh us know what perfection is, and yet our infected will keepeth us from reaching unto it'.[42]

What might make Marlowe a dissident? He circulated what makes Machiavelli so dangerous, not just his maxims but his *Ideologiekritik*. From the 'Baines libel' we remember 'The first beginning of religion was only to keep men in awe' (quoted O'Neill, 1969, 10; see Dollimore, 1984, 11–13) and this is paraphrased in the plays: 'I count religion but a childish toy, And hold there is no sin but ignorance' (*Jew*, Prologue, 14–15) and, from the mouth of the Guise, 'My policy hath fram'd religion' (*The Massacre at Paris*, 2.65) (Minshull, 1982, 35–54). More subtly, Tamburlaine's 'sweet felicity of an earthly crown' (*1 Tamburlaine*, 2.6.29) is not just 'Scythian bathos' as Una Ellis–Fermor, in moralizing vein, termed it, but a demonstration of the bad faith of the philosophizing tyrant. With respect to *The Jew of Malta*, we recognize that on Malta the cash nexus has displaced any mystic sinew – that conceit is John Donne's – between ruler and ruled. And in the domain of private desire he seems to 'make strange' the metaphoric traffic between sexual and economic transactions in *Faustus*.

A vulgar Marxist or biographically oriented critic might place Marlowe along with his Faustus among categories of alienated intellectuals deprived of power (Faustus was born to parents base of stock) and alienated from the energies of demotic life.[43] This reading was rendered into stage terms by playing Faustus as a melancholic in a wonderful production by John Barton with Ian McKellen as Faustus (1976). Or, if you consider that Faustus displays the imperfections rather than the perfection of his learning, you may think that Faustus has failed to grasp the new philosophy and new discoveries of the period (Mephistophilis is more informed than he) and plumps for *material* wealth instead. Marlowe, however, had the power he needed – in the playhouse.

For he is, I think, more radical. If we are prepared to concede the category of the homosexual character in the period and associate Marlowe with it we might want to see him looking quizzically at gender roles and ideas of manliness. Indeed I find enough in Marlowe to question the current orthodox opinion that in the early modern period – or at least in literary texts – there was homosexual activity without the emergence of homosexual

210

identity.[44] In *2 Tamburlaine* the hero has become a monster as he describes the unwarlike appearance of his sons:

> Their hair as white as milk and soft as down,
> Which should be like the quills of porcupines,
> As black as jet, and hard as iron or steel
> (1.3.25–7)

Calyphas, the third, a bit like Cordelia, resists his father and is slain. In *Edward II* we witness a particular concatenation of the political and the sexual. Gaveston and Spencer are doubly marginal: by virtue of both sexual and social difference. The barons claim to hate them because they are upstarts and then demonize them. (From a contrary point of view, Edward II is seen through the eyes of Gaveston and Baldock who manipulate the desire of the king in order to manipulate themselves into power.) They are socially mobile:

> My name is Baldock, and my gentry
> I fetched from Oxford, not from heraldry.
> (3.2.242–3)

The sight of Edward and Gaveston on the throne together generates immediate hatred which is difficult not to construe as partly based on homophobia – as with Tamburlaine. The proximate is constructed as the 'other' (Dollimore, 1991, 33), which in turn generates the male bonding among the barons that is used to consolidate political authority.

The execution of Edward is peculiarly and horribly sexual: disturbing in that, by making his executioner Lightborn, the barons have legitimized their murder of a political enemy. Only a devil will do. What is noble about the king is that Edward refuses the role of the abject so often filled by the homosexual. There is no confession of guilt of the sort made by Richard II. However, he does not seem to be able to admit, even to himself, that his sexuality makes him different from other men.

Dissidence or ideological subversion is not just associated with particular personalities but is located within texts, particularly in Brechtian 'gests'. Let us look at one more obvious example. It comes from the opening of *The Tragedy of Dido* (1585–6?) where we see Jupiter dandling Ganymede on his knee. Jupiter is prepared to overturn the order of heavens for Ganymede's love. Marlowe was not attempting to evoke disgust at a pathological condition by showing that Jupiter with his minion: it is not a matter of morals. Marlowe asks, by implication, whether any political question is a moral matter. Ganymede will wreak as much havoc in heaven as the feuds of Gods did on earth – that is the point of 1.1.

I should like to propose a model: Marlovian texts are infused with dissident *ideologies* but, perhaps because of the ironic perspective that he adopted upon the genres within which he chose to write, his *characters* constitute a gallery of delinquents. Charles Nicholl has made the challenging but controversial proposal that Marlowe was an intelligencer or even a spy (Nicholl, 1992): maybe his point of view as an author was like that of one who chronicles the tawdry lives of the great. Characters in Marlowe, have, it turns out, internalized the dominant ideology. Tamburlaine may claim that 'Will and Shall best fitteth Tamburlaine' (*1 Tamburlaine*, 3.3.41), but he crowns Zenocrate in a way that makes the scene a pastiche of the coronation of the Virgin, and at the end we see him, in Greene's phrase, compulsively 'daring God out of heaven'.[45] Maybe Marlowe's own hegemony as a mocking author makes it inevitable that his characters will be enclosed by the forms and pressures of their literary milieux. (This is certainly something we notice in Marlowe's jesting refusal to maintain one tone in *Hero and Leander*.) Like Ben Jonson he may have loved and loathed the stage in equal measure, enjoyed its capacity to evoke wonder while despising the cheap tricks of the illusionist and the way that mere properties were metamorphosed into 'ceremonies' and objects of desire.

I prefer this theory to the new historicist orthodoxy that 'Marlowe and his heroes ... live in the recognition of the void, in the realisation that rebellion never manages to find its own space, but always acts in the space that society has created for it' (Goldberg, 1991, 75–82). The trouble with this is that it derives from a method of reading that concentrates on endings – Aristotelian, Brecht termed it – and does not allow for variant theatrical realisations (see below), dramatic tone, or even humour.

Yet, in another general sense his characters are mere delinquents, because they want some *thing*, they are consumers, their desires are reified, generally something more than they have been assigned, be it love, power, or wealth. As Greenblatt has demonstrated, their aspirations are fostered by nascent capitalism (Greenblatt, 1980, 194ff). They do not seek an authentic self: that is Hamlet's problem, the greatest delinquent who failed to be a dissident. Rather they wish to supplement their being: it should be complete, but the fact of desire demonstrates its incompleteness. This Derridean impasse is hauntingly phrased in *Massacre* when the Guise speaks of his wish 'To bring the will of our desires to end' (2.84). It all seems to be summed up in another formulation of Gabriel Harvey who wrote of: 'The whole brood of venerous libertines that know no reason but appetite, no law but lust'.[46]

5. Marlowe and Liberty

But this catalogue of moral observations upon his characters makes Marlowe unexciting. I think this author is 'larger' than his characters and I want to take further my comparison with Rabelais and place him in the category of the libertine. That is another difficult word: obviously I want to rescue it from being a mere term of abuse, and to conflate its non–pejorative meaning 'free thinker' with that of the sexual dissident. I am implying that this writer may stand for liberty in a larger sense, for something more than relief from political oppression, something that need not be defeated by a morally triumphalist ending to a mere play. I thought I would end by thinking about Marlowe and liberty – and relating these speculations to the theatre.

After Foucault, it has become orthodoxy to argue that delinquency and possibly deviance are not only repressed by the dominant order but produced by it, 'consolidating the powers which it ostensibly challenges' (Dollimore, 1991, 27). 'Liberty' was, of course, a key word in the early modern period, one that was changing its meaning. It may not have been an absolute categorical imperative but something to be granted, a privilege, charter, or franchise. In Rabelais, the Thelemites, whose motto was 'Do what thou wilt' (*Works*, I.47, 163), inhabit a place contained, an abbey founded by Gargantua. In the world of Hobbes, the liberty of the subject was praetermitted by the sovereign power.[47] The playhouses were contained within the 'Liberties' of London. It is for reasons like this that cultural theorists have displaced the designation 'Renaissance', which implies a brave new world, for the designation 'early modern period'.

Now Jacques in *As You Like It* is described as a libertine. Here he is on liberty:

> I must have liberty
> Withal, as large a charter as the wind,
> To blow on whom I please:
> (2.7.47–9)

Liberty, in other words is possible only within a designated, contained space.[48] Doctor Faustus gains his liberty only by signing a compact with a devil, who, when you think about it, is much more like a politician than a supernatural being. Faustus's stage punishment of dismemberment (seen in the B text only) is corporal: what we see accorded to a sinner by the devils was what Elizabethan hangmen accorded to criminals.

However, I want to quote here another passage from Gabriel Harvey, writing, in 1592, an invective letter – marked, however, with understanding and compassion – against Robert Greene. It is an interesting text, full of references to Greene as clown, one given to 'Tarltonizing' – a descendant of the stage clown Richard Tarlton – and as a disciple of Aretine, whose reputation in the early modern period was as a sexual and political libertine, a true dissident.

213

> But ... Zoilus [a fourth century BC pedantic critic of Homer] in his
> spiteful vein will so long flirt [scoff] at Homer, and Thersites in
> his peevish mood so long fling at Agamemnon that they will
> become extremely odious and intolerable to all good learning and
> civil government; and, in attempting to pull down or disgrace other
> without order, must needs finally overthrow themselves without
> relief. Orators have challenged a special liberty, and poets claimed
> an absolute licence – but no liberty without bounds nor any licence
> without limitation.[49]

Are these phrases of Harvey just the reflex utterances of the good safe
university man, or does this last phrase say something about the
'Renaissance'? This text seems to call into question that element of new
historicism known as containment theory. Harvey is conceding that poets,
wits, and dramatists *were* able to think the unthinkable, move so far beyond
the borders of delinquency that they were truly seditious. No limit is
comprehensible unless it is capable of being exceeded or transgressed.[50]
Now, if Marlowe was a dissident, what positives does he claim, to what ends
does he subvert? Is it liberty that he seeks? Nashe wrote of Aretine, 'His life
he contemned in comparison of the liberty of speech.'[51]

Liberty, in fact, is an early aim of Tamburlaine: in the first scene in
which he appears he claims that he loves 'to live at liberty' (1.2.26) and that
he seizes wealth to maintain his life 'exempt from servitude' (1.2.31)

A play like *Edward II* makes obvious points about court corruption and,
by implication, political and personal liberty. *The Massacre at Paris,* the *Ubu
Roi* of its age, a pantomime version of the politics of the French wars of
Religion – the French wars of religion provided a seedbed for ideas about
liberty – goes further and invokes notion of liberty of conscience. (The phrase
is first cited in *OED* in passages from John Knox's *History of the
Reformation* of 1572):

KING CHARLES my heart relents that noble men,
        Only corrupted in religion,
        Ladies of honour, knights, and gentlemen,
        Should for their conscience taste such ruthless ends.
        (4.9–12)

François Hotman, probably the author of Marlowe's source, *A True and Plain
Report of the Furious Outrages of France* (1573) (Oliver, 1968, lxi), allows
himself a reflective digression upon the Massacre of St Bartholomew which
aligns itself with the play: 'Why was not orderly enquiry and judicial
proceeding used according to the custom and laws and general right of

nations, and witness produced according to the form of law? But be it that the Admiral and a few other of his confederates and followers had conspired, why yet proceeded the outrageous cruelty upon the rest that were innocent ...'(quoted in Oliver, 1968, 178). This accords with the report in the Baines libel about St Paul's advice to the primitive Christians (Romans 13.1–7): 'That all the apostles were fishermen and base fellows neither of wit nor worth, that Paul only had wit, but he was a timorous fellow in bidding men to be subject to magistrates against his conscience' (quoted in O'Neill, 1969, 10).[52] Marlowe from this, it may, be judged, was an advocate of political liberty, an advocate of what is termed resistance theory.

To put this in a historical perspective, we might invoke Kierkegaard, writing about the differences between ancient and modern tragedy. In the ancient world, 'even if the individual moved freely, he still rested in the substantial categories of state, family, and destiny. This substantial category is exactly the fatalistic category in Greek tragedy, and its exact peculiarity. The hero's destruction is, therefore, not only a result of his own deeds, but is also a suffering, whereas in modern tragedy, the hero's destruction is not really suffering but is action ... Our age has lost all the substantial categories of family, state, and race. It must leave the individual entirely to himself, so that in a stricter sense he becomes his own creator' (Kierkegaard, 1971, I, 141, 147)

6. Two Versions of *Doctor Faustus*

The difficult text, of course, is *Faustus*. Marlowe, it seems to me, may well have been a true but tentative atheist[53] – the kind who is going to need to blaspheme – standing above and beyond that desolate battlefield between good and evil that defines the religious life in Faustus. (This at least is a model from which a viable critical interpretation might emerge). From the Olympian position of an author, he chose to tell the story of a man who was unable to escape from the prison–house of Manichean ideology in which he was confined: Marlowe, in other words, may be detached not just from his hero but from what, to adapt Plato, we might call the cave of ideology. He has something to say about a *kind of tale* rather than a *kind of hero*. This hero, it now seems to me, is scarcely autonomous; rather he is constructed by what 'heavenly *power* permits' (Epilogue, 8, emphasis added) and social constraints like that described by Mephistophilis as the 'ceremonial toy' of marriage (2.1.147).[54] Faustus's engagement with the rituals of both worship and demonism may have seemed as comic to his author as the antics of Tamburlaine and Barabas. Faustus is not only wicked but he is, disappointingly to some critics, very naughty: he has recourse to necromancy, what the Baines libel dismisses as 'juggling', and is possibly guilty of 'demoniality', sexual congress with demons (Greg, 1946, 97–107). These actions are narrated in a way little different from that when we hear of how his rough magic confronts the Pope[55] – although there we hardly think of liberty of conscience.

If Marlowe had lived, he may, I conjecture, have been amused by the tales that accreted to his text: the report that Alleyn played the role in a surplice with a cross upon his chest, and the tale of extra devils on the stage at a performance of the play in Exeter. This detachment, of course, does not prevent Marlowe creating a tragedy. He is perhaps dramatizing his own doubt but also showing the magnificent dithering of his hero, vacillating as he does between brave scepticism about the fables by which he lives and moments when he seems to recognize both divine presence and the validity of religious codes. The problem is, does Marlowe allow his delinquent to grow into a dissident, or does he simply offer a parable in which Christian orthodoxy both generates and contains the actions of his hero?

As always, answers to problems like this are best to be found in the theatre. I want to restore an element of agency to Marlowe, but, at the end of the day, am forced to concede that he is unavailable, that I cannot reach him. I have to abandon not only the answers but the questions of the new historicism and become a cultural materialist, using evidence about staging that derives, unfortunately, from texts printed eleven and twenty–seven years after his death respectively.

Yet I want to conclude by proposing a provisional and tentative answer to these questions concerning the extent of Marlowe's subversion by considering briefly the variant *stage directions* in the A (1604) and B (1616) texts of *Faustus*.[56] The B text, which partly records performances in professional London playhouses, is, I submit, a text of containment in that devils aloft frame Faustus's actions, ironize his intentions. This turns him into a mere delinquent (and may be a 'non–authentic' theatrical interpretation[57]). So we read in the conjuring scene, '*Thunder. Enter* LUCIFER *and* FOUR DEVILS [*above*]: *Faustus to them with this speech*' (1.3.0SD) Later, in middle of his spell, we find that mysterious word *Dragon* (1.3.19). It is conceivable, of course, that a hell mouth stood on stage throughout the performance, a silent but ironic commentator on the action.

The A Text, in contrast, which records performances by players driven out of London by the plague to play on open one–level stages, reads simply '*Enter Faustus to conjure*'. At the end of the play, before Faustus confesses, B reads '*Thunder. Enter* LUCIFER, BEELZEBUB, MEPHISTOPHILIS *above*' (5.2.0SD). This, and twenty–five lines, beginning

LUCIFER   Thus from infernal Dis do we ascend
                To view subjects of our monarchy ...

(5.1.1–2)

do not appear in A. It is obvious that B, by offering a frame of containment, creates a visual, dramatic irony. In A Faustus is man alone, more of a hero, a braver dissident.

This conclusion of course, must remain provisional. It may well be that this great text, by escaping from the containment of the public playhouses of early modern London and falling first into the hands of strolling players, then into the hands of a twentieth–century reader like myself, someone who is inclined to be 'oppositional', has turned early modern delinquency into contemporary deviance, libertinism to liberty. Marlowe's texts have been, despite our best endeavours, released from history, and my act of reading is inevitably an act of interpretation. It is difficult to avoid the temptations of whiggish history and of appropriating a great mind like Marlowe's to our cause: I might well have turned an early modern and rather sheepish delinquent into a contemporary and almost heroic dissident.

Notes

1. An early version of this paper was given as a lecture at Corpus Christi College, Cambridge on 12 May 1993 as part of the Corpus Marlowe Celebrations. I am grateful to the Master and Fellows for the invitation to this occasion.

2. 'John Ford' (1932) in *Selected Essays*, London, 1951 edn, 202.

3. Quotations are taken from *The Plays of Christopher Marlowe*, ed. Roma Gill, (Oxford, 1971).

4. As Leonard Tennenhouse writes, plays provided 'a site where the iconography of state power was formulated in tension with various forms of representation that contested the ideology of the Renaissance court' (1986, 14).

5. Compare Michel Foucault: 'Rather than ask ourselves how the sovereign appears to us in his lofty isolation, we should try to discover how it is that subjects are gradually, progressively, really and materially constituted through the multiplicity of organisms, forces, energies, materials, desires, thoughts etc. We should try to grasp subjection in its material instance as a constitution of subjects' (1980, 88, 97).

6. As, for example, in a text of 1590, Edward Webbe, *Edward Webbe ... his Troublesome Travels*, ed. E. Arber, London, 1868; see also Shepherd, 1986, 142–77.

7. Moving laterally to material history, we might remind ourselves of how new military technology – a paraphrase of part of Paul Ive's *Practise of Fortification* (London, 1589) – is rather self–consciously worked into *2 Tamburlaine*, 3.2.54ff. However, see also Nicholas de Somogyi's essay in the present volume.

8. Gaveston's 'cullions' wear 'proud fantastic liveries' (*Edward II*, 1.2.409).

9. See Stephen Gosson, *The Schoole of Abuse*, London, 1579, 39: 'Overlashing in apparel is so common a fault that the very hirelings of some of our players ... jet under gentlemen's noses in suits of silk'.

10. Such a constitution is tersely described by Matrevis to Edward II: 'The court is where Lord Mortimer remains.' (5.3.60) and by Machiavel in *The Jew of Malta*: 'Might first made kings, and laws were then most sure/ When, like the Draco's, they were writ in blood.' (Prologue, 20–1); compare too a line from Marlowe's translation of Lucan's *Pharsalia*, 'Dominion cannot suffer partnership' (93).

11. Recent writings on the relation between ritual and power are surveyed in Cannadine, 1992, 1–19.

12. Witness a stage image from *1 Tamburlaine*, 2.4.0SD: *'To the battle, and Mycetes comes out alone with his crown in his hand, offering to hide it'*; compare Hattaway, 1990, 147–74.

13. See Hattaway, 1968, 95–112; in the case of Tamburlaine we must remember that he is a figure of the scourge of God – whose claim that he is 'the scourge of the immortal God' (*1 Tamburlaine*, 2.4.80) sounds, because of its grammatical ambiguity, like a symptom of acute hybris.

14. For diatribes against the Pope's power to make kings, see *Edward II*, 1.4.96ff, *The Massacre at Paris*, 25.56ff, *Doctor Faustus*, 3.1.149–60; for a survey of the doctrine of the divine right of kings, see Sommerville, 1986, 9–56.

15. He prays for 'The plagues of Egypt, and the curse of heaven, Earth's barrenness, and all men's hatred' (1.2.161–2), and exclaims 'But mark how I am blessed for plaguing them' (2.3.197).

16. Barabas's appearance *'above'* at 3.2.4SD is a device in the intrigue and does not suggest moral authority or dramatic irony.

17. See, for example, *Edward II*, 5.1.41–2, 5.1.9–13, 5.2.116, 5.3.6–7, 5.3.34–5.

18. For a recent study, see Pye, 1990.

19. For Gaveston as peasant, see *Edward II*, 1.4.218, and for the category of 'peasant' see Palliser, 1983.

20. Compare, for example, Philisides (a figure for Sidney himself) at the tilt in *Arcadia*, II, 21 (Sidney, *The Countess of Pembroke's Arcadia*, ed. M. Evans, Harmondsworth, 1977, 353).

21. *The City of God,*, tr. J. Healey, London, 1610, 4.4, Everyman edition, I, 115.

22. Pertinent plays are surveyed by Peter Berek who, however, fails to detect the more radical ideology that operates in Marlowe's texts (1982, 55–82).

23. Pyrrhus appears in Seneca's *Troades* ; Marlowe's own description of Pyrrhus comes in *Dido*, 2.1.213ff.; he is also invoked as an archetype of tyranny in Marlowe's translation of Lucan, *First Booke*, l.30.

24. *The Works of Mr Francis Rabelais ... 1653*, tr. T. Urquhart and P. Motteux, London, 1931 edition, I. 46.

25. *The Schoole of Abuse*, ed. E. Arber, London, 1868, 37–8.

26. Meaning to 'pass over' as well as to 'draw'.

27. See, for example, *The Jew*, 1.1.106–7: 'What more may heaven do for earthly man/Than thus to pour out plenty in their laps,/Ripping the bowels of the earth for them...?'.

28. *Fovre Letters and certeine Sonnets, 1592*, Edinburgh, 1966, 67.

29. Weil compares Marlowe with Rabelais but does not refer to the passage in Harvey (1977, *passim*).

30. Greenblatt calls his chapter in *Renaissance Self–Fashioning* 'Marlowe and the will to absolute play' (1980, 193–221).

31. In *1 Tamburlaine* he uses the stock phrase 'play the orator' (1.2.129), also used by Shakespeare's Edward IV (*3 Henry VI*, 1.2.2).

32. Robert Greene, *Friar Bacon and Friar Bungay*, ed. J.A. Lavin, London, 1969, 9.83SD; for contexts of a carnival hell see Bakhtin, 1984, 393.

33. Karl Marx, 'On the Jewish question', cited in Greenblatt, 1990, 50.

34. *Letter–Booke of Gabriel Harvey, AD 1573–1580*, ed. E.J.L. Scott, Westminster, 1884, 79; Robert Sidney's heavily annotated copy of Lipsius's 1585 edition of the *Opera* is in the British Library; compare Dean, 1941, 161–83 and Jardine and Grafton, 1990, 30–78.

35. Tacitus, *The End of Nero and Beginning of Galba. Four books of the Histories of Cornelius Tacitus*, tr. Sir Henry Savile in 1591. The *Annals* appeared in 1598 (see n.38). The translator Richard Greneway's Epistle Dedicatory, also to the Earl of Essex, reads in part: 'For if history be the treasure of times past and, as well as a guide, a[n] image of man's present estate, a true and lively pattern of things to come, and, as some term it, the work–mistress of experience which is the mother of prudence, Tacitus may by good right challenge the first place among the best'. The influence of Tacitus on later drama is set out in Bradford, 1983, 127–51; see also Salmon, 1991, 169–88.

36. It may have been written by Anthony Bacon.

37. After narrating how Augustus had refashioned the state, Tacitus wrote 'How many were there which had seen the ancient form of government of the free commonwealth' (*The Annales of Cornelius Tacitus*, tr. R. Greneway, London, 1598, 3)

38. *Annales*, I,IV,7; the phrase is used of Asinius Gallus who 'plusquam civilia agitaret' (*Tacitus in Five Volumes*, ed. C. Moore and J. Jackson, 5 vols, Cambridge, Mass., 1969, III, 268).

39. In the epistle we read 'In these four books ... thou shalt see all the miseries of a torn and declining state: the empire usurped, the princes murdered, the people wavering, the soldiers tumultuous, nothing unlawful to him that hath power, and nothing so unsafe as to be securely innocent ... If thou dost detest their anarchy, acknowledge our own happy government, and thank God for her, under whom England enjoys as many benefits as ever Rome did suffer miseries under the greatest tyrant' (*Histories*, sig. ¶3^{r-v}).

40. In Book 1 we find a marvellous sentence on one Percennius, leader of the revolt in Pannonia, 'who had been sometimes a ringleader of factious companions on stages and theatres, afterward a common soldier, an impudent and saucy prater, well practised in disturbing assemblies, to show favour unto such actors as he favoured' (*Annales*, I. 5, 8).

41. 'For Gide transgression is in the name of a desire and identity rooted in the natural, the sincere, and the authentic; Wilde's transgressive aesthetic is the reverse: insincerity, inauthenticity, and unnaturalness become the liberating attributes of decentered identity and desire, and inversion becomes central to Wilde's expression of this aesthetic...' (Dollimore,

1991, 14). The author deals with *Faustus* on 285–6, but his reading does not seem sufficiently open to the semantics of stage performance (see below).

42. *An Apology for Poetry*, ed. G. Shepherd, Manchester, 1965, 101.

43. 'Marlowe demystifies the power he craves but cannot obtain, a not uncommon strategy of frustrated social ambition on the Elizabethan political scene' (Cox, 1989, 98).

44. This is not the conclusion of, for example, Bruce Smith who writes well about the 'master and minion' relationship in *Edward II* (1991, 209–23).

45. *Perimides the Blacksmith*, Robert Greene, London, 1588, Sig.A3^r.

46. *Pierce's Supererogation*, Gabriel Harvey, London, 1593. 45.

47. *Leviathan*, ed. M. Oakeshott, New York, 1962, 161.

48. We can perform a similar semantic exercise on the word 'licentious': it means guilty of the abuse of license. Baldock boasts to Spenser that he was 'curate–like in mine attire, Though inwardly licentious enough And apt for any kind of villainy' (*Edward II*, 2.1.49–51).

49. *Fovre Letters* , 15; compare Gosson, who, in the course of discussion of the effects of plays, wrote: 'I cannot liken our affection better than to an arrow which, getting liberty, with wings is carried beyond our reach; kept in the quiver, it is still at commandment' (*Schoole of Abuse*, 44).

50. Compare passages to this effect from Foucault and Montaigne in Dollimore, 1989, 114–15.

51. *The Unfortunate Traveller and Other Works*, Thomas Nashe, ed. J. Steane, Harmondsworth, 1985, 310; I see no reason to endorse the conjecture that here and in Harvey 'Aretine' is, in fact, Marlowe – see, for example, Nicholl, 1992, 55.

52. See Oliver, 1968, 180, for François Hotman's account of Henri III's revocation of edicts permitting 'liberty of religion'.

53. Joseph Cresswell notes in 1592, 'Sir Walter Ralegh's school of atheism by the way, and of the conjurer that is master thereof, and of the diligence used to get young gentlemen to this school wherein both Moses and our Saviour, the Old and New Testaments are jested at, and the scholars taught among other things to spell God backward' (*An Advertisement written to a Secretary of my Lord Treasurers of England by an English Intelligencer as he passed through Germany towards Italy*, n.p. 1592). See also Nicholas Davidson's discussion in the present volume.

54. Dollimore calls it 'an exploration of subversion through transgression ... Faustus' pact with the devil, because an act of transgression without hope of liberation, is at once rebellious, masochistic, and despairing'(1989, 109 and 114).

55. See Kermode, 1971, 44, for a discussion of popes as magicians.

56. Useful material on historical and ideological implications of the variant readings in the dialogue is to be found in Marcus, 1990, 1–29; Clare, 1990, 27–30; and Healy, 1992, 117–20.

57. Glynne Wickham, however, claims that no London theatre before the late 1590s had the technical capacity to produce the final scenes of the play in the B version (1964, 184–94).

13. 'What meanes this shew?': Theatricalism, Camp and Subversion in *Doctor Faustus* and *The Jew of Malta*

DARRYLL GRANTLEY

An article in *The Independent* in 1992 described a procession of Anglican clergy at the shrine of Our Lady of Walsingham.[1] This was very much a high church 'bells and smells' affair and and involved the parading of an effigy of the Virgin Mary through the streets of the town, referred to by the participants as 'taking Mother for a walk'. The journalist observed that the priests, called in the article 'gin and lace clergymen', were 'conservative doctrinally and enjoy the pageantry of their faith' and he quickly became aware that the whole event was infused with a homosexual subtext. What he was witnessing was one of the many manifestations of high camp in the Church of England's Anglo–Catholic wing. The Walsingham procession clearly had many aspects of the mode of representation and perception that can be defined as camp: an engagement with the orthodox, but in a way that is theatricalized and which recognizes its own theatricality, a *mechant* interplay between an awareness of the profound orthodoxy of the ceremony on the one hand, and a recognition of its grotesqueness on the other, a realization too on the part of the participants of their position at the centre of the ritual and its ideology (for instance, in their doctrinal conservatism), and at the same time substantially outside of the system of values which construct and infuse it. What emerges is a powerful sense of the provisionality of all appearance as an attestation of identity, a provisionality which allows for dramatic playfulness in the process of self–representation.

A theoretical history of the trope of camp has yet to be written, but such a project could do worse than begin with Marlowe.[2] His dramatic method in the two plays under present discussion can be seen to operate in the same ironizing way as the ceremony just referred to; in both the Walsingham procession and the plays the way in which orthodoxy is embraced and even celebrated, ultimately becomes a subversive strategy, illustrating Foucault's observation that resistances to power are the more real and effective for being 'formed right at the point where relations of power are exercised' (1980, 142). In these two plays it is (ironically) without the homosexual element, but questions arise about sexual deviance and its implications for the experience of all identity and 'reality' as provisional and constructed, to which this particular kind of manoeuvre might be related, theoretical questions which unfortunately fall outside the scope of this essay.

In *The Jew of Malta* and *Doctor Faustus*, theatricality and theatrical tactics are especially foregrounded, and they suggest themselves as the basis of the subversive project of Marlowe's work. The essence of these strategies lies in theatricalism – the selfconscious use of theatre – and the sabotaging ironies which that produces. Marlowe's own position in relation to his society and its religious ideologies, on the one hand centrally part of them, and on the other marginal and even oppositional, might be considered in some ways analogous to that of the gay priests in the Walsingham procession, and that position could be argued to be a significant factor in his approach. However, what also needs to be brought into view are the determinants present in the writing culture in which he found himself. The very emergence and availability of certain types of theatre in the sixteenth century yields, in itself, a revealing perspective on the prevailing modes of perception and representation in the early modern period, and Marlowe's choice, exploitation and development of these contributes a particular dimension to this perspective.

At the climax of Kyd's *Spanish Tragedy*, the murderous revenge of Hieronymo is enacted in the course of a dramatic presentation that he has mounted, in which the dramatized murder conceals the 'real' murder. This collapse of the boundaries between layers of representation is just one of many features of this play that disclose a theatricalist imagination which is not simply a predeliction for staginess and spectacle, but which constantly brings into play the question of dramatic representation, its modes and implications. It seems perfectly appropriate that such issues should arise in an historical period when figurative or quasi–allegorical modes of theatre and historical modes were both current within the theatrical culture, and issues of identity and representation were significant concerns of the broader culture. Marlowe is a dramatist whose relatively small *oeuvre* ranges over a number of very different generic categories, and the texture and theatrical design of whose plays indicate a remarkable interest in the signifying possibilities of dramatic form as distinct from content, and the implications of theatrical representation as a process. In *The Jew of Malta* and *Doctor Faustus*, religious and other forms of power are interrogated precisely by re–producing them as theatrical constructs – therefore as both contingent rather than absolute – and compromised by the essentially illusory nature of theatre. This project entails an awareness of the possibilities and constraints of the medium itself, and the ironies which are produced by the competing requirements of, or transactions between narrative substance and dramatic form.

Related to the issue of representation is the question of the construction of the hero or central persona of the plays. Here complications arise, since the problem engages the history of the subject in drama. They involve a distinction between the dramatic persona as a discursive category, as in allegorical moralities on the one hand, and the interiority and defined psychological integrity of the subject on the other. Discussions of this, such as those of Catherine Belsey (1985) and Francis Barker (1984), locate the emergence of the subject as occurring substantially in the seventeenth century.

Nonetheless, even materialists like Jonathan Dollimore and Stephen Greenblatt who accept this and are fully aware of the weight of the discursive determinants of the dramatic persona in Marlowe, have some difficulty in restraining the impulse to respond to Marlowe's heroes as psychological entities. This is illustrated by the following extract from Greenblatt:

> . . . if the heart of Renaissance orthodoxy is a vast system of repetitions in which disciplinary paradigms are established and men gradually learn what to desire and what to fear, the Marlovian rebels and skeptics remain embedded within this orthodoxy: they simply reverse the paradigms and embrace what society brands as evil. In so doing, they imagine themselves set in diametrical opposition to their society where in fact they have unwittingly accepted its crucial structural elements.
> (Greenblatt, 1980, 209)

Here Greenblatt recognizes the paradigmatic in Marlowe's representation of the world, but his discussion of the dramatic heroes does not significantly present a view of the persona as paradigm. The nearest he comes to it is in his description of Barabas's Judaism in Marx's words as, 'a universal antisocial element' (1978, 297). The problem is the fact of the material incarnation of the heroes on stage, as Belsey recognizes, and the response which this invites from, or imposes upon the audience (1985, 43–4). This is true of texts for reading as well as those for performance. Reading Bunyan's *Grace Abounding to the Chief of Sinners* alongside *Pilgrim's Progress* throws up some useful perspectives on the question of representation, characterization and the subject in early modern discourse, and modern consumption of this literature. While *Grace Abounding* is an autobiographical record of Bunyan's own mental crises and their resolution, the allegorized *Pilgrim's Progress* removes the subjective and reconstitutes the experience in terms of the conceptual processes of theological argument. In the course of thus allegorically recasting his experience, Bunyan also concretizes the process of struggle, which then becomes an abstract argument constructed in material images. This replaces the subjectivity, interiority and the sense of psychological particularity found in the autobiographical text. However, the modern reader, and no doubt the majority of contemporary readers too, eschew the more directly subjective text for the more colourful allegory but, in the process of consuming that text, reinscribe the subject. Christian does not function simply as a concretized concept; in order to operate as a narrative hero, the figure has to have his subjectivity recuperated. Indeed, with the passage of time, as the original theological frame of reference becomes ever more remote and exotic, this becomes all the more necessary for the continued acceptability of the text.

In her discussion of *Faustus*, Catherine Belsey identifies elements of interiority and remarks:

> the shrunken personifications and the pliant Vice are diminished in proportion to the dominance of the human hero whose conflict is largely internalized.
> (Belsey, 1985, 43–4)

David Aers has more recently objected to the location by early modernists of the origins of the history of the subject in the seventeenth century, and he cites considerable evidence for a medieval conception of the subject (Aers, 1992, 177–202). It could be argued that what we see in Marlowe, and indeed in drama right up to the end of the eighteenth century, is effectively a simultaneity and coexistence of what might be termed the figural impulse, i.e. towards dramatic persona as paradigm or discursive category, and the subjective impulse, i.e. towards interiority and psychological integrity, in short that dramatic *persona* in Marlowe operates as *both* figure *and* character. I would further suggest that the theatrical design and strategies in Marlowe's plays, and particularly the two under consideration, involve a negotiation between these two representational modes. As modern consumers of sixteenth century drama, we have also to be aware of the historical and cultural determinants of our own habits of reception, habits which privilege the subjective over the figural. In the light of the work on early modern iconography of Frances Yates (1975), Roy Strong (1977) and others, including the more recent collection of essays on Renaissance bodies, edited by Gent and Llewellyn (1990), an argument needs hardly be made for the importance of the figural and iconographic as a mode of perception and reception in the period.

In both plays the first indication of the process by which the central figures are constructed to embody arguments are the inductive devices of Machevill in *The Jew* and the Chorus in *Faustus*. Machevill becomes the mouthpiece for a version of machiavellian ideas and then claims that he is not here to deliver a 'lecture in Britain', but to present the tragedy of a Jew. The play thus becomes a substitute for the lecture, a function which privileges the discursive as a determinant of the construction of a hero. On the other hand, the Machevill prologue also ends in a request that the audience:

> Grace [Barabas] as he deserves,
> And let him not be entertain'd the worse
> Because he favours me.
> (Prologue 33–5)[3]

227

in a tone which suggests the same sort of conspiratorial relationship with the audience as Greenblatt has identified in relation to Barabas, the character (1980, 216). In *Faustus* the Chorus is present from the outset, at two further points during the play and at the end, not only to outline the course of Faustus's life but to draw attention to it as an example, functioning rather like the Expositors of early scriptural drama.

In *The Jew* the theatricalist approach engages the issue of power in opposing paradigms and realizes these in terms of theatrical display. The setting of the play is itself a significant contribution to this because, as in Kyd, or Shakespeare's *Titus Andronicus* and later Jacobean revenge drama, the Mediterranean setting constitutes a hermetic, histrionic, machiavellian world, where normal principles governing social intercourse give way to principles which are essentially theatrical in conception: a constant process of dramatized concealment and spectacular revelation which appear to have their chief justification in their theatrical effect. The construction of dramatic persona as both figure and character plays a significant part in the dual process of exemplification and audience engagement in this theatre which constantly exposes its own workings.

In *The Jew* the exemplificative process is apparent in the distortion of the narrative to point up certain climactic moments of display which occur throughout the play. These consist of conflicts, spectacular intrigues, intricately contrived strategies or other striking actions illustrating one form of power or another. Act 1 Scene 2 contains two sequences of display: in the first Barabas is confronted by Ferneze and divested of his fortune, and in the second he hatches the plot to put his daughter in the house as a nun. Between the two, his house is expropriated and set up as a nunnery. All this takes place within a single scene and in the course of a continuous unit of dialogue, the implausibility occasioned by the extreme narrative compression being less important than the juxtaposition of the contending points of display.[4]

These points of display disclose two contending forms of power which attach to the two machiavellian figures, Ferneze and Barabas. Ferneze's is the military, governmental and ritualized form, while Barabas's is exercised covertly through accommodation, avoidance of sovereignty, and self effacement. The distinction between these two configurations is made by Barabas early on in the play when describing his own people, and lists wealthy Jews throughout Europe:

> I must confesse we come not to be Kings:
> That's not our fault: Alas, our number's few,
> And Crownes come either by succession,
> Or urg'd by force; and nothing violent,
> Oft have I heard tell, can be permanent.

Give us peacefull rule; make Christians Kings,
That thirst so much for Principality.
(1.1.129–35)

The phrase, 'Infinite riches in a little roome' (1.1.37) succinctly encapsulates
the combination of privacy and power. Later in the play, Ferneze is confirmed
as representing the latter set of principles by his speech at the end of Act 2
scene 2 on his change of plan in respect of the tribute to Calymath, when he
receives Del Bosco's support:

> *Calymath*, instead of gold,
> Wee'll send thee bullets wrapt in smoake and fire:
> Claime tribute where thou wilt, we are resolv'd –
> Honor is bought with bloud, and not with gold.
> (53–6)

Both paradigms of power are not only exemplified, but are actually conceived
of in particular theatrical terms, so that they constitute two competing modes
of theatre. The theatre which constructs Ferneze is essentially ceremonial and
state centered, while' that which constructs Barabas is one of intrigue and
solitary machination; the one exists in the overt exercise of power, while the
other is based on the concealment of power. The two instances referred to
from Act 1 Scene 2 exemplify them. In the incident of the confiscation of
Barabas's wealth, the law is read by an officer as an official decree. In the
twists that follow, by which Barabas is made to forfeit all his wealth, the
subterfuges are legitimized by the legalistic tone of the decree, and the decree
by its interdiction of resistance, brooks no negotiation of its power. Ferneze's
remark to Barabas, 'Content thee, Barabas, thou hast nought but right'
(1.2.157) deliberately obscures the sense of real justice in a legalistic
interpretation of the term. Ferneze's theatre is also visual, however: he is
constantly surrounded by knights who constitute the symbolic trappings and,
indeed, the substance of power.

Barabas's error in this incident is not to be consistent with the basis of
his power, which is accommodation. However, his real power is exercised in
the next display sequence in the scene in which he engineers his daughter's
entry into the nunnery. Not only is this subterfuge, but whereas Ferneze's
power resides in institutional structures, Barabas's relies on his own particular
resources, here not only his cunning, but his daughter. Barabas's theatre is
theatrical in a different way to that of Ferneze, in that it involves the necessity
for representation which is improvised rather than institutionalized: he has to
devise acts rapidly in response to situations, such as his feigned horror at his
daughter's entering the nunnery, whereas Ferneze's theatre is previously

scripted, both culturally and in terms of legal structures of authority. Barabas is also thrown back upon intrigue in the same sense as the revengers of Jacobean tragedy when the mechanisms of state and other manifestations of *force majeure* block their way. Here the intriguer enters an authorial role within the play, since his planning constructs the dramatic situations which follow and the terms 'plot' and 'intrigue' function simultaneously in their two senses of 'narrative' and 'conspiratorial action'. There are also implications here for the audience's engagement with the central figure, to be discussed below.

Barabas's Jewishness also has a particular theatrical dimension since it helps to actualize in performance the justifying ideological frame of reference of the two forms of power: Barabas is an 'other' and his presence defines the majoritarian status of Ferneze and the other Christians. While not denying the real anti–Semitic virulence of the portrait, I would suggest that Jewishness is less of interest in any social or theological sense than as a representational category which conveniently fits the particular theatricalization of power here: his Jewishness defines his power as minoritarian: as Barabas points out in the opening scene, 'I must confesse we come not to be Kings:/ That's not our fault: Alas our number's few' (129–30). It also cuts Barabas off from the recourse to conventional justice, and other stereotypes such as cunning and ruthlessness are able to be brought into play. The relative absence of real Jews in late sixteenth century England combined with the tradition in the dramatic literature and elsewhere of the demonization of Jews provides Marlowe with a ready made theoretical construct, which allows him to make Barabas a complex signifier.[5] It is no less a form of dramatic shorthand than the setting of plays in Mediterranean countries and is a further illustration of persona as figure. There seems an element of playfulness in Marlowe's having Barabas describe himself to Ithamore in a self subverting way which piles one Jewish stereotype upon another to an extent which becomes farcical:

> As for my selfe, I walke abroad a nights
> And kill sicke people groaning under walls:
> Sometimes I goe about and poyson wells;
> And now and then, to cherish Christian theeves,
> I am content to lose some of my Crownes;
> That I may, walking in my Gallery,
> See 'em go pinion'd along by my doore.
> Being young, I studied Physicke, and began
> To practise first upon the Italian;
> There I enrich'd the Priests with burials,
> And alwayes kept the Sexton's armes in ure
> With digging graves and ringing dead men's knels:

And, after that, was I an Engineere,
And in the warres 'twixt *France* and *Germanie*,
Under pretence of helping *Charles* the fifth,
Slew friend and enemy with my stratagems.
Then after that was I an Usurer,
And with extorting, cozening, forfeiting,
And tricks belonging unto Brokery,
I fill'd the Jailes with Bankrouts in a yeare,
And with young Orphans planted Hospitals;
And every Moone made some or other mad,
And now and then one hang himselfe for griefe,
Pinning upon his breast a long great Scrowle
How I with interest tormented him.
(2.3.174–98)

This sort of almost comically hyperbolic speech is very much in keeping with Marlowe's autodeconstructive theatre; in so exaggeratedly embracing the stereotype, it turns it into pure theatrical grotesque.

The scripted, Christian theatre of power is scarcely less machiavellian, however. As a Vice–like truthteller, Barabas says of Christians:

I can see no fruits in all their faith,
But malice, falshood, and excessive pride,
Which me thinkes fits not their profession.
(1.1.116–18)

This is borne out by the machinations of the Christians who, unlike Barabas, never tell the truth to the audience. One instance of malice and falsehood is Barnardine's exploitation of Abigail's confession which, on the one hand, illustrates the institutional and legitimized process of regulation and control, and on the other exposes its possibilities for oppression. This both discloses the theatrical nature of the supposed sacrament, and reveals the institutional basis of Christian power.

Most instances of the scripted Christian theatre centre around Ferneze and include the meetings with Calymath, and Del Bosco. These are conducted on a level of diplomatic ceremony, but Ferneze double crosses Calymath twice, once when Del Bosco offers him help, and the other when he detains him at the end of the play. The betrayals are less spectacular than the machinations of Barabas, but are no less part of a world of hard–edged *realpolitik*. The contrast between Barabas and Ferneze in their responses to their children's deaths is also interesting: Ferneze's talk is of 'sacred monuments of stone' on the one hand, and a legal enquiry leading to

231

vengeance. His frame of reference is the public theatricalization of death and structures of law available for formal retribution. Barabas's grief is at his daughter's real conversion, not her death: his loss of a daughter from the theatrical category which defines him (i.e. Jew).

Barabas's displays of power all reside in theatrical effects and devices. He sets up comedies of errors in the duel between Lodowick and Mathias, and the deception of Friar Jacomo. He uses disguise in the house of Bellamira and when he 'disguises' himself as dead in Act 5 Scene 1, and Barnardine as alive in the sequence just referred to. He employs acting techniques at his pretended horror at Abigail's entry into the nunnery, in his apparent favouring of Lodowick as a suitor to Abigail, (2.3), in his professed 'adoption' of Ithamore (3.4), in his sudden proposed 'conversion' (4.1), and with his French accent in the house of Bellamira (5.1). He even erects a stage set in the traps for Calymath in Act 5 Scene 2. His manipulation of others also gives him an authorial role, as suggested above, and a directorial one. His downfall comes when he allows the directorial role to pass to Ferneze.

The focus on the protagonists as figures allows recognition of them as facilitators and pivots of the competing theatrical discourses of power. Though they are theatrically differentiated, the state authorized paradigm of power is interrogated precisely through the relationship between the Ferneze–centred, scripted discourse and its 'other', the improvised Barabas–centred Jewish/private/conspiratorial discourse. Barabas's stratagems are more complex and theatrical than those of Ferneze precisely because there are no fixed structures to conceal his exercise of power. Barabas's theatre of intrigue is actually necessitated by Ferneze's actions; his machinations are always finally a response to what Ferneze does.

The very complexity of Barabas's manoeuvres, however, give him a dramatic dominance, a certain psychological consistency and most significantly of all, a relationship with the audience which is produced by the fact of the sophisticated intelligence operating on stage. This does not perhaps quite add up to interiority, but he is also given several asides which add to his conspiratorial relationship with the audience and signal a distinction between public face and private motivation. Roger Sales compares him to the Vice in the old drama (Sales, 1991, 99). All this has significance for the subversive project, since it invites the audience into an engagement with Barabas that, by definition, distances them from the Ferneze paradigm. Thomas Cartelli has effectively described this in terms of the imaginative pleasure of transgression (Cartelli, 1991, 162–80).

The theatricalist reflexivity which presents power as theatre also offers an interrogation of the relationship between authorized power and its legitimizing principle. There is irony at the end of the play when Ferneze attributes his victory, 'Neither to Fate, nor Fortune, but to Heaven', but it is irony based firstly on the recognition of the theatrical and therefore contingent and essentially duplicitous nature of power, secondly on the play's subversion of the legitimacy of the formal manifestations of state power by associating its processes with those of intrigue theatre, and thirdly by the recognition (compelled by its own spectacular staginess) of the play's status as a conventional theatrical composition with the requirement for this type of narrative closure. The orthodoxy of the ending is ironized by its very conventionality.

In *Faustus* the theatricalism of the play is related to the very obvious fact of the choice of the morality form. That Marlowe should choose an obviously outdated form is striking and raises a question that needs addressing. In an early article Nicholas Brooke suggested that Marlowe's choice of this form was made in order to subvert it by turning it into an inverted morality play through having the hero actually choose his damnation (Brooke, 1952, 662–87). Jonathan Dollimore sees it in Foucauldian terms as a structure of oppression defining Faustus's transgression and sees the play's subversive value in the dramatization of transgression (Dollimore, 1984, 16). Thomas Cartelli has more recently called it a 'formally defensive strategy' (Cartelli, 1991, 16). The choice of this highly formal and intrinsically orthodox form can also, however, be seen as the basis of a theatricalist project of deconstruction. Just as the exemplificatory theatre of proto–revenge tragedy in *The Jew* foregrounds the mechanics of theatrical display in the course of confronting the whole question of power and representation, so the morality form in *Faustus* engineers an engagement with the question of theatre in its relation to the processes of religious authority, and religious authority, in turn, as a product of theatricalized representation.

The theatricalism of *Faustus* is a little different from that of *The Jew* but not markedly so in principle. The emphasis on the mechanisms and operations of theatrical representation resides not only in the selfconsciousness of the dramatic form, but in the repeated occurrence of image making in the play. The opposing discourses are represented in different images and sequences of theatre–within–theatre. The Seven Deadly Sins sequence (2.2), and the image of Hell (5.2 – apparently a hell–mouth, to judge from the reference to the 'jawes of hell' l. 1908), are both elements of the old religious drama. The sequences created by Faustus, with Alexander and Darius (4.1) and Helen of Troy (5.1) have, by contrast, more reference to an academic, neoclassical lineage of drama. The play thus makes reference to the history of its own genre and the cultural history of the century, of which it is very much a part. The Emperor's enchantment by the visions presented to him in Act 4 Scene 2, and Faustus's warning to him, 'These are but shadows, not substantial' can stand as the implicit comment of Marlowe's play on the genre of drama which it incorporates so ironically, and by implication the structure of divine power which it imaginatively actualizes.

This selfconsciousness about dramatic form is also very much present in the dramatization of stage devils. The very outdatedness of the devils as a dramatic device underlines their identity as theatrical mechanisms, in a sort of alienation effect and this is further underlined by the fact that Marlowe pulls out all the technical stops: they enter with thunder and lightning, and on occasion with fireworks. These instances recall the description of the entry of Belyal in the manuscript of the 15th century morality play, *The Castle of Perseverance*: 'And he pat schal pley Belyal loke pat he have gunne powder brennyng in pypys in his handys and in his erys.'[6] They are spectacular, but are thus in a way which makes them at best quasi–comic and at worst a theatrical excess of camp preposterousness.[7] As signifiers in a philosophical discourse they are therefore not only self–defeating, but call into question the very foundation of the discourse which determines their existence.[8] If, as Michael Hattaway says, they were more likely to be of interest to the audience than the mind of Faustus in the popular theatre, this effect is further reinforced.[9]

Another interesting piece of theatre is the excommunication of Faustus at the end of Act 3 Scene 3. The ceremony is represented fully and it is difficult not to take it as comic, especially in the dispersal of the Friars by Faustus at the end. The audience is presented with a piece of religious theatre, but the contrast between the solemn formality of the process and both the words of the friars and the riotous end, turns the whole thing into farce. However, the episode produces some additional implications. At the end of it, Faustus is damned by the Friars and this is in fact his true fate at the end of the play. But the Friars are manifestly Catholic, and an audience's approval of the fate of Faustus will mean complicity with these people. It is difficult to imagine a Protestant audience not making some association between the theatre of the excommunication ceremony and the old fashioned religious drama which informs the structure of this play. As in *The Jew*, power is again articulated through theatre as a way of ordering and regulating perception, and is exposed as such.

The role of Faustus as protagonist is of obvious importance and is probably the source of the greatest difficulty when it comes to viewing this play as transgressive, given Faustus's horrifying end. However, if the construction of the hero is seen in terms of a dramatic process, an argument can be made for a multifaceted engagement of the audience which is wholly in keeping with a transgressive agenda. Again, the hero must be seen as operating in terms both of figure and character. It is useful to draw an analogy here with Shakespeare's use of Lady Macbeth as a figure. Early in the play, she is used to maintain a sympathy for Macbeth by drawing the fire, as it were. In Act 5 she is the exact converse, again in the interests of shaping contrasts. She is, however, frequently cited as a character of psychological complexity. What emerges from this is that the unity or integrity of a dramatic character, even one with some interiority, is often largely invested by audience expectation, while the representation at different points in a play is frequently shaped to serve more immediate and localized dramaturgical ends. In the case of Faustus, it is possible to see three distinct figures, perhaps more. There is firstly the humanist philosopher whose rhetorical and imaginative energy powerfully establishes the presence of a humanist discourse in the play. Secondly there is Faustus the entertainer and clown who, like Barabas, becomes the dramatic author by devising the theatrical substance of the play, and engages the audience by so doing, while facilitating the imaginative pleasure of transgression that Cartelli identifies. Finally, there is Faustus the victim of a theocratic discourse of terror. Considering Faustus in terms of figure involves viewing him as constituting the centre of an argument. He can be seen as being the locus of conflict between a theocratic and humanist views of man. He is not so much a transgressive figure as the exemplification of conflict, which necessarily involves a dualism or even multiple identity in the figure. His representation incorporates a debate: his several speeches of humanist aspiration and questioning are a rhetorical and dramatic realization of that position, while his terror of damnation is a realization of the opposing, theocratic view. However, what becomes apparent in both the construction of Faustus, and the play generally, is that the argument is not presented evenhandedly. His terror at the end, rather than justifying the religious world view, is revelatory of its processes of operation. If the 'first beginning of religion was but to keep man in awe', this is a graphic representation of that awe.[10]

The figure of Faustus as an embodiment of the oppressive operation of religious fear also depends, as the dramatization of humanist aspirations does, on experiencing him as a subject, characterized through interiority. It is this interiority that sits particularly ill with the uncompromisingly different forms of theatre represented by the devils, the pageant of the Seven Deadly Sins, and Hell mouth. A very telling instance of the figural and subjective impulses working through contrast is the *psychomachia* of the good and bad angels. This device appears several times during the play, and against Faustus's soliloquies constitutes a powerful contrast of dramatic discourses. As a device which is overtly theatrical and visual, it discloses the Manichean basis of the theocratic discourse as a theatrical stratagem, whereas the humanism of Faustus is allowed the complexity and psychological authenticity conferred by soliloquy as a rhetorical vehicle of philosophical discourse. It is here entirely through the contrast of dramatic models that religious discourse is delegitimized and exposed as theatrical, and the essential old fashionedness of the theological mode of theatre by the late sixteenth century further serves to emphasize this.

Doctor Faustus and *The Jew of Malta* have always posed the problem of reconciling what appears to be conventional support for the dominant social and religious order with what is known of Marlowe's life and opinions. By viewing these two plays, not simply as tragic narratives inhabited by psychologically defined protagonists, but as autodeconstructive theatricalizations of power, transgression and repression articulated by means of dramatic figures constructed through a mode of correlative and exemplificative representation fully available in the writing and theatrical culture of the period, it is possible to see these texts as in fact powerfully dissident. As in the Walsingham pageant, embracing the orthodox framework is actually necessary to the subversive process, since it is by this means that it can be effectively turned into theatrical grotesque. An observation on the nature of camp is of relevance here:

> [The] piggy–backing upon the dominant order's monopoly on the authority of signification explains why Camp appears, on the one hand, to offer a transgressive vehicle yet, on the other, simultaneously involves the specter of dominant ideology within its practice, appearing in many instances, to actually reinforce the dominant order.
> (Meyer, 1994, 11)

The theatricalism and reflexive engagement with power as theatre involve, in the case of *The Jew* a study of the ironies of power, authority and representation, and in the case of *Faustus* the text reconstitutes divine authority as a theatrical construct, and one which is by turns ridiculous and terrifying, the visual and conceptual terms of reference of which are exotic and crude. The powers in place *have* to triumph, Barabas and Faustus *have* to die spectacularly (as Marlowe's Edward II has to), in order for the texts satisfactorily to function in this subversive way.[11]

Notes

1. 29th May. The article by Jim White was 'Gin and Lace and a High Time for All'.

2. Since this essay was presented as a paper in 1993, a volume of essays has appeared (Meyer, 1994) which, though not strictly a history, does contain some historical perspectives on the phenomenon, and provides considerable theoretical discussion. See also Dollimore, 1991.

3. References for both *The Jew of Malta* and *Doctor Faustus* are to the 1971 edition of Marlowe's Complete Works by Fredson Bowers.

4. Thomas Cartelli talks of Marlowe's conditioning his audience to the ironic and logical discontinuities of the type of play he is writing and accommodate itself to the freedom of the play's theatrical mode (Cartelli, 1991, 164–8).

5. On the relative absence of Jews from England in the period, see Roth, 1941, 132–48. For discussions of early representations of Jews in England, see Rosenberg, 1960, 21–7, and Panitz, 1981, 23–63.

6. Folger MS V. a. 354, fo. 191v., reproduced as frontispiece of *The Macro Plays* ed. M. Eccles, EETS, London, 1969.

7. Roger Sales sees the playfulness of the play residing in a series of dramatic parodies which render Lucifer and the devils as much figures of fun as terror (Sales, 1991, 144).

8. Marlowe's reputation for atheism is obviously germane, though not indispensable to this argument. For a discussion of Marlowe and Renaissance scepticism, see Nicholas Davidson's essay in the present volume.

9. Hattaway, 1982, 165–7. Compare also: 'A traveller in 1790 . . . goes on to relate that in other villages near Innsbrück, St Mary Magdalene and St Sebastian were being performed; and he was assured that these pieces possessed superior attractions to that of St Pancras, inasmuch as more devils appeared in them' (Pichler, *Über das Drama des Mittelalters in Tirol*, quoted in Baring–Gould, 1879, vol.1, 16–17).

10. Baines deposition, May 1593, reproduced in Wraight and Stern, 1965, 308–9.

11. Greenblatt, by contrast, sees the Marlovian rebels and sceptics as 'embedded within the orthodoxy of the Renaissance: they simply reverse the paradigm and embrace what is evil.' Greenblatt does, however, go on to discuss Marlowe's 'suspicion that objects of desire are fictions, theatrical illusions, shaped by human subjects. And these subjects are themselves fictions, fashioned in reiterated acts of self naming.' He also remarks that Catholic and Protestant polemicists were always pointing out that each other's religion was a cunning theatrical illusion, a demonic fantasy, a piece of poetry (Greenblatt, 1980, 209, 218–9).

14. Marlowe and the Internalization of Irony

ALEXANDER SHURBANOV

It is hardly possible and indeed unnecessary to try and decide whether Marlowe's creative thinking was shaped by the scholastic tradition of the *argumentum in utramque partem*, argued by Joel Altman (1978) to lie as a model at the fountainhead of early Renaissance drama, or whether it was informed by a much more fundamental attitudinal predisposition of the age, which Leonid Batkin defines as the 'dialogical principle' of humanist culture, its unwillingness or even virtual inability to reconcile conflicting views on any given topic of discussion (1978, esp. ch. 3). What becomes apparent is that a powerful sense of irony informs his writing, through which every intellectual position is problematized and demystified. This is, in many ways, a hallmark of the age. The gradual penetration of irony into the dramatic structure and particularly its contribution to the shaping of the early modern dramatic character is what I propose to examine briefly in this essay.[1]

Tamburlaine the Great opens with the characteristic words of the hero's first antipodal antagonist, Mycetes, King of Persia:

> Brother Cosroe, I find myself aggrieved;
> Yet insufficient to express the same,
> For it requires a great and thundering speech:
> Good brother, tell the cause unto my lords;
> I know you have a better wit than I.
> (1.1.1–5)

Here we find in a nutshell everything that Tamburlaine is not, everything that he despises in the others and deems unworthy of a ruler: the inability to wield the 'high astounding terms' of triumphant rhetoric, a lack of self confidence and self esteem, feeblemindedness, pusillanimity, and the inclination to delegate responsibility.

The speech introduces the chief type of irony that accompanies the protagonist throughout the play, and which I call *parallelistic*. It is based on the contrastive pairing of the great Scythian with his adversaries or inadequate imitators, including Cosroe, Bajazeth and his son Callapine, Agydas and the Governor of Babylon, but also some of those closest to the hero: his own immature sons, Amyras and Celebinus, and even the almost faultless Theridamas (in his unfortunate attempt in Balsera to repeat Tamburlaine's conquest of a fair lady). The most striking contrast to the hero is perhaps his eldest son and heir apparent, Calyphas, whose nature brings him closer to Mycetes than to his father. All these strains of parallelistic irony tend to point away from the protagonist towards other figures, undermining the latter and thus bolstering the speaker. This is almost invariably the case in the first three acts of Part One. After that, however, the contrast starts fading away from the parallelistic patterns leaving more and more room for subversive analogy. The irony becomes double–edged and is equally levelled at the protagonist's opposites and at his own person. This is especially true of the confrontation between Tamburlaine and Calyphas, who cannot appreciate his father's endless preoccupation with war and who subverts the Scythian's rhetorical heroism with the necessary dose of plain commonsense pragmatism.[2]

The re–emergence of the previously defeated Mycetes in Calyphas is also an instance of the other central type of irony in the play, the one contained in the abrupt reversals of dramatic action known as peripeteia and therefore best termed *peripeteic*. It becomes increasingly prominent in the play and passes through a series of losses and unexpected betrayals culminating in the death of fair Zenocrate and the execution of Tamburlaine's appointed successor. Thus the entire triumphant march of the world conqueror is undermined, until his ultimate adversaries, Hell and Darkness, borrow his own military colour symbolism and 'pitch their pitchy tents' so that Death can put an end to his exploits. Parallelistic and peripeteic ironies appear frequently in conjuction and are not easy to separate.

The workings of these two kinds of plot irony are responsible for the dual impression of the protagonist with which we are left: the invincible warrior whose final defeat is inescapable and the nonpareil of war heroism continuously verging on the ludicrous or the monstrous.

The methodical subversion of Doctor Faustus's heroic stature is achieved in much the same way. This time, however, the parallelistic and peripeteic ironies are more compact and salient. They inform the entire central part of the play. Each of them is allotted a series of humorous scenes: in the one a number of clowns provide grotesque analogues for the protagonist's deeds while the other features Faustus himself transformed into an itinerant court jester. The two strains are skilfully intertwined in the remarkable Horse Courser episode. It is here that the would–be master of the universe and sole possessor of all its riches sinks to the lowest depths of his career, trying to cheat an ignoble rogue out of some forty dollars and in the process subjecting himself to utter physical humiliation. It is here too that Faustus seems to step into the role of Mephistophilis leaving his own part to be played by the Horse Courser. And through this transformation of the main plot of the tragedy we are made aware of its central delusion: the hero's futile and self–destructive attempt to outwit the superior powers of Hell. The parallelistic irony is further reinforced by the introduction of the Old Man as a foil for the hero and by the allusions to Icarus and Lucifer as the Doctor's prototypes. Needless to say, it is now levelled primarily at the protagonist. The peripeteic variety is similarly pervasive. It makes its first appearance on the crucial conjuring night, when Faustus's confidence that he has managed to raise the devil through the power of his magic is exploded by Mephistophilis's prompt revelation of its auxiliary (*per accidence*) function. And it gathers momentum in the later scenes, attaining full sway in the closing section, where the hero's erstwhile self assurance is turned into utter despair and his overwhelming ambition 'to gain a deity' is converted into an urge to seek refuge in beasthood.[3]

But *Doctor Faustus* couples the already familiar plot irony with a new, character irony, almost non–existent in *Tamburlaine* and produced either by the interaction of characters or by a single character's inner duality – which I will call respectively *interpersonage* and *intrapersonage* irony. Even in this play the said forms remain rather peripheral. The interpersonage variety is chiefly confined to the ambiguous partnership between Faustus and Mephistophilis – and its grotesque imitations in the horseplay episodes – whose essence is discovered to be the reverse of its spurious appearance. Intrapersonage irony moulds the opening scenes, in which the protagonist's impressive 'resolution' can again and again be interpreted as immaturity and improvidence, while the grounds for his rebellion against traditional authority seem little more than quibbles.[4] Both types of character irony in this play remain dependent on plot structure. The first is tied up with the parallelistic and the second with the specifically dramatic irony which presupposes superior audience awareness.

Plot irony continues to be of paramount importance in *The Jew of Malta*. Its parallelistic variant makes itself known in the analogies established between Barabas's cupidity and the centrality of this characteristic in the overall strategy of the Christian government of the island. A scheme of ironic correspondences is superimposed on the differentiation of dramatic action into a political overplot and a low–life underplot[5], both of which turn out to be propelled by the same greed and covetousness. The protagonist, who can hardly be seen as heroic on a par with Tamburlaine and Faustus, is nonetheless provided with a grotesque double. Unlike Faustus's distant underplot caricatures, this character, the mercenary Turk Ithamore, is the hero's trusted slave, involved in a continuous intricate relationship with him, which transforms the parallelistic scheme into an interpersonage one. Whatever we choose to call it, it is obviously double edged and Barabas is seldom spared its acid stings. Interpersonage irony certainly informs most of the hero's relations with the remaining characters in a world of pervasive hypocrisy and mutual duplicity.

The peripeteic variety is perhaps even more essential to this 'tragic farce'. Time and again the protagonist is inadvertently reduced from agent to patient, from doer to sufferer, until, at the end, he tumbles down into the boiling cauldron he has himself prepared for the ultimate destruction of his enemies. At the same time, this is the first of Marlowe's plays to rely so heavily on character irony. The interpersonage scheme involving Barabas and Ithamore is in fact triple, because Abigail is also drawn into it. The Jew's ill advised choice of the treacherous slave instead of his loving daughter for a trusty companion reflects unfavourably on his overrated intelligence. Abigail is herself an important source as well as target of interpersonage irony. Her unquestioning filial devotion to her plotting father turns her into a tool for his criminal designs and ruins her personal happiness. Even after her death, the girl's moral idealism is bitterly ironized by the self seeking cynicism of her environment. Her last confession gives a corrupt monk the necessary information to blackmail Barabas. Poisoned by her own father, with her last breath she wishes that the caitiff might be converted into Christianity like herself to save his soul. The Jew pretends to be willing to follow her advice only in order to outwit the avaricious monks and beat them at their own game. Thus Abigail, despite her best intentions, continues unwittingly to serve the villain's ends from the beyond. But even Barabas, who is sure he can hoodwink everybody else, falls victim to the same strange blindness twice over. Having already been betrayed by Ithamore, now he confides most unexpectedly in his bitterest enemy, Ferneze and supplies him with all the means for his own destruction. Obviously, this interpersonage irony is inextricably connected with the structural peripeteic pattern.

Intrapersonage irony also pervades the play, though it is chiefly of the simplest possible kind typical of the thoroughly Machiavellian world of Marlowe's Malta: most of its denizens have to wear prim masks meant to conceal their predatory nature. Barabas is, of course, a candidate for absolute supremacy in this social art. The mechanism of a peculiar dramatic irony is consistently used to sustain the intrapersonage variety: from the very first, the protagonist attempts to collude with us against everybody else on the stage through his many characteristic asides, which change radically the meaning of all his cues and make his communication dangerously devious. Barabas is perhaps Marlowe's most 'Gorgian' creation, for he exhibits most clearly of all what Stephen Greenblatt calls 'the unavoidable distance between the particular actor and his role' (Greenblatt, 1980, 217).

This fundamental ironic ambivalence of character, the constant attempt to hide the unseemly truth behind a socially acceptable façade leads to its disintegration into a number of incompatible forms jostling together with their rival claims for authenticity. Now the Jew is a magnificent tycoon, almost a poet of wealth, who is above all petty considerations of meagre gains ('Fie, what a trouble 'tis to count this trash!'), and at the next moment he takes good care to buy a slave 'that's sickly, an't be but for sparing victuals'. Now nothing is dearer to him than his riches, and then he is ready to sacrifice everything for a Burckhardtian exquisite revenge on the entire world. This is how we arrive at the specifically Renaissance 'discontinuity' of dramatic character (Dollimore, 1984, 30–36), not just contradictory, but almost 'dispersed' in Barthes's sense of the word (Barthes, 1977, 143). Marlowe's next, and probably last, play will make ample use of this approach.

Plot irony is not altogether marginal in *Edward II*. There is, first of all, the systematic contrastive parallelism between the King and his chief antagonist, the young Mortimer, that is pivotal to the entire drama. In addition, it is interspersed with peripeteic irony at all crucial junctures of the action, such as Mortimer's imprisonment which directly becomes a springboard for his aggrandizement. Thenceforth the progress of each of the two is punctuated with a series of such turns. Thus Edward, who has always yearned for true friendship, is finally handed over to a gang of foes who beguile him with their mock–sympathy driving him ever closer to his horrible end. Mortimer, for his part, is arrested and turned over to the executioner at the moment when he seems most secure in his power.

What is much more fundamental to the construction of this play, however, is its character irony often free from all structural props. The interpersonage variety can be found at every step. Gaveston's opening speech offers the first characteristic example. The minion is entranced by Edward's amorous letter, which invites him to England to 'share the kingdom with [his] dearest friend'. Yet his reaction warns us of a striking difference in the attitudes of the two lovers. While Edward's genuine affection is beyond doubt, Gaveston's reply betrays an opportunistic bent that will continue to cast an ironic light on their further liaison. The Frenchman's rapturous exclamation – 'What greater bliss can hap to Gaveston / Than live and be the favourite of a king! (1.1.4–5) – with its indefinite article before the last word, is soberingly impersonal and egotistic. Such subtle nuances become apparent at various points in the relations of many characters in the play. One of the most striking instances is the final encounter of the protagonist and his murderer Lightborn, who takes it upon himself to play the ironic role of the King's sympathetic confidant and confessor. Such dualities inform most of the action, and we watch in bewilderment the struggle between the two irreconcilable camps, the monarch's and that of his rebellious nobles, each claiming moral superiority over the other and vehemently denounced by its opponent.

It is in the midst of this interpersonage irony that its intrapersonage counterpart comes into play. In the absence of a reliable moral centre, not only the relations between characters but the very characters themselves become ambivalent or 'discontinuous'. It is impossible to decide with any certainty whether Gaveston is, at least potentially, a true friend or a mere wily parasite; whether Mortimer's patriotic rhetoric is an absolute sham and whether he can be reduced to a stage Machiavel; whether Isabella does try to be a loving wife in spite of her husband's indifference or whether she is a

243

scheming hypocrite and a cruel villain throughout irrespective of all sentimental speeches (including a few confessional soliloquies!); or whether Pembroke, Gaveston's escort to death, is the most humane or the most perfidious of all the rebels. Even Kent's integrity is punctured by occasional surprising glimpses of self interest.[6] And above all else – like Barabas, but in a much more complex and intriguing way – Edward rises as the central enigma of the play, a figure of powerful outbursts of passion invariably subverted by irony but undefeated to the end; a weakling of immense stamina, a stoical coward, a selfish individualist who, alone among his Marlovian kin, is capable of self–sacrifice but resorts to it only when other options are no longer available.[7]

This is discontinuity proper, yet, at least in Edward's case, not the irreconcilable kind imposed by the structural mechanism of parallelistic irony on Tamburlaine and Faustus or, by the inchoate thrusts of intrapersonage irony, on Barabas. It is a kind of discontinuity capable of suggesting the inextricable complexity of life as the great *concordia discors*. For, while it is true that the principle of 'misalignment' (Dollimore, 1984, 39) is at the heart of all mature Renaissance tragedy, the striving towards a new, larger aesthetic harmony that would contain disparity rather than subdue it is also there and is responsible for its greatest feats.

One important way towards this new uneasy integration seems to be suggested by Marlowe in *Edward II*. The inner contradiction in characters like Isabella, Mortimer and, to a certain extent, even the protagonist himself, can be seen as either discontinuity or transformation, either in a synchronic or in a diachronic perspective, the former providing the basis for the latter, its potential existence. Thus the ironic polarization and decentralization of character prepares the way for its dynamization, its study as a process rather than as a state, a shift that also points forward to its fruition in Jacobean drama.

Notes

1. I have considered this topic in greater detail elsewhere; see Shurbanov, 1992.

2. Pace Kocher (1946, 263), it is difficult not to agree with the majority of commentators, broadly in accord with Una Ellis–Fermor who argues convincingly that, 'Calyphas comes very near persuading us that he is the only sane man in a group of madmen, or that Marlowe had had a sudden movement of impatience with the absurdity of his conception and had joined the audience in laughing at his chief characters' (Ellis–Fermor, 1927, 42).

3. For a very clear outline of this ironic scheme see Mahood, 1950, 73.

4. Douglas Cole lays these tricks bare as effectively as anyone else (Cole, 1962, 197).

5. The structural terminology used here was coined by Harry Levin (1954, 87).

6. Note, for instance, how in 5.2.16–19 Kent springs into action for no other reason than to avenge himself on his foe, Mortimer. Bearing in mind the exceptional nobility of this character, one might have expected his motive to be the safety of his captive brother rather than his own petty satisfaction.

7. Compare the abdication scene where, forced by untoward circumstances, Edward relinquishes his crown, so that it may be passed on to his beloved son (5.1).

BIBLIOGRAPHY

Publication details of early texts are provided in endnotes.

Aarssen, P. (1969) 'Tot Middelburgh by Richard Schilders', *Zeeuws Tijdschrift*, 4.

Adams, H. (1967) *Catalogue of Books Printed on the Continent of Europe 1501–1600 in Cambridge Libraries*, 2 vols., Cambridge.

Aers, D. (1992) 'A Whisper in the Ear of the Early Modernists: Reflections on Literary Critics Writing "The History of the Subject"' in *Culture and History 1350–1600*, ed. D. Aers, Hemel Hempstead.

Agnew, J.–C. (1986) *Worlds Apart: The Market and the Theater in Anglo–American Thought 1550–1750*, Cambridge.

Akrigg, G. (1975) 'The Literary Achievement of King James I', *University of Toronto Quarterly*, 44.

Allen, D. (1943) 'Henry Vaughan's "The Ass"' *MLN* 58 (1943). London.

Alpers, S. (1983) *The Art of Describing: Dutch Art in the Seventeenth Century*, London.

Altman, J. (1978) *The Tudor Play of Mind: Rhetorical Inquiry and the Development of Elizabethan Drama*, Berkeley.

Anderson, M. (1955) 'English Views of Russia in the Seventeenth Century', *Slavonic and Eastern European Review*, 13.

Andrews, K. (1964) *Elizabethan Privateering: English Privateering during the Spanish War, 1585–1603*, Cambridge.

Andrews, K. (1984) *Trade, Plunder and Settlement: Maritime Enterprise and the Genesis of the British Empire, 1480–1630*, Cambridge.

Ashe, T. (1907) ed. Coleridge, *Lectures and Notes on Shakespeare and Other English Poets*, London.

Auerbach, E. (1984) 'Figura' in *Scenes from the Drama of European Literature*, Manchester.

Aylmer, G. (1978) 'Unbelief in Seventeenth–Century England' in *Puritans and Revolutionaries: Essays in Seventeenth–Century* History presented to Christopher Hill, ed. Donald Pennington and Keith Thomas, Oxford.

Bakeless, J. (1937) 'Christopher Marlowe and the Newsbooks', *Journalism Quarterly*, 14.

Bakeless, J. (1942) *The Tragicall History of Christopher Marlowe*, 2 vols., Cambridge Mass.

Bakhtin, M. (1984), *Rabelais and his World*, tr. Helene Iswolsky, Bloomington.

Bald, R. (1970) *John Donne: A Life*, Oxford.

Baldwin Smith, L. (1986) *Treason in Tudor England: Politics and Paranoia*, London.

Baring–Gould, S. (1879) *Germany Present and Past*, London, 2 vols.

Barish, J. (1981) *The Antitheatrical Prejudice* , Berkeley.

Barker, F. (1984) *The Tremulous Private Body*, London.

Barnavi, E. (1980) *Le parti de Dieu*, Brussels/Louvain.

Baron, S. (1978) 'Ivan the Terrible, Giles Fletcher and the Muscovite Merchantry', *Slavonic and Eastern European Review*, 56.

Bartels, E. (1993) *Spectacles of Strangeness: Imperialism, Alienation, and Marlowe*, Philadelphia.

Barthes, R. (1977) *Roland Barthes*, tr. R. Howard, London.

Barthes, R. (1982) 'The reality effect' in *French Literary Theory Today*, ed. T. Todorov, tr. R. Carter, Cambridge.

Baskerville, E. (1993) 'A Religious Disturbance in Canterbury, June 1561: John Bale's Unpublished Account,' *Historical Research*, 65.

Batkin, L. (1978) *Italyanskie Gumanisty: Stil Zhizni i Stil Myshleniya*, Moscow.

Baumgartner, F. (1973) *Radical Reactionaries: the Political Thought of the French Catholic League*, Geneva.

Belsey, C. (1985) *The Subject of Tragedy*, London.

Ben–Amos, I. (1994) *Adolescence and Youth in Early Modern England* , New Haven and London.

Berdan, J. (1924) 'Marlowe's *Edward II*' *Philological Quarterly*, 3.

Berek, P. (1982 *'Tamburlaine's* weak sons: imitation as interpretation before 1593', *Renaissance Drama*, n.s. 13.

Berry, L. and Crummey R., (1968) *Rude and Barbarous Kingdom: Russia in the Accounts of Sixteenth–Century English Voyagers*, Madison, Wisc.

Besancon, A. (1988) 'The Russian Case' in *Europe and the Rise of Capitalism*, ed. J. Baechler, J. Hall and M. Mann, Oxford.

Bevington, D. (1962) *From 'Mankind' to Marlowe. Growth of Structure in the Popular Drama of Tudor England*, Cambridge, Mass.

Bingham, C. (1968) *The Making of a King: the Early Years of James VI and I*, London.

Bishop, C. (1972) 'Raleigh satirized by Harington and Davies', *Review of English Studies*, 23.

Boas, F. (1940) *Christopher Marlowe: a bibliographical and critical study*, Oxford.

Bono, P. (1979–81) 'The Massacre at Paris (1592): Contributi del gruppo di ricerca sulla communicazione teatrale in Inghilterra', in *Le forme del teatro* ed. G. Melchiori, Rome.

Bossy, J. (1991) *Giordano Bruno and the Embassy Affair*, New Haven and London.

Boucher, J. (1981) *Société et mentalités autour de Henri III*, Lyon thesis, 4 vols., Lille (Archives Nationales, Paris, K 1539 microfilm).

Boucher, J. (1985) 'Culture des notables et mentalités populaires dans la propagande qui entraina la chute de Henri III', in *Mouvements populaires et conscience sociale* ed. J. Nicolas, Paris.

Boucher, J. (1986) *La cour de Henri III*, Ouest France.

Boulton, J. (1987) 'Neighbourhood migration in early modern London' in *Migration and Society in Early Modern England*, ed. P. Clark and D. Souden, London.

Bourilly, V–L. and Vindry, F. (1908–9) eds., *Mémoires de Martin et Guillaume du Bellay*, 4 vols., Paris.

Bowen, B. (1972) 'Cornelius Agrippa's *De Vanitate*: Polemic or Paradox', *Bibliothèque d'Humanisme et Renaissance*, 34.

Bowers, F. (1972) 'The Early Editions of Marlowe's *Ovid's Elegies'*, *Studies in Bibliography*, 25.

Boyer, C. (1914) *The Villain as Hero in Elizabethan Tragedy*, London and New York.

Bradbrook, M. (1963) 'Marlowe's *Doctor Faustus* and the Eldritch Tradition', *Essays ... in Honor of Hardin Craig*, ed. R.H. Hosley, London.

Bradford, A. (1983) 'Stuart absolutism and the "utility" of Tacitus', *HLQ* 46, 127– 51;

Braudel, F. (1982) *Civilization and Capitalism, 15th–18th Century: The Wheels of Commerce*, tr. S. Reynolds, London.

Bray, A. (1982) *Homosexuality in Renaissance England*, London.

Bray, A. (1990) 'Homosexuality and the Signs of Male Friendship in Elizabethan England' *History Workshop*, 29, 1–19.

Bredbeck, G. (1991) *Sodomy and Interpretation: Marlowe to Milton*, Ithaca and London.

Brenner, R. (1993) *Merchants and Revolution: Commercial Change, Political Conflict, and London's Overseas Trade, 1550–1653*, Cambridge.

Brigden, S. (1984) 'Youth and the English Reformation', in *Rebellion, Popular Protest and the Social Order in Early Modern England*, ed. P. Slack, Cambridge.

Briggs, J. (1983) 'Marlowe's *Massacre at Paris*: a reconsideration', *The Review of English Studies*, new ser. 34.

Brook, V. (1962) *Matthew Parker*, London.

Brooke, C. (1987) 'Allocating Rooms in the Sixteenth Century,' *The Caian*, Nov.

Brooke, N. (1952) 'The Moral Tragedy of Dr Faustus', *Cambridge Journal* V.

Brown, L. (1951) *The Story of Maps*, London.

Brown, R. and Cavendish Bentinck G. (1890) eds., *Calendar of State Papers ... Venice*, vol. 7, London.

Buckley, G. (1932) *Atheism in the English Renaissance*, Chicago.

Butcher, A. (1979) 'Canterbury's earliest rolls of freemen admissions, a reconsideration', in *A Kentish Miscellany*, Kent Records (Kent Archaeological Society), ed. F. Hull, Chichester.

Butcher, A. (1989) 'Marlowe goes missing', *Kent Society Bulletin* 13.

Calder, I. (1949) 'A Note on the Magic Squares in the Philosophy of Agrippa of Nettesheim' *JWCI* 12.

Calderwood, D. (1843) *The History of the Kirk of Scotland*, ed. T. Thompson, 8 vols, The Wodrow Society, Edinburgh, 1842–9, vol.3.

Cameron, K. (1974) 'Henri III – the Antichristian King', *Journal of European Studies*

Cameron, K. (1978) *Henri III: Maligned or Malignant King?*, Exeter.

Campbell, G. (1992) 'Popular Traditions of God in the Renaissance' in *Reconsidering the Renaissance*, ed. M. Di Cesare, Binghampton.

Cannadine, D. (1992) 'Introduction: divine rights of kings', *Rituals of Royalty*, ed. D. Cannadine and S. Price, Cambridge.

Cartelli, T. (1991) *Marlowe, Shakespeare, and the Economy of Theatrical Experience*, Philadelphia.

Chambers, E. (1923) *The Elizabethan Stage*, Oxford.

Champion, P. (1939) 'Henri III: la légende des mignons', *Humanisme et Renaissance*, 6.

Champion, P. (1941–2) *La jeunesse de Henri III*, 2 vols, Paris.

Chevallier, P. (1985) *Henri III. Roi shakespearien*, Paris.

Clare, J. (1990) *'Art Made Tongue–tied by Authority': Elizabethan and Jacobean Dramatic Censorship*, Manchester.

Clark, P. (1977) *English Provincial Society from the Reformation to the Revolution: Religion, Politics and Society in Kent, 1500–1640*, Brighton.

Clark, P. (1983) *The English Alehouse*, London and New York.

Clulee, N. (1988) *John Dee's Natural Philosophy: Between Science and Religion*, London and New York.

Cocula, A.–M. (1992) 'Brantôme ou la mauvaise réputation du duc d'Anjou, futur Henri III', in *Henri III et son temps*, ed. R. Sauzet, Paris.

Cohen, A. (1994) *Self Consciousness. An Alternative Anthropology of Identity*, London and New York.

Cole, D. (1962) *Suffering and Evil in the Plays of Christopher Marlowe*, Princeton, N.J.

Collinson, P. ([1967] 1982) *The Elizabethan Puritan Movement*, London and New York.

Collinson, P. (1988) *The Birthpangs of Protestant England. Religious and Cultural Change in the Sixteenth and Seventeenth Centuries*, Basingstoke.

Collinson, P. Ramsay N. and Sparks, M., (1995) eds., *History of Canterbury Cathedral*, Oxford.

Cortés, H. (1986) *Letters from Mexico*, ed. and tr. A. Pagden, New Haven.

Cowper, J. (1900) *Lives of the Deans of Canterbury, 1541–1900*, Canterbury.

Cox, J. (1989) *Shakespeare and the Dramaturgy of Power*, Princeton.

Crewe, J. (1982) *Unredeemed Rhetoric: Thomas Nashe and the Scandal of Authorship*, Baltimore and London.

Crosskey, R. (1983) 'Hakluyt's Accounts of Sir Jerome Bowes' Embassy to Ivan IV', *Slavonic and East European Review*, 61.

Cruickshank, C. (1966) *Elizabeth's Army*, 2nd ed., Oxford.

Crummey, R. (1987) 'New Wine in Old Bottles?: Ivan IV and Novgorod', in *Ivan the Terrible: A Quatercentenary Celebration of His Death, Russian History*, 14.

Cunningham, K. (1990) 'Renaissance Execution and Marlovian Elocution: The Drama of Death', *Publications of the Modern Language Association of America*, 105.

Curtis, M. (1959) *Oxford and Cambridge in Transition, 1558–1642*, Oxford.

Curtius, E. (1953) *European Literature and the Latin Middle Ages*, tr. W. Trask, London.

Dasent, J. (1890–1907) ed. *Acts of the Privy Council of England*, new series, 32 vols., London.

Davidson, N. (1992) 'Unbelief and Atheism in Italy, 1500–1700' in Wootton and Hunter, 1992.

Dawson, G. (1965) ed., *Records of Plays and Players in Kent, 1450–1642: Malone Society Collections*, VII, 17–18.

Dean, L. (1941) 'Sir Francis Bacon's theory of civil history–writing', *ELH*, 8, 161–83.

Descimon, R. (1983) *Qui étaient les seize?*, Paris.

Dickens, A. (1974) 'The Elizabethans and St. Bartholomew' in *The Massacre of Saint Bartholomew*, ed. A. Soman, The Hague.

Dickens, B. (1966) 'The Emergence of a College Portrait' *Letter of the Corpus Association*, no.45, Michaelmas.

Dimock, A. (1813) 'The Conspiracy of Dr Lopez', *English Historical Review*, ix.

Dodu, G. (1930) 'Henri III', *Revue historique*, 165.

Dodu, G. (1934) *Les Valois. Histoire d'une maison royale (1328–1589)*, Paris.

Dollimore, J. (1984) *Radical Tragedy: Religion, Ideology and Power in the Drama of Shakespeare and His Contemporaries*, London.

Dollimore, J. (1991), *Sexual Dissidence: Augustine to Wilde, Freud to Foucault*, Oxford.

Donaldson, G. (1965) *Scotland: James V to James VII*, Edinburgh.

Dover Wilson, J. (1912) 'Richard Schilders and the English Puritans', *The Library*, 11, 3–20.

Du Maurier, D. (1977) *Golden Lads: Anthony Bacon, Francis, and their Friends*, London.

Duncan, E. (1942) 'Alchemy in Jonson's *Mercury Vindicated*', *Studies in Philology*, 39.

Dunning, C. (1989)(1) 'A Letter to James I Concerning the English Plan for Military Intervention in Russia', *Slavonic and Eastern European Review*, 67.

Dunning, C. (1989)(2) 'James I, the Russia Company, and the Protectorate over North Russia', *Albion* 21.

Dutton, R. (1993) 'Shakespeare and Marlowe: Censorship and Construction', *The Yearbook of English Studies*, vol. 23.

Dyer, G. (1824) *The Privileges of the University of Cambridge*, 2 vols., London.

Earle, E., Craig, G. and Gilbert, F. (1944) eds., *Makers of Modern Strategy: Military Thought from Macchiavelli to Hitler*, Princeton.

Eccles, M. (1982) 'Brief Lives: Tudor and Stuart Authors', *Studies in Philology*, vol. 79, no. 4.

Edwards, D. (1957) *A History of the King's School, Canterbury*, London.

Eliot, T. (1932) *Selected Essays, 1917–1932*, London.

Ellis–Fermor, U. (1927) *Christopher Marlowe*, London.

Emmison, F. (1973) *Elizabethan Life: Morals and the Church Courts, mainly from Essex Archidiaconal Records*, Chelmsford.

Erikson, R. (1981) 'Construction in Marlowe's The Massacre at Paris', in *Papers from the First Nordic Conference for English Studies*, ed. S. Johansson and B. Tysdahl, Oslo, 1981, 41–54.

Esper, T. (1967) 'A Sixteenth–Century Anti–Russian Arms Embargo' *Jahrbücher für Geschichte Osteuropas* 15.

Febvre, L. (1982) *The Problem of Unbelief in the Sixteenth Century: The Religion of Rabelais*, London.

Ferguson, J. (1924) 'Bibliographical Notes on the Treatises *De Occulta Philosophia* and *De Incertitudine et Vanitate Scientiarum* of Cornelius Agrippa', Edinburgh [reprinted from *The Publications of the Edinburgh Bibliographical Society*].

Fischer, D. (1971) *Historians' Fallacies: Towards a Logic of Historical Thought*, London, 1971.

Fischer, M. (1986) 'Ethnicity and the Post–Modern Arts of Memory', in *Writing Culture. The Poetics and Politics of Ethnography*, ed. J. Clifford, and G. Marcus, Berkeley, Los Angeles, London.

Fleay, F. (1890) *A Chronicle History of the London Stage, 1559–1642*, London.

Forker, C. (1994) Introduction to edition of *Edward II*, The Revels Plays, Manchester.

Foucault, M. (1978) *The History of Sexuality: An Introduction*, tr. R. Hurley, New York.

Foucault, M. (1980) 'Two Lectures', in *Power/Knowledge: Selected Interviews and Other Writings*, ed. C. Gordon, Brighton.

Foucault, M. (1984) *The Foucault Reader*, ed. P. Rabinow, Harmondsworth.

Fraser, A. (1974) *King James VI of Scotland, I of England*, London.

Freeman, A. (1973) 'Marlowe, Kyd and the Dutch Church Libel', *English Literary Renaissance*, vol. 3.

French, P. (1972) *John Dee: the World of an Elizabethan Magus*, London.

Fuhrmann, J. (1972) *The Origins of Capitalism in Russia: Industry and Progress in the Sixteenth and Seventeenth Centuries*, Chicago.

Fumerton, P. (1991) *Cultural Aesthetics: Renaissance Literature and the Practice of Social Ornamentation*, Chicago.

Garber, M. (1984) '"Here's Nothing Writ": Scribe, Script, and Circumscription in Marlowe's Plays', *Theatre Journal* 36.

Genette, G. (1969) 'Vraisemblance et motivation', *Figures II*, Paris.

Gent, L. and Llewellyn, N. (1990) eds. *Renaissance Bodies: The Human Figure in English Culture c.1540–1660*, London.

Gill, R. and Krueger, R. (1971) 'The Early Editions of Marlowe's Elegies and Davies's Epigrams: Sequence and Authority', *The Library*, vol. 26, No 3.

Goldberg, J. (1983) *James I and the Politics of Literature: Jonson, Shakespeare, Donne and their Contemporaries*, Baltimore and London.

Goldberg, J. (1991) 'Sodomy and society: the case of Christopher Marlowe' in *Staging the Renaissance*, ed. D. Kastan and P. Stallybrass, London, 75–82.

Goldberg, J. (1992) *Sodometries: Renaissance Texts, Modern Sexualities*, Stanford, California.

Goldberg, J. (1994) (ed.) *Queering the Renaissance*, Durham and London.

Graham, H. (1975) '"A Brief Account of the Character and Brutal Rule of Vasil'evich, Tyrant of Muscovy": Albert Schlichtling on Ivan Grozni', *Canadian–American Slavic Studies*, 9.

Greenblatt, S. (1978) 'Marlowe, Marx and Anti–Semitism' *Critical Inquiry* 5:2, Winter.

Greenblatt, S. (1980) *Renaissance Self–Fashioning: From More to Shakespeare*, Chicago.

Greenblatt, S. (1981) 'Invisible Bullets: Renaissance Authority and its Subversion', *Glyph*, 8.

Greenblatt, S. (1990) *Learning to Curse. Essays in Modern Culture*, London.

Greenblatt, S. (1992) 'Marlowe and the Will to Absolute Play', in *New Historicism and Renaissance Drama*, eds. R. Wilson and R. Dutton, London.

Greg, W. (1946) 'The Damnation of Faustus', *MLR* 41, 97–107.

Grey, I. (1962) 'Ivan the Terrible and Elizabeth of England', *History Today*, 12.

Grotowski, J. (1969) *Towards a Poor Theatre*, ed. E. Barba, London.

Gwyer, J. (1952) 'The Case of Dr Lopez' *Transactions of the Jewish Historical Society of England*, 16, 163–84.

Hale, J. (1993) *The Civilization of Europe in the Renaissance*, London.

Hale, W. (1847) ed., *A Series of Precedents and Proceedings in Criminal Causes*, London.

Hallam, Elizabeth, (1994) 'Crisis and Representation: Gender and Social Relations in Canterbury, 1580–1640', unpublished Ph.D. thesis, University of Kent at Canterbury.

Hamilton, A. (1956) 'Sidney and Agrippa' *RES*, ns. 7.

Harlow, C. (1961) 'Thomas Nashe and Robert Cotton the Antiquary', *Review of English Studies*, 12.

Harte, N. (1976) 'State control of dress and social change in pre–industrial England', in *Trade, Government and Economy in Pre–Industrial England*, ed. D. Coleman and A. John, London.

Hartley, T. (1995) ed., *Proceedings of the Parliaments of Elizabeth I*, vol. 3, Leicester.

Hattaway, M. (1968) 'Marlowe and Brecht', in *Christopher Marlowe*, ed. B. Morris, London.

Hattaway, M. (1970) 'The Theology of Marlowe's *Dr Faustus' Renaissance Drama* n.s. 3.

Hattaway, M. (1982) *Elizabethan Popular Theatre*, London.

Hattaway, M. (1987) *Hamlet, The Critics Debate*, London.

Hattaway, M. (1990) '"For now a time is come to mock at form": *Henry IV* and ceremony', in *Henry the Fourth, Milton, Gay, pouvoir et musique*, ed. J.–P. Teissedou, Cahiers du Groupe de Recherches et d'Études sur le Théâtre d'Élisabeth I et des Stuarts, Lille.

Hazlitt, W. (1904) *The Spirit of the Age*, ed. W. Carew Hazlitt, London.

Healy, T. (1992) *New Latitudes: Theory and English Renaissance Literature*, London.

Helgerson, R. (1992) *Forms of Nationhood: the Elizabethan Writing of England*, Chicago.

Henderson, P. (1953) 'Marlowe as a Messenger', *T.L.S*, 12 June.

Henrichs, A. (1970) 'Pagan Ritual and the Alleged Crimes of the Early Christians: a Reconsideration', in *Kyriakon: Festschrift Johannes Quasten*, ed. P. Granfield and J. Jungman, 2 vols., Münster.

Herr, M. (1978) *Dispatches*, London.

Heywood, J. and Wright, T. (1854) *Cambridge University Transactions during the Puritan Controversies of the Sixteenth and Seventeenth Centuries*, 2 vols., London.

Hill, C. (1984) 'Irreligion in the "Puritan" Revolution', in *Radical Religion in the English Revolution*, ed. J. McGregor and B. Reay, Oxford.

Hill, D. (1982) *The Six Preachers of Canterbury Cathedral, 1541–1982*, Ramsgate, 1982.

Hillebrand, H. (1964) *The Child Actors: a Chapter in Elizabethan Stage History*, New York.

Hotson, L. (1925) *The Death of Christopher Marlowe*, London.

Hughes, P. and Larkin, J. (1964–9) eds. *Tudor Royal Proclamations*, 3 vols., New Haven.

Hunter, M. (1985) 'The Problem of "Atheism" in Early–Modern England', *Trans. Royal Hist. Soc.*, vol. 35.

Hunter, M. and Wootton, D. (1992) eds. *Atheism from the Reformation to the Enlightenment*, Oxford.

Huttenbach, H. (1971) 'New Archival Material on the Anglo–Russian Treaty of Queen Elizabeth I and Tsar Ivan IV' *Slavonic and Eastern European Review*, 49.

Jardine L. and Grafton, A. (1990) '"Studied for action": how Gabriel Harvey read his Livy,' *Past and Present*, 129, 30–78.

Jeaffreson, J. (1972) ed. *Middlesex County Records vol.1: 1550–1603*, London.

Jenkins, C. (1911) 'An Unpublished Record of Archbishop Parker's Visitation in 1573', *Archaeologia Cantiana*, vol. 29.

Johnson, F. (1942) 'Thomas Hood's Inaugural Address as Mathematical Lecturer of the City of London (1588)', *Journal of the History of Ideas*, 3.

Jordan, W. and Cherry, P. (1995) *Spanish Still Life from Velázquez to Goya*, London.

Jorgensen, J. (1956) 'Alien Military Doctrine in Renaissance England', *Modern Language Quarterly* 17.

Jouanna, A. (1992) 'Faveur et favoris: l'exemple des mignons de Henri III' in Sauzet, 1992.

Jouanna, A. (1993) 'La crise monarchique des années 1574–1576 en France', *Proceedings of the Western Society for French History*, 20.

Judson, A. (1926) 'Cornelius Agrippa and Henry Vaughan' *MLN* 41.

Keefer, M. (1983) 'Verbal Magic and the Problems of the A and B Texts of *Dr Faustus*,' *JEGP* 82.

Keefer, M. (1988) 'Agrippa's Dilemma: Hermetic "Rebirth" and the Ambivalences of *De vanitate* and *De occulta philosophia*', *Renaissance Quarterly*, 41.

Kermode, F. (1971) *Shakespeare, Spenser, Donne*, London.

Kierkegaard, S. (1971) *Either/Or*, tr. D. Swenson and L. Swenson. 2 vols., Princeton.

Kirchner, W. (1956) 'Entrepreneurial Activity in Russian–Western Relations During the Sixteenth Century', in *Explorations in Entrepreneurial History*, 8.

Kocher, P. (1941) 'François Hotman and Marlowe's *The Massacre at Paris*', *Publications of the Modern Language Association of America*, 56.

Kocher, P. (1942) 'Marlowe's Art of War' *Studies in Philology*, 39.

Kocher, P. (1946) *Christopher Marlowe: A Study of his Thought, Learning and Character*, Chapel Hill.

Kocher, P. (1947) 'Contemporary pamphlet backgrounds for Marlowe's *The Massacre at Paris*', *Modern Language Quarterly*, 8.

Kocher, P. (1953) *Science and Religion in Elizabethan England*, San Marino, California.

Korkowski, E. (1976) 'Agrippa as Ironist' *Neophilologus* 60.

Kuriyama, C. (1980) *Hammer or Anvil: Psychological Patterns in Christopher Marlowe's Plays*, New Brunswick, N.J.

Lebigre, A. (1980) *La révolution des curés: Paris, 1588–94*, Paris.

Levin, H. (1954) *Christopher Marlowe: The Overreacher*, London.

Lloyd, C. (1981) *English Corsairs on the Barbary Coast*, London.

Lubimenko, I. (1914) 'A Project for the Acquisition of Russia by James I', *English Historical Review*, 29.

Lynn Martin, A. (1973) *Henri III and the Jesuit Politicians*, Geneva.

Macdonald, M. (1981) *Mystical Bedlam*, Cambridge.

McClure, J. (1990) '"O Phoenix Escossois": James VI as Poet' in *A Day Estivall*, ed. A. Gardner–Medwin and J. Williams, Aberdeen.

Maclure, M. (1968) ed. *The Poems: Chrisopher Marlowe*, The Revels Plays, London.

Maclure, M. (1979) ed. *Marlowe: The Critical Heritage*, London.

Mahood, M. (1950) *Poetry and Humanism: An Analysis of Seventeenth–Century English Poetry*, London.

Marcus, L. (1989) 'Textual Indeterminacy and Ideological Difference: The Case of *Doctor Faustus*', *Renaissance Drama*, n.s. 20.

Massie, R. (1981) *Peter the Great: His Life and World*, London.

Masters, R. (1753) *A History of the College of Corpus Christi and the Blessed Virgin Mary... at Cambridge*, Cambridge.

Meyer, E. (1897) *Machiavelli and the Elizabethan Drama*, Weimar.

Meyer, M. (1994) ed. *The Politics and Poetics of Camp*, London.

Moore Smith, G. (1908–9) 'Marlowe in Cambridge', *Modern Language Review*, 4.

Moore Smith, G. (1913) *Gabriel Harvey's Marginalia*, Stratford–upon–Avon.

Moore Smith, G. (1923) ed. *The Academic Drama at Cambridge: Extracts from College Records. Malone Society Collections*, 2 vols., Oxford.

Minshull, C. (1982) 'Marlowe's "Sound Machevill"', *Renaissance Drama* n.s. 13.

Mullaney, S. (1988) *The Place of the Stage: License, Play and Power in Renaissance England*, Chicago and London.

Murray, J. (1910) *English Dramatic Companies, 1558–1642*, 2 vols., London.

Nauert, C. (1965) *Agrippa and the Crisis of Renaissance Thought*, Urbana, Ill.

Nauert, C. (1979) 'The Author of a Renaissance Commentary on Pliny: Rivius, Trithemius or Aquaeus?', *JWCI* 42.

Neale, J. (1957) *Elizabeth I and her Parliaments, 1584–1601*, London.

Nelson, A. (1989) ed. *Records of Early English Drama:Cambridge*, 2 vols., Toronto, Buffalo, London.

Nicholl, C. (1984) *A Cup of News*, London.

Nicholl, C. (1992) *The Reckoning: The Murder of Christopher Marlowe*, London.

Nicholl, C. (1995) *The Creature in the Map*, London.

Nicolls, D. (1988) 'The Theatre of Martyrdom in the French Reformation', *Past and Present*, 121, 49–73.

Normand, L. (1994) 'Irigaray's Hom(m)osexuality and Gay Writing in Marlowe and Gunn', in *Political Gender: Texts and Contexts*, ed. S. Ledger et al., Hemel Hempstead.

Nowotny, K. (1949) 'The Construction of Certain Seals and Characters in the Work of Agrippa of Nettesheim', *JWCI* 12.

O'Mara, V. (1987) 'A Middle English Sermon preached by a Sixteenth–Century "Athiest"', *Notes and Queries*, vol. 34.

O'Neill, J. (1969) ed. *Critics on Marlowe*, London.

Osborne, J. (1962) ed. *The Autobiography of Thomas Whythorne*, London.

Outhwaite, R. (1985) 'Dearth, the English Crown and the "Crisis of the 1590s"' in *The European Crisis of the 1590s: Essays in Comparative History*, ed. P. Clark, London.

Page, R. (1990) 'Audits and Replacements in the Parker Library 1590–1650', *Trans. Cambridge Bibliographical Soc.* 10.

Palliser, D. (1983) *The Age of Elizabeth: England under the Later Tudors, 1547– 1603*, London.

Palmer, P. and More, R. (1966) *The Sources of the Faust Tradition from Simon Magus to Lessing*, New York, (1936, repr. 1966).

Panitz, E. (1981) *The Alien in their Midst: Images of Jews in English Literature*, East Brunswick, N.J.

Parker, G. (1975) 'The Economic Costs of the Dutch Revolt', in *War and Economic Development: Essays in Memory of David Joslin*, ed. J. Winter, Cambridge.

Parker, G. (1988) *The Military Revolution: Military Innovation and the Rise of the West, 1500–1800*, Cambridge.

Parr, J. (1971) *Tamburlaine's Malady and Other Essays on Astrology in Elizabethan Drama*, Westport, Conn.

Peck, D. (1985) *Leicester's Commonwealth*, Ohio.

Perrie, M. (1978) 'The Popular Image of Ivan the Terrible', *Slavonic and Eastern European Review*, 56.

Pérotin–Dumon, A. (1991) 'The Pirate and the Emperor: Power and the Law on the Seas', in *The Political Economy of Merchant Empires: State Power and World Trade*, ed. J. Tracy, Cambridge.

Petti, A. (1959) ed., *The Letters of Richard Verstegan (c.1550–1640)*, London.

Pollen, J. (1908) ed. *Unpublished Documents relating to the English Martyrs 1584– 1603*, Catholic Record Society, vol.5, London,

Potter, D. (1995) 'Kingship in the Wars of Religion: the Reputation of Henri III' in *European History Quarterly*, October.

Prideaux, W. (1885) 'Marlowe's *Hero and Leander*', *Notes & Queries*, 6 ser., xii

Prouty, C. (1942) *George Gascoigne: Elizabethan Courtier, Soldier, and Poet*, New York.

Purdon, N. (1967) '*Quod Me Nutrit Me Destruit*', *The Cambridge Review*, 4 March.

Pye, C. (1990) *The Regal Phantasm*, London.

Quinn, D. and Ryan, A. (1983) *England's Sea Empire*, London.

Raab, F. (1964) *The English Face of Machiavelli: A Changing Interpretation, 1500– 1700*, London.

Ramel, J. (1979) '*Le massacre de Paris* de Christopher Marlowe et les *Mémoires de l'estat de France sous Charles neuvième*', *Confluents*, 5.

Rebhorn, W. (1988) *Foxes and Lions: Machiavelli's Confidence Men*, Ithaca.

Ricoeur, P. (1992) *Oneself as Another*, Chicago and London.

Roberts, G. (1976) 'A New Source for Barnabe Barnes's *The Devil's Charter*' *Notes and Queries*, June.

Roberts, P. (1994) 'Elizabethan Players and Minstrels and the Legislation of 1572 against Retainers and Vagabonds,' in *Religion, Culture and Society in Early Modern Britain*, ed. A. Fletcher and P. Roberts, Cambridge.

Robin, G. (1964) *L'énigme sexuelle de Henri III*, Paris.

Rosenberg, E. (1960) *From Shylock to Svengali: Jewish Stereotypes in English Fiction*, London.

Roth, C. (1941) *A History of the Jews in England*, Oxford.

Rowse, A. (1964) *Christopher Marlowe: A Biography*, London.

Rowse, A. (1971) *The Elizabethan Renaissance: the Life of the Society*, London.

Said, E. (1991) *Orientalism: Western Concepts of the Orient*, Harmondsworth.

Sales, R. (1991) *Christopher Marlowe*, Basingstoke.

Salmon, J. (1991) 'Seneca and Tacitus in Jacobean England', in *The Mental World of the Jacobean Court*, ed. L. Levy Peck, Cambridge.

Sauzet, R. (1992) *Henri III et son temps*, Paris

Scott, W. (1912) *The Constitution and Finance of English, Scottish and Irish Joint– Stock Companies to 1720*, 2 vols., Cambridge.

Seaton, E. (1924) 'Marlowe's Map', *Essays and Studies* 10.

Shaaber, M. (1929) *Some Fore–Runners of the Newspaper in England, 1476–1622*, London.

Shammas, C. (1978) 'English commercial development and American colonization 1560-1620', in *The Western Enterprise*, ed. K. Andrews, N. Canny and P. Hair, Liverpool.

Sharpe, J. (1985) 'Last Dying Speeches: Religion, Ideology and Public Executions in Seventeenth–Century England', *Past and Present*, 107, 144–67.

Shepherd, S. (1986) *Marlowe and the Politics of Elizabethan Theatre*, Brighton.

Shurbanov, A. (1992) *Mezhdu Patosa i Ironiyata: Kristofer Marlou i Zarazhdaneto na Renesansovata Drama*, Sofia.

Simpson, A. (1987) *A History of the Common Law of Contract: The Rise of the Action of Assumpsit*, Oxford.

Sinfield, A. (1992) *Faultlines: Cultural Materialism and the Politics of Dissident Reading*, Oxford.

Smith, B. (1991) *Homosexual Desire in Shakespeare's England: A Cultural Poetics*, Chicago and London.

Smith, L. (1986) *Treason in Tudor England: Politics and Paranoia*, London.

Smith, R. (1984) 'Some issues concerning families and their property in rural England 1250–1800', in *Land, Kinship, and Lifecycle*, ed. R. Smith, Cambridge.

Sommerville, J. (1986) *Politics and Ideology in England, 1603–1640*, London.

Spampanato, V. (1921) *Vita di Giordano Bruno, con documenti editi e inediti,* Messina.

Spierenburg, P. (1984) *The Spectacle of Suffering: Executions and the Evolution of Repression: from a Preindustrial Metropolis to the European Experience,* Cambridge.

Spottiswoode, J. (1847–51) *the History of the Church of Scotland ... to the End of the Reign of James VI,* Bannatyne Club and Spottiswoode Society, 3 vols, Edinburgh, Vol 2.

Stern, V. (1972) 'The *Bibliotheca* of Gabriel Harvey' *Renaissance Quarterly,* 25.

Strong, R. (1969) *The English Icon: Elizabethan and Jacobean Portraiture,* London.

Strong, R. (1973) *Splendour at Court: Renaissance Spectacle and Illusion,* London.

Strong, R. (1977) *The Cult of Elizabeth: Elizabethan Portraiture and Pageantry,* London.

Stuart, A. (1917) 'Early Russian Embassies to Britain', *Twentieth Century Russia,* 2.

Summers, C. (1992) ed., *Homosexuality in Renaissance and Enlightenment England: Literary Representations in Historical Context,* New York.

Summers, C. (1994) 'Marlowe and Constructions of Renaissance Homosexuality', *Revue Canadienne de Littérature Comparée,* 21.

Summers, C. (1995) 'Christopher Marlowe' in *The Gay and Lesbian Literary Heritage: A Reader's Companion to the Writers and their Works, from Antiquity to the Present,* ed. C Summers, New York.

Summerson, J. (1967–8) 'Three Elizabethan Architects', *John Rylands Library Bulletin* 40.

Taunton, E. (1901) *History of the Jesuits in England, 1580–1773,* London.

Taylor, E. (1935) *The Original Writing and Correspondence of the Two Richard Hakluyts,* 2 vols., Hakluyt Society, London.

Tennenhouse, L. (1986) *Power on Display: the Politics of Shakespeare's Genres,* London.

Thomas, K. (1971) *Religion and the Decline of Magic,* London.

Thomas, V. and Tydeman W. (1994) *Christopher Marlowe: the Plays and their Sources,* London and New York.

Thorndike, L. (1919) 'Peter of Abano: a Medieval Scientist' *Annual Report of the American Historical Society,* 1.

Thorndike, L. (1923–58) *A History of Magic and Experimental Science,* 8 vols., New York.

Thornton Burnett, M. (1987) 'Tamburlaine: An Elizabethan Vagabond', *Studies in Philology,* 39.

Tilley, M. (1950), *A Dictionary of the Proverbs in England in the Sixteenth and Seventeenth Centuries*, Ann Arbor.

Traub, V. (1992) *Desire and Anxiety: Circulations of Sexuality in Shakespearean Drama*, London and New York.

Tuck, R. (1993) *Philosophy and Government 1572–1651*, Cambridge.

Tucker Brooke, C. (1930) *The Life of Marlowe and The Tragedy of Dido Queen of Carthage*, London.

Urry, W. (1988) *Christopher Marlowe and Canterbury*, ed. A. Butcher, London.

Van Dorsten, J. (1962) *Poets, Patrons and Professors: Sir Philip Sidney, Daniel Rogers and the Leiden Humanists*, Oxford.

Vaughan, R. and Fines, J. (1960) 'A Handlist of Manuscripts in the Library of Corpus Christi College, Cambridge, not Described by M R James', *Trans. Cambridge Bibliographical Soc.* 3.

Venn, J. (1897) *Biographical Dictionary of Gonville and Caius College*, London, 7 vols.

Von Staden, H. (1967) *The Land and Government of Muscovy*, tr. T. Esper, Stanford.

Waith, E. (1962) *The Herculean Hero in Marlowe, Chapman, Shakespeare, and Dryden*, London.

Wallerstein, I. (1983) *Historical Capitalism*, London.

Weil, J. (1977) *Christopher Marlowe: Merlin's Prophet*, Cambridge.

Wernham, R. (1976) 'Christopher Marlowe at Flushing in 1592', *English Historical Review*, 91.

White, P. (1993) *Theatre and Reformation. Protestantism, Patronage, and Playing in Tudor England*, Cambridge.

Wickham, G. (1964) '*Exeunt to the cave*: notes on the staging of Marlowe's plays', *Tulane Drama Review* 8.

Willan, T. (1953) *The Muscovy Merchants of 1555*, Manchester.

Willan, T. (1956) *The Early History of the Russia Company, 1553–1603*, Manchester.

Williams, G. (1994) *A Dictionary of Sexual Language and Imagery in Shakespearean and Stuart Literature*, 3 vols., London.

Williams, P. (1979) *The Tudor Regime*, Oxford.

Williamson, J. (1969) *Hawkins of Plymouth*, London.

Willson, D. (1956) *King James VI and I*, London.

Wirth, J. (1977) '"Libertins" et "Epicuriens": Aspects de l'Irréligion au XVIᵉ Siècle', *Bibliothèque d'Humanisme et Renaissance*, 39

Wolf, L. (1924–7) 'The Jews in Elizabethan England', *Trans. Jewish Historical Society of England*, xi.

Woodruff, C. and Cape, H. (1908) *Schola Regia Cantuarienses: a History of Canterbury School*, London.

Woodruff, C. and Danks, W. (1912) *Memorials of the Cathedral and Priory of Christ in Canterbury*, London.

Woods, G. (1992) 'Body, Costume, and Desire in Christopher Marlowe' in Summers, 1992, 69–84.

Wootton, D. (1985) 'Unbelief in Early–Modern Europe', *History Workshop Journal*, vol. 20.

Wootton, D. (1988) 'Lucien Febvre and the Problem of Early–Modern Unbelief', *Journal of Modern History*, vol. 60.

Wootton, D. (1992) 'New Histories of Atheism' in Hunter and Wootton, 1992.

Wraight, A. (1965) *In Search of Christopher Marlowe*, London.

Wraight, A. (1993) *Christopher Marlowe and Edward Alleyn*, Chichester.

Wretts–Smith, M. (1914) 'The English in Russia During the Second Half of the Sixteenth Century', *Trans. Royal Hist. Soc.*, 4th ser., vol. 3.

Wright, T. (1754) *Memoirs of the Reign of Queen Elizabeth*, 2 vols., London.

Yakobson, S. (1935) 'Early Anglo–Russian Relations, 1553–1613', *Slavonic and Eastern European Review*, 13.

Yardeni, F. (1992) 'Henri III sorcier', in Sauzet, 1992.

Yates, F. (1947) *The French Academies of the Sixteenth Century*, London.

Yates, F. (1975) *Astraea: the Imperial Theme in the Sixteenth Century*, London.

Zambelli, P. (1960) 'A Proposito del *De Vanitate Scientiarum et Artium* di Cornelio Agrippa', *Rivista Critica di Storia di Filosofia*, 15.

EDITIONS OF MARLOWE PLAYS

(Referred to in the text)

Bawcutt, N. (1978) *The Jew of Malta*, Manchester.

Bennett, H. (1931) *The Jew of Malta and The Massacre at Paris*, London.

Bevington, D. and Rasmussen, E. (1993) *Doctor Faustus: A– and B–Texts* (1604, 1616) Manchester.

Bowers, F. (1981) *The Complete Works of Christopher Marlowe*, 2nd edn., 2 vols., Cambridge.

Bullen, A. (1884–5) *The Works of Christopher Marlowe*, 3 vols., London.

Cunningham, J. (1981) *Tamburlaine the Great*, London.

Forker, C. (1994) *Edward II*, Manchester.

Ellis–Fermor, U. (1930) *The Life and Works of Christopher Marlowe: Tamburlaine the Great*, London.

Gill, R. (1971) *The Plays of Christopher Marlowe*, Oxford.

Gill, R. (1989) *Dr Faustus*, 2nd. edn., London and New York.

Greg, W. *Marlowe's Doctor Faustus, 1604–1616: Parallel Texts*, Oxford, 1950.

Oliver, H. (1968) *Dido Queen of Carthage and The Massacre at Paris*, London.

Pendry, E. and Maxwell, J. (1976) *Christopher Marlowe: Complete Plays and Poems*, London.

Ribner, I. (1977) *The Complete Plays of Christopher Marlowe*, Indianapolis.

INDEX